Competing for Soft Power

Through the critical case study of Ethiopia, Maria Repnikova examines the ambitious but disjointed display of Chinese diplomatic influence in Africa. In doing so, she develops a new theoretical approach to understanding China's practice of soft power, identifying the core mechanisms as tangible enticement with material and experiential offerings, ideational promotion of values, visions, and governance practices, and censorial power over the production and dissemination of China narratives. Through in-depth fieldwork, including interviews and focus groups, Repnikova builds a clear picture of the uneven implementation and reception of this image-making, in which Chinese messengers can improvise official agendas, and Ethiopian recipients can strategically appropriate and negotiate Chinese power. Contrary to popular claims about China replacing the West in the Global South, this innovative research reveals the successes, but also the inconsistencies and limitations of Chinese influence, as well as the ever-present shadow of the West in mediating soft power encounters.

Maria Repnikova is associate professor in Global Communication and the William C. Pate Endowed Chair in Strategic Communication at Georgia State University.

Competing for Soft Power

China's Image-Making in Africa

MARIA REPNIKOVA

Georgia State University

Shaftesbury Road, Cambridge CB2 8EA, United Kingdom

One Liberty Plaza, 20th Floor, New York, NY 10006, USA

477 Williamstown Road, Port Melbourne, VIC 3207, Australia

314–321, 3rd Floor, Plot 3, Splendor Forum, Jasola District Centre,
New Delhi – 110025, India

Cambridge University Press is part of Cambridge University Press & Assessment,
a department of the University of Cambridge.

We share the University's mission to contribute to society through the pursuit of
education, learning and research at the highest international levels of excellence.

www.cambridge.org
Information on this title: www.cambridge.org/9781009710312

DOI: 10.1017/9781009710275

First published 2026

Cover Image: Original artwork by Matt Rota

A catalogue record for this publication is available from the British Library

*A Cataloging-in-Publication data record for this book is available from the Library
of Congress*

ISBN 978-1-009-71031-2 Hardback
ISBN 978-1-009-71029-9 Paperback

Cambridge University Press & Assessment has no responsibility for the persistence
or accuracy of URLs for external or third-party internet websites referred to in this
publication and does not guarantee that any content on such websites is, or will remain,
accurate or appropriate.

For EU product safety concerns, contact us at Calle de José Abascal, 56, 1°, 28003
Madrid, Spain, or email eugpsr@cambridge.org

Contents

Figures and Tables

Preface and Acknowledgments

The six-year journey of this book manuscript was invigorating, challenging, and certainly not linear. After researching Chinese domestic media politics and journalism practices for nearly a decade, I was ready for a new adventure. Having witnessed China's quest for positive global image through academic, media, and policy discussions in China, it felt timely and logical to adjust my lens from domestic to the global. I initially considered a multi-case study on China's export of its "model," but I ended up both narrowing and expanding my focus. I chose to largely dive into a single case of Ethiopia, and to incorporate different facets of China's diplomatic image-making, including but not limited to the promotion of its political values.

My approach of theorizing from the "ground-up" meant adopting an open-minded and open-ended attitude toward my data collection. Studying a new complex polity, Ethiopia, was both exciting and intimidating. I discuss this in detail in my ethnographic reflection (Appendix I). The journey included several multi-month fieldwork trips, at least three complete rewrites of the entire manuscript, a few dark moments of wanting to give up entirely, as well as the overcasting shadow of COVID-19 disruptions and dramatic political transformations in both China and Ethiopia (and more recently, in the United States).

Research and writing, of course, is always a collaborative process, shaped by many lucky interactions in and out of the field. As a novice in Ethiopian and African studies, several colleagues have facilitated my immersion, helped correct and anticipate my mistakes, and carved out larger networks for my interviews and visits. Johannes Gedamu, an Atlanta-based Ethiopian scholar, opened the very first doors into the circles of Ethiopian elites and entrepreneurs on my visits, and gave me practical advice on living in Addis. Lahra Smith, an expert on Ethiopian politics and society at Georgetown University, also made many important introductions, and taught me about the intersections of class, gender, and power in Ethiopian society. Mekuria Mekasha and Jonas Ashine Demisse both hosted me as a visiting scholar at Addis Ababa University and created spaces for me to present my work to their colleagues and students.

Tensae Berhane, Tesfaye Alemayehu, and Shimellis Hailu have been my true collaborators in the field – helping with translations and research meetings, but also with sharing ideas, reflections, and friendships during my stay in Ethiopia. I have many fond memories of our colorful lunch meals of injera and yellow lentils (*yekik alicha*) at cafes and cafeterias, flavorful tiny coffees (*buna*), and long, rainy walks to different ministries and media outlets across the city. Shimellis was especially instrumental in deciphering Ethiopian bureaucracies and conducting focus groups in multiple Ethiopian languages. In China, I am especially grateful to Xu Liang and Liu Haifang for hosting me and making introductions, as well as for inviting me to speak to their students and colleagues. Meseret Techane and Xifan Yang offered warm friendships in Addis and Beijing, and soothed loneliness that often accompanied the intensity of fieldwork. Of course, the biggest gratitude in the field goes to the many interlocutors who trusted me to share their insights and stories, took hours out of their days to speak to me, showed up at my lectures with inquisitive questions, and tolerated my linguistic and cultural barriers.

Embarking on and persisting on a new and unpredictable endeavor was only possible with intellectual support of like-minded colleagues, many of whom I consider friends. Ching Kwan Lee – a pioneer of Global China studies – has inspired my turn from domestic to the global – and remained a consistent supporter throughout. From brainstorming field observations and theoretical framings to inviting me to workshops in Taiwan and South Africa that transpired in new ideas and networks, CK has influenced not only the progression of this book but also my own intellectual transformation into a scholar of Global China. Publishing the inaugural Element book, *Chinese Soft Power*, in her Global China Cambridge University series also cemented my expertise and visibility on this topic.

My writing exchanges with Miriam Driessen, a much more experienced China-Ethiopia scholar and ethnographer, have both inspired me and held me through the many revisions and efforts to "make sense" of the data. It was especially magical to work "alongside" with Miriam as she was also developing her second book on China in Ethiopia (*Immunity on Trial*). On several occasions, Cheryl Mei-ting Schmitz – another ethnographer of China in Africa (working in Angola) – has joined us and offered astute feedback on our work. This intellectual camaraderie also had an affective dimension as we talked through challenges in the field, as well as in life, lockdown, love, and many other spheres that inevitably intersect with our research.

Several friends and colleagues paused the endless busyness of academia to read and comment on the earlier iterations of my work. Kristen Looney, a dear friend and an exceptional scholar of Chinese politics, read multiple chapters and has consistently urged me to "let go" and submit the manuscript for review and publication. "It is ready," she said to me with confidence during one of our get-togethers in Georgetown. I didn't quite have the faith in it myself, but her encouragement pushed me over the edge of doubt.

Edward Schatz and Rachel Silvey – Asian studies scholars at the University of Toronto, who are well-versed in fieldwork in challenging contexts – have generously workshopped two of my chapters and provided lively feedback over a long lunch at the university faculty club. Their new edited volume, *Seeing China's Belt and Road*, also enriched the approach of my book. Juliet Lu – a rising star in Global China research – shared some of the most detailed and fascinating comments on my introductory chapter, reminding me that when it comes to ethnographic storytelling, the details are as important as the analysis. Xiaoyu Pu, a prominent scholar of China's international relations and foreign policy, offered much enthusiasm for my work and constructive suggestions on how to make it conceptually clearer. Nina Sylvanus, a political and economic anthropologist of West Africa (and China's influence there), helped refine and sharpen my storytelling. Andrea Pollio, another fellow co-journeyer and ethnographer of China–Africa relations, has become a true champion of my work in the critical final stages of revisions. My study hopes to be in conversation with his ethnographic reflections and creative approaches to the field captured in his forthcoming book *Silicon Elsewhere*. Nicholas Loubere, an important, innovative voice and leader in Global China research, has given relentless patient advice on my project, and new ideas with his *Global China as a Method* Element book. I am, of course, also deeply grateful to the two anonymous reviewers for the Cambridge University Press, who provided timely and very helpful comments that made the work much stronger.

Many colleagues have generously hosted me to present earlier versions of this book. Andrew Mertha, a long-standing mentor and friend, invited me to take part in his series at SAIS that engaged with different strategies of studying China from afar. His excitement for this book gave me fresh bursts of energy. Rongbin Han, Aynne Kokas, Timothy Cheek, and

Tommy Tse have all created invaluable opportunities to share the work, meet new colleagues, and gather feedback. I have also benefited from written correspondence and sharp and soulful conversations with Tim Barouch, Carwyn James Morris, Natalia Roudakova, Silvia Lindtner, César Jiménez-Martínez, Sarah Gonzalez, Fan Yang, Marwan Kraidy, Marina Krikorian, Omar Al Ghazzi, Stas Budnitsky, Christian Sorace, Alvin Camba, Alexander Gabuev, Tabitha Speelman, and many other friend-colleagues I met at conferences and in the hallways of my department.

As I prepared for my research trips, revised and polished the manuscript for submission, I received enormous support from my graduate students. Wendy (Weile) Zhou, who has now graduated and launched a career of her own, helped with mapping my China fieldwork, as well as the intellectual landscape of China–Africa research at Chinese universities. Xiyuan Li has been instrumental in checking and scoping for Chinese official and academic sources for this book. Solomon Elusoji, whose own research also focuses on China in Africa and whose journalistic writings have initially brought us together, has been through all the steps of this project, from locating the impossible citations to reading over the entire manuscript. Alexander Lloyd helped bring in the US context into my research, and Luwen Qiu did remarkable work on finding Chinese sources in the earlier stages.

Lucy Rhymer at Cambridge University Press has been wonderful to work with throughout the process. From my younger years as a PhD candidate to my evolution into an Associate Professor, Lucy has supported my ideas, found potential in my unusual scholarly trajectories, and ensured that the path from submission to publication is smooth and expedient. Working with Rosa Martin at CUP has also been timely and productive.

Logistically, multi-sited fieldwork and writing time is costly. The Social Science Research Council gave the first financial (and moral) boost for my research with the Transregional Junior Research Fellowship. In 2020–21, I had benefited enormously from the Wilson Fellowship. It provided a beautiful setting for research and writing and brought me into the "Covid cohort" with two wonderful African Studies scholars who became close friends, Khalid Medani and Aili Tripp. Sadly, at the time of writing, this institution has been shut down by the Trump administration. My home institution, Georgia State University, offered additional support over the years through internal grants, and my department (Communication) has granted me the flexibility to travel for prolonged periods. I am also very honored and lucky to serve as the Inaugural Endowed William C. Pate Chair in Strategic Communication – a position that came with generous research funding that supported my latest field research, writing, and editing process.

Solitary, multiyear, book projects can take an emotional toll. Any writer and scholar can share in the delicate balance between isolation and social engagement, withdrawal and interaction. Friends and family have been my cushion of support and love over the years. Tuesday home-cooked Russian meals and heartfelt talks with Tanya Walter, evening walk-calls with Mackenzie Wood, conversations with my mother, Tatiana, and babushka, Galina, bobbing and singing with Ben Cohen, cheerful visits from my brother Dmitri, Baltic pastries with Tiina D'Souza, and weekly restorative yoga and chats with Jessica von Schlichten have provided a consistent rhythm of support and inspiration. "How is the book?" was the question I heard almost daily from my loving mother, Tati, reminding me to stay focused, but also to exercise, eat well, and stay joyful. The flow of loving voice notes on everything from work to love to fashion with Ariele Le Grand inspired me to continue to envision and redefine myself beyond my work. My lifelong friendship with Elena Minina, the rare carrier of a perfect fusion of sarcasm and optimism, reminded me of what's possible during difficult times. My regular, caring check-ins and storytelling with Elina Pavlova, Natalia Roudakova, and Nadiya Kravets have nourished my spirit. Ilya Rozenberg has stimulated me with his work ethic and diligence to help the most vulnerable. Jeremy Dell supported me in my earlier stages of the project with his wisdom, scholarly insights, and delicious meals, and Evan Martin was there for the later stage, listening to my many presentations, dancing in the kitchen, and leaving the marks of love on my journey. Sassy the Cat, my daily green-eyed writing companion, reminded me with her stares and scratches to take breaks and not take myself too seriously – the habits that proved invaluable as I was completing the book.

PART I

THEORETICAL AND CONTEXTUAL FOUNDATIONS

I

Introduction

Grasping China's Uneven Image-Making

1.1 INTRODUCTION

On July 15, 2023, a group of Ethiopian policy experts, officials, and journalists, as well as several Chinese embassy personnel, gathered to celebrate the launch of the first book on China–Ethiopia relations written by an Ethiopian expert.[1] The launch took place in the grand ballroom of a large hotel in central Addis, with participants seated at round tables, and journalists from Ethiopian and Chinese state media hovering in the corner with cameras and notebooks. The event featured a long exchange of mutually celebratory speeches. "China is the largest developing country in the world. Now this diplomatic relationship has reached the level of a comprehensive strategic partnership," noted one of the Ethiopian speakers. "In the words of Xi Jinping, we, China, respect Africa, we love Africa, and we support Africa," proclaimed a Chinese embassy official in his passionate remarks. The speeches concluded with book signings and a lunch banquet.

Although, officially, an Ethiopian think tank organized the event, closer observation revealed Chinese actors' heavy-handed involvement. As soon as I took my seat at the start of the ceremony, an Ethiopian participant leaned over and whispered to me: "This is paid by China." The sponsorship covered the launch, but also the actual publication of the

---

[1] The author attended the event and took careful notes of the proceedings. The event was also featured in Chinese state media. See "Ethiopian Scholar Highlights Deepening China-Africa Ties in New Book," Xinhua, July 17, 2023, https://english.news.cn/20230716/ce c63013e41947ccbf68285285dcdd14/c.html.

3

book. The author noted in his introductory remarks: "Special thanks to the embassy of China who supported in the publication of the book." A similar note of gratitude appears in the acknowledgments of the book, with the Chinese Ambassador to Ethiopia at the time (Zhao Zhiyuan) thanked directly.[2] The book itself emerged from the author's multiple training and educational trips to China – all paid for by the Chinese government.

The Chinese embassy also took advantage of the launch to promote China's political visions for all of Africa. The embassy speaker mentioned and commended the book briefly, but he mainly underscored China's benevolent ambition in Africa and the parity in China–Africa relations. "China is not coming here for geopolitical gains; we don't seek hegemonic power … geopolitics should have no place in this great continent – resource-rich, talented continent. … We want to extend our cooperative hand to all African countries, including Ethiopia in particular," he stated. The embassy official further referred to China and Ethiopia as "developing countries" that can extend mutual support. The rhetoric of depoliticized engagement (implicitly differentiating China from the West), noninterference, and mutuality is part of China's ideational arsenal or promotion of political values and ideals in appealing to African elites, with China positioned as an equitable and sincere partner.

At the same time, some Chinese officials embarked in subtle disciplining of the event's agenda. As the presentations and remarks proceeded, the younger staff from the embassy communicated with Ethiopian participants at my table about my presence. In one of the text messages relayed to me later by an Ethiopian colleague, she asked for my name and background. She then quickly looked up my publications (ironically, the Element book on Chinese soft power) and continued to question the participant on whether I am Russian or American. "What is her position on China? If she is friendly to China, then she is welcome," was the final message shared with me. As I was one of the only unfamiliar faces to the Chinese embassy staff, my presence sparked concern. By questioning and setting the rules for my participation, the embassy signaled to Ethiopians that the Chinese side was in charge.

Throughout the ceremony, however, Ethiopian participants did not serve as passive bystanders. They actively engaged with and at times appropriated and even tilted China's influence in their favor. Responding to material enticement, for instance, one Ethiopian speaker suggested that it

---

[2] Melaku Mulualem K., *Africa-China Relations: Ethiopia as a Case Study* (2023).

would be valuable to translate the book into Amharic, the national language of Ethiopia, to spread more publicity across the Ethiopian public on China–Ethiopia relations. The speaker left it open as to which side should be covering the costs, seemingly alluding to the Chinese officials to take it up. Some Ethiopian speakers underscored the importance of Africa for China by mentioning Ethiopia's favorable voting at the United Nations. One speaker even said: "Africa needs China, but China needs Africa most," without further elaborating. Reacting to the efforts to screen me by the young Chinese embassy employee, Ethiopian participants I spoke to didn't seem too bothered. They laughed off and partially ignored the requests for information. Many Ethiopians treated the spectacle as entertainment – they shared smiles and smirks across the tables, used the breaks to catch up with friends, and especially lingered at the immaculate buffet spread that followed the official proceedings.

This lively gathering, aimed at fostering bilateral ties, also featured a tacit presence of the West. At the reception, the second in command of the Chinese embassy approached me directly, addressed me by my first name, and quickly switched from China–Africa politics to US politics. He noted with concern that he is afraid that the US democracy is relapsing and moving into "a black hole," and further emphasized the intensity of American polarization. I kept trying to bring the discussion back to Ethiopia, but the official persisted to discuss the threats to American democracy and the instability it could bring to the world. When we finally returned to the topic of the book launch, he stressed that China is trying to help Ethiopia progress in the right direction, and then quickly pointed fingers at the West, calling its debt-trap accusations of China "absolute nonsense." When the embassy official finally left and the reception was winding down, my Ethiopian interlocutors invited me for a simple coffee ceremony (*jebena buna*) outside the fancy hotel. As we chatted, they didn't dwell in the performative speeches witnessed earlier. Some of them, instead, took the opportunity to ask me more about the position of the United States vis-à-vis Africa, the upcoming US presidential election cycle, and how to access professional and educational opportunities in America.

This event – one of many Sino-Ethiopian diplomatic encounters – captures the central arguments of this book. Namely, the gathering highlights the ambitious yet uneven nature of China's image-making in Africa. The book launch illuminates China's multidimensional reach via key influence mechanisms, including *tangible enticement, ideational persuasion,* and *censorial power.* At the same time, Chinese messengers at this event are at once deliberate and spontaneous. They combine rehearsed political narratives and strategic funding of important elites with more ad hoc acts like the junior official's coercive on-the-spot reaction to my presence. The engagement of Ethiopian participants further showcases the dynamic reception toward Chinese diplomatic influence, as they welcome, but also selectively appropriate, negotiate, and neglect Chinese power. Both, the Chinese and Ethiopian participants also continue to express intrigue with the West alongside their bilateral engagements. In the chapters that follow, I draw on extensive ethnographic fieldwork in Ethiopia and China, including over 130 interviews and focus groups with key stakeholders (primarily elites), to examine these characteristics of China's image-making in detail. I illuminate China's ambitious and chaotic practices, the contested reception they encounter in Ethiopia, as well as the role of the West in further complicating these dynamics.

1.2 WHY IT MATTERS: CHINA'S IMAGE-MAKING IN POLICY AND THEORETICAL DEBATES

Grasping how China engages in image-making and the varied responses it generates, especially targeting influential elites in Africa, is critical to ongoing debates on China-US competition, transnational authoritarianism, and South–South communication flows. First, China-US competition has increasingly morphed into struggles over values, norms, or what Evan Osnos, the former China correspondent for the *New Yorker*, has described as contestation over a "moral vision of the future."[3] While much of this rivalry takes place within Western liberal democracies, with the United States itself halting some of China's diplomatic initiatives like Confucius Institutes[4] and state-owned media broadcasting,[5] the competition over image and narratives has also escalated in the Global South.

---

[3] Evan Osnos, "The Future of America's Contest with China," *The New Yorker*, January 6, 2020, https://www.newyorker.com/magazine/2020/01/13/the-future-of-americas-contest-with-china.

[4] The majority of Confucius Institutes and Classrooms have been shut down in the United States since 2019. See Bonnie Girard, "The Rise and Fall of Confucius Institutes in the US," *The Diplomat*, November 28, 2023, https://thediplomat.com/2023/11/the-rise-and-fall-of-confucius-institutes-in-the-us/.

[5] In 2020, the US government designated five major Chinese media organizations operating within the United States as "foreign missions," requiring them to register with the State Department. See for instance Jonathan Landay, "U.S. Imposes New Rules on State-Owned Chinese Media over Propaganda Concerns," *Reuters*, February 19, 2020, https://www.reuters.com/article/us-usa-china-media/u-s-imposes-new-rules-on-state-owned-chinese-media-over-propaganda-concerns-idUSKBN20C2G1/.

In the past several years, considering the pushback and ambivalence of many Global South countries to Western efforts to quell Russia's ongoing invasion of Ukraine,[6] as well as to stand by Israel in its war against Hamas,[7] Western media and policy experts started to invoke this region more forcefully as an important battlefield for global public opinion. Popular writings underscore the danger of "losing the Global South."[8] Academic experts like Tanina Zappone suggests that China's diffusion of alternative and often anti-Western narratives about Russia's war in Ukraine succeeded in influencing the "fence-sitting position" of Global South countries.[9] Some experts further argue that the synergy between China and the rest of the Global South in these geopolitical conflicts is an indication of the larger trend of China taking over the West's position as "the world's leading influencer."[10] President Trump's latest dismantlement of the US diplomatic apparatus,[11] and his embrace of coercive power in foreign policy through relentless trade wars, has given more fuel to these arguments. Joseph Nye, the most influential scholar of and the "founder" of soft power, for instance, has written that Trump's abandonment of "attraction" in foreign relations will make it challenging to beat

---

[6] Chris Alden, "The Global South and Russia's Invasion of Ukraine," in Michael Cox (editor), *Ukraine: Russia's War and the Future of the Global Order* (LSE Press: 2023).

[7] Jorge Heine, "International Reaction to Gaza Siege Has Exposed the Growing Rift between the West and the Global South," *The Conversation*, November 8, 2023, http s://theconversation.com/international-reaction-to-gaza-siege-has-exposed-the-growing-rift-between-the-west-and-the-global-south-216938.

[8] On Ukraine, see for instance Howard French, "Why Ukraine Is Not a Priority for the Global South," *Foreign Policy*, September 19, 2023, https://foreignpolicy.com/2023/09/19/unga-ukraine-zelensky-speech-russia-global-south-support/; On Gaza, see H. A. Hellyer, "The West Is Losing the Global South over Gaza," *Time Magazine*, November 3, 2023.

[9] Tanina Zappone, "Reinventing Soft Power: The Strong Impact of China's Soft Power 'Shortcomings' on the Global South," IAI Papers 23, July 19, 2023, p. 11.

[10] Collin Meisel, Jonathan Moyer, and Mathew J. Burrows, "The US Is Losing the Global South: How to Reverse Course," *The Hill*, June 13, 2023, https://thehill.com/opinion/in ternational/4046182-the-us-is-losing-the-global-south-how-to-reverse-course/.

[11] As of June 2025, President Trump has dismantled USAID and called for the shutdown of Voice of America (this order has thus far been blocked in courts). The State Department has also announced a major reorganization, including large-scale job cuts (see Simon Lewis, Humeyra Pamuk, and Jonathan Landay, "State Dept Overhaul Will Cut Thousands of Jobs, Push 'Western values'," *Reuters*, May 29, 2025, https://www .reuters.com/world/us/state-dept-broad-reorganization-plan-submitted-congress-2025-0 5-29); and a halt on visa interviews for international students (Joseph Gedeon, "Trump Administration Orders US Embassies to Stop Student visa Interviews," *The Guardian*, May 27, 2025, https://www.theguardian.com/us-news/2025/may/27/international-stu dent-visa-trump).

China's already influential position in the Global South.[12] Ironically, the obsession with losing the Global South to China in contemporary policy and media narratives echoes the concern of "losing" China to communism in the 1940s.[13]

Scholars and experts who take a longer view on China-US competition in the Global South abstain from such definitive claims but still underscore China's ambitions and practices in shaping and leading the region. Nadége Rolland, for instance, positions domination over the Global South as part of China's grand strategy vis-à-vis the United States (and Western hegemony more broadly) – a vision that she traces back to the Mao era, and that she sees as coming into a new fruition under Xi Jinping.[14] Dawn Murphy, in her comprehensive book on China's rise in the Middle East and sub-Saharan Africa, argues that China "builds spheres of influence" and promotes an alternative vision of an international order in these regions as part of great power competition.[15] She pays special attention to major diplomatic tools, like the Cooperation Forums and Special Envoys to the regions, as facilitating China's geopolitical influence. Maria Adele Carrai, in a recent article, takes the lens of infrastructure diplomacy to showcase that China already significantly overshadows the influence of the United States in the Global South.[16]

By empirically focusing on both, the implementation and reception toward Chinese diplomatic influence though the critical case of Ethiopia – the second largest country in Africa and one of China's key partners on the continent – this book complicates these dramatic characterizations, and the treatment of Global South as a pawn in great power competition. Rather than replacing the West, China's image-building is an ambitious, but also a fractured project, featuring uneven implementation from within and complex external responses in the form of selective acceptance, as well as appropriation and negotiation of Chinese influence.

---

[12] Joseph Nye, "Trump Is Liquidating America's Reserves of Soft Power: The United States Can't Beat China with Hard Power Alone," *The Washington Post*, March 25, 2025.

[13] See for instance: "Who Lost China," Harry S. Truman Library Museum, National Archives, https://www.trumanlibrary.gov/education/presidential-inquiries/who-lost-china.

[14] Nadege Rolland, "China's Southern Strategy: Beijing Is Using the Global South to Constrain America," *Foreign Affairs*, June 2, 2022, https://www.foreignaffairs.com/articles/china/2022-06-09/chinas-southern-strategy.

[15] Dawn C. Murphy, *China's Rise in the Global South: The Middle East, Africa, and Beijing's Alternative World Order* (Stanford University Press: 2022), p. 8.

[16] Maria Adele Carrai, "Is America Losing the Global South? Assessing the Dynamics of Sino-American Rivalry in Infrastructure Diplomacy," Orbis 67(4) (2023): 524–43.

Echoing recent survey-based studies of mixed and contradictory public perceptions of China in critical regions like Latin America and Southeast Asia,[17] this book underscores the complexity and fluidity of on-the-ground engagement with China's diplomatic outreach in the Global South. It further demonstrates (in its final chapter) how the shadow of the West still looms large in China's image-making project, as both Chinese and Ethiopian participants view the West as a professional destination and a standard setter. In other words, China is increasingly influential in the Global South, but the way it exerts its influence is not linear nor zero-sum, leaving much space for other major powers to compete. Even in the age of weakened US diplomacy, China's complete "take over" of the region should not be taken for granted.

Second, the analysis of China's diplomatic outreach in Ethiopia also speaks to related debates on transnational authoritarianism and specifically on whether China is diffusing and promoting autocracy outside its borders. In policy writings and media reports, China's image-making efforts are increasingly associated with sharp power or manipulative and co-optive efforts aimed more at disinformation than at inspiring attraction.[18] Leading American think tanks, like the Hoover Institute, fuse China's illicit and routine political and cultural engagements under a blanket category of influence operations.[19] Globally, but especially in developing countries, policy and media writings regularly frame China as an exporter of authoritarianism. Niva Yau, for instance, writes for the Atlantic Council that China is "training future authoritarians" through its extensive training programs of Global South elites.[20] Bethany Allen-Ebrahimian, in her investigation of the Mwalimu Julius Nyerere Leadership School in Tanzania – a partnership between the CCP and the six ruling parties of major African countries – concludes that Chinese

---

[17] Kerry Ratigan, "Are Peruvians Enticed by the 'China Model'? Chinese Investment and Public Opinion in Peru," *Studies in Comparative International Development* 56(1) (2021): 87–111. https://doi.org/10.1007/s12116-021-09321-0; Selina Ho and Terence Lee, "Elite Perceptions of a China-Led Regional Order in Southeast Asia," *Journal of Current Southeast Asian Affairs* 44(1) (2025).

[18] Christopher Walker, Shanthi Kalathil and Jessica Ludwig, "Forget Hearts and Minds," *Foreign Policy*, September 14, 2018, https://foreignpolicy.com/2018/09/14/forget-hearts-and-minds-sharp-power/.

[19] Larry Diamond and Orville Schell (cochairs), "China's Influence & American Interests: Promoting Constructive Vigilance," *Report of the Working Group on Chinese Influence Activities in the United States* (Hoover Institution Press: 2019).

[20] Niva Yau, "A Global South with Chinese Characteristics," *Atlantic Council*, June 13, 2024, https://www.atlanticcouncil.org/in-depth-research-reports/report/a-global-south-with-chinese-characteristics/.

officials are spreading an authoritarian alternative to democracy.[21] Some experts further position the Global South as a testing ground for China's larger plan to legitimize its model. "Chinese leaders recognize that to achieve legitimacy as a responsible great power without democratizing – a prospect not welcomed by the developed West – they must first popularize China's model in the developing world," David Shullman argues in his analysis of China in the developing world published by the Brookings Institute.[22]

Scholars of Global China who conduct empirical work in the field critique what they see as an overemphasis on China's authoritarian features as a form of "othering" and essentializing China, which inhibits deeper knowledge production about its external activities.[23] Scholars of Chinese foreign policy and authoritarian politics caution against presuming China's strategic and deliberate mission of autocracy export, and argue that China's increasingly assertive involvement in global governance is "making the world safe for autocracy."[24] "The CCP welcomes democratic dysfunction abroad, as it makes the party look better by comparison. But democratic backsliding does not reflect a grand strategic plan in Beijing," argues Weiss in her influential essay in *Foreign Affairs*.[25] These arguments echo the consensus in the larger literature on transnational authoritarian diffusion that contemporary autocracies mainly pursue their strategic interests rather than directly export their models.[26]

In examining how China attempts to build and guard a positive image with elites in a major autocratic country in Africa, this study adds an

[21] Bethany Allen-Ebrahimian, "In Tanzania, Beijing Is Running a Training School for Authoritarianism," *Axios*, August 21, 2023, https://www.axios.com/2023/08/21/chin ese-communist-party-training-school-africa.

[22] David O. Shullman, "Protect the Party: China's Growing Influence in the Developing World," *Brookings*, January 22, 2019, https://www.brookings.edu/articles/protect-the-party-chinas-growing-influence-in-the-developing-world/.

[23] See Ivan Franceschini and Nicholas Loubere, *Global China as Method*, Global China Cambridge Element Series (Cambridge University Press: 2022); Jessica DiCarlo and Meredith DeBoom, "Six Paths of Global China: A Genealogy of Contested Geographical Imaginary," *Dialogues in Human Geography* (2025): 1–23.

[24] Jessica Weiss first popularized this phrase (and argument) in her 2019 Foreign Affairs article. See Jessica Chen Weiss, "A World Safe for Autocracy? China's Rise and the Future of Global Politics," *Foreign Affairs* (July/August 2019). Dukalskis used a similar phrasing in his 2021 book, with the book itself titled as *Making the World Safe for Dictatorship*, but his argument extended beyond China to motivations of other authoritarian regimes.

[25] Weiss, "A World Safe for Autocracy?"

[26] In his book, Dukalskis presents a summary of this debate. See Alexander Dukalskis, *Making the World Safe for Dictatorship* (Oxford University Press: 2021).

empirical slice to these ongoing debates. It cautions against a sweeping aggregation of China's diplomatic efforts into "sharp power," and uncovers the prominence of both promotional and more coercive and defensive practices. It further demonstrates the subtlety of China's authoritarian features in its diplomatic engagements, as they aim to legitimize its governance and protect it against external criticisms. Chinese officials and educators, for instance, actively promote China's version of "democracy" as exceptional and at times even superior to that in the West (see Chapter 4), and (along with some company representatives) practice and encourage censorship and self-censorship when it comes to media and public discourse on China in Ethiopia (see Chapter 5). While not reaching the level of sophistication and coercion of targeting ethnic Chinese diasporas,[27] the Chinese state's shaping of public opinion among elite, non-diasporic audiences can still indirectly enhance and mask the appeal of authoritarian governance.

Finally, the study of China's image-making efforts in Ethiopia helps us critically recenter the Global South as part of global communication flows. There is a growing interest in the study of communication in and from the Global South; however, these studies tend to analyze it through the prism of or in juxtaposition to the Global North. In particular, the existing scholarship underscores the creative and at times subversive response of Global South audiences to Western content,[28] as well as the increasing power of the Global South as a cultural and media producer, exporting to, not solely importing from the Global North.[29] Pushing

[27] For conceptual and theoretical frameworks on autocratic diaspora management, see Gerasimos Tsourapas, "Global Autocracies: Strategies of Transnational Repression, Legitimation, and Co-optation in World Politics," *International Security Review* 23(3) (2021): 616–44; and Marlies Glasius, "Extraterritorial Authoritarian Practices: A Framework," *Globalizations* 15(2) (2018): 179–97. For a detailed empirical study of transnational repression, see for instance Dana Moss and Saipira Furstenberg (editors), *Transnational Repression in the Age of Globalization* (Edinburgh Studies on Diasporas and Transnationalism, 2024).

[28] See for instance Kalyani Chadha and Anandam Kavoori, "Media Imperialism Revisited: Some Findings from the Asian Case," *Media, Culture & Society* 22(4) (2000).

[29] For film industry in the Global South, major production hubs include Nigeria and India. On Nollywood, see Matthias Krings and Onookome Okome (editors), *Global Nollywood: The Transnational Dimensions of an African Video Film Industry* (Indiana University Press: 2013). On Bollywood, see Aswin Punathambekar, *From Bombay to Bollywood: The Making of a Global Media Industry* (New York University Press: 2013). For global journalism, see for instance Vivien Marsh, *Seeking Truth in International TV News: China, CGTN and the BBC* (Routledge: 2023); William Youmans, *An Unlikely Audience: Al Jazeera Struggle in America* (Oxford University Press: 2017); Bilge Yesil,

against the earlier scholarship on media imperialism that underscored the dominance of the Global North over the Global South, these innovative studies showcase the presence of "contra-flows"[30] that originate from the Global South, and as such have the potential to reshape global communication dynamics.

The focus on emancipatory power of the Global South, however, risks romanticizing and homogenizing it, and thereby eclipsing the complex power relations and new hierarchies that emerge horizontally, within the Global South itself.[31] Responding to Willems' call for studying "media and communication from the vantage point of the everyday lives of ordinary people in the Global South,"[32] this book further de-Westernizes and deromanticizes our analysis of communication flows in the Global South through the lens of the China–Ethiopia diplomatic encounter. The chapters that follow reveal the layered South–South interactions across different groups of communicators, including officials, students, journalists, and educators in China and Ethiopia. Chinese actors and initiatives encounter contested power dynamics and ambivalent solidarities in their efforts to build and guard China's image on the ground. The grounded fieldwork also complicates the positionality of the Global North vis-à-vis the Global South, as my interlocutors continue to simultaneously build both South–South and North–South connections. They appear to exist in what Doyle termed as "interimperality" or an overlapping of different hegemonic processes[33] and occupy what Rofel and Rojas describe as "spaces where different worlds become mutually entangled."[34]

By illustrating China's multidimensional, ambitious, and uneven image-making through the case of China in Ethiopia, this book challenges and complicates the claims about China's inevitable dominance over the Global South, the associations of China's image promotion with direct authoritarian export, and the subversive character of South–South

---

Talking Back to the West: How Turkey Uses Counter-Hegemony to Reshape the Global Communication Order (University of Illinois Press: Forthcoming).

[30] Daya Kishan Thussu, "Contra-flow in Global Media: An Asian Perspective," *Media Asia* 3-4(33) (2006): 123–9.

[31] It's important to acknowledge here that China's positioning of itself as a "developing" country is also complicated by the fact that its economy is now on par with major Western economies on some metrics.

[32] Wendy Willems, "Beyond Normative De-Westernization: Examining Media Culture from the Vantage Point of the Global South," *The Global South* 8(1) (2014): 16.

[33] Laura Doyle, "Inter-imperiality: Dialectics in a Postcolonial World History," *Interventions* 16(2): 159–96.

[34] Lisa Rofel and Carlos Rojas (ed.), *New World Orderings: China and the Global South* (Duke University Press: 2022).

communication flows. The deep empirical analysis demonstrates the vast scope, as well as the contradictions and limitations of China's diplomatic influence in developing countries, its fusion of promotional power mechanisms with subtle authoritarian legitimation, and the coexistence of South–South synergies with frictions and continuous interactions with the West. We now shift to a more in-depth engagement with China's influence in Africa, how it has been studied over the decades, and the gaps in our grasp of China's diplomatic influence in the region.

1.3 CHINA IN AFRICA: FROM ECONOMIC INFLUENCE TOWARD WIELDING SOFT POWER

China's contemporary influence in Africa and more broadly in the Global South layers on rich historical legacies, especially from the Cold War era. Under Mao's rule, China primarily pursued political relations with the continent.[35] Historians of that period document China's competition over status and ideological visions in Africa. In his recent book, *Winning the Third World*, for instance, Brazinsky argues that Maoist China promoted what he describes as "revolutionary evangelism" or China's experience of breaking away from colonialism as instructive to other nations seeking independence.[36] In her analysis of Mao's charm offensive in Africa, Lovell demonstrates that he had directly promoted China's revolution in Africa by providing guerrilla warfare training to selective African visitors as part of the foreign aid program.[37] In his book on China's relations with Africa between 1949 and 1970, Larkin identified "ideological commitment to world revolution" as the core impetus for China's engagement with the continent.[38]

China's "return" to Africa in the past several decades has initially centered on its economic agenda. China has positioned itself as a new and reliable economic partner to African nations. In the past two decades, it has emerged as Africa's largest bilateral trade partner[39]

[35] David H. Shinn, "China-Africa Ties in Historical Context," in Arkebe Oqubay and Justin Yifu Lin (editors), *China-Africa and an Economic Transformation* (Oxford University Press: 2019).

[36] Gregg A. Brazinsky, *Winning the Third World: Sino-American Rivalry During the Cold War* (University of North Carolina Press: 2017).

[37] Julia Lovell, *Maoism: A Global History* (Vintage: 2020).

[38] Daniel Large, "Beyond 'Dragon in the Bush': The Study of China-Africa Relations," *African Affairs* 107(426) (2008): 45–61.

[39] "China remains Africa's largest trading partner, key contributor to dev't: officials,' Xinhua, April 17, 2025; https://english.news.cn/20250417/2a10d6dbda13437 ba2370395076f24a0/c.html.

and creditor,[40] as well as a major foreign direct investor.[41] Competing moral claims continue to overshadow the analyses of China's vast economic activities. Whereas Chinese media, scholars, and officials tend to highlight their economic approach to Africa as mutualistic and responsive to local demands,[42] many popular and policy writings in the West invoke concerns about its neocolonial behavior[43] manifested in resource extraction, "debt-trap diplomacy," or deliberately predatory lending,[44] as well as labor[45] and environmental violations.[46] Some of these accusations are also voiced by members of African civil society, media, and political elite. In 2018, for instance, a major Kenyan newspaper, the *Standard*, published explosive accounts about physical abuse taking place during the Mombasa railway construction, with Kenyan workers reporting physical assaults by their Chinese employees.[47] In Zambia, China

[40] According to SAIS-CARI research, as of 2021, China was the largest bilateral lender in terms of volume of loans to Africa, but its overall lending to Africa has been on decline in recent years. See: Zainab Usman, "What Do We Know About Chinese Lending in Africa?" Carnegie Endowment for International Peace, June 2, 2021; https://carnegieen dowment.org/research/2021/06/what-do-we-know-about-chinese-lending-in-africa? lang=en.

[41] "Data: Chinese Investment in Africa, 2003-2024," China Africa Research Initiative, https:// www.sais-cari.org/chinese-investment-in-africa.

[42] "China-Africa: Mutual Gains, Not One-Sided Aid," The State Council Information Office, September 7, 2023, http://english.scio.gov.cn/videos/2023-09/07/con tent_113357168.htm.

[43] "China in Africa: The New Colonialism?" Hearing before the Subcommittee on Africa, Global Health, Global Human Rights, and International Organizations of the Committee on Foreign Affairs House, House of Representatives, March 7, 2018, https://www .govinfo.gov/content/pkg/CHRG-115hhrg28876/pdf/CHRG-115hhrg28876.pdf.

[44] For a good overview of debt-trap diplomacy debate, including in Africa, please see Lucas Niewenhuis, "The 'Debt-Trap Diplomacy' Debate: Are China's Loans Predatory?" SupChina, September 18, 2019, https://signal.supchina.com/the-debt-trap- diplomacy-debate-are-chinas-loans-predatory/.

[45] "Zambia: Workers Detail Abuse in Chinese-Owned Mines," Human Rights Watch, November 3, 2011, https://www.hrw.org/news/2011/11/03/zambia-workers-detail- abuse-chinese-owned-mines#.

[46] On discussion about negative linkages between trade with China and environmental degradation in developing countries, see Jonas Gamso, "Is China Worsening the Developing World's Environmental Crisis?" *The Conversation*, August 22, 2018, https://theconversa tion.com/is-china-worsening-the-developing-worlds-environmental-crisis-100284.

[47] Eyder Peralta, "A New Chinese-Funded Railway in Kenya Sparks Debt-Trap Fears," All Things Considered, NPR, October 8, 2018, https://www.npr.org/2018/10/08/6416251 57/a-new-chinese-funded-railway-in-kenya-sparks-debt-trap-fears.

has been accused of taking over the country's economy "informally and deceptively."[48]

Many important academic works on China–Africa relations, in turn, have complicated and challenged these polarizing assessments of China's economic engagement on the continent. In her groundbreaking work on Chinese mining and construction companies in Zambia, for instance, Ching Kwan Lee counters the popular depictions of Chinese capital as "colonialist" and demonstrates how it can be more adaptive and responsive to public pressures than private Western companies that tend to pursue a more uncompromising position.[49] A study led by Carlos Oya at SOAS, drawing on fieldwork in Angola and Ethiopia, reveals a high degree of localization of Chinese companies, including hiring and training of local labor.[50] Deborah Brautigam dispels the popular claims about China exploiting Africa for agricultural resources, and illustrates how China is still a minor player in the agricultural sector on the continent.[51] Brautigam and Meg Rithmire also repeatedly tackle the narrative of debt-trap diplomacy,[52] showing how Chinese lending practices are more experimental and limited than presumed in popular narratives. Anthropologists Miriam Driessen and Cheryl Mei-ting Schmitz indirectly push back against the claims of China as an exploitative economic power by illuminating the challenges and disappointments faced by Chinese workers in Africa,[53] as well as by showcasing the contested power dynamics, whereby African counterparts attempt to defy Chinese developmental norms and practices.[54]

---

[48] Kalima Nkonde, "How China Slowly Colonizing Zambian Economy," *Lusaka Times*, July 27, 2018, https://www.lusakatimes.com/2018/07/27/how-china-slowly-colonizing-zambian-economy/.

[49] Ching Kwan Lee, *The Specter of Global China: Politics, Labor, and Foreign Investment in Africa* (The University of Chicago Press: 2017).

[50] Carlos Oya and Florian Schaefer, "Chinese Firms and Employment Dynamics in Africa: A Comparative Analysis," *IDCEA Research Synthesis Report* (SOAS, University of London: 2019).

[51] Deborah Brautigam, *Will Africa Feed China?* (Oxford University Press: 2015).

[52] Deborah Brautigam, "A Critical Look at Chinese 'Debt-Trap Diplomacy': The Rise of a Meme," *Area Development & Policy* 5(1) (2019): 1–14; Deborah Brautigam and Meg Rithmire, "The Chinese 'Debt Trap' Is a Myth," *The Atlantic*, February 6, 2021, https://www.theatlantic.com/international/archive/2021/02/china-debt-trap-diplomacy/617953/.

[53] Miriam Driessen, *Tales of Hope, Tastes of Bitterness: Chinese Road Builders in Ethiopia* (Hong Kong University Press: 2019); Cheryl Mei-Ting Schmitz, "Doing Time, Making Money at a Chinese State Firm in Angola," *Made in China Journal*, January 25, 2021.

[54] Driessen, *Tales of Hope, Tastes of Bitterness*; George Ofosu and David Sarpong, "China in Africa: On the Competing Perspectives of the Value of Sino-Africa Business

More recently, China's influence in Africa has shifted beyond the economic realm into the political and cultural spheres. China has taken correcting Western misconceptions into its own hands, and to promote its image in Africa through educational, cultural, and media channels, in addition to economic ones. In the past two decades, for instance, China has launched 67 Confucius Institutes in Africa,[55] set up major regional state media operations in Nairobi (and many branches across the continent),[56] launched digital diplomacy outreach on Twitter,[57] and trained thousands of African journalists and officials,[58] among other initiatives. The Chinese government has held regular large-scale diplomatic summits[59] and vastly expanded its publicity work across Africa.[60] Chinese companies have also embraced more active branding and publicity of their initiatives, including via engagement in corporate social responsibility projects, while other non-state actors, such as Chinese NGOs and volunteers, have launched their pathways into the continent.[61] As already discussed in the context of debates on Sino-US

Relationships," *Journal of Economic Issues* 56(1) (January 2, 2022): 137–57, https://doi.org/10.1080/00213624.2022.2020025.

[55] "Experts Commend China's Role in Advancing Quality Education in Africa," *Xinhua*, May 18, 2024, https://english.news.cn/20240518/822ed216d11d49939704fc55301996b3/c.html.

[56] Since the turn of the twenty-first century, China has expanded its media operations in Africa. See Bob Wekesa, "China Global Television Network's Debate Show, 'Talk Africa': Conflict, Economics, and Geopolitics," in George Ogola (editor), *The Future of Television in the Global South* (Palgrave Macmillan: 2023), 107–28, https://doi.org/10.1007/978-3-031-18833-6_7.

[57] Dani Madrid-Morales, "China's Digital Public Diplomacy towards Africa: Actors, Messages and Audiences," in Kathryn Batchelor and Xiaoling Zhang (editors), *China-Africa Relations: Building Images through Cultural Co-operation, Media Representation and Communication* (Routledge: 2017), 129–46.

[58] Lily Kuo, "Beijing Is Cultivating the Next Generation of African Elites by Training Them in China," *Quartz*, December 14, 2017, https://qz.com/africa/1119447/china-is-training-africas-next-generation-of-leaders; Xi Jinping, "Full Text: Keynote Speech By Chinese President Xi Jinping at Opening Ceremony of 8th FOCAC Ministerial Conference," *Forum on China-Africa Cooperation*, December 2, 2021, https://www.focac.org/eng/gdtp/202112/t20211202_10461080.htm.

[59] Ian Taylor, *The Forum on China-Africa Cooperation* (Routledge: 2011).

[60] Joshua Kurlantzick, *Beijing's Global Media Offensive: China's Uneven Campaign to Influence Asia and the World* (Oxford University Press: 2023).

[61] Hangwei Li and Yuan Wang, "African Media Cultures and Chinese Public Relations Strategies in Kenya and Ethiopia," Carnegie Endowment for International Peace, February 27, 2023, https://carnegieendowment.org/research/2023/02/african-media-cultures-and-chinese-public-relations-strategies-in-kenya-and-ethiopia/.

competition in the Global South and on China's authoritarian diffusion, in popular and policy writings, what China promotes as "win-win" initiatives is associated with a multidimensional threat to Western interests in Africa,[62] as well as to democratic governance more broadly.[63] The moral claims about China's domination and exploitation of Africa have now expanded from the economic onto the political and cultural layers of Sino-African encounter.

In contrast to studies of China's economic activities, however, our empirical understanding of China's soft power in Africa is still limited. In particular, the existing scholarship, especially book-length studies, is concentrated on Chinese media as a soft power channel. These innovative works present broad overviews of modalities of Chinese media diplomacy, including the workings of the core media "channels,"[64] as well as the historical legacies, motivations, and journalistic genres of Chinese media in Africa.[65] Several studies delve into the implications, revealing mixed outcomes of China's media outreach. Multicountry survey studies about correlations between Chinese media and public perceptions of China, for instance, showcase a positive impact over time.[66] Interview-based works, in contrast, point at inherent limitations of Chinese media diplomacy, including mistrust from African audiences,[67] as well as

---

[62] "Countering China in Africa," *The Economist*, May 20, 2022, https://www .economist.com/special-report/2022/05/20/countering-china-in-africa; Glenn Tiffert and Oliver McPherson-Smith, "China's Sharp Power in Africa: A Handbook for Building National Resilience," *Hoover Institution*, March 21, 2022, https://www .hoover.org/research/chinas-sharp-power-africa-handbook-building-national-resilience

[63] Carolyn Logan and Josephine Appiah-Nyamekye Sanny, "China Has Invested Deeply in Africa: We Checked to See Whether that Is Undermining Democracy," *The Washington Post*, October 29, 2021, https://www.washingtonpost.com/politics/2021/10/29/china-has-invested-deeply-africa-we-checked-see-whether-that-is-undermining-democracy/.

[64] Shubo Li, *Mediatized China-Africa Relations: How Media Discourses Negotiate the Shifting of Global Order* (Palgrave Macmillan: 2017).

[65] Xiaoling Zhang, Herman Wasserman, and Winston Mano, *China's Media and Soft Power in Africa: Promotions and Perceptions* (Palgrave Macmillan: 2016).

[66] Catie Snow Bailard, "China in Africa: An Analysis of the Effect of Chinese Media Expansion on African Public Opinion," *The International Journal of Press/Politics* 21(4) (2016); Dani Madrid-Morales and Herman Wasserman, "How Effective Are Chinese Media in Shaping Audiences' Attitudes towards China? A Survey Analysis in Kenya, Nigeria and South Africa," *Online Media and Global Communication* (2022).

[67] Herman Wasserman and Dani Madrid-Morales, "How Influential Are Chinese Media in Africa? An Audience Analysis in Kenya and South Africa," *International Journal of Communication* 12 (2018).

editorial constraints of Chinese journalists in Africa[68] and the emerging hierarchies in Sino-African collaboration as part of journalistic production.[69]

Other than media diplomacy, some scholars look to education aid and capacity building as part of China's power projection in Africa. Kenneth King's work on China's education aid,[70] Wei Ye's study of domestic politics of China's education diplomacy,[71] and Lina Benabdallah's influential book on China's knowledge production through state-sponsored professionalization trainings[72] all showcase the expansive scope, richness, and limitations of these initiatives. Benabdallah's book makes a larger theoretical argument about the central role that "network-building" or relational power plays in China's rise in Africa and beyond.[73] Selective works on Confucius Institutes in Africa also demonstrate the importance of skill diffusion and relationship-building beyond teaching Chinese language and culture,[74] as well as some challenges that Confucius Institutes (CIs) face in Africa, including transactional[75] and suspicious[76] reception on the ground.

Overall, our existing empirical grasp of China's image-making in Africa (and arguably more broadly in the Global South) is limited to specific tools or channels (primarily the media), and either to the top-down layer of resources and strategies (and in rare cases, practices) or the bottom-up level of outcomes, mostly linked to the impact of Chinese media. The evolving literature demonstrates the ambitious trajectory of China's diplomacy and its uncertain implications for China's influence in

---

[68] Iginio Gagliardone and Nyiri Pal, "Freer But Not Free Enough? Chinese Journalists Findings their Feet in Africa," *Journalism* 18(8) (2016).

[69] Emeka Umejei, *Chinese Media in Africa: Perception, Performance, and Paradox* (Lexington Books: 2020).

[70] Kenneth King, *China's Aid and Soft Power in Africa: The Case of Education and Training* (Boydell & Brewer: 2013).

[71] Wei Ye, *China's Education Aid to Africa: Fragmented Soft Power* (Routledge: 2023).

[72] Lina Benabdallah, *Shaping the Future of Power: Knowledge Production and Network-Building in China-Africa Relations* (University of Michigan Press: 2020).

[73] Joshua Eisenman has also developed parallel arguments in his recent writings. See, for instance: "China's relational power in Africa: Beijing's 'new type of party-to-party relations,'" *Third World Quarterly* 44 (12): 2441–2461.

[74] Maria Repnikova, "Rethinking China's Soft Power: 'Pragmatic Enticement' of Confucius Institutes in Ethiopia," *The China Quarterly* 250 (2022): 440–463.

[75] Ibid.

[76] A. Wheeler, "Cultural Diplomacy, Language Planning, and the Case of the University of Nairobi Confucius Institute," *Journal of Asian and African Studies* 49(1) (2014): 49–63; M. Procopio, "The Effectiveness of Confucius Institutes as a Tool of China's Soft Power in South Africa," *African-Asian Affairs* 2 (2015): 98–125.

the region. This study draws on this important scholarship but diverges in its analytical scope and aspirations. Specifically, it expands from the study of soft power tools to dissecting the core tentacles of China's image-making by identifying and examining the workings of its dominant mechanisms. It also weaves together the top and bottom layers by equally prioritizing China's dynamic image projection and reception in the context of Ethiopia. As such, the book presents a holistic analytical picture and a rich empirical account of Sino-African engagement, with a special focus on China's outreach to African elites. I explain my analytical approach and the core arguments in detail in the next section.

1.4 CHINA'S UNEVEN IMAGE-MAKING: ANALYTICAL FRAMEWORK AND ARGUMENTS

1.4.1 China's Image-Making and Its Core Mechanisms

In this book, I build on and move beyond "soft power" conceptualization in theorizing China's state-led and state-linked diplomatic initiatives in Africa by introducing a broader term, "image-making" – a mosaic of distinct but entwined power mechanisms that include both promotional and defensive functions aimed at boosting and guarding China's image. The focus on the "making" captures the relational, dynamic, and multi-directional nature of this process, including uneven implementation, and contested responses on the ground, discussed in the following section.

In my study of China's state-led diplomatic influence in Ethiopia, I identify and empirically analyze three core image-making mechanisms: *tangible enticement, ideational persuasion,* and *censorial power* (see Table 1.1). *Tangible enticement* refers to centering tangible or material access at the heart of elite diplomacy, whereby China offers educational,

TABLE 1.1 *The core mechanisms of China's image-making*

Core Mechanisms	China's Image-Making Mechanisms
Tangible enticement	Providing tangible resources through diplomatic channels (i.e., education, trainings, media partnerships)
Ideational persuasion	Promoting China's political and cultural ideals, values, and governance practices
Censorial power	Guarding the production and dissemination of China narratives

training, and employment opportunities, as well as media and infrastructure resources as part of its diplomatic initiatives. This tangible appeal is foundational to China's promotion of its image, as it lures influential groups into engagement with China and presents China as an accessible power. *Ideational persuasion* signifies the promotion of China's political and cultural ideals, values, and governance practices – something that is most clearly on display in China's elite training programs, but also present in China's media and cultural diplomacy, among other channels. This lever of influence gets at deeper meaning-making or diffusion of knowledge and understanding of what China is about beyond its projected generosity. *Censorial power* encompasses active efforts to guard China's narratives, including through controlled publicity and varied censorship tactics aimed at Ethiopian communication professionals and other influential actors. While treated as analytically distinct, these mechanisms tend to overlap, reinforce, and at times contradict each other, as already showcased in the opening vignette. The promotional efforts by the Chinese embassy at the book launch, for instance, were in part undercut by sudden surveillance directed at Ethiopian participants.

The use of the term "image-making" is not meant to "displace" soft power as an analytical tool, but rather to build on it and to accommodate for some of its limitations in capturing Chinese, and arguably, more broadly authoritarian realities. Soft power concept, coined by Joseph Nye in 1990 and widely popularized since, is rooted in the US context. It emerged from his analysis of American influence in the post-Cold War era, as Nye advocated for the US reliance on "attraction" in foreign policy. In his seminal 2004 book, he identified culture, values, and morally sound foreign policy as the key characteristics or ingredients of soft power, prioritizing examples from the United States, and referring to American culture as "universalistic."[77] Nye also delineated economic influence from soft power, associating the former with co-optation and hard power.[78]

---

[77] Joseph S. Nye Jr, *Soft Power: The Means to Success in World Politics* (PublicAffairs: 2005).

[78] Nye Jr, *Soft Power: The Means to Success in World Politics*, p. 13. His definition transpired in critiques from international relations scholars. Some scholars, like Mattern, for instance, argue against the assumption that attraction is "natural" and instead suggest that it is inherently relational and even coercive. See Janice Bially Mattern, "Why 'Soft Power' Isn't So Soft: Representational Construction of Attraction in World Politics," *Millenium: Journal of International Studies* 33(3) (2005). Some scholars also highlight the weakness of his resource-based and transmission-based approach, and instead offer a discursive lens to studying soft power. See Chengxin Pan, Benjamin Isakhan, and Zim Nwokora,

As I write about in my Chinese Soft Power Element book, while the concept of soft power "travelled" to China starting in mid 2000s, it was reimagined for the local context. Chinese thinkers tend to merge economic prowess (i.e., technological advancement and China's economic model) with cultural power and treat boundaries between hard and soft power as malleable and interactive.[79] Chinese soft power writings frequently invoke economic governance, material opportunities, and political ideology and culture as China's core resources, and the conceptualization of culture tends to intermingle with that of ideology.[80] In addition to promoting China's image, Chinese experts also emphasize the defensive nature of Chinese soft power, arguing for protecting China's narratives against those infiltrating from the West.[81] I discuss this in more detail in the context of Africa in the following chapter. Chinese analytical framings of "soft power," therefore, are fundamentally distinct from what we associate with it in the West, problematizing the direct applicability of this concept to China.

My own intellectual journey from "soft power" toward "image-making" and its core mechanisms also emerged inductively – from the experiences and practices observed and studied on the ground. The extensive fieldwork in Ethiopia and China discussed in detail in the next section, which focused on China's diplomatic and communication strategies in Ethiopia, revealed the simultaneous prevalence of practical inducements, ideational outreach, and disciplining or censoring. I found that Chinese diplomacy draws heavily on material power and attraction to lure in participants, selectively channels China's political ideal and values, and relies on nuanced modalities of control to guard against potential criticisms (especially those publicly expressed) across its communication channels. "Soft power" in the traditional, Western-centric sense is misfitting to explain and capture these dynamics. Some readers may wonder whether "sharp power" is the term that would more readily apply here. However, as I already discussed in section 1.1, "sharp power" is laden

"Othering as Soft-Power Discursive Practice: China Daily's Construction of Trump's America in the 2016 Presidential Election," *Politics* 40(1) (2020): 54–69.

[79] Zheng Yongnian and Zhang Chi, "Guoji zhengzhi zhong de ruanliliang yiji dui ruanliliang de guancha" ("Soft Power in International Politics and the Implications for China"). *Shijie Jingji Yu Zheng Zhi (World Economics and Politics)* (7) (July 14, 2007): 6–12; 3; Mingjiang Li, ed., *Soft Power: China's Emerging Strategy in International Politics* (Lexington Books: 2009).

[80] Maria Repnikova, *Chinese Soft Power* (Cambridge Element Series: 2022).

[81] Ibid.

with ideological biases and presumes coercion as the core modus operandi of Chinese diplomacy. My empirical work speaks against this, and instead advocates for a careful fusion of "softer" and "sharper" edges of Chinese diplomacy. Rather than apply an "oppositional" term of "sharp power" to assess China, my hope is that my analytical choices can stimulate other scholars of Global China to reimagine "soft power" from Chinese perspectives and practices and to lend a new vocabulary to do so.

My use of the term "image-making" also builds on other studies of authoritarian external legitimation. I especially take inspiration from Dukalskis' "authoritarian image management" framework that calls for a more comprehensive study of how authoritarian regimes attempt to legitimize themselves in the international arena.[82] In his book, Dukalskis puts forward "promotional" and "obstructive" categories of authoritarian image management that align with my fusion of softer and sharper modes of China's diplomacy in Africa. The mechanisms I identify are more limited and specific to my empirical case (though they can arguably be applied to other authoritarian cases), but the overarching motivation of moving away from Western-centric lenses in documenting the complex authoritarian global engagements is the same.

1.4.2 Unpacking the Mechanisms: Tracing Uneven Practices and Processes

In analyzing the workings of China's image-making mechanisms, this book abstains from determining linear outcomes and instead grapples with the practices or the "how" of implementation and reception. My interest in studying the process itself resonates with the public relations approach to nation branding, which emphasizes relational and co-creational dimensions of image projection, in contrast to the more top-down practices of "image management."[83] This analytical direction is also in line with the practice-centered approach to studying China's domestic governance articulated by Shue and Thornton as "capable of accommodating, if not 'patterned anarchy,' then at the very least the mixed effects of multidirectionality observable within processes of

---

[82] Alexander Dukalskis, *Making the World Safe for Dictatorship* (Oxford University Press: 2021).

[83] Szondi Gyorgy, "From Image Management to Relationship Building: A Public Relations Approach to Nation Branding," *Place Branding and Public Diplomacy* 6(4) (2010): 333–43.

political change."[84] In their analysis, they introduce the "braided stream" metaphor to account for the dynamism and fluidity of China's evolving governance, with change continuously taking place, "but almost never change in just one direction."[85]

In this book, I argue that these considerations of fluidity and multi-layered, uneven transformation are also critical in understanding China's global governance, especially given the diverse interests and actors involved in constructing, shaping, and responding to China's global encounters. In my analysis, I build on other studies in Global China that endeavor to systematize its chaotic governance practices. Some scholars, like Min Ye and Wei Ye, for instance, document the fragmented implementation of China's major global initiatives like the Belt and Road Initiative (BRI) and education diplomacy, as rooted in complex domestic politics.[86] Others, including Lee and Driessen, demonstrate the varied motivations and the ensuing practices of Chinese actors partaking in state-led (and private) economic projects in Africa.[87] Some empirical studies also unveil mixed outcomes of China's economic expansion, including backlash, acceptance, and the dynamic negotiations on the ground.[88]

In my analysis, I disaggregate both the top-down layer of implementation and the bottom-up level of reception across the core mechanisms and showcase the "unevenness" of China's image-making project. As for implementation, far from a linear or a monolithic effort, China's "soft power" is at once strategic and disjointed, targeted and random, systematic and opportunistic, as a diverse set of Chinese actors are driven by varied agendas, including the party-state's visions, but also bureaucratic and personal ambitions. These contradictions or disparities in governance are notable across different power mechanisms and diplomatic initiatives. In promoting the tangible benefits of China's diplomacy, for instance,

---

[84] Vivienne Shue and Patricia M. Thornton (editors), *To Govern China: Evolving Practices of Power* (Cambridge University Press: 2017), p. 13.

[85] Ibid, p. 14.

[86] Min Ye, "Fragmentation and Mobilization: Domestic Politics of the Belt and Road in China," *Journal of Contemporary China* 28(119) (2019): 696–711. Wei Ye, *China's Education Aid to Africa: Fragmented Soft Power* (Routledge: 2023).

[87] Lee, *The Specter of Global China*; Driessen, *Tales of Hope, Tastes of Bitterness*.

[88] Margaret M. Pearson, Meg Rithmire, and Kellee S. Tsai, "China's Party-State Capitalism and International Backlash: From Interdependence to Insecurity," *International Security* 47 (2022): 135–76; Selina Ho, "Infrastructure and Chinese Power," *International Affairs* 96(6) (2020): 1461–85; Edward Schatz and Rachel Silvey (ed.), *Seeing China's Belt and Road* (Oxford University Press: 2025); Bradley Jardine and Edward Lemon, *Backlash: China's Struggle for Influence in Central Asia* (Hurst: 2025).

Chinese diplomats at once target specific elite groups and institutions, as well as improvise in approaching individual candidates and even delegate resource allocation to their Ethiopian partners. In spreading China's ideals and visions, Chinese educators promote some recurrent frameworks and practices, such as China's distinctive democracy and performance legitimacy, but also present patchy, disjointed accounts of specific governance spheres like the media. In disciplining narratives about China in Ethiopia, Chinese embassy and company representatives proactively engage in structured publicity and information control but also issue sporadic punishments and threats. Mirroring the writings on China's domestic governance that underscore experimentation and improvisation as the underlying feature,[89] my analysis presents ad hoc practices as critical to China's image-making project, alongside with more strategic or directed governance. This makes China's image initiatives somewhat unruly, taking on a zigzag shape rather than a linear direction.

The reception or engagement by Ethiopian elites is also fluid and contradictory, evading the labels of outright resistance to or co-optation and seduction by China, or that of antagonism and solidarity. Ethiopian actors, like their Chinese counterparts, contain multitudes of interests and creatively and selectively take part in China's orbit. Specifically, the study of Ethiopian perspectives through interviews and focus groups reveals a mix of responses, including selective acceptance of Chinese influence, as well as initiation, appropriation, and negotiation of Chinese offerings. These practices point at the agency of Ethiopians as direct participants in shaping the Sino-Ethiopian encounter, but also the asymmetric power structures at play, whereby Ethiopians (while at times initiating the engagement) are still largely adjusting to and reacting to China – the more dominant partner. The complex responses by Ethiopian elites, often enacted simultaneously, also underscore the contingent nature of China's image-making, as relative success in some areas, such as in publicly guarding China's storytelling can also backfire in mistrust and private questioning of China's objectives.

The unevenness and multidirectionality of China's image-making project in Africa is further evident in its intersections with and subjugations to global power hierarchies, namely the influence of the West, as explored in

[89] Yuen Yuen Ang, *How China Escaped the Poverty Trap* (Cornell University Press: 2016); Sebastian Heilmann, "Policy Experimentation in China's Economic Rise," *Studies in Comparative International Development* 43(1) (2008): 1–26, https://doi.org/10.1007/s 12116-007-9014-4.

the final empirical chapter. The analysis of perspectives of both selective Chinese image practitioners and Ethiopian recipients revealed a surprising synergy in their shared aspiration toward the West as part of their encounter. Chinese practitioners, including diplomats, journalists, and educators, often mediate their interactions with Ethiopians through Western benchmarks, and treat Africa as a step toward careers in the West. Ethiopian elites engage with China's offerings and ideals through a comparative prism of the West and often treat China as a secondary (but accessible) option and destination. Returning to the opening vignette, both Chinese and Ethiopian interlocutors chose to focus more on American politics and opportunities rather than on China–Africa relations in conversing with me after the book launch. One of the unanticipated realities of China's so-called soft power in the Global South, this book argues, is that thus far it remains entwined with the power of the Global North. China's uneven "worldmaking"[90] is still challenged by the shadows of Western dominance.

1.5 METHODOLOGICAL APPROACH: GLOBAL CHINA THROUGH LOCAL ENCOUNTERS

1.5.1 Why Ethiopia

While big data approaches are increasingly popular across political science, communication and international relations disciplines, in-depth ethnographic work that allows for theorizing and conceptualizing complex and elusive power dynamics is best afforded by immersion into a specific, but carefully selected context. This approach has been adopted in several groundbreaking works that now make up the emerging interdisciplinary field of Global China. Lee's highly regarded study of China's global capital, for instance, is centered in Zambia,[91] Driessen's illuminating analysis of China-led development is grounded in Ethiopia,[92] Huang's study of China's racial capitalism is an ethnography of "China malls" in South Africa,[93] and Hubbert's important book on the contested Sino-globalization project is an

---

[90] I borrow the formulation of "worldmaking" from Rofel and Rojas and their edited volume, *New World Orderings: China and the Global South* (Duke University Press: 2023).

[91] Lee, *The Specter of Global China.*

[92] Driessen, *Tales of Hope, Tastes of Bitterness.*

[93] Mingwei Huang, *Reconfiguring Racial Capitalism: South Africa in the Chinese Century* (Duke University Press: 2024).

in-depth ethnography of the workings of Confucius Institutes and Classrooms in the United States.[94]

I selected Ethiopia as a critical case for examining the potential for China's image-making in Africa and more broadly in the Global South. China's high stakes for crafting a positive image in Ethiopia – combined with its deep-seated economic and political influence in the country over the past three decades, and Ethiopia's relatively favorable political context – can render visible the full scope of China's image-making that would be more challenging to discern in other contexts. First, Ethiopia is of unique importance in China's larger Africa and Global South outreach. Other than being the second most populated country in Africa and an influential regional actor,[95] Ethiopia is a gateway for China's larger diplomatic influence on the continent both symbolically and logistically. As a nation proudly carrying a unique history of not surrendering to colonial conquest, Ethiopia is an important symbol of Pan-Africanism.[96] As a home to the African Union (its new quarters are Chinese-funded and constructed),[97]

[94] Jennifer Hubbert, *China in the World: An Anthropology of Confucius Institutes, Soft Power, and Globalization* (Hawaii University Press: 2020).

[95] Claire Klobucista, "Ethiopia: East Africa's Emerging Giant," *Council on Foreign Relations*, November 4, 2020, https://www.cfr.org/backgrounder/ethiopia-east-africas-emerging-giant.

[96] Harcourt Fuller, a scholar of international history of Africa, highlights the importance of Ethiopia's defeat over Italy in the famous 1896 battle of Adowa as "a symbol of inspiration and hope for the next generation of African nationalists and Pan-Africanists." See Hacrourt Fuller, *Building the Ghanaian Nation-State: Kwame Nkrumah's Symbolic Nationalism* (Palgrave Macmillan: 2014), p. 134; first found in Jan Záhořík, Aleksi Ylönen A, and Jonah Lego, "Multiple Layers of Pan-Africanism and Pan-Ethiopianism in Current Debates on Nationalism and Ethnicity in Ethiopia," *Nationalities Papers*, published online 2025:1–16. Ethiopia was occupied by Italy between 1936 and 1941 but not officially colonized. In the 1950s and 1960s, Haile Selassie further reinforced the centrality of Ethiopia in Pan-Africanism by establishing Addis Ababa as the headquarters of the UN Economic Commission for Africa (UNECA) in 1959 and by initiating and hosting the Organization of African Unity in 1963 (the organization later became the African Union). For a detailed analysis on Ethiopia as "unifier" of conflicting Pan-African factions and on Haile Selassie's presentation of Ethiopia as "neutral," see Fikru Gebrekidan, "From Adwa to OAU: Ethiopia and the Politics of Pan-Africanism, 1896–1963," *International Journal of Ethiopian Studies* 6(1/2) (2012): 71–86. More recently, under the leadership of Prime Minister Abiy Ahmed, Ethiopian leaders and elites have strategically invoked Pan-Africanism to promote their agendas. See "Multiple Layers of Pan-Africanism and Pan-Ethiopianism in Current Debates on Nationalism and Ethnicity in Ethiopia" and Abiy Ahmed's recent speech at the African Union: "Speech of the Federal Democratic Republic of Ethiopia (FDRE); H. E. Dr. Abiy Ahmed," February 18, 2023, https://au.int/ar/node/42610.

[97] On the complex and contested symbolism of the AU headquarters, please see the fascinating analysis by Daniel Mulugeta: "Pan-Africanism and the Affective Charges of the

Ethiopia is a pathway for a wider diplomatic outreach. As one of the central hubs for China's BRI initiatives, featuring flagship projects like the Addis-Djibouti Railway and the Addis Light Rail, among others, China's "success" in Ethiopia matters for the larger projection of its power.

Second, China's extensive influence in Ethiopia across economic and political spheres presents a fertile foundation for its image production. In the economic domain, Ethiopia is China's second largest loan recipient in Africa and a destination of nearly 700 private Chinese enterprises (see Figure 1.1 of Chinese company advertisements on Ethiopian roads).[98] Described as the "China of Africa" in Western[99] and Chinese analyses,[100] Ethiopia has been considered as one of the most assiduous students of China's economic governance, taking advantage of its population leverage to create a manufacturing hub housed in China-constructed industrial parks across the country.[101]

On the political level, Sino-Ethiopian diplomatic relations date back to 1970, but have deepened in the post-Cold War era. In the past three decades, the Chinese Communist Party has built close ties with the Ethiopian People's Revolutionary Democratic Front (EPRDF, renamed as the Prosperity Party in 2019), with bilateral visits and briefings taking place on a regular basis.[102] Even during Ethiopia's controversial war in

---

African Union Building in Addis Ababa," *Journal of African Cultural Studies* 33(4) (2021): 521–37.

[98] Hairong Yan and Barry Sautman, "China, Ethiopia and the Significance of the Belt and Road Initiative," *The China Quarterly*, July 20, 2023.

[99] See for instance Tyler Cowen, "Ethiopia Already Is the 'China of Africa'" Bloomberg, May 29, 2018, https://www.bloomberg.com/view/articles/2018-05-29/ethiopia-already -is-the-china-of-africa?embedded-checkout=true.

[100] See for instance Qing Ying, "Aisabiya: cankao zhongguo moshi de 'feizhoubanzhong-guo' zouleduoyuan" (Ethiopia: Relying on China model, how far the African version of China has gone), *Caixin*, August 18, 2017, https://pit.ifeng.com/a/20170818/5167599 3_0.shtml.

[101] See for instance "Chinese-Built Industrial Parks Drive Ethiopia's Ambition in Manufacturing Sector, Job Creation," Xinhuanet, August 30, 2019, https://www .xinhuanet.com/english/2019-08/30/c_138351330.htm; for a Western perspective, see "Can Ethiopia Become a Manufacturing Powerhouse?" UNDP Working Paper Series, December 2023, https://www.undp.org/sites/g/files/zskgke326/files/2023-12/undp_e thiopia-_working_paper_series_4_2023_online_version_finanl.pdf.

[102] According to Hackenesch and Bader's study of the CCP's most important political party partners between 2002 and 2017, EPRDF was twelfth globally, and only second to Sudan on the African continent in terms of total number of contacts. See "The Struggle for Minds and Influence: The Chinese Communist Party's Global Outreach," *International Studies Quarterly* (2020) 64: 723–33.

FIGURE 1.1 Chinese company advertisement on a road bridge.

Tigray, the Chinese government abstained from criticizing the Ethiopian regime, in contrast to more punishing reactions from Western partners.[103]

As for Ethiopia's political context, despite the promises for democratic reforms in 2018,[104] Ethiopia remains authoritarian.[105] This can translate into fewer ideological barriers for Chinese influence. Of special importance for China's capacity to contain negative narratives, Ethiopian media sphere is tightly controlled and co-opted by the state, with most major outlets, such as the Ethiopian News Agency, Ethiopia Broadcasting Corporation, and

---

[103] See for instance Jevans Nyabiage, "China Votes 'No' on Tigray Abuses Probe by UN Team, Calls It Interference in Ethiopia's Affairs," *South China Morning Post*, December 19, 2021, https://www.scmp.com/news/china/diplomacy/article/3160246/ch ina-votes-no-tigray-abuses-probe-un-team-calls-it.

[104] Jason Burke, "'These Changes Are Unprecedented': How Abiy Is Upending Ethiopian Politics," *The Guardian*, July 8, 2018, https://www.theguardian.com/world/2018/jul/0 8/abiy-ahmed-upending-ethiopian-politics.

[105] According to the 2024 Freedom in the World report by Freedom House, Ethiopia is marked as "not free" – a consistent rating in the past five years. See "Freedom in the World 2024: Ethiopia," *Freedom House*. Accessed on August 16, 2025. https://freedom house.org/country/ethiopia/freedom-world/2024.

influential newspapers like the Ethiopian Herald, directly owned by the government. In contrast to other major African countries, such as South Africa, Nigeria, and Kenya, where there is a relatively vibrant media capable of contesting Chinese influence,[106] Ethiopia's domestic public sphere is more subdued, posing fewer risks to China's image promotion. I analyze this in detail in Chapter 5. Ethiopia's legacies of a "developmental state" model of state-driven economic growth under the EPRDF (which some argue are still present under the current leadership)[107] can also facilitate synergies between Ethiopian and Chinese elites.[108]

While the Ethiopian case can illuminate the potential for China's image-making, it can also reveal its limitations and frictions that translate to other Global South contexts. Specifically, Ethiopia like many Global South nations has a long history of negotiating and balancing its relationships with major and rising powers.[109] Scholars of Ethiopian diplomatic history argue that even Ethiopia's initiation of diplomatic ties with China in 1970 was driven by a "hedging strategy" vis-à-vis the United States.[110] In recent years, under the leadership Abiy Ahmed, the Ethiopian government has tilted more toward the West after a long period of proximity to

[106] In countries like South Africa and Kenya, critical stories about Chinese activities routinely appear in the media. For example, see Ross Anthony, "China's R370bn 'Gift' Demands Scrutiny," *Mail and Guardian*, September 17, 2018, https://mg.co.za/article/2018-09-17-chinas-r370bn-gift-demands-scrutiny/; Yash Pal Ghai, "Is Kenya a Beneficiary or Victim of Chinese Belt and Road Initiative?," *The Star*, April 28, 2019, https://www.the-star.co.ke/siasa/2019-04-28-is-kenya-a-beneficiary-or-victim-of-chinese-belt-and-road-initiative/.

[107] Some Ethiopian scholars and officials argue that despite publicly abandoning the "developmental state model" in favor of liberalizing the economy, the Ethiopian government under Abiy Ahmed still remains heavily involved in economic governance. See Tsegab Kebebew Daka, "Understanding the Shift in Ethiopia's 'Developmental State' Trajectory: A Political Settlement Perspective," master's thesis, CERIS-ULB Diplomatic School of Brussels, January 2021, https://www.ceris.be/wp-content/uploads/2021/11/Understanding-the-Shift-in-Ethiopias-DS-trajectory.pdf.

[108] Some scholars argue that between 2005 and 2012 Ethiopian elites were learning and engaging with China's developmental successes. See Elsje Fourie, "China's Example for Meles' Ethiopia: When Development 'Models' Land," *Modern African Studies* 53(3): 289–316.

[109] Vijay Prashad, *The Poorer Nations: A Possible History of the Global South* (Verso: 2012); Erica Hogan and Stewart Patrick, "A Closer Look at the Global South," Carnegie, May 20, 2024, https://carnegieendowment.org/research/2024/05/global-south-colonialism-imperialism?lang=en.

[110] Mesafinkt Tarekegn Yalew, "Development of Relations between Ethiopia and China during Emperor Haile Selassie: A Product of Timing or the Leadership?" *Cogent Social Sciences* 10(1) (2024).

China under EPRDF.[111] China's outreach to Ethiopia, like that to other Global South states, therefore, faces strategic and noncommittal dispositions among ruling elites, as well as the persisting influence of the West. The Sino-Ethiopian encounter also allows us to grapple with Global China as a "moving story." China's lending to Ethiopia, similarly to other major African countries, has slowed in recent years[112] – reflecting the larger trends of the BRI.[113] Grasping whether and how this more cautious economic approach translates into image-making is important for understanding the larger tribulations of China's rise. The follow-up fieldwork in 2023, interestingly, had showcased that despite the economic slow-down and the COVID pandemic, China's diplomatic reach has persisted and has bounced back to pre-2020 levels, including large-scale educational and training exchanges that will be discussed in the following chapters.

1.5.2 Data Gathering: Expanding China's Empirical Boundaries

Adding to collective effort of Global China scholars to "[push] the empirical boundary of China studies beyond China's territorial borders,"[114] this study is rooted in multi-sited and transnational fieldwork (2018–23), including research across Ethiopia and China. The fieldwork traced China's major diplomatic initiatives, with a special focus on outreach to elites, primarily via training and educational access, Confucius Institutes, and media and public relations diplomacy. In Ethiopia, the research took place in multiple cities, including the capital, Addis Ababa, but also Mekelle, Adama, Bahir Dar, and Jimma. In China, I was based in Beijing but traveled to Shanghai, Changsha, and Guangzhou for field visits. For a wider geopolitical context, I also carried out some research

---

[111] Simon Marks, "How an African State Learned to Play the West off China for Billions," *Politico*, February 7, 2020, https://www.politico.com/news/2020/02/07/ethiopia-china-west-power-competition-110766.

[112] "A New State of Lending: Chinese Loans to Africa," Global Development Policy Center Report, September 18, 2023, https://www.bu.edu/gdp/2023/09/18/a-new-state-of-lending-chinese-loans-to-africa/.

[113] The BRI is now shifting toward "small" and "beautiful" projects, signaling more caution about large-scale loans and investments. See "Why China Is Rebooting the Belt and Road Initiative," The United States Institute of Peace Report, October 26, 2023, https://www.usip.org/publications/2023/10/why-china-rebooting-belt-and-road-initiative.

[114] Ching Kwan Lee, *The Specter of Global China: Politics, Labor, and Foreign Investment in Africa* (University of Chicago Press: 2017), p. xiv, citation also found in *Global China as a Method*, p. 7.

into how the US policy community views China–Africa relations, as part of my participation in discussions and events at think tanks and with government officials.

As part of this fieldwork, I conducted in-depth semi-structured interviews and focus groups, collected participant observations, and studied policy and archival documents, media reports, and social media content. My interviews involved nearly 130 participants in Sino-Ethiopia image-making encounters, including Chinese diplomats, state media practitioners, Confucius Institute directors and volunteers, educators in charge of organizing and training African officials and journalists, and Chinese experts and scholars of China–Africa relations, among other actors. On the Ethiopian side, I interviewed party and state officials, journalists, university deans and former deans in charge of launching and managing Confucius Institutes and Classrooms, and Ethiopian students enrolled in Chinese language study, as well as recent graduates from these programs, and experts working at major Ethiopian think tanks, among other actors. In addition to interviews, I conducted focus groups on diverse opinions on China among university students, including social science undergraduate and graduate students, journalists, and officials whose work intersects with China. Please see the Appendix II for more details.

I was also fortunate to attend events that captured Sino-Ethiopian and Sino-African diplomatic encounters. The opening vignette about the book launch is one of many examples. Others include Chinese embassy cultural events, provincial diplomacy events, such as the China–Africa trade fair hosted by Hunan province, lectures about China delivered to multiple African audiences in Ethiopia and China, and major Sino-Africa forums, among others. I also held numerous workshops across Ethiopia on China's soft power and China–Africa diplomacy, including at major universities, think tanks, and government offices. Through questions and engagements from the audiences, I was able to gauge diverse perspectives on China from a range of Ethiopian stakeholders.

Other than interviews and observations, I draw on selective analyses of Chinese academic, think tank, and official publications about Africa and China's image in Africa, presented in the next chapter, as well as content analysis of Ethiopian media coverage of China discussed in Chapter 5. In some chapters, I incorporate my analysis of policy documents and academic writings produced by Ethiopian, but also other African journalists and experts about China. Finally, as part of the study of Chinese trainings of Ethiopian elites, I did qualitative content analysis of lecture materials generously shared with me by some Ethiopian participants. The fieldwork journey was incredibly rich but also challenging and uneven – just like the project of China's image-making itself. I discuss these moments of discovery and tribulations, as well as my reflections on my positionality as a researcher in Appendix I (my ethnographic reflections).

1.6 SUMMARY OF CHAPTERS

The book is organized in three parts. Part I presents the larger context for this study. Following the Introduction that examined the relevant scholarly and policy debates, as well as the analytical and methodological choices underpinning this study, Chapter 2 looks at China's ongoing quest for recognition and image-building, and the importance that Africa plays in it. Part II – the crux of the book – illuminates the workings of the core image-making mechanisms, including China's material, ideational, and censorial influence in Ethiopia. Finally, in Part III, I expand to more transnational and comparative directions by bringing in the role of the West in the China–Ethiopia encounter (Chapter 6) and by offering comparative applications of this study to other contexts (Chapter 7).

Chapter 2 examines the positionality of Africa in China's larger pursuit of image and recognition. Drawing on high-level official speeches, academic and policy writings, as well as on selective interviews with China–Africa experts in Beijing and Shanghai, this chapter shows China's dualistic visions for Africa. It is at once treated as an important pathway for China's construction of its global image as a major responsible power, but also as a sensitive context in competing for narratives with the West. China's activities in Africa are frequently the target of Western criticisms that feed into the larger Western narrative of the "China threat." Chinese scholars and experts, in turn, advocate for both offensive and defensive image-making in Africa – strengthening its diplomatic reach and debunking Western narratives on neocolonialism and imperialism.

Chapter 3 delves into the material facet of China's image-making or attraction through tangible offerings. Drawing on the analysis of China's core diplomatic initiatives in Ethiopia, namely elite training and education diplomacy, Confucius Institutes, and media outreach, this chapter illuminates how offering access to opportunities and resources is at the heart of initiating participants into China. It also examines the uneven deployment of "tangible enticement" by demonstrating how Chinese actors, including embassy personnel and Confucius Institute directors, among others, are at once strategic and methodical about presenting targeted opportunities, as well as spontaneous and hands-off in promoting and allocating resources. The chapter then analyzes the reception from Ethiopian target audiences, finding a mix of opportunistic engagement and negotiation of China's offerings.

In Chapter 4, I engage with China's ideational power as part of its image-making in Ethiopia and more broadly in Africa. The chapter directly speaks to the ongoing debates about the export of the China model to the Global South by delving into the content of and perceptions toward China's official training programs of African elites. Rather than exporting a model, I find that Chinese educators and officials attempt to legitimize China's governance (both domestic and global) and to show off China. The actual delivery of these trainings carries some consistency, such as the presentation of China as an alternative type of democracy and an economic success story, as well as some arbitrary content diffusion in specific governance domains like journalism. Far from passively buying into the "China model," Ethiopian participants soften their perceptions of China, but also negotiate and reject some of its persuasion narratives and strategies.

In Chapter 5, I explore the sharper edges of China's image-making and illuminate the subtle, multifaceted silencing that permeates China's diplomacy. The experiences of Ethiopian journalists, PR professionals, officials, and scholars point to the core feature of censorship as controlled information release. This includes proactive selective publicity and information withdrawals, as well as spontaneous and reactive silencing, at times carried out by non-state actors. Ethiopian elites reinforce the efforts of Chinese stakeholders and co-discipline China narratives out of their own strategic interest in upholding a positive relationship with China. At the same time, in private spaces, these same elites also articulate and spread negative stories about China through satire and rumors.

In Chapter 6, I bring in a transnational dimension to the study of China's image-making in Ethiopia by examining the role of the West in conditioning this encounter. Drawing on interviews with core participants in Chinese initiatives, including Ethiopian elites and Chinese diplomatic professionals, the analysis reveals their shared aspirations for the West, and especially for the United States. Ethiopian participants tend to treat the West as a quality marker, and China as a secondary choice, and at times even as a pathway to experiencing the West. Ironically, Chinese soft power promoters also appear to uphold and aspire to Western hierarchies and use Ethiopia and Africa as a channel toward more desired professional destinations in the West. While Chinese official narratives invoke competition with the West, the actual participants in the Sino-African encounter still strive to be part of it.

Finally, Chapter 7 summarizes the core findings of this book and positions them in a larger comparative context by examining how they translate to other contexts in Africa and in the Global South. The chapter further discusses future research pathways in the field of China's diplomacy and image-making in the Global South, including comparative directions, and provides some practical considerations for policymakers.

2

Africa in China's Quest for Global Image and Recognition

2.1 INTRODUCTION

On August 18, 2022, at the Coordinators' Meeting following the Eighth Ministerial Conference of the Forum on China–Africa Cooperation (FOCAC) in Beijing, Wang Yi, China's Foreign Minister, expressed his firm confidence in the future of Sino-Africa relations: "Fruitful China-Africa cooperation will add fresh impetus to global development, generate more positive energy for world stability, and bring new hopes to people around the world. China-Africa friendship will stand any test of winds and storms. It will continue to be the backbone in South-South cooperation and a fine example in international relations."[1] This statement, echoed in other high-level speeches on China–Africa relations introduced later in this chapter, captures the aspirational vision for Africa in China's diplomatic ambitions. Wang Yi describes engagement with Africa as significant for accomplishing China's larger global objectives and presents China–Africa relations as representative and core to China's engagements with the Global South and with the world at large.

This chapter delves deeper into this idealized imagery of Africa by contextualizing it in China's broader soft power and diplomatic

---

[1] "Wang Yi: Women jianxin zhongfei youhao yiding hui jixu chengwei nannan hezuo de jiliang, guoji guanxi de dianfan" (Wang Yi: We Firmly Believe China–Africa Friendship Will Continue to Be the Backbone in South–South Cooperation and a Fine Example in International Relations), Ministry of Foreign Affairs of the People's Republic of China. August 18, 2022, https://www.fmprc.gov.cn/web/wjb_673085/zzjg_673183/xws_674681/ xgxw_674683/202208/t20220818_10745566.shtml.

objectives. While the previous chapter articulated how the analytical framework in this book moves away from "soft power" toward more grounded practices of "image-making" in studying China's diplomatic influence in Africa, in this chapter, I still analyze official invocations of soft power to show how image and attraction, loosely defined, have entered the official and academic lexicon. Drawing on high-level official speeches, selective academic, and policy writings,[2] as well as interviews with China–Africa experts in Beijing and Shanghai, this chapter demonstrates the centrality of image and status in China's self-conceptions of itself as a rising power and the important positioning of Africa in this pursuit. Soft power and discourse power are increasingly prominent in official and academic rhetoric, and Africa appears as a crucial pathway for China's construction of its global image, as well as a sensitive context in competing for narratives and public opinion with the West.

Specifically, while Chinese official speeches and writings frame Africa as a third-tier diplomatic priority (following major and neighboring countries),[3] they highlight its prominence in the Global South, and its role in constructing China's global identity as a major responsible power. At the same time, Chinese experts also express concerns about the West as threatening its image ambitions in Africa. Africa is both a potential vessel for China's soft power and discourse power, as well as a site of production and dissemination of the "China threat" narrative. In these writings, African publics and elites are at once glorified as natural allies and treated with concern as potential victims of Western propaganda. Chinese experts, further, call on strengthening China's diplomatic outreach in Africa, both to reinforce its benevolent image and to push back against attacks from the West.

The chapter proceeds with a discussion of the prioritization of image promotion, often referred to as "soft power" in Chinese official and academic narratives as part of China's rise, followed by the analysis of Africa in China's larger pursuits for recognition. Competition with the West features strongly in this analysis, as it appears to both drive and hinder China's image work.

---

[2] The policy writings include high-level pronouncements on soft power and image-building, as well as invocations of Africa in speeches by China's Foreign Minister. Academic writings include articles on China's image diplomacy in Africa and Global South published in top Chinese political science, international relations, communication and area studies journals, as well as by well-known experts in this field (the author compiled a list of experts through prior fieldwork in China).

[3] As will be discussed further in the chapter, major countries are deemed as the biggest geopolitical players, namely, the United States, Russia, and the European Union.

2.2 PROMOTION OF POSITIVE IMAGE AS CENTRAL TO CHINA'S RISE

Whereas scholars of Global China and China's foreign policy have largely prioritized its economic and security statecraft,[4] the pursuit of a favorable image has long preoccupied Chinese officials and experts. International relations scholars like Yong Deng and Xiaoyu Pu underscore China's obsession with status in the international system.[5] Writing in 2008, Deng argues that "the Chinese are intensely sensitive to their nation's 'international status,' treating it as an overriding foreign policy agenda."[6] Writing nearly a decade later in 2019, Xiaoyu Pu notes that Chinese elites are concerned about China's management of its "role and image on the world stage."[7] He further argues that China deploys mixed signals in "status-signaling," including projections of itself as both a major power and a developing country. Communication scholars and historians, Burcu Baykurt and Victoria de Grazia, in their analysis of "soft-power internationalism" write that despite the overarching global enthusiasm for soft power waning in the past decade, China "continues its commitment to soft power, much reframed but also much more ambitious in scale."[8]

---

[4] For recent books on China's economic statecraft in the context of Global China, see for instance: Min Ye, *The Belt Road and Beyond: State-Mobilized Globalization in China: 1998–2018* (Cambridge University Press: 2020); David M. Lampton, Selina Ho, and Cheng-Chwee Kuik, *Rivers of Iron: Railroads and Chinese Power in Southeast Asia* (University of California Press: 2020); Richard W. Carney, *China's Chance to Lead: Acquiring Influence via Infrastructure Development and Digitalization* (Cambridge University Press: 2024); and Ching Kwan Lee, *The Specter of Global China: Politics Labor, and Foreign Investment in Africa* (University of Chicago Press: 2017). On geopolitical and security influence, see Scott L. Kastner, Margaret M. Pearson, and Chad Rector, *China's Strategic Multilateralism: Investing in Global Governance* (Cambridge University Press: 2019); M. Taylor Fravel, *Active Defense: China's Military Strategy since 1949* (Princeton University Press: 2020); Fiona S. Cunningham, *Under the Nuclear Shadow: China's Information-Age Weapons in International Security* (Princeton University Press: 2025). On books that co-examine economic and security nexus, see Jacques de Lisle and Avery Goldstein (editors), *China's Global Engagement: Cooperation, Competition, and Influence in the 21st Century* (Brookings Institution Press: 2017); and Oriana Skylar Mastro, *Upstart: How China Became a Great Power* (Oxford University Press: 2024).

[5] Yong Deng, *China's Struggle for Status: The Realignment of International Relations* (Cambridge University Press: 2008); and Xiaoyu Pu, *Rebranding China: Contested Status Signaling in the Changing Global Order* (Stanford University Press: 2019).

[6] Deng, *China's Struggle for Status: The Realignment of International Relations*, p. 8.

[7] Pu, *Rebranding China: Contested Status Signaling in the Changing Global Order*, p. 10.

[8] Burcu Baykurt and Victoria de Grazia, *Soft Power Internationalism: Competing for Cultural Influence in the 21st-Century Global Order* (Columbia University Press: 2021), p. 4.

The analysis of official pronouncements and selective Chinese academic writings reveals the continuity and acceleration in China's image pursuit, as well as the persisting sentiment that China still hasn't realized its full potential. As for the official rhetoric, high-level concern with image promotion was already notable in the 1980s and 1990s. At the Expanded Meeting of the Central Military Commission in 1985, for instance, Deng Xiaoping promoted the building of a peaceful, anti-war national image.[9] At the 1999 Conference on External Propaganda Work, Jiang Zemin called for "fostering different countries' understanding of China" and "defending the international image of China as a socialist country."[10]

In 2000s, in the Hu-Wen era, showing and explaining China to the world became more prominent in official speeches. At the 2003 National Propaganda Thought Work Meeting, for instance, Hu Jintao urged to: "…comprehensively and objectively introduce to the world the continuous development of our country's socialist material civilization, political civilization, and spiritual civilization … create a beneficial international public opinion environment for the construction of a moderately prosperous society."[11] In his 2007 address at the 17th Party Congress, Hu invoked the term soft power (*ruan shili*) for the first time. He stressed the need for China to "…stimulate the cultural creativity of the entire nation, enhance the country's cultural soft power, and better protect the basic cultural rights and interests of the people…"[12]

In the past thirteen years, under Xi Jinping, the official endorsement of China's image promotion has gained further prominence, as evident in his numerous references to image-building, soft power, discourse power,

---

[9] "1985 nian 6 yue 4 ri, deng xiaoping zai zhongyang junwei kuoda huiyi shang" ("June 4, 1985, Deng Xiaoping at the Expanded Meeting of the Central Military Commission"), *People's Daily Online*, May 5, 2016, http://cpc.people.com.cn/BIG5/n1/2016/0505/c69 113-28326613.html.

[10] "Jiang zemin zai quanguo duiwai xuanchuan gongzuo huiyi shang qiangdiao, zhanzai genggao qidian shang ba waixuan gonguo zuo de geng hao" ("Jiang Zemin Emphasizes at Conference on External Propaganda Work, Strive for Greater Success from a Higher Starting Point"), *People's Daily*. February 27, 1999, https://cn.govopendata.com/renmin ribao/1999/2/27/1/.

[11] "Hu jintao zai quanguo xuanchuan sixiang gongzuo huiyi shang fabiao zhongyao jianghua" ("Hu Jintao Delivers Important Speech at the National Propaganda Thought Work Meeting"), *Sina News*, December 9, 2003, https://news.sina.com.cn/o/2003-12-0 9/214111299177s.shtml.

[12] "Hu jintao guanyu wenhua jianshe he wenhua tizhi gaige de zhongda lilun guandian" ("Hu Jintao's Major Theoretical Views on Cultural Development and Cultural System Reform"), *China Daily*, October 21, 2011, www.chinadaily.com.cn/dfpd/17jlzqh/2011-10/21/content_13949506_2.htm.

and international communication among other interrelated concepts. In 2013, at the 12th Study Group of the Political Bureau of the Central Committee, Xi Jinping juxtaposed image-making with soft power, arguing that enhancing soft power necessitates "paying attention to the construction of country's national image" – presenting China as "…politically transparent, economically developed, culturally prosperous …"[13] Xi Jinping also invoked soft power at the 2017 19th Party Congress,[14] and the 2018 address on propaganda, among other important party sessions.[15] As part of advocating for bolstering China's soft power, Xi often stressed the importance of international communication and discourse power. At the 2018 National Propaganda Thought Work Meeting, for instance, Xi Jinping called for Chinese communicators to "…display a real, multi-dimensional, and all-round image of China to the world…"[16] At the 2021 30th Study Group of the Political Bureau of the Central Committee, Xi called for elevating China's "international discourse rights," which he equated with "a beneficial public opinion environment" and China's construction of the community of shared destiny.[17] In his 2022 report to the 20th Party Congress, Xi associated "strengthening international communication capability" with "…achieving an international discourse power

<hr>

[13] "Xi jinping: jianshe shehuizhuyi wenhua qiangguo, zhuoli tigao guojia wenhua ruanshili" ("Xi Jinping: Build a Socialist Cultural Powerhouse, Enhance Cultural Soft Power"), *Xinhua*, December 31, 2013, www.xinhuanet.com/politics/2013-12/31/c_118788013.htm.

[14] "Xi jinping: juesheng quanmian jiancheng xiaokang shehui, duoqu xinshidai zhongguo tese shehui zhuyi weida shengli-zai zhongguo gongchandang di shijiu ci quanguo daibiao dahui shang de baogao" ("Xi Jinping: Secure a Decisive Victory in Building a Moderately Prosperous Society in All Respects and Strive for the Great Success of Socialism with Chinese Characteristics for the New Era-Report at the 19th National Congress of the Communist Party of China"), *Xinhua*, October 27, 2017, www.xinhuanet.com/politics/leaders/2017-10/27/c_1121867529.htm.

[15] "Ju qizhi ju minxin yu xinren xing wenhua zhan xingxiang geng hao wancheng shixia xuanchuan sixiang gongzuo shiming renwu" ("Raise the Banner, Gather the people, Cultivate New Talents, Develop Culture, and Promote the National Image: Better Fulfilling the Mission of Propaganda and Ideological Work in the New Situation"), *People's Daily Online*, August 23, 2018, http://media.people.com.cn/n1/2018/0823/c40606-30245183.html.

[16] "Jianghao zhongguo gushi rang shijie geng liaojie zhongguo" ("Tell China Stories Well, Let the World to Better Understand China"), *Xinhua*, September 2, 2018, www.xinhuanet.com/politics/2018-09/02/c_1123367300.htm.

[17] Tang Jia. "Tisheng guoji huayu quan, zhongguo xuyao zheyang zuo" ("Improve China's International Discourse, China Needs to Do Like This"), *People's Daily*, June 7, 2021, www.people.com.cn/n1/2021/0607/c437595-32124020.html.

that matches China's national strength and international status (*guoji diwei*)."[18]

A large body of academic and policy writing that accompanied official pronouncements[19] underscores the urgency of China's image-building by highlighting its shortcomings in comparison to hard power, as well as in contrast to the West. As for hard versus soft power assessments, in the words of Yu Guoming, a highly regarded communications expert: "The strength of our voice does not match our position in the world. That affects the extent to which China is accepted by the world. If our voice does not match our role, we remain a crippled giant."[20] Yu links voice to acceptance and acceptance to status of a major power. In a more recent article, Ye Shulan, the director of the International Relations Institute at East China Normal University, articulates a similar view. Integrating the concepts "image," "soft power," and "hard power," she argues that while China's "hard image," characterized by economic strength, has been steadily improving, its "soft image," defined by perception and appraisal, has declined to its lowest level since 1978. She expresses concern about the growing disparity between these two dimensions of China's rise.[21]

The assessments of China's image work also invoke the problematic relative dominance of the West and measure China against the United States. Shi Anbin, a Tsinghua University global communication scholar, influential in policy circles, argues that despite improvements in China's international image since the 18th Party Congress, the narrative of China's "decline" and "collapse" promoted by Western media still dominates international public opinion about China, overshadowing China's remarkable achievements since the Reform and

---

[18] "Jiaqiang guoji chuanbo nengli jianshe, cujin wenming jiaoliu hujian" ("Strengthen International Communication Capability, Promote Mutual Learning and Exchange among Civilizations"), *Xinhua*, December 27, 2023, www.xinhuanet.com/politics/202 31227/c21a7e5c88404d1cb86a4515b5da5815/c.html.

[19] Over 11,000 article titles with the word "soft power" in the title came up with the title search on CNKI. On CNKI, a title search for "national image" yields over 4,000 articles and more than 1,700 dissertations. I discuss some selective examples from these writings here, but not a systematic analysis. For more systematic analysis, see Maria Repnikova, *Chinese Soft Power* (Cambridge University Press: 2022).

[20] Guo and Lye 2011, cited in Zhao 2013, p. 22. Originally quoted in my earlier work, *Chinese Soft Power*.

[21] Ye Shulan, "Zhongguo guojia xingxiang de xianshi tiaozhan yu youhua celue" ("Practical Challenges and Optimization Strategies of China's National Image"), *Xueshu Qianyan (Academic Frontiers)* (24) (2023): 15–23.

Opening-up.[22] Feng Tianyu, the Director of the National Center for Collaborative Innovation in Cultural Soft Power at Wuhan University, in his article on soft power, directly points at Western superiority or the notion of "the West is strong, China is weak" (*xi qiang zhong ruo*), and calls for further development of Chinese culture and cultural conscience.[23] Yan Xuetong, a well-known international relations theorist at Tsinghua University, in his earlier writings cautions that economic wealth does not automatically equate to great power status,[24] and urges China to enhance its soft power to compete with the United States.[25]

In this brief overview of official discourse and selective academic studies, it is evident that the official focus on constructing a favorable global image has intensified over time, especially in the Xi Jinping era, with Xi himself referring to it more frequently at high-level meetings. Chinese academic scholarship in international relations and global communication further underscores the urgency of elevating China's image. Chinese scholars articulate weak soft power as a major vulnerability in China's rise, especially in contrast to its growing hard power and to the relative favorability of the United States. In some ways, the concern with competition for image and the quest for recognition as part of China's rise as a major power reflects the concept of "reputational security" coined by the renowned public diplomacy scholar Nicholas J. Cull, whereby "image plays at the core of statecraft, invoking statecraft's highest purpose: defense."[26] In his analysis, Cull primarily focuses on the United States, but the centrality of promoting and guarding China's image in high-level official narratives and objectives makes "reputational security" applicable

---

[22] Shi Anbin, "Xinshidai guoji chuanbo nengli jianshe de xin silu xin zuowei" ("New Strategies and Innovations in Building International Communication Capabilities in the New Era"), *Guoji Chuanbo (Global Communication)* (1) (2018): 8–15.

[23] Feng Tianyu, "Ruanshili chuyi" ("On Soft Power"). *Wenhua Ruanshili Yanjiu (Studies on Cultural Soft Power)* 1(1) (2016): 11–13. https://doi.org/10.19468/j.cnki.2096-1987 .2016.01.003.

[24] Yan Xuetong, "Zhongguo jueqi de shili diwei" ("The Rise of China and its Power Status"), *Guoji Zhengzhi Kexue (Quarterly Journal of International Politics)* (2) (2005): 1–25.

[25] Yan Xuetong and Xu Jin, "Zhongmei ruanshili bijiao" ("A Comparative Study of Chinese and American Soft Power"), *Xiandai Guoji Guanxi (Contemporary International Relations)* (1) (2008): 24–29.

[26] Nicholas J. Cull, "Public Diplomacy and the Road to Reputational Security: Analogue Lessons from US History for a Digital Age," Background Research, Gates Forum I, November 2022, p. 3.

to China. We now shift to the analysis of how the Global South and Africa fit into the larger puzzle of China's image-making.

2.3 AFRICA IN CHINA'S PURSUIT FOR GLOBAL RECOGNITION

2.3.1 Africa in China's Larger Diplomatic Priorities

Before delving into the significance of Africa for China's image ambitions, this section positions it in the larger regional hierarchies of China's diplomatic visions. In China's diplomatic rhetoric over the past decade, Africa is at once downplayed and elevated. It is relegated into the category of "developing countries," which follows major global power and regional diplomacy. At the same time, Africa stands out as the crux of the Global South.

As for the hierarchical positioning of Africa and developing countries more broadly, the key diplomatic addresses of China's Foreign Minister, Wang Yi, from 2015 to 2024,[27] all adhere to the same pattern of highlighting relations with other major powers, followed by neighborhood diplomacy, and then relations with developing countries. In Wang Yi's 2021 address, for instance, he first presents a more detailed account of diplomacy with Russia, the United States, and the European Union, and then offers a more limited discussion of diplomatic engagements with neighboring countries, and finally with developing countries.[28] At the Second Session of the 14th National People's Congress in 2024, Wang

---

[27] From January to July 2023, during his brief tenure as the foreign minister, Qin Gang also adhered to this diplomatic framework. At the First Session of the 14th National People's Congress in March 2023, in response to a journalist's question about the future direction of China's foreign policy, Qin Gang emphasized China's commitment to building "a new type of international relations," a concept contrived by Xi Jinping. See "Waijiao buzhang qingang jiu zhongguo waijiao zhengce he duiwai guanxi huida zhongwai jizhe tiwen" ("Foreign Minister Qin Gang Answers Questions from Chinese and Foreign Journalists on China's Foreign Policy and International Relations"), Ministry of Foreign Affairs of the People's Republic of China, March 7, 2023, www.fmprc.gov.cn/web/wjdt_674879/wjbx w_674885/202303/t20230307_11037046.shtml. According to official explanations, fostering this new type of international relations involves maintaining positive relations with major countries, subsequently with neighboring countries, and then with developing countries. See "Tuidong goujian xinxing guoji guanxi shenhua tuozhan quanqiu huoban guanxi" ("Advancing the Building of a New Type of International Relations and Deepening Global partnerships"), *Global Times*, December 12, 2022, https://baijiahao .baidu.com/s?id=1752012131036694262&wfr=spider&for=pc.

[28] "2021 nian zhongguo waijiao: bingchi tianxia xionghuai, jianxing weiguo weimin" ("China's Diplomacy in 2021: Embracing a Global Vision and Serving the Nation and Its People"), The Ministry of Foreign Affairs of the People's Republic of China,

reiterates this diplomatic stance, emphasizing China's efforts to maintain stable relations with major powers, cooperate closely with neighboring countries, and seek rejuvenation alongside Global South countries.[29] The major official statements about Xi Jinping's diplomatic thought by Yang Jiechi, the Director of the General Office of the Central Foreign Affairs Commission, and a member of the Politburo, point at the same priorities. In analyzing what he refers to as China's "global network of partnerships," he calls to "deepen coordination and cooperation with major countries and promote global stability as a whole … advance the building of community with a shared future with our neighbors … make continuous efforts to enhance solidarity and cooperation with developing countries."[30]

Similar implicit hierarchies are also present in some policy and academic writings. Feng Weijiang, then the Deputy Director of the General Office at the Chinese Academy of Social Sciences (CASS), in his analysis of China's strategic diplomatic presence divides China's diplomatic presence into three layers, with big countries, including the United States and Russia, positioned in the first layer.[31] In his study of China's future diplomatic strategic layout, Men Honghua at Tongji University argues that China should first stabilize its relations with major powers, including the United States, Russia, and Europe, then strategically engage with neighboring countries, and finally expand cooperation with developing countries.[32] Some Chinese scholars advocate for simultaneously pursuing

December 20, 2021, www.fmprc.gov.cn/web/wjbzhd/202112/t20211220_10471837 .shtml.

[29] "Zhonggong zhongyang zhengzhiju weiyuan, waijiao buzhang wang yi jiu zhongguo waijiao zhengce he duiwai guanxi huida zhongwai jizhe tiwen" ("Politburo Member and Foreign Minister Wang Yi Answers Questions from Chinese and Foreign Journalists on China's Foreign Policy and International Relations"), Ministry of Foreign Affairs of the People's Republic of China, March 7, 2024, www.mfa.gov.cn/web/ziliao_674904/zyj h_674906/202403/t20240307_11255225.shtml.

[30] Yang Jiechi, "Shenru xuexi guanche xi jinping waijiao sixiang jinyibu kaituo duiwai gongzuo xin jumian" (Studying and Implementing Xi Jinping Thought on Diplomacy in a Deep-Going Way and Opening up New Horizons in China's External Work), *People's Daily*, May 16, 2022, http://politics.people.com.cn/n1/2022/0516/c1001-32422054 .html.

[31] Feng Weijiang, "Xinshidai zhongguo tese daguo waijiao: kexue neihan zhanlue buju yu shijian yaoqiu" ("On Major Country Diplomacy with Chinese Characteristics in a New Era: Vision, Planning, and Practice"), *Guoji Zhanwang (Global Review)* 10(3) (2018): 13–28.

[32] Men Honghua, "Goujian mianxiang weilai de zhongguo waijiao zhanlue xin buju" ("Building a New Layout of China's Diplomatic Strategy for the Future"), *Tansuo yu Zhengming (Exploration and Free View)* (1) (2022): 43–50, 177.

all three layers (or objectives), but rhetorically, they tend to still invoke major powers before neighboring and developing countries.[33]

Within the category of the Global South, however, Africa is granted a priority. In Wang Yi's diplomatic speeches, Africa is discursively positioned before other developing contexts. In his 2022 address, for instance, he discusses Africa first, under the theme of South–South relations, followed by Latin America and the Arab States.[34] In his detailed interview with the Xinhua News Agency on the state of China's diplomacy in 2021, the question on China–Africa relations directly followed the question about neighboring countries (ASEAN). Other parts of the Global South were omitted in the interview.[35]

Some official statements also highlight Africa (along with China) as the symbol of the Global South. In February 2024, in a congratulatory message to the 37th Summit of the African Union, for instance, Xi Jinping depicts China and Africa as representatives of the Global South, emphasizing that the vigorous development of the Global South profoundly impacts the course of world history.[36] A month later, at the Two

---

[33] Li Boyi, "Zhongguo huoban waijiao de bianhua" ("Changes in China's Partner Diplomacy"), *Zhanlue Juece Yanjiu (Journal of Strategy and Decision Making)* 12 (3) (2021): 36–66, 102; Wang Fan, "Zhongguo tese daguo waijiao: xietiao, biange yu wanshan" ("Big Country Diplomacy with Chinese Characteristics: Coordination, Change and Perfection"), *Tansuo yu Zhengming (Exploration and Free View)* (1) (2022): 12–15; Yang Jinwei, "Zhongguo tese daguo waijiao de lilun chuangxin he shijian jinlu" ("The Theoretical Innovation and Practical Approach of Great Power Diplomacy with Chinese Characteristics"), *Dong Yue Luntan (Dong Yue Tribune)* 44(3) (2023): 5–12; Guo Hongwei, "Zou heping fazhan daolu: zhongguoshi xiandaihua daguo waijiao de hexin luoji" ("Pursuing a Path of Peaceful Development: The Core Logic of Great Power Diplomacy with Chinese Characteristics"), *Lilun Yanjiu (Theoretical Research)* (1) (2024): 7–14; Zhao Kejin, "Zhongguoshi xiandaihua de waijiao luoji: jiyu shengtai zhidu zhuyi zhengzhixue de fenxi" ("The Diplomatic Logic of Chinese Modernization: An Analysis Based on the Politics of Eco-Institutionalism"), *Guoji Zhanwang (Global Review)* 16(4) (2024): 1–20, 165.
[34] Wang Yi, "Gaoju renlei mingyun gongtongti qizhi kuobu qianxing" ("Striding Forward Holding High the Banner of Building a Community with a Shared Future for Mankind"), The Central Government of the People's Republic of China, January 2, 2022, www.gov.cn /guowuyuan/2022-01/02/content_5666074.htm.
[35] "Wang yi guowu weiyuan jian waizhang jiu 2021 nian guoji xingshi he waijiao gongzuo jieshou xinhuashe he zhongyang guangbo dianshi zongtai lianhe caifang" ("State Councilor and Foreign Minister Wang Yi Gives Interview to Xinhua News Agency and China Media Group on International Situation and China's diplomacy in 2021"), Ministry of Foreign Affairs of the People's Republic of China, December 30, 2021, www .fmprc.gov.cn/web/wjbz_673089/zyjh_673099/202112/t20211230_10477288.shtml.
[36] "Xiandaihua daolu shang xieshou xiangqian, gongzhu gao shuiping zhongfei mingyun gongtongti: xi jinping zhuxi xiang di 37 jie feizhou lianmeng fenghui zhi hedian zai feizhou yinfa qianglie fanxiang" ("Jointly Advancing on the Path of Modernization to

Sessions, Wang Yi tells journalists that the Chinese foreign minister's first overseas visit each year is always to Africa, a tradition followed for thirty-four years because China and Africa are inseparable (*gan dan xiang zhao*) and are "brothers who share a common destiny."[37] Academic writings also often invoke Africa as the representative of developing countries.[38] An in-depth analysis of the diplomatic visions for Africa, as articulated in official, academic, and policy writings on soft power, and public diplomacy further reveals that Africa is seen as a key enabler of China's global visions, as well as an important context for competing for discourse power with the West. I turn to this discussion next.

2.3.2 Constructing China through Africa

In academic and policy writings, Chinese scholars further position African countries as enabling China's global influence through direct tactical support, but more importantly by showcasing China as a responsible power that strives to create a more equitable global order. As for tactical visions, some scholars like Zhou Shuqing, a research fellow at the Institute of African Studies, Zhejiang Normal University, explicitly argue that Africa can help promote and amplify China's political agendas and interests. Zhou invokes the importance of Africa in curbing Taiwan's plight for independence, as well as Japan's quest for membership in the UN Security Council.[39] Luo Jianbo, a Diplomacy expert at the Central Party School, in his articulation of the strategic importance of Africa, highlights Africa's support for China at the United Nations, as well as in fulfilling China's Belt and Road Initiative (BRI) – a key diplomatic project of the Xi Jinping

Build a High-Level China-Africa Community of Shared Future: President Xi Jinping's Congratulatory Message to the 37th African Union Summit Receives Warm Response in Africa"), *People's Daily Online*, February 19, 2024, http://politics.people.com.cn/n1/20 24/0219/c1001-40178907.html.

[37] "Wang Yi: zhongfei lingdaoren jiang zaici jushou beijing, gongshang weilai fazhan daji" ("Wang Yi: China-Africa Leaders to Reunite in Beijing to Discuss Future Development Cooperation"), *Xinhua*, March 7, 2024, www.xinhuanet.com/politics/20240307/dcc8 b436a56b44cf884222a6fe4e476b/c.html.

[38] Luo Jianbo, "Ruhe tuijin zhongguo duifei duobian waijiao" ("How to Advance China's Multi-lateral Diplomacy towards Africa"), *Xiandai Guoji Guanxi (Contemporary International Relations)* (11) (2006): 24–29; Yao Yao, "Zhongfei mingyun gongtongti de lishi yiyi yu lilun jiazhi" ("Historical Significance and Theoretical Value of China–Africa Community with a Shared Future"), *Zhongguo Feizhou Xuekan (Journal of China-Africa Studies)* 2 (1) (2021): 3–23, 154.

[39] Zhou Shuqing, "Zhongguo zai feizhou de liyi jiqi weihu zhanlue" ("Chinese Interests and the Safeguard Strategies"), *Guoji Guancha (International Review)* (2) (2009): 21–28.

era.[40] Wang Lijuan, an international relations scholar at Hebei Normal University, associates China's assistance to Africa with African pro-China voices helping China increase its global influence. She specifically referred to Africa's support in holding major diplomatic events like the Beijing Olympics and the Shanghai Expo.[41] These studies frame African countries as amplifiers of China's discourse power by directly supporting and magnifying China's diplomatic positions.

Another, more prominent theme in the analyses of Africa's positioning in China's narratives on public diplomacy and soft power is the indirect role or what Luo Jianbo refers to as the "stage" that Africa (and developing countries more broadly) presents in facilitating a construction of China's identity and image.[42] In the Hu-Wen period, engagement with Africa was seen as propelling China's vision of a "harmonious world" – a major political slogan of that era. In his analysis of China–Africa relations under Hu Jintao, for instance, Wei Xuemei, an international relations scholar at the Central Party School, argues that China's assistance to Africa was a way of realizing "the harmonious world" by highlighting coexistence, equal dialogues, and developmental prosperity.[43] Under Xi Jinping, Chinese scholars characterize China's relations with Africa as embodying China's practice of "major country diplomacy" – a proactive diplomatic leadership in the international system[44] that includes a pursuit of justice, not solely interests.[45] Justice in the context of China's diplomacy is the promotion of

---

[40] Luo Jianbo, "Tisheng zhongguo duifei huayuquan de xinjiyu yu xinsikao" ("Promote New Opportunities and New Thinking of China's Discourse Power toward Africa"), *Guoji Chuanbo (International Communications)* (4) (2017): 32–35.

[41] Wang Lijuan, "Ershiyi shiji zhongguo duifei yuanzhu de biyaoxing ji duice" ("The Necessity of China's Foreign Aid in Africa and Solutions in the 21st Century"), *Dangdai Shijie Yu Shehui Zhuyi (Contemporary World and Socialism)* (3) (2014): 88–92.

[42] Luo Jianbo, "Zhongguo tese daguo waijiao xinlinian xinzhanlue yu xintese" ("Major - Country Diplomacy with Chinese Characteristics: New Concepts, Strategy and Characteristics"), *Xiya Feizhou (West Asia and Africa)* (4) (2017): 28–49.

[43] Wei Xuemei, "Zhongguo yuanzhu feizhou yu tisheng zhongguo ruanshili" ("China's aid to Africa and Improvement of China's Soft Power"), *Guoji Guanxi Xueyuan Xuebao (Journal of University of International Relations)* (1) (2011): 31–36.

[44] Jianwei Wang, "Xi Jinping's 'Major Country Diplomacy:' A Paradigm Shift?" *Journal of Contemporary China* 28(115) (2018): 5.

[45] "Major country diplomacy" is the key diplomatic concept of the Xi Jinping era, and it is understood as China's more proactive diplomatic stance that breaks with Deng's tradition of "conceal one's abilities and hide one's intention" and calls for China's leadership in the international system. See Dai Changzheng, "Zhongguo tese daguo waijiao de neihan yu jiazhi" ("Connotation and Value of Major-Country Diplomacy with Chinese Characteristics"), *China's Diplomacy in the New Era*, April 29, 2022, http://cn.chinadiplomacy.org.cn/2022-04/29/content_78193494.shtml; Jianwei Wang, "Xi

mutuality and fairness, as encapsulated by another important slogan of the Xi era – "the community with a shared future for mankind."[46] Referring to China's outreach to the Global South, including Africa, Wu Zhicheng at the Central Party School and Li Jiaxuan at Nankai University argue that "…friendly cooperation with developing countries presents the basic pathway for China to practice the correct 'justice-benefit view' and realize the integration of national interest and international justice."[47]

Specifically, by demonstrating China's capacity to deliver development to Africa, Chinese scholars argue that China can also promote a more benevolent or just image of itself as a major power. Hao Yuanyuan and Shuang Chuanxue at Nanjing University, for instance, write that for China to construct a "responsible big country image," it needs to demonstrate that it is willing to shoulder responsibility for human development. They further invoke Africa as an opportune context for showcasing this commitment, and for improving China's image by helping Africa develop.[48] In their analysis of the BRI, Liu Zaiqi and Wang Manli at Wuhan University characterize Africa as the region that manifests its effective outreach and exemplifies China's more active engagement in global affairs. The authors attribute many benefits of BRI to African countries, including economic and technological development.[49] More directly referring to China's soft power ambitions, Yin Yue's report

Jinping's 'Major Country Diplomacy:' A Paradigm Shift?" *Journal of Contemporary China* 28(115) (2018): 5.

[46] "The Community of Shared Human Destiny," first proposed at the 18th CPC National Congress in 2012, is considered China's guiding principle of international relations under the leadership of Xi Jinping. Its main principle is to "consider the legitimate concerns of other countries while pursuing national interests, and promote common development among all countries while seeking national development." See Wang Zhimin and Chen Zonghua, "Goujian renlei mingyun gongtongti: lilun tanyuan, shidai yihan yu shijian jinlu" ("Constructing a Community with a Shared Future for Mankind: Theoretical Origin, Time Implication and Practical Approach"), *Guizhousheng Dangxiao Xuebao (Journal of Guizhou Provincial Party School)* (4) (2022): 5.

[47] Wu Zhicheng and Li Jiaxuan, "Xi jinping waijiao sixiang zhong de zhengque yiliguan" ("The Pursuit of Shared Interests and Common Good in Xi Jinping Thought on Diplomacy"), *Guoji Wenti Yanjiu (International Studies)* (3) (2021): 41.

[48] Hao Yuanyuan and Shuang Chuanxue, "Renlei mingyun gongtongti shiyu xia de guojia wenhua ruanshili jianshe" ("National Cultural Soft Power Construction from the Perspective of Shared Destiny of the Mankind"), *Zhongguo Tese Shehui Zhuyi Yanjiu (Study of Socialism with Chinese Characteristics)* (6) (2017): 65–71.

[49] Liu Zaiqi and Wang Manli, "Yidai yilu zhanlue yu zhongguo canyu quanqiu zhili yanjiu yi huayu quan he huayu tixi wei shijiao" ("Study of 'Belt and Road' Strategy and China's Engagement in Global Governance – from a Perspective of Discourse Power and Discourse System"), *Xuexi Yu Shijian (Study and Practice)* (4) (2016): 68–74.

about the significance of Wang Yi's visit to Africa in 2018 argues that "Africa is an important testing field to improve China's soft power" as it is the first region where China has shifted its foreign policy from passive to active in constructing its national image and discourse power.[50] Ma Hanzhi and Yu Jiang at the China Institute of International Studies underscore that Africa has the largest number of developing countries and that the China–Africa community of a shared destiny can serve as a fine model for the construction of similar communities with the Arab world, Latin America, and the ASEAN region.[51]

In positioning it as the channel for projecting China's benevolent image, Chinese scholars tend to treat Africa as an enthusiastic partner, sharing a similar pursuit of elevating the plight of developing countries. Wu Zhicheng and Li Jiaxuan, for instance, in their endorsement of cooperation with developing countries, point to their synergies with China in terms of shared developmental ambitions and historical suffering.[52] In his work, Yu Jiang, the Deputy Director of the China Institute of International Studies, argues that Africa is a crucial component of the Global South and harbors the most urgent desire to establish an equitable global order among other Global South countries, which makes Africa a natural ally of China.[53] Liu Hongwu, a renowned African Studies scholar and the Director of the Institute of African Studies at Zhejiang Normal University, notes that following centuries of global dominance of the West accompanied by the marginalization of developing countries, it is timely for the rise of Asian and African countries to participate more actively in international affairs and global knowledge production.[54] Long Xiaonong at the China Communication University argues that under Xi Jinping, the China Dream

[50] Yin Yue, "Wang yi xinnian shoufang tuxian feizhou zhanlue zhongyaoxing" ("Wang Yi's First Visit in the New Year Highlights Africa's Strategic Importance"), China-Africa Friendly Economic and Trade Development Foundation. January 22, 2018, www.cnafrica.org/cn/zfxw/14707.html.

[51] Ma Hanzhi and Yu Jiang, "Lun goujian gaoshuiping zhongfei mingyun gongtongti" ("On Building a High-Level China-Africa Community with a Shared Future"), *Guoji Guancha (International Review)* (3) (2024): 1–28.

[52] Wu Zhicheng and Li Jiaxuan, "Xi jinping waijiao sixiang zhong de zhengque yiliguan" ("The Pursuit of Shared Interests and Common Good in Xi Jinping Thought on Diplomacy"), *Guoji Wenti Yanjiu (International Studies)* (3) (2021): 23–46.

[53] Yu Jiang, "Zai duojihua jincheng zhong gongzhu gaoshuiping zhongfei mingyun gongtongti" ("On Building a High-Level China-Africa Community of a Shared Future in the Process of Multipolarization"), *Guoji Guanxi Yu Diqu Qushi (International Relations and Regional Situation)* (2) (2024): 50–55.

[54] Liu Hongwu, "Xifang zhengzhi jingji lilun fansi yu yafei zhishi huayuquan chongjian" ("Retrospections on Western Political and Economic Theories and the Reconstruction of

and the Africa Dream are interconnected as part of the "community with a shared future for mankind." Long quotes Xi Jinping's statement that China and Africa share "historical experiences, developmental missions and strategic interests," and that their relationship cannot be interpreted solely through the lens of Western-framed power struggle and competition for interests.[55] In Long's understanding (that draws directly on Xi Jinping's thought), China's and Africa's global visions are naturally entwined, and together make up a more equitable vision of international relations than the status quo pushed by the West. In these writings, the evolution of China–Africa relations is presented as linear, with compatible worldviews evolving from joint struggles against colonialism and imperialism toward mutual ambitions of creating a more balanced global order that prioritizes the interests of developing countries.

These narratives of "sameness" that underpin the endorsement of Africa as a site for China's image-making may obfuscate some implicit hierarchies whereby China speaks for Africa and assumes responsibility for African countries' future. Carrozza and Benabdallah in their study of representations of Africa in Chinese international relations scholarship theorize this production of hierarchies through invoking similarities as a practice of "selving." In contrast to Western international relations scholarship that tends to treat Africa through the "othering" lens or through "a position of inferiority or backwardness," they argue that in Chinese writings, hegemony is manifested through inclusion rather than exclusion.[56] In the articles and reports analyzed in this section, it is notable that Chinese experts tend to project China's grievances with the current world order onto African countries, fusing China and Africa into a shared identity of marginalized developing countries. Similar themes are also invoked in China's elite diplomacy toward Ethiopia, as I explain in Chapter 4. These writings rarely include African voices or differentiate across African countries in their experiences with development and colonial legacies. Most scholars tend to refer to either Africa or the African

Power of Discourse in Asian-African Knowledge"), *Xiya Feizhou (West Asia and Africa)* (1) (2011): 11–16, 79.

⁵⁵ Long Xiaonong, "Cong xiongdi dao mingyun gongtongti zhongguo jiangou dui feizhou huayu tixi de linian yu shijian" ("From Brothers to a Community with a Shared Future for Mankind-Principles and Practices of China's Discourse Construction towards Africa"), *Xiandai Chuanbo (Modern Communication)* 38 (1) (2016): 79.

⁵⁶ Ilaria Carrozza and Lina Benabdallah, "South–South Knowledge Production and Hegemony: Searching for Africa in Chinese Theories of IR," *International Studies Review* 24(1) (2022): 6.

continent as a monolithic category and offer brief summations of Africa's experiences and visions as echoing those of China. More broadly, by articulating its image of a responsible power through helping and supporting Africa, China positions itself as enacting justice for Africa and thereby improving its image in the international system.

2.3.3 Defending Africa from the West

Another major theme in Chinese writings on diplomatic relations with Africa is competition with the West. While some scholars, drawing on public opinion surveys, acknowledge relatively favorable public perceptions of China in Africa,[57] others emphasize the threatening influence of the West for Chinese soft power on the continent. Western media and its dissemination of neocolonialism narrative is treated as especially problematic for China's image promotion in Africa and beyond. These concerns echo larger arguments in Chinese writings on soft power and public diplomacy that underscore the West as a hindrance to China's recognition and acceptance by the international community.

Chinese think tanks, such as the party-affiliated CASS, have produced extensive reports about Western influence in Africa. A report written in 2013 by Zhang Yongpeng, for instance, analyzes Western soft power in Africa as a significant force for China to reckon with. Zhang describes Western countries as "...using historical culture and ideologies as its basis, as well as multiple kinds of bilateral or multilateral agreements, meetings, and partnerships as its bonds."[58] In his analysis of US policies in

---

[57] You Guolong's study based on a report from the Pew Research Center in 2014, for instance, found that African respondents expressed the highest favorability toward China among global survey participants. See You Guolong, "Ruanshili de pinggu lujing yu zhongguo ruanshili de xiyinli" ("Evaluation Paths of Soft Power and Attraction of Chinese Soft Power"), *Xiandai Guoji Guanxi (Modern International Relations)* (9) (2017): 18–26. Jiang Changjian's analysis of earlier public opinion polls from 2005 to 2011 similarly found that whereas citizens in developed countries tend to have relatively low ratings of China's image, respondents from African countries shared more positive impressions. See Jiang Changjian, "Bodong zhong de ruanshili yu xin gonggong waijiao" ("Soft Power and New Public Diplomacy amid Changes"), *Xiandai Chuanbo (Zhongguo Chuanmei Daxue Xuebao) (Modern Communication, Journal of Communication University of China)* (8) (2011): 55–60.

[58] Zhang Yongpeng, "Xifang dui feizhou yingxiang shenhua yu kuoda xin taishi-zhongfei guanxi mianlin de xin tiaozhan" ("New Situation of Deepening and Expansion of the Influence of the West on Africa – New Challenges for China-Africa Relations"), Institute of West-Asian and African Studies, Chinese Academy of Social Sciences, April 16, 2013, www.focac.org/lhyj/yjcg/201304/t20130416_7877479.htm.

Africa, Li Nan, a researcher at the American Institute at the CASS, argues that the United States is attempting to squeeze China's influence by supporting civil society and corporations for the sake of "great power competition."[59] Another recent CASS report suggests that the aim of the Biden administration's Africa policy was not just to address the competition among major powers in the region but also to undermine China's "diplomatic foundation" (*waijiao genji*) and diminish the strategic role of Africa in China's international relations by disrupting China's economic initiatives and squeezing its diplomatic space in Africa.[60]

Chinese experts highlight the production of critical narratives by Western media and politicians as especially detrimental to China's image. In their study of China–Africa media relations, Li Xinfeng and Li Yujie at the Institute of West-Asian and African Studies (CASS) note that attacks and smearing of China in Western media are commonplace and can partially explain the deficit in China–Africa discourse power.[61] Some scholars emphasize the damaging trope of China as a neocolonial power.[62] Hu Zongshan in his study of stigmatization of China in Western narratives, for instance, laments China's extensive efforts at uplifting developing countries being interpreted as "new colonialism."[63]

---

[59] Li Nan, "Daguo jingzheng xia meiguo dui feizhou zhengce de tezheng yu zouxiang" ("The Characteristics and the Prospect of US Policy towards Africa under the 'Great Power Competition'"), *Meiguo Yanjiu (The Chinese Journal of American Studies)* 36(3) (2022): 9–24.

[60] Zhang Hongming, "Bai deng zhengfu de feizhou zhengce: youxian shixiang yu benzhi neihan" ("The Biden Administration's Africa Policy: Priorities and Essential Implications"), *Xiya Feizhou (West Asia and Africa)* (4) (2022): 67–94; 157-158.

[61] Li Xinfeng and Li Yujie, "Xinmiankong yu xinbiange: zhongguo meiti gaibian feizhou chuanmei geju" ("China's Media Engagement in Africa: Influences and Changes"), *Hunan Shifan Daxue Shehui Kexue Xuebao (Journal of Social Science of Hunan Normal University)* 47(3) (2018): 131–140.

[62] See for instance: Li, "The Characteristics and the Prospect of US Policy"; Li and Li, "China's Media Engagement in Africa"; Hu Zongshan, "Zhongguo guoji huayuquan chuyi: xianshi tiaozhan yu nengli tisheng" ("On China's International Discourse Power: Realistic Challenges and Ability's Enhancement"), *Shehui Zhuyi Yanjiu (Socialism Studies)* (5) (2014): 127–135; Hu Nan, "Zhongguo dui feizhou ruanshili yanjiu: zhanlue fenxi yu duice jianyi" ("Analysis on China's Soft Power in Africa: Strategic Analysis and Solution Recommendations"). *Changchun Shiwei Dangxiao Xuebao (Journal of the Party School of CPC Changchun Municipal Committee)* (4) (2011): 67–71; Li Anshan, "Wei zhongguo zhengming: zhongguo de feizhou zhanlue yu guojia xingxiang" ("In Defense of China: China's Africa Strategy and State Image"), *Shijie Jingji Yu Zhengzhi (World Economics and Politics)* (4) (2008): 6–15, 3; Wang Yiwei, "Ruhe kefu zhongguo gonggong waijiao beilun" ("How to Deal with the Paradox of China's Public Diplomacy?"), *Dongbeiya Luntan (Northeast Asia Forum)* 23(3) (2014): 42–50.

[63] Hu Zongshan, 129.

In their analysis, Zhang Xinping and Zhuang Hongtao at Lanzhou University give an example of Western media ignoring China's economic assistance to Sudan, and instead labeling China as a "neo-colonial" power and accusing it of aiding rogue regimes.[64]

Some scholars associate the neocolonial label with Western resentment toward China's influence in Africa. Hu Nan's study of Chinese soft power in Africa, for instance, links negative commentaries from the West, including neocolonialism accusations, to the successful development of China–Africa relations over the past thirty years.[65] Li Anshan at Beijing University goes as far as to argue that China's presence in Africa upends the existing world order that benefits the West and that the West is eager to maintain the status quo.[66] Other experts interpret the neocolonial framing as part of Western media's larger production of the "China threat" narrative aimed at harming China's global image. Zhao Qizheng, the former Minister of the State Council Information Office, in his book on China's public diplomacy strategy, for instance, links the invention of the "China threat" by Western news outlets to negative perceptions of China among international audiences. In listing serious distortions about China published in Western media under the rubric of the "China threat," Zhao includes the portrayal of "China's perfectly normal national defense construction" as military dominance, and the wrongful labeling of China's aid policy in Africa as neocolonialism.[67]

In characterizing Western media and Western governments as endangering China's image of a benevolent, justice-oriented power in Africa, Chinese writings appear to treat global, and especially African, audiences as passive recipients of Western messaging. In discussing the so-called buzz topics that make up the "China threat coverage," Zhao Qizheng, for instance, writes that they are "spread through the powerful media groups, resulting in widespread misconceptions about China amongst

---

[64] Zhang Xinping and Zhuang Hongtao, "Zhongguo guoji huayuquan: licheng, tiaozhan ji tisheng celue" ("China's International Discourse Power: History, Challenges and Promotion Strategies"), *Nankai Xuebao (Zhexue Shehui Kexue Ban) Nankai Journal (Philosophy & Social Sciences)* (6) (2017): 1–10.

[65] Hu Nan, "Zhongguo dui feizhou ruanshili yanjiu: zhanlue fenxi yu duice jianyi" ("On China's soft power in Africa: Strategic analysis and policy recommendations"), *Changchun Shiwei Dangxiao Xuebao (Journal of the Party School of CCP Changchun Municipal Committee)* (4) (2011): 67–71.

[66] Anshan, "Wei zhongguo zhengming: zhongguo de feizhou zhanlue yu guojia xingxiang."

[67] Zhao Qizheng, *How China Communicates: Public Diplomacy in a Global Age* (Foreign Language Press: 2012), p. 24.

foreign publics."[68] Zhao associates the efforts of Western media directly with effective persuasion over their audiences, echoing a linear model of media effects in communication studies, whereby messages transmitted through the media are accepted and internalized by target audiences.[69] In invoking African audiences, some Chinese writings specifically point to their potential susceptibility to Western narratives. Wang Hongyi, a research fellow at the Institute of West Asian and African Studies at CASS, for instance, argues that while most African leaders tend to have a positive attitude toward China, some ordinary people are deceived by the "China threat" narrative and hold a biased or limited understanding of China.[70] He further contends that African media are promoting the "China threat" because they tend to reprint stories about Africa from Western news agencies. The few politicians that endorse an anti-China stance, according to Wang, are also indirectly influenced by the West through previous education experiences that shape their pro-Western identities. Wu Chuanhua, Guo Jia, and Li Yujie, from the same institute, in their study on challenges in China–Africa cultural and educational exchanges, invoke deep immersion of Africans into Western culture as problematic and quote some African scholars characterizing it as "brainwashing" by the West.[71] Zhou Shuqing similarly argues that African elites tend to receive Western education and have a better understanding of Westernized political culture, which poses challenges to the articulation and circulation of the China model.[72] The immersion into Western education and culture is discussed in detail in Chapter 6. Some Chinese studies do acknowledge Africans' grievances about China, such as self-interested practices of Chinese enterprises, but still tend to conflate these concerns with negative Western narratives about China in Africa.[73]

---

[68] Ibid, p. 8.

[69] Harold Lasswell's Model of Communication is a classic example of a linear model of media effects in communication studies. For a more recent analysis of the model, which was proposed in 1948, see Zachary S. Sapienza, Narayanan Iyer, and Aaron S. Veenstra, "Reading Lasswell's Model of Communication Backward: Three Scholarly Misconceptions," *Mass Communication and Society* 18(5) (September 3, 2015): 599–622.

[70] Wang Hongyi, "Shilun zhongguo weixie lun" ("On China Threat Theory"), *Xiya Feizhou (West Asia and Africa)* (8) (2006): 28–32.

[71] Wu Chuanhua, Guo Jia, and Li Yujie. 2018. *Zhongfei renwen jiaoliu yu hezuo (China-Africa People-to-People and Cultural Exchanges and Cooperation)* (China Social Science Press, 2018), p. 33.

[72] Shuqing, "Zhongguo zai feizhou de liyi jiqi weihu zhanlue."

[73] See for instance Luo Jianbo, "Youhua zhongguo zai feizhou de ruanshili" ("Optimizing China's Soft Power in Africa"), *Yafei Zongheng (Asia & Africa Review)* (6) (2007): 18–24, 63; Liu Yumei, "Ruanshili yu zhongfei guanxi de fazhan" ("Soft Power and

This section explained the heightened sensitivity of the Chinese party-state about its image in Africa, especially about how it is communicated through the West. Accusations of neocolonialism channeled by Western media are seen as threatening not only to China's reputation in Africa but also to China's global image as a responsible power that aims to compete with the West for morality and justice, not solely for material gains. In contrast to the positioning of African publics and elites as China's natural allies, as described in the previous section, in these studies, they are portrayed as allies of the West that need to be won over by China.

2.3.4 Calls for Improving China's Image in Africa

As part of promoting China's benevolent image through Africa and counteracting negative Western influence, Chinese experts call for more extensive soft power outreach on the continent, including by demonstrating its generosity, sharing lessons and values, and refuting harmful narratives. As for practical offerings, in an interview with a professor at the Central Party School in Beijing, who specializes in public diplomacy in Africa, he stressed the importance of generosity in winning trust – the idea that he associated with China's traditional cultural norms.[74] Some scholars of China–Africa relations, like Liu Qianqian and his co-authors at the International Poverty Reduction Center, attempt to delineate between hard aid, which includes infrastructure and direct financial assistance, and what they describe as "soft aid," which focuses on human resources, capabilities, and technology.[75] Other scholars, like Zhao Yating at the

Development of Sino-African Relations"), *Guoji Wenti Yanjiu (China International Studies)* (3) (2007): 16–21; Luo Chen and Wang Yirong, 'Meijie jiechu, jiazhiguan yu zhongguo zai feizhou yingxiangli pingjia' ('Media Exposure, World Values, and Evaluation of China's Influence in Africa'), *Quanqiu Chuanmei Xuekan (Global Media Journal)* 7(4) (2020): 24–38.

[74] Interview CHPD02, Beijing, 2019. Scholars of societal relations in China also associate giving or gifting with gaining face or respect in Chinese society and with relationship building (*guanxi*). "By losing or giving away part of one's substance in guanxi exchange, one paradoxically gains or increases one's face," writes Mayfair Mei-Hui Yang. She argues in her book about the role of gifts and favors in China's social relationship building. See Mayfair Mei-hui Yang, *Gifts, Favors, and Banquets: The Art of Social Relationships in China* (Cornell University Press: 1994), p. 196.

[75] Liu Qianqian, Zhu Jiming, and Wang Xiaolin, "Zhongguo weisheng ruanyuanzhu: shijian wenti yu duice-yi duiwai weisheng renli ziyuan hezuo weili" ("China's Soft Aid for Health: Practices, Issues and Implications: A Case of Health Human Resource Cooperation"), *Zhongguo Weisheng Zhengce Yanjiu (Chinese Journal of Health Policy)* 7(3) (2014): 58–63.

Institute of West-Asian and African Studies (CASS), highlight supporting African infrastructure development and providing aid in addressing poverty, food security, education, and health issues as two major priorities in advancing China–Africa cooperation.[76] Others suggest that China's approach has shifted from providing infrastructure to offering training and educational resources.[77] Ma Jianchun, the Chinese Ambassador to the Gambia (2018–22), for instance, believes that China should optimize its assistance model by considering further bringing technology, methodology, and talent to Africa based on existing infrastructure projects.[78]

Some experts also highlight the diffusion of China's ideals and practices as a way of creating a more inspirational image of China. Yan Xiaoxiao at the Institute of International Studies at the Shanghai Academy of Social Sciences, in his analysis of China's image construction in Africa, for instance, argues that China's economic contributions, development models, experiences, and lessons can be used as a soft power resource foundation.[79] Liu Yumei at Tongji University, similarly, suggests that China's economic development and attractiveness constitute important resources for its soft power in Africa.[80] Zhou Yuyuan, then a senior research fellow at the China Institute of International Studies, advocates for promoting China's economic development model, such as the establishment of free trade zones, to Africa, arguing that China's experience in lifting over a billion people out of poverty is highly attractive to African nations.[81] Other experts call for boosting the attractiveness of Chinese culture and its economic model, binding the projection of culture with

---

[76] Zhao Yating, "Goujian xinxing nan nan hezuo: quanqiu fazhan changyi yu '2063 nian yicheng' quanmian duijie" ("Constructing a New Model of South-South Cooperation: Aligning Global Development Initiatives with Agenda 2063"), *Zhongguo Feizhou Xuekan (Journal of China-Africa Studies)* 4 (3) (2023): 24–44, 155-156.

[77] Lijuan, "Ershiyi shiji zhongguo duifei yuanzhu de biyaoxing ji duice."

[78] Ma Jianchun, "Ershida yihou de zhongfei jingmao hezuo: xingshi yu jianyi" ("China-Africa Economic and Trade Cooperation after 20th Party Congress of Communist Party of China: New Circumstances and Suggestions"), *Guoji Jingji Hezuo (Journal of International Economic Cooperation)* 39 (6) (2023): 1–8.

[79] Yan Xiaoxiao, "Yingdui 'zhongguo ruishili shuo': waijiao shijiao xia zhongguo de ruanshili yunyong yu guoji xingxiang suzao" ("To Refute that 'China Is a Sharp Power': China's Soft Power Application and International Image Construction from the Perspective of Culture Diplomacy"), *Journal of Central South University (Social Sciences)* 26(5) (2020): 167-176.

[80] Yumei, "Ruanshili yu zhongfei guanxi de fazhan."

[81] Zhou Yuyuan, "Dabianju shidai zhongfei hezuo de xinzhengcheng yu xinsikao" ("China-Africa Cooperation in the Era of Global Changes: New Journey and New Thinking"), *Xiya Feizhou (West Asia and Africa)* (3) (2023): 3–25.

that of China's economic success stories.[82] Belt and Road Initiative, for instance, is presented as fostering prosperity by sharing China's developmental lessons, as well as its language and cultural symbols.[83] China's educational training and funding are also seen as facilitating Africa's cultivation of talent in multiple industries, for example, agriculture, healthcare, and technology, to empower both individuals and nations to realize their development goals and boost China's soft power.[84]

Some Chinese experts also call for a more proactive effort at refuting Western narratives. Luo Jianbo, for instance, had long advocated for a "timely and refined global propaganda strategy" to push back on Western claims, such as China's neocolonialism in Africa,[85] and He Wenping has similarly explicitly framed China's efforts at improving soft power in Africa as directed at debunking slanderous accusations from the West.[86] Others call for more discourse channels to counter Western narratives. For instance, Li Hongfeng, the Dean of the School of African Studies at Beijing Foreign Studies University, believes that China should not only address and mitigate the influence of negative Western narratives in Africa but also promote the circulation of friendly Western narratives toward China.[87]

Chinese experts don't go into extensive detail in explaining the optimal strategies (and outcomes) of China's image-making efforts in Africa. Their writing often reads as constructive, suggestive, and aspirational, formulated in broad strokes. The core suggestions can be grouped into promotional strategies that include practical and ideational (mixed with cultural)

---

[82] Hu Nan, "Zhongguo dui feizhou ruanshili yanjiu: zhanlue fenxi yu duice jianyi" ("Analysis on China's Soft Power in Africa: Strategic Analysis and Solution Recommendations"). *Changchun Shiwei Dangxiao Xuebao (Journal of the Party School of CPC Changchun Municipal Committee)* (4) (2011): 67–71.

[83] Hu Jian, "'Yidai yilu' yu zhongguo ruanshili de tisheng" ("'Belt and Road' and the Improvement of Chinese Soft Power"), *Shehui Kexue (Social Science)* (1) (2020): 3–18.

[84] Cheng Weihua, Liu Aijun, and Dong Weichun, "Zhongguo jiaoyu yuanzhu feizhou xiangmu youxiaoxing yanjiu" ("Study of Effectiveness of China's Educational Aid Programs in Africa"), *Gaodeng Nongye Jiaoyu (Higher Agricultural Education)* (3) (2015): 29–32.

[85] Luo, "Optimizing China's Soft Power," 23.

[86] He Wenping, "Tuidao gaoqiang: lun zhongfei guanxi zhong de ruanshili jianshe" ("To Pull down the Wall: Building Soft Power in China-African Relations"), *Xiya Feizhou (West Asia and Africa)* (7) (2009): 5–12, 79.

[87] Li Hongfeng, "Zhongguo guojia xingxiang zai feizhou de goujian yu chuanbo: tiaozhan yu yingdui" ("The Construction and Dissemination of China's National Image in Africa: Challenges and Responses"), *Duiwai Chuanbo (International Communications)* (3) (2021): 27–31.

diffusion, as well as the more defensive tactics of pushing back against what is perceived as Western misinformation. As we will examine in the following empirical chapters, tangible and ideational diffusion is very present in the case of Ethiopia. As for defensive image-making, there is a practical effort on the ground to guard China's image, but in Ethiopia, it is rarely directly aimed at refuting Western narratives, but more so at preempting criticisms and negative reporting on the ground.

2.4 CONCLUSION

This chapter demonstrated the importance that Chinese officials and scholars place on image-making as part of China's rise and examined the role that Africa (and Africans) plays in this larger quest for recognition. The analysis of Chinese writings on China–Africa relations, and especially on China's soft power in Africa, reveals that Africa is both idealized as foundational to China's global diplomacy and treated as a sensitive and contested terrain for China's image. On the one hand, Africa is prioritized in the larger category of the Global South as a platform for fulfilling and showcasing China's ideals-based ambitions in the international system. Africa is a key context for persuading the rest of the world that China is a responsible power, helping other developing countries rise alongside it by distributing its economic welfare to construct a more equitable world. At the same time, Chinese scholars underscore Africa as a site of struggle over moral claims with the West, as Western media portray China as a neocolonial power and use China's engagements in Africa as illustrations of the "China threat."

African countries and publics in these analyses are depicted in conflicting terms: They are at once inseparable allies of China, sharing similar grievances and ambitions oriented in part against the West, and as easily malleable targets of Western influence. They are both preordained partners naturally embracing Chinese visions and pro-Western actors that need to be persuaded to shift their allegiances. These tensions are not resolved in the Chinese scholarship. Instead, Chinese scholars emphasize the importance of further improving its image in Africa, including via practical assistance, ideational diffusion, and defending against Western narratives. The following chapters examine how China's image-making works in practice, and the complex responses it incites from Ethiopian audiences.

PART II

CHINA'S IMAGE-MAKING MECHANISMS IN ETHIOPIA

3

Tangible Enticement or the Power of Material Offerings

Mrs. Zhao,[1] the Director of a Confucius Classroom in Ethiopia's scenic city, Bahir Dar, shared a story of her encounter with a German embassy representative. While on a hike together, the German official asked Mrs. Zhao why Bahir Dar University launched a Confucius Classroom but declined a German cultural center. Mrs. Zhao explained to her colleague that rather than seeing it as a discriminatory choice by the university, it was more of a practical decision. She clarified that they are entirely sponsored by the Chinese government and don't require anything from the university.[2] The German embassy, in contrast, expected the university to cosponsor the center.

Dr. Yu, the Director of the Confucius Institute at Addis Ababa University, recalled a similar experience of interacting with Western embassy representatives curious about the success of her initiative and how they manage to recruit the students. In addition to the full sponsorship by the Chinese government, she explained that they attract students with favorable job prospects and scholarship opportunities. In contrast, learning European languages doesn't lead to jobs, and getting to Europe is a slim chance for most students.[3] My visit to the registrar's office at Addis

---

[1] All the names used are pseudonyms.

[2] Visit to Confucius Classroom and informal discussion with the director and Ethiopian colleagues, Bahir Dar, 2018, with a follow-up in 2019.

[3] Informal group discussion with Addis Ababa Confucius Institute Director, a Chinese embassy staff, and a Chinese volunteer, Addis Ababa, 2018, with a follow-up in 2019. The same narrative was relayed by another former director of the same institute in 2019 (Interview CI07).

Ababa University in May 2019 confirmed this: There were almost no new enrollments in European languages in recent years, whereas the Chinese language had steady enrollments. When I asked the registrar official why European languages are so unpopular, her response was curter than the explanations offered by the Chinese directors: "There are no jobs."[4]

These encounters illustrate the importance of practical appeal or what I describe as "tangible enticement" in initiating engagement with China. The positioning of China as an opportunity creator, of course, is often reflected in China's high-level diplomatic narratives. Xi Jinping's core concept, "community with a shared future for mankind," introduced in the previous chapter, for instance, underscores the importance of achieving "common well-being" and China as facilitating better life prospects for citizens in other countries.[5] In his 2021 speech at the United Nations General Assembly, Xi advocated for improvement of people's livelihoods and vowed to "protect and promote human rights through development."[6] In his major addresses at Belt and Road Forums, Xi further underscored the mission of his signature policy as that of enhancing connectivity and creating "new opportunities for global development," with a special focus on the Global South.[7] Increasing practical opportunities in Africa as part of elevating China's image was also advocated by Chinese experts and scholars, as discussed in the previous chapter.

While the most direct channeling of these directives comes in the form of loans and investments, this chapter demonstrates how tangible offerings are also embedded in China's elite diplomacy in Ethiopia. Specifically, Chinese soft power practitioners entice Ethiopians with practical opportunities across different diplomatic initiatives, including as part of education and training diplomacy, Confucius Institute outreach, and media relationship building. The analysis in this chapter further illustrates the uneven deployment of "tangible enticement" by different Chinese institutions and

---

[4] Visit to the Addis Ababa University registrar office in the spring of 2019.

[5] "Ten Years on, Concept of Community with Shared Future for Mankind Injects New Impetus into World," CGTN, March 14, 2023, https://news.cgtn.com/news/2023-03-15/ Concept-of-community-with-shared-future-injects-new-impetus-into-world-1ibrNlsemo U/index.html.

[6] "Statement by President Xi Jinping at the General Debate of the 76th Session of the United Nations General Assembly," Permanent Mission of the People's Republic of China to the UN, September 21, 2021, http://un.china-mission.gov.cn/eng/zt/20210921/202109/t202 10922_10410004.htm.

[7] "Full Text of Xi Jinping's Keynote Speech at 3rd Belt and Road Forum for Int'l Cooperation," *Xinhua*, October 18, 2023, https://english.news.cn/20231018/7bfc16a c51d443c6a7a00ce25c972104/c.html.

individual actors, featuring strategic and consistent promotion practices, as well as disjointedness and improvisation. The appeal of practical empowerment resonates with Ethiopian elites,[8] as they strategically engage with and accept Chinese diplomatic offerings. At the same time, they also attempt to appropriate and negotiate Chinese power, occasionally pushing Chinese officials and educators to adapt to their demands. I now proceed to discuss the centrality of tangible enticement in China's core diplomatic channels, followed by the modalities of allocation and promotion of these opportunities and resources, and finally, the opportunistic reception in Ethiopia.

3.2 THE OFFERINGS: RESOURCES AND ACCESS AT THE HEART OF CHINA'S SOFT POWER

The promotion of tangible benefits is notable across China's major diplomatic initiatives in Ethiopia. Starting with elite training and education diplomacy, based on some estimates, over 5,000 Ethiopian officials have now been trained in China, including through long-term and short-term visits.[9] Hundreds of students are also getting their graduate and undergraduate degrees in China every year.[10] In contrasting the United States' and China's capacity building efforts, a US diplomat in Ethiopia described the latter as training en masse, in comparison to the former, which only offers selective opportunities to very few top-ranked applicants.[11] According to the interviews with both Chinese and Ethiopian stakeholders, China is now the number one destination for getting free capacity building and education experience. Most of my interlocutors already have

---

[8] I include students under "elites" here too as they are based at top universities in the country, and many end up working as facilitators for Chinese companies or joining the government.

[9] "Ethiopia, China enjoy strong cooperation on human resource dev't: officials," Xinhua News, March 31, 2018; http://www.xinhuanet.com/english/2019-10/27/c_138505711.htm. These numbers are broad estimates. Since 2018, many more officials have visited China for short-term trainings. In 2019, an Ethiopian Foreign Ministry Spokesperson claimed that thousands of Ethiopians were attending trainings in China at that time. See: "Ethiopia-China ties set for further boost: official," Xinhua News, October 26, 2019; http://www.xinhuanet.com/english/2019-10/26/c_138503431.htm. After a pause during Covid, trainings resumed in full scale, as I discuss further in the chapter.

[10] The numbers on scholarships are not precise. According to an interview with a Ministry of Education official in February 2019, there were about 200 Ethiopian students at that time studying in China on Chinese Ministry of Finance (MOFCOM) scholarships. Because of the relatively low cost of Chinese education, many students also go on self-funded route. Interview ETHOF06, Addis Ababa.

[11] Informal discussion with US embassy personnel in Addis Ababa, 2018 and 2019.

traveled to China or know someone who has. Ethiopia is part of China's larger capacity building and educational mission in Africa. At the China–Africa Forum in 2018, the Chinese government pledged 50,000 scholarships and 50,000 training opportunities to Africans. In 2021, this number decreased to 10,000 "training and seminar opportunities for high-end talents."[12] However, in 2024, China raised the ante and pledged 60,000 training opportunities, focusing on African women and youth. Chinese officials also agreed to provide training for 6,000 African military personnel and 1,000 police officers.[13]

As for Confucius Institutes (CIs) and Classrooms (CCs), as already noted in the introduction, their accessibility and facilitation of material (namely employment) opportunities are critical to their expansion in Ethiopia. CIs and CCs cover the salaries of teachers and the costs of educational materials and events, with Ethiopian universities only responsible for Chinese teachers' accommodation and classroom spaces. Chinese lessons are also affordable. In my research I found that they are free for university students and staff and offered at a low cost for other members of the community, including Ethiopian chefs, drivers, waiters, and entrepreneurs who have business ties with China. For a brief period, CI teachers even gave free lessons to Ethiopian officials.[14] Located on university campuses, Confucius Institutes and Classrooms are also more physically accessible to students than other cultural and language institutes. In her research on CIs in Ethiopia, Benabdallah, for instance, contrasts the more elitist space occupied by the French Institute, serving the upper-class community in a secluded fenced-up building in the old city, and the more people-oriented outreach of Confucius Institutes located in the middle of campuses and targeting students and university staff (see Figure 3.1, a banner for a Confucius Institute at Addis Ababa University).[15] Up until the Tigray War broke out in Ethiopia in 2020, Confucius Classrooms were embedded in major universities across the country, including in Mekelle, Bahir Dar, Hawassa, Jimma, Asella, and

<hr>

[12] Yun Sun, "FOCAC 2021: China's Retrenchment from Africa?" *Brookings*, December 6, 2021, www.brookings.edu/articles/focac-2021-chinas-retrenchment-from-africa/.

[13] "Full text: Keynote Address by Chinese President Xi Jinping at Opening Ceremony of 2024 FOCAC Summit," *China Daily*, September 5, 2024, www.chinadaily.com.cn/a/2 02409/05/WS66d95a04a3108f29c1fca5c0.html.

[14] The reason these stopped, according to both Chinese and Ethiopian interlocutors, is that Ethiopian officials found the study of Chinese language too challenging and time-consuming.

[15] Lina Benabdallah, *Shaping the Future of Power: Knowledge Production and Network-Building in China-Africa Relations* (University of Michigan Press: 2020).

FIGURE 3.1 A Confucius Institute at Addis Ababa University.

Adama, in addition to the capital, Addis Ababa, that's home to two Confucius Institutes. The Ethiopian context reflects the vitality of Confucius Institutes in non-Western contexts. In contrast to their closures across Western universities, in Africa, and other parts of the Global South, they remain vibrant, according to Chinese officials interviewed in Beijing.[16]

Other than being relatively cost-efficient and physically accessible, Confucius Institutes and Classrooms in Ethiopia also attach tangible incentives to Chinese language learning, including promises of employment at Chinese companies, as well as scholarships to Chinese universities for selective students, as I discuss further in this chapter. Some Chinese educators dedicate significant effort toward both promoting these opportunities and preparing students for specific jobs and industries. The access to jobs, as already noted, strongly differentiates Confucius Institutes from their Western counterparts that don't have the advantage of large-scale company presence in Ethiopia.

---

[16] Interview CHPD03, Beijing, 2019.

In the context of media diplomacy, Chinese state media offers access to its resources and paid-for advertising as part of its outreach to local media outlets. Echoing the larger trends of China's global media practices,[17] one of the outreach strategies I observed in Ethiopia is that of signing content-sharing agreements with major news outlets, as well as paying for inserts in Ethiopian print media. The agreements technically signify content exchange, but in practice they provide Ethiopian media practitioners with free access to Xinhua's global news database – something that Western news agencies like Reuters and AP typically charge for.[18] Chinese state media also routinely place paid-for content in major Ethiopian news outlets, and China Daily is regularly delivered (for free) across many Ethiopian institutions. The Chinese embassy also donates or sponsors technology equipment and furniture for major Ethiopian news outlets, such as the Ethiopian News Agency (ENA), in addition to providing training opportunities for the journalists.[19]

Finally, though it's not the focus of this study, some infrastructure projects and medical assistance fall under "tangible enticement" diplomacy in Ethiopia. While most of the China-constructed infrastructure is financed through loans (as noted in Chapter 1, Ethiopia is the second largest China loan recipient in Africa), some selective projects are considered "gifts" from the Chinese government. These include the spectacular constructions of several urban parks across Addis Ababa,[20] the Science Museum,[21] and the African Union building,[22] among other projects. These constructions are often marked with "China Aid" signs to signal their philanthropic nature in comparison to the many commercial projects marked solely by company logos. These projects can be seen as symbolic, fostering the beautification of Addis Ababa through

---

[17] Joshua Kurlantzick, "Xinhua and Content-Sharing Deals: A Success Story," in *Beijing's Global Media Offensive* (Oxford University Press: 2023), 181–200.

[18] Eisenman has described access to Xinhua's stories as a possible "economic lifeline" for some cash-strapped African news publications. See Joshua Eisenman, "China's Media Propaganda in Africa: A Strategic Assessment," *US Institute of Peace*, 2023, www.jstor.org/stable/resrep48506, 11.

[19] Interview ETJ13, Addis Ababa, 2019.

[20] For an example of China's beautification projects in Ethiopia, see "Chinese-Aided Project Transforms Heart of Ethiopia's Capital," *Xinhua*, August 12, 2021, www.xinhuanet.com/english/2021-08/12/c_1310123458.htm.

[21] The Science Museum was launched on October 4, 2022. See "Feature: China-Aided Science Museum Wins Hearts of Science-Enthusiast Ethiopians," Xinhua, November 19, 2022, https://english.news.cn/20221119/20306acce7ce4d0a90aed208c65311b3/c.html.

[22] "African Union Opens Chinese-Funded HQ in Ethiopia," *BBC*, January 28, 2012, www.bbc.com/news/world-africa-16770932.

FIGURE 3.2 African Union building built by and financed by China.

Chinese infrastructure, but they also carry tangible value, as they provide access to new public spaces like parks, as well as gathering spaces for Ethiopian and African convenings. Some projects, like the African Union building (see Figure 3.2), have also been mired in controversy, with Chinese surveillance technology later discovered in the compound.[23] Ethiopian media, however, did little to investigate it, operating in a censored environment when it comes to China reporting – something I discuss in a separate chapter on censorship (Chapter 5).

As for medical or public health diplomacy, the Chinese government has provided extensive medical equipment and testing supplies during COVID-19, with Ethiopian state media, FANA, noting that "China was the first nation to respond to Ethiopia's urgent health needs" during this crisis.[24] Chinese medical teams have also carved out a more permanent

[23] Abdi Latif Dahir, "China 'Gifted' the African Union a Headquarters Building and then Allegedly Bugged It for State Secrets," *Quartz*, January 30, 2018, https://qz.com/africa/1192493/china-spied-on-african-union-headquarters-for-five-years.

[24] "Chinese Medical Center Pledges Support to Ethiopia's Efforts to Become Regional Medical Tourism Hub," Fana, September 22, 2024, www.fanamc.com/english/chinese-

presence at the China-built Addis Ababa Silk Road General Hospital, which extends free healthcare services to local community and trains local medical practitioners, among other services. In 2024, the Ethiopian prime minister inaugurated a high-tech China-supported military hospital in Bishoftu – a hospital that boasts Chinese medical equipment and China-trained medical practitioners.[25]

3.3 DEPLOYMENT OF TANGIBLE ENTICEMENT: TRACING UNEVEN PRACTICES

Building on the discussion in the previous section about the centrality of tangible opportunities and resources as part of China's diplomatic outreach in Ethiopia, this section analyzes the diffusion and promotion of these offerings. I examine the distribution of education scholarships and training invitations, the spread of the CI initiative, as well as student recruitment strategies and job facilitation by CI directors, and finally, the allocation of Chinese state media resources, including physical and digital content. The key theme that cuts across the analysis is the uneven promotion – a combination of both strategic and coordinated practices, as well as improvised, ad hoc, and decentralized approaches.

3.3.1 Recruiting into Trainings and Scholarships

The recruitment into China's elite training and educational initiatives follows at once a methodical and piecemeal strategy. On the one hand, as part of fulfilling the quota for trainings and scholarships set out by China's Ministry of Finance and Commerce (MOFCOM), the Chinese embassy consistently targets a range of important institutions that shape Ethiopian politics. At the same time, Chinese diplomats and adjacent actors practice a mix of opportunistic and hands-off recruitment – inviting

medical-center-pledges-support-to-ethiopias-efforts-to-become-regional-medical-tourism-hub/.

[25] "Ethiopian PM Inaugurates China-Supported Military Hospital," Xinhua, May 19, 2024, https://english.news.cn/20240519/158f522b50e7430ca08282135eb1b71a/c.html. According to Fana news, this hospital received a total of $18 million of hospital furniture and medical equipment from China. See "Defense High-Tech Hospital Receives $18 million Worth of Medical Equipment Assistance from China," Fana News, November 12, 2022, www.fanamc.com/english/defense-high-tech-hospital-receives-18 mln-worth-of-medical-equipment-assistance-from-china/.

individual participants on an ad hoc basis, as well as delegating selections to Ethiopian institutions.

As for methodical recruitment, the Chinese embassy and its partners appear to prioritize certain strategic institutions, many of which are part of the Ethiopian government (party and state ministries) or closely aligned with it. Other than the members of the main political party, the Prosperity Party (and in the past, the Ethiopian People's Revolutionary Democratic Front), official records from Ethiopia's Ministry of Finance indicate that officials working in the agriculture sector, social governance and development, as well as in infrastructure planning, technology and science projects, and trade and investment initiatives have thus far received the most training and long-term educational opportunities.[26]

In my visits to political, educational, and media institutions between 2018 and 2023, I found a wider institutional targeting than what showed up in the Ministry of Finance records. Specifically, in the political sphere, in addition to the officially-listed entities, the Ministry of Finance, the Planning Commission, the Investment Commission, the Ministry of Infrastructure, the Ministry of Agriculture, the Women and Social Affairs Bureau, the Mayor's Office, and the Ministry of Education, among others, all take part in China-sponsored training programs.[27] These institutions present the bedrock of Ethiopian political governance, responsible for everything from approving new infrastructure projects to carrying out new social and poverty alleviation initiatives. During my visits to these institutions, I also learned that communication, public relations, and international relations offices are more likely to receive frequent and extensive opportunities. These departments are most directly involved in disseminating information about China to internal and external audiences.

In the education sector, top university officials, including university presidents and deans from major nationally reputable universities, such as

---

[26] Finding accurate data on the exact number of training opportunities for specific ministries and departments is challenging in Ethiopia, as the trainings are distributed in a decentralized manner and Ethiopian officials don't keep close track of the numbers. Ministry of Finance officials have shared with me data received from MOFCOM from 2017 and 2018 that differentiates training numbers by sector rather than by a specific ministry. The MOFCOM table, however, does not include journalist trainings, as well as the think tank and educational sector that are also an important part of Chinese capacity building in Ethiopia, and something I incorporate into my analysis in this chapter.

[27] According to the author's visits and interviews with officials at these institutions, regular training and long-term educational opportunities are provided to them on annual bases, with the numbers varying by year, as well as by institution.

the Addis Ababa University, Bahir Dar University, Arba Minch University, and several others, have routinely received invitations to visit and study in China. Targeting of top-tier universities may be in part connected with the establishment of Confucius Institutes and Classrooms. I learned from university deans, for instance, that trips to China played an important role in solidifying institutional relationships and launching Confucius Institutes and Classrooms.[28] In addition to universities, up until 2020, the Meles Zenawi Academy – a government-affiliated civil servants training academy that had branches in three cities in addition to Addis – received many training opportunities.[29] Representatives at prestigious think tanks that produce nationally notable policy analysis, including the Institute for Peace and Security Studies (IPSS), the Policy Studies Institute, and the Institute of Foreign Affairs (part of the Ministry of Foreign Affairs), are also regular recipients of Chinese scholarships. In the media sphere, major state-owned and party-affiliated national media outlets, including the Ethiopian News Agency (ENA), the Ethiopian Herald, Addis Zemen, Walta, and Ethiopian Broadcasting Corporation (EBC), have been relatively more exposed to Chinese training and fellowships, but the Chinese embassy has also extended invitations to regional outlets, such as the Oromia Network, Oromia TV, and even influential private media, including the Reporter and Addis Fortune newspapers.

While the Chinese embassy prioritizes strategic sectors and institutions, recruitment of scholarship recipients can also proceed in a sporadic and decentralized manner. As for spontaneous targeting, some Ethiopian journalists shared that they received invitations to China training trips and graduate programs on the spot, following a particular encounter with Chinese officials. Several state media journalists, for instance, were invited by the Chinese embassy days after attending a Chinese cultural event at the Sheraton Hotel in Addis Ababa.[30] An Ethiopian expert working on

---

[28] Informal discussions with university Deans and interviews across Ethiopia. See Appendix II for more details.

[29] Visits to the Academy, including its three regional offices in Bahir Dar, Adama, and Mekelle in 2018 and 2019, revealed that the top administrative personnel (i.e., directors of training and research, and presidents of the academy) were all offered three-week training trips to China, hosted by the Chinese Academy of Governance. Meles Zenawi Academy was essentially a civil servants training institution, akin to China's party schools, which explains the alignment with China's Academy of Governance. In recent years, this academy got downsized, as well as renamed, restructured, and reoriented as Abiy Ahmed's leadership carved out more distance from Meles Zenawi's legacy and vision.

[30] Focus Group ETJFG02, Addis Ababa, 2019.

China at a major think tank disclosed that his first opportunity for a China trip was offered at a dinner with a Chinese diplomat. The diplomat asked him if he was interested in going to China and if so, to send him his CV for a scholarship consideration. Four months later, he was notified that he was selected.[31]

At times, non-embassy actors also engage in their own, spontaneous targeting for recruitment of Ethiopian, but also other African elites into specific events held in China. Some academic and official participants at the 2019 Guangzhou Forum on People-to-People Diplomacy that I attended, for instance, were invited to attend the forum after a serendipitous meeting with a Chinese professor in their respective countries. "Days after my very exciting conversation with Professor X, I receive an email about coming to China! I was shocked. I have never been, and of course, I immediately accepted it," one participant relayed on a bus journey to the trade expo in Guangzhou.[32] At that same conference, an Ethiopian expert who publicly expressed some mild criticism of Chinese development strategies in Africa was swiftly invited to apply for a PhD program at Beijing University by a Chinese faculty member on his panel.[33] At times, the same individuals receive recurrent invitations from specific institutions they already established contact with in China. In the middle of my interview with the then vice director of the Oromo Leadership Academy (a branch of the former Meles Zenawi Academy located in Adama), an email popped up from the Chinese Academy of Governance with an invitation to attend another training in China. "It will be my fourth time in China!" he exclaimed.[34]

This opportunistic recruitment proceeds alongside with a laissez-faire approach, whereby the selection of participants is delegated to Ethiopian institutions, with vague criteria provided by the Chinese embassy. An example of recruitment correspondence with the Chinese embassy, shared by an Ethiopian expert, reads as the following: "With a view to further promoting human resources cooperation between Chinese embassy in

---

[31] Interview ETEX05, Addis Ababa, 2023.

[32] Informal discussions about the China trip with participants in the 2019 Guangzhou Forum on People-to-People Diplomacy.

[33] This invitation was extended publicly during the panel that the author was attending. After the Ethiopian participant made his critical remarks (concerning the detrimental effects of China's infrastructure projects in the country), the Chinese professor from Beijing University invited him to come to study there for a doctoral program. The Ethiopian participant also confirmed with the author that the Chinese academic followed up with him and he was seriously considering the possibility.

[34] Interview ETOF08, Adama, 2019.

Ethiopia and your Institute and contributing to capacity building efforts of the Ethiopian Institute, the Embassy of China in Ethiopia sincerely invites your Institute to recommend 5 qualified candidates for Master programs for MOFCOM Scholarship programs listed in the Attachment 1."[35] The letter from the Embassy further notes that the Chinese Scholarship Council and the relevant universities make the final admission decisions, advising the institute to select "competent" candidates. The letter, however, doesn't specify what "competent" means or how the selection process works in China, delegating the nomination to the Ethiopian director.

Many interviewees across Ethiopian institutions recounted a similar process. In response to my question about competing for China fellowships, an Ethiopian journalist shared that there was no clear competition. He was simply tasked to go by his editor. The editor, in turn, clarified that this journalist had decent English language skills and was covering international affairs, thereby deemed as competent to travel to China.[36] For some fellowships, Ethiopian applicants had to submit a brief application letter to the Chinese embassy, along with other documentation. In previewing one such letter, it appeared as hastily written, with glaring grammatical mistakes. When I pointed this out to the applicant, he waved off my editorial suggestions and reassured me that the letter would pass as is. For longer fellowships and graduate programs, applicants are invited to a brief interview with the embassy's commercial office (MOFCOM). According to the participants, the interviews are more of a formality and tend to be relatively brief and at times even comical. "Do you want to go to China? Do you like China? Can you speak English OK?" a former Ethiopian media fellow recalled the interview details with the embassy personnel.[37] In informal chats with Chinese embassy officials doing these interviews, they noted their busy schedules, and the limited time allocated to each applicant. For the most part, they treated these as symbolic routine procedures used to finalize the application process rather than to seriously assess the candidates.

---

[35] This correspondence dates to April 2023. Similar formulations were also used in previous correspondence from the Chinese embassy to this think tank: notifying about the number of available opportunities and urging the Ethiopian interlocutors to make a swift selection and send the selected names back to the embassy staff. At times, the invitations were sent last minute, and the selection was particularly rushed.

[36] Interview ETJ11, Addis Ababa, 2019.

[37] Interview ETJ15, Beijing, 2019.

A close look at the recruitment practices into Chinese education and training opportunities shows a mix of methodical targeting with ad hoc and decentralized recruitment processes. This palette of tactics is likely linked to the overarching motivation of the Chinese embassy staff in meeting the targets for sponsored training and educational opportunities already allocated by MOFCOM. As such, they resort to large-scale strategic outreach and individual opportunistic targeting but also delegate recruitment to Ethiopian counterparts. The fusion of methodical and opportunistic recruitment can also be attributed to the multiplicity of actors involved in distributing these opportunities, with the more sporadic invitations often extended by specific individuals, as well as institutions doing their independent outreach.

3.3.2 Promoting and Recruiting into Confucius Institutes and Classrooms

The diffusion of and recruitment into Confucius Institutes and Classrooms, as well as the facilitation of employment opportunities as part of these programs, also features a combination of deliberate, consistent practices, and some adaptive and improvised strategies. Starting with the expansion of the CI initiative across Ethiopia, as noted in section 3.1, before the escalation of the security conflict in 2019, Confucius Institutes and Classrooms had a remarkable presence in different regions of the country. At first glance, this regional diffusion may reflect a grand plan of Hanban (previously in charge of managing the Confucius Institutes) or specifically of Tianjin University of Technology and Education, which has served as the key partner institution in Ethiopia. A closer look, however, shows that the distribution of these Institutes and Classrooms is a product of strategic vision, as well as some improvised adaptiveness to requests from Ethiopian counterparts.

As for deliberate targeting, the launch of the first flagship Confucius Institute in 2010 grew out of a larger bilateral collaboration – the Ethio-China Polytechnic College (later renamed as the Federal Technical and Vocational Education and Training Institute, FTVETI) – that initially aimed at technical training modeled on the Chinese experience.[38] The subsequent expansion, namely the establishment of the CI at Addis Ababa University and Confucius Classrooms at major reputable regional universities, featured targeted persuasion efforts from the Chinese side.

---

[38] Interview ETUAD11, Addis Ababa, 2023.

Some Ethiopian university administrators, like the former dean at AAU, were directly approached by the CI director at FTVETI and by the Chinese embassy.[39] Other deans and high-level personnel at selected universities were invited for a trip to China to learn more about the initiative, including by attending an international CI conference.[40] The head CI (at FTVETI) would also assess the applications by these Ethiopian universities to host a Confucius Institute or Classroom for feasibility prior to approval, including whether these universities already host other language centers.[41]

In some cases, however, as with the initiation of Chinese language teaching at the boarding school in Adama, the Chinese counterparts largely reacted to Ethiopian requests. The former principal of the school learned about the CI initiative from Addis Ababa University and approached the director of AAU CI himself to help establish a Confucius Classroom at his boarding school.[42] More recently, the Oromia Education Bureau requested more Ethiopian Chinese language teachers to be trained and sent to boarding schools across the region – a request that the Chinese side has thus far obliged.[43] Some Ethiopian university deans I spoke to also shared that they approached the Chinese side themselves to initiate collaboration.

In recruiting students, the Confucius Institutes and Classrooms consistently entice them with jobs and scholarships but vary in their promotion efforts. As for the strategic focus on practical benefits, field observations across CI and CCs highlight the "material" sell of studying Chinese. From curricula descriptions to advertising posters, practical benefits are visible across the promotion materials. A Chinese major curriculum designed by the CI in Hawassa, for instance, articulated the rationale for establishing a BA program in Chinese language major in transactional terms: "The communication in economy, culture, and other fields between two countries has been enhanced in recent years with a large number of Chinese

---

[39] Interview ETUAD02, Addis Ababa, 2019; and informal discussions and site visits in 2018 and 2019.

[40] Specifically, the former Deans at the AAU University, Mekelle University, Arba Minch University, as well as the President of Jimma University shared that they received invitations to visit China as part of getting to know the Confucius Institute initiative. I didn't get a chance to interact with the officials at Arsi University and Bahir Dar University. It is also unclear whether other universities were targeted but didn't end up applying to host a Confucius Classroom.

[41] Ethiopian university officials shared that their application was typically followed by a visit from the CI director at FTVETI in Addis.

[42] Interview ETUAD06, Adama, 2019.

[43] This was confirmed during the visit to the Oromia boarding school in Adama in 2019, as well as to the FTVETI CI in 2023.

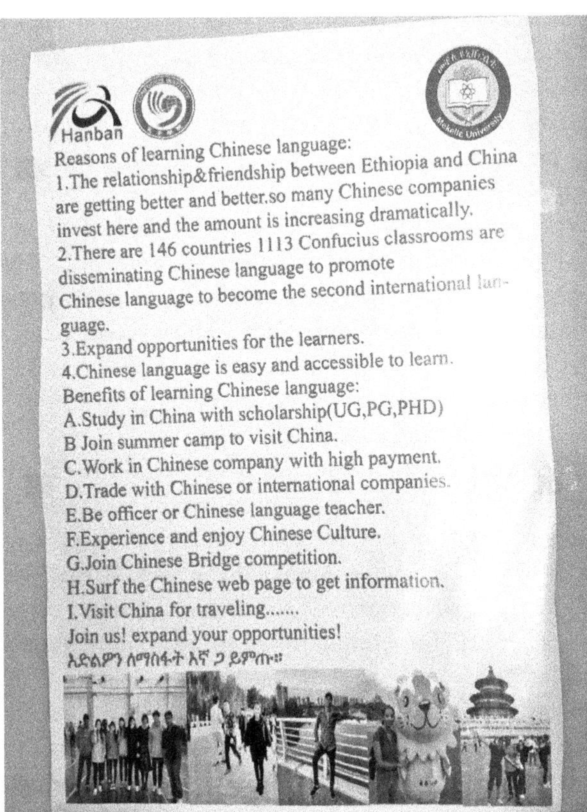

FIGURE 3.3 Confucius Classroom promotion poster at Mekelle University.

companies coming into Ethiopia to invest and research, which necessitates badly for more Ethiopian and local translators."[44]

An advertising poster hung up on the door of a Confucius Classroom in Mekelle University details all the advantages of studying Chinese, with practical gains listed at the top (see Figure 3.3). The number one reason for learning the Chinese language is articulated in pragmatic terms: "The relationship & friendship between Ethiopia and China are getting better and better and better. So many Chinese companies invest here, and the

[44] "Curriculum of B.A. Program in Chinese Language," Hawassa University, December 2012, page 3. The document was obtained from an Ethiopian student teaching at the Confucius Institute.

amount is increasing dramatically."[45] This description depicts Chinese companies as carriers of lucrative opportunities. Further down the poster, under the benefits of learning Chinese language, material opportunities for students are outlined more explicitly and are hierarchically positioned above the perks of cultural exchange: "A: Study in China with a scholarship; B: Join summer camp to visit China; C: Work in Chinese company with high payment; D: Trade with Chinese or international companies; E: Be officer or Chinese language teacher …." The first four benefits feature material enticement, including free education, China touring, and desirable employment with Chinese companies, or as part of learning Chinese. The Chinese directors and volunteers I interviewed also noted that they emphasize jobs and scholarships to university officials and students in introducing their programs.

At the same time, Chinese directors and teachers differ in their initiative to promote these benefits, with some engaging in more active and visible outreach, while others settling for a more restrained approach. During some of my visits, including to Addis Ababa and Mekelle Universities, I learned about invitations extended to Chinese company representatives to big cultural events on campus to raise awareness about attractive employment options for potential (as well as existing) students. In Mekelle, according to the director and teachers, some events attracted nearly 100 participants from across the campus.[46] As part of other field observations, I also spotted directors actively trying to increase the visibility of Confucius Classrooms and their offerings. After hearing from an Ethiopian colleague that it would be attractive to put photos of past participants in Chinese scholarship exchanges on the banner, for instance, a CC director in Bahir Dar included images of smiling Ethiopians on the Great Wall and in Tiananmen Square, and posted them on large banners at the university entrance.[47] Other directors I encountered, such as one formerly based in Hawassa, were relatively hands-off in targeting students, promoting the practical benefits of learning Chinese only once the students already enrolled or took an interest in the program, according to former students there. It is also worth noting that in informal conversations with students on university campuses that host Confucius Institutes

---

[45] Confucius Classroom Poster photographed at Mekelle University Confucius Institute in the spring of 2018.

[46] Informal discussion with the author and Ethiopian colleagues, Mekelle, 2018.

[47] Informal group discussion with the author and Ethiopian colleagues, Bahir Dar, 2018. The author also spotted the banners on her visit.

and Classrooms, many were unaware of their existence and the opportunities they carry until meeting me, which again signals the inconsistency in advertising and promotion by the Chinese side.

The work of connecting students and preparing them for employment also differed across Confucius Institutes and Classrooms. In Bahir Dar, the director developed close relationships with Chinese companies in the area and transformed her Classroom into a de facto employment center, as company representatives regularly held interviews with applicants there.[48] In Mekelle, Bahir Dar, Jimma, and Addis Ababa, the directors and some students recalled visits to Chinese company headquarters during special holidays to network and inspire the students to keep learning Chinese. In other Confucius Classrooms, job networking was less notable. When hearing about such active engagement in other CIs and CCs, for instance, the Ethiopian codirector of a Confucius Classroom in Hawassa noted, with disappointment, that he didn't witness such activities there.[49] A graduate from Hawassa Classroom further shared that his teachers were primarily instrumental in providing recommendation letters for jobs, less so in directly organizing and facilitating the interviews or connections with Chinese enterprises.[50]

Some directors also selectively incorporated new teaching tools to prepare students for the jobs. At the FTVETI CI, Chinese language teaching includes specialized courses in technical subjects, such as "mechanics basic professional vocabulary" and "reading and writing of electronic and electricity testing equipment in Chinese," among other subjects.[51] Considering that the FTVETI specializes in vocational training, the institute endeavored to combine students' technical skills with specialized Mandarin fluency that could prepare them for jobs at Chinese companies in Ethiopia.[52] Some CCs, such as those in Jimma and Bahir Dar, emphasized soft skills, like punctuality, as a way of disciplining students for Chinese company employment. Teachers, for instance, would explain the potential criticisms or punishments that students would face if they arrived late to work at a Chinese company.[53] In other Confucius Classrooms like the one I visited at the Oromia boarding school, as well

---

[48] Site observations in Bahir Dar, 2018.
[49] Interview ETUAD09, Hawassa, 2019.
[50] Interview CIST05, Addis Ababa, 2019.
[51] The author initially gathered this information from the Facebook page of the institute, and it was further confirmed by the director (interview CI09, Addis Ababa, 2023).
[52] Interview CI09, Addis Ababa, 2023.
[53] Interview CI02, Jimma, 2019; Informal discussion and observations, Bahir Dar, 2018.

as in Mekelle University, teachers appeared to mostly stick to basic Chinese language training.

Overall, the spread of the Confucius Institutes and Classrooms in Ethiopia is both methodical and ad hoc. The evolution of CIs and CCs in part reflects a strategic vision, as major reputable universities in different regions of the country were encouraged to participate. At the same time, the expansion of Chinese language offerings carries some flexibility and adaptiveness to unanticipated local demands, as in the case of the Oromia boarding schools and some universities that later joined the initiative. Beyond establishing the programs, the recruitment of students features recurrent emphasis on scholarships and jobs, but the promotion of these benefits varies by director, with some seeking more visibility and exerting more effort than others. This variation also extends into the Chinese educators' initiative in procuring employment connections and skills for Ethiopian students.

The tactical and responsive strategy in expanding CIs in Ethiopia is likely a product of limited resources and the underlying motivations to localize CI operations. In contrast to large-scale quotas for trainings and scholarships, the resources for Confucius Institutes are tied to the partner university in Tianjin. During my visits to Confucius Institutes and Classrooms in Ethiopia over the years, I observed that some lacked teachers in part due to the challenges of recruiting young volunteers to go to Africa. Targeting several most reputable universities in different regions, therefore, may present a cost-efficient approach to maximize visibility and outreach. At the same time, CIs and CCs, according to Hanban officials,[54] are encouraged to respond to local demands, which explains the relative flexibility extended to some requests from Ethiopian educators.

Loose performance objectives of Confucius Institutes and Classrooms, combined with their decentralized operations, in turn, can explain the variation in recruitment and job-facilitating strategies. Less driven by specific metrics than their Chinese embassy counterparts, the CI initiative does not appear to have a synchronized recruitment strategy, except for the emphasis on practical appeal. In contrast to the more centralized (though still disjointed) operations of the Chinese embassy, moreover, Confucius Institute and Classroom directors are scattered across the country, with limited interactions with each other. Officially, the CI at TVETI in Addis Ababa is considered the head Confucius Institute in

---

[54] Interview CHPD03, Beijing, 2019.

charge of managing the Confucius Classrooms, but in practice, there is little oversight due to travel restrictions and limitations.[55] Faced with vague guidance from Beijing and even from Addis Ababa, the Chinese directors can improvise some of their strategies, including the extent of their creativity and effort in recruiting students. We now shift to the discussion of the workings of pragmatic enticement in media diplomacy.

3.3.3 Distributing Media Resources

The tangible enticement in the context of media diplomacy is primarily aimed at expanding the visibility and accessibility, and eventually at increasing the consumption of Chinese state media.[56] The core techniques deployed here include subsidizing access to Chinese state media, such as through content-sharing agreements, distributing free Chinese media publications, and paying for Chinese state media content placement in Ethiopian media. Multiple, and at times dispersed, actors are involved in tangible media diplomacy, including representatives of Chinese state media like Xinhua News Agency, as well as of the Chinese embassy, and even Confucius Institutes, as I explain further in this section. As with other initiatives, China's material media diplomacy is both cohesive and coordinated, as well as partially disjointed.

As for strategic and deliberate efforts, the targets of media offerings include important media and political actors. For instance, Xinhua News Agency signed a content-sharing agreement with ENA – the largest state-owned news agency. ENA produces media content across the country that in turn filters into many other media outlets, especially at the regional and local levels. During my last field visit in 2023, representatives from EBC and Ethiopia's National Television Network (ETV) also shared that they are considering signing an agreement with Xinhua and are frequently relying on Xinhua reporting in their China coverage.[57] A former Xinhua journalist in Ethiopia shared that the goal of these agreements is to directly subsidize access to the Xinhua

---

55 Most directors interviewed by the author rarely met or corresponded with their counterparts in other cities during their Ethiopia stay.

56 Visibility was underscored as an important aspect of China's media diplomacy by Chinese editors and journalists at state media. Informal discussion with the author, Addis Ababa, 2018; Interview CHJ02, Beijing, 2019.

57 Interviews ETJ17 & ETJ19, Addis Ababa, 2023.

database for strategic media partners,[58] which suggests that more agreements may be signed in the future.

The China Daily newspaper is delivered to most major Ethiopian media outlets, including to well-regarded private media like Fortune, according to its editors, as well as to major government and party offices across the capital city. Given that there is no China Daily bureau in Addis, the delivery coordination is likely carried out by the Chinese embassy personnel, according to Ethiopian editors. Both Xinhua and China Daily have also regularly placed paid-for content in Ethiopia's major national newspapers – Xinhua content in the state-owned Ethiopian Herald, and China Daily content in the private national paper, Reporter.

Alongside this strategic targeting, some of China's pragmatic media diplomacy appears rather arbitrary. For instance, in addition to delivering China Daily to governmental and media sectors, copies of the paper (including older copies) are dropped off at large- and medium-sized international hotels in Addis Ababa, rarely frequented by Ethiopian visitors. Some Confucius Institute volunteers are also instructed to drop off copies of the paper with university administrators – a seemingly strategic tactic, but only carried out selectively, at the determination of the individual Confucius Institute or Classroom director. I observed this practice only at the Confucius Institute in Addis Ababa, where volunteers made regular deliveries to the president's office. Some Ethiopian journalists shared that China Daily was occasionally available at supermarkets, but I never encountered a copy of the paper in public spaces (outside of hotels).

The distribution of paid Chinese media content is also in part sporadic. First, my analysis of all Xinhua inserts in the Ethiopian Herald found some gaps in placement, with occasional months or weeks missing over the years.[59] Editors at the newspaper acknowledged the irregularity of Xinhua inserts but confirmed that payments for inserts are typically collected every month, which means that Xinhua simply didn't take advantage of the space it purchased. Some of the content placed was also jumpy, with little direct relevance to Ethiopia or Ethiopian realities. The title of the main paid-for article on June 29, 2018, for instance, reads: "The UN police is happy with China's peacekeeping."[60] October 19,

---

[58] Interview CHJ05, Beijing, 2019.

[59] This is based on detailed analysis of all placements by examining printed copies of the paper at Ethiopia's National Archive from 2018 to 2023. The research was carried out in the summer of 2023.

[60] "The UN Police Is Happy with China's Peacekeeping," *Ethiopian Herald*, June 29, 2018.

2018 headline is: "China Built dam heralds end to water supply challenges in Mauritius."[61] Another insert, a few weeks later carries a story titled: "Shanghai import expo to promote Egypt's exports to China: Egyptian businessman."[62] Most of the inserts analyzed either highlight China's leadership speeches or various accomplishments in Africa or other parts of the world, with Ethiopia itself rarely mentioned in the articles.

The promotion of Chinese media resources in Ethiopia is generally less extensive than that of capacity building or China exposure experiences and Confucius Institutes. Kenya is a more vibrant center of China's media diplomacy in Africa – widely documented by other China–Africa media scholars.[63] In the context of media diplomacy in Ethiopia, however, we can still discern the centrality of tangible enticement or practical offerings as part of engaging local audiences (mainly elites). As with other initiatives, this tangible promotion is both coordinated and partially improvised. This can be attributed to the relatively vague overriding objective of enhancing Chinese media visibility, as well as to the multiplicity of actors involved on the Chinese side, including non-media stakeholders like Confucius Institute directors occasionally mobilizing volunteers to distribute Chinese media, and the Chinese embassy as mediating the deliveries of China Daily. We now shift to the engagement with tangible enticement by Ethiopian counterparts.

3.4 ENGAGING WITH TANGIBLE ENTICEMENT: FROM STRATEGIC ACCEPTANCE TO NEGOTIATION

Ethiopian elites are active recipients, as well as initiators and negotiators of China's tangible diplomacy. The fluid distribution of opportunities and resources discussed throughout this chapter leaves space for creative engagement. I examine these different forms of engagement next, starting with strategic acceptance.

---

[61] "China Built Dam Heralds End to Water Supply Challenges in Mauritius," *Ethiopian Herald*, October 19, 2018.

[62] "Shanghai Import Expo to Promote Egypt's Exports to China: Egyptian Businessman," *Ethiopian Herald*, July 27, 2018.

[63] See for instance Herman Wasserman and Dani Madrid-Morales, "How Influential Are Chinese Media in Africa? An Audience Analysis in Kenya and South Africa," *International Journal of Communication* 12 (2018): 2212–31.

3.4.1 Strategic Acceptance

Interviews with officials, journalists, university administrators, and students, among other groups targeted by Chinese diplomatic initiatives, reveal a generally enthusiastic, utilitarian response, whereby participants distill their own practical benefits from consuming Chinese offerings. In terms of China-sponsored training and education, most institutions analyzed in this book readily accepted these opportunities, whether for short-term or long-term stays. The only institution I came across that deliberately declined a China visit is a major private newspaper. An editor at the news outlet shared that the trip itinerary proposed by the Chinese embassy didn't align with their professional objectives of gaining more journalistic skills.[64] As will be discussed in the next chapter, China trainings tend to focus more on explaining China rather than on teaching professional skills. Except for this outlet and a few independent journalists, however, editors and reporters at major Ethiopian media, as well as Ethiopian officials across the government spectrum, accepted the trips, mainly as channels for international exposure. Traveling to China, for many, was the first time going abroad, and for some, even the first time on an airplane. Trainings and graduate degrees in China are seen as rare no-cost global adventures, especially in the context of pressing challenges of going to Europe, Canada, or the United States – something explained in more detail in Chapter 6. In the words of an Ethiopian media practitioner: "It is better to see China than to stay at home and see nothing."[65]

In engaging with Confucius Institutes and Classrooms, beyond the appreciation for the cost subsidies (i.e., most expenses covered by China), Ethiopian counterparts expressed enthusiasm about the scholarships and especially jobs promoted by Chinese directors and teachers. A vivid illustration of positive reactions to tangible benefits associated with Chinese language study was shared by the vice-principal of the Adama boarding school in Oromia region, which introduced Chinese language (cosponsored by Addis Ababa CI) as an elective language class. According to him, the parents at first expressed resistance and dismay at their kids having to learn Chinese – a language that appeared at once remote and esoteric. They were quick to change their minds when they learned about the tangible opportunities that came with studying Chinese. "Once they heard about the summer camp opportunity, however, and

---

[64] Interview ETJ10, Addis Ababa, 2019. Interview ETJ28, Addis Ababa, 2023.
[65] Interview ETJ13, Addis Ababa, 2019.

other scholarships in China, they were put at ease," shared the vice-principal.[66]

The responsiveness to job offerings as part of learning Mandarin was even more powerful. Confucius Institutes and Classrooms have enjoyed steady enrollment over the years, according to the Chinese directors. The enrollment data provided by some Ethiopian universities supports this. As noted in the introduction to this chapter, Chinese language was the only foreign language with continuous enrollments at Addis Ababa University, and the registrar official directly linked this to job aspirations at Chinese companies. Ethiopian students also shared that perceived job possibilities drew them to explore Confucius Institutes even before they came across the promotions or met the Chinese directors. "I observed lots of miscommunication between Chinese employers and Ethiopian workers around Hawassa Industrial Park, with locals not listening to Chinese bosses, as well as at the airport where Chinese were frequently cheated by local drivers. I thought that if I learned Chinese, I could help fix this problem, so I embarked on studying it,"[67] recalled a CI graduate, now an established translator and broker at a Chinese company. The marketing of CIs as employment generators, as well as the linkages to Chinese companies provided by some Chinese directors, therefore, matched the students' preexisting motivations for learning Chinese. Some students interviewed especially appreciated the visits to Chinese companies organized by their teachers. "They gave us food and told us 'Come work for us!',," recalled a Chinese language student at Mekelle University in slight disbelief.[68] Even those students initially attracted to Chinese culture shared that they persisted in studying Chinese mainly for practical reasons.

The practical attraction to Chinese language, of course, is not unique to Ethiopia or to Africa at large. Hubbert's in-depth study of Confucius Classrooms in the United States, for instance, found that American students also embarked on the journey of learning Mandarin for strategic reasons, such as that of adding a flourish to their CVs and being more competitive for jobs and graduate programs.[69] In Ethiopia, however, this

---

[66] Interview ETUAD09, Adama, 2019. "Rethinking Soft Power: 'Pragmatic Enticement' of Confucius Institutes in Ethiopia".

[67] Interview CIST02, Addis Ababa, 2019. "Rethinking Soft Power: 'Pragmatic Enticement' of Confucius Institutes in Ethiopia".

[68] Interview CIST04, Mekelle, 2019. "Rethinking Soft Power: 'Pragmatic Enticement' of Confucius Institutes in Ethiopia".

[69] Jennifer Hubbert, *China in the World: An Anthropology of Confucius Institutes* (University of Hawaii Press: 2020).

pragmatic pull is more visceral given China's large-scale economic presence in the country, the high youth unemployment rate,[70] and the notable need for Chinese language speakers at Chinese enterprises across the country. The enticement by Chinese directors is also made more convincing by translators' salaries – amounting to an average of $500 a month, which is double if not triple of university professors' salaries, according to my interviewees. Chinese language students learn about this through the word of mouth and connections with current translators, as well as from their teachers who make these practical aspirations appear as realistic and their pursuit of Chinese language as worthwhile.

In engaging with material media offerings from Chinese state media, Ethiopian news outlets and editors also accept them out of practical considerations. When discussing the ENA-Xinhua content sharing agreement, for instance, the editor at ENA acknowledged its ambiguity, but still found it useful for signaling the internationalization of the news agency (they recently signed a similar deal with Russia's TASS agency), as well as for having access to a free international news database.[71] The ENA editors (as well as editors at other major state media outlets) admitted to regularly relying on Xinhua for China-related stories – something that might be linked to these content-sharing agreements,[72] but also to self-censorship on China stories, as will be discussed in Chapter 5. Officials and journalists who receive free copies of China Daily shared that they occasionally glance through them for layout inspiration (in the case of journalists) and for stories about China (in the case of journalists and officials). While not reading the newspaper, even Ethiopian hotel managers found China Daily deliveries helpful for their image branding. In the words of one manager, "China Daily displays make us look more international."[73] Given that China Daily is the only international English-language paper delivered for free, it presents the main "international" branding material for these hotel managers. As for paid adverts, editors at the Ethiopian Herald and the Reporter were not preoccupied with the content, but rather treated them as good sources of advertising revenue, especially with alternative revenue channels shrinking across the media sphere.[74] Overall, while the pragmatic

---

[70] According to Ethiopian official data, as of 2022, youth unemployment rate in urban areas reached 27.2 percent. See www.statsethiopia.gov.et/wp-content/uploads/2024/02/Abstract-3-2.pdf.

[71] Interview ETJ11, Addis Ababa, 2019.

[72] Interviews ETJ12, Addis Ababa, 2019; ETJ18, Addis Ababa, 2023.

[73] Informal discussion with the author, Addis Ababa, 2019.

[74] Interviews ETJ28 & ETJ02, Addis Ababa, 2023 and 2019.

appeal of material media offerings is less explicit than in training diplomacy and Confucius Institute outreach, the recipients still found some utility in China "gifts," from branding to free content usage to income generation.

3.4.2 Negotiation and Push-Back

In addition to actively accepting and utilizing China's tangible diplomatic offerings, Ethiopian elites also attempt to exploit and negotiate these opportunities, especially in the context of education diplomacy and Confucius Institutes' outreach. Ethiopian interlocutors, for instance, take advantage of the delegated and ad hoc recruitment into training and education opportunities by skewing the selection criteria and bargaining for increasing the participation quota. Some Ethiopian officials distribute trainings internally based on subjective rather than competitive rationale. An Ethiopian official partaking in a one-year fellowship in China, who also frequently served as an interpreter for short-term Ethiopian delegations to China, for instance, underscored the randomness of the selection system when it comes to internal institutional nominations.[75] In attending a training program in China for public relations officials from Ethiopia, he was surprised that most officials there were secretaries instead of heads of public relations units. Over time, he observed that some offices would send someone to China for personal reasons, such as to get medicine for a sick relative, rather than to study or to gain new skills. Other times, he noted that the journalists chosen for China fellowships from Ethiopian media vary by age and experience, signaling a lack of systematic criteria. As discussed earlier in the chapter, many Ethiopians selected by their institutions weren't informed about the criteria used by their supervisors. They were simply asked to go.

Other Ethiopian officials play into China's spontaneous allocation of trainings by initiating more opportunities for their institutions. Some editors and marketing directors of official media shared that they maintain regular contact with the Chinese embassy and bring up their requests for more training and fellowships to be granted to their news outlets during these meetings.[76] Rather than quietly waiting for invitations from the embassy, these enterprising Ethiopian professionals initiate or directly request the diplomatic "gifts" from China.

---

[75] Interview ETHST03, Beijing, 2019.
[76] Interviews ETJ03 & ETJ13, Addis Ababa, 2019.

Some Ethiopian participants also attempt to stretch the decentralized workings of Chinese initiatives and the power dynamics that occasionally favor Ethiopia, as in the case of Confucius Institutes and Classrooms, to negotiate for more resources. A former dean at Addis Ababa University described this as "try to get more out of them" attitude. During his time as dean and codirector of the Confucius Institute, he proposed to the Chinese director to engage a Chinese company to build a large building that would host the institute on one floor, and the two other floors would be used by Ethiopian departments.[77] The Chinese counterparts refused out of cost considerations, but the effort from the dean is still noteworthy.

At times, these negotiations can even take a form of conditionality for further engagement. In considering the expansion from certificate programs into Chinese language majors (a key aspiration of Confucius Institute directors), for instance, Ethiopian deans placed challenging preconditions on Chinese directors in terms demonstrating job feasibility. In Jimma, the Chinese director was tasked with conducting an independent feasibility study with Chinese companies in neighboring areas to map out their needs for Ethiopian translators, as part of applying for a Chinese language major program.[78] In Bahir Dar, the Chinese director was asked to guarantee employment for all their graduates – a much tougher challenge – something she was unable to do as part of her effort to promote and institute a Chinese language major.[79] To my knowledge, the Chinese language major was not approved.

Ethiopian administrators have also threatened to downsize the CI program if their requirements were not met. A former Ethiopian director of the FTVETI CI wanted the Chinese colleagues to sponsor more PhD fellowships for his staff and students, or else scale down the program that he saw as of limited practical utility to his students who were mainly training to be teachers in Ethiopia.[80] Other Ethiopian directors and deans expressed an intent to change the Chinese language major programs back into certificate programs out of concern for saturation of translator jobs. A former dean and codirector at Mekelle University conveyed a worry about long-term prospects of translator jobs and

---

[77] Interview ETUAD03, Addis Ababa, 2019.

[78] Interview CI01, Jimma, 2019.

[79] Discussion with the author and Ethiopian colleagues, Bahir Dar, 2018, and correspondence with university officials in 2019.

[80] In a follow-up visit five years later, in 2023, the program was still running, but the leadership planned for more language offerings, including Korean (ETUAD11).

considered turning the Chinese major back into a minor or a certificate program.[81] In this case, it would be up to the Confucius Classroom director to push-back and demonstrate that the job feasibility is still viable. The Mekelle Confucius Classroom has closed anyway due to the civil war in the Tigray region and the safety concerns of Chinese teachers. Deans from other universities that host Confucius Institutes and Classrooms, however, also communicated long-term caution when it comes to training Chinese language speakers at their schools. When asked what would happen to the Confucius Classrooms if the translator jobs were to run out, several deans simply stated: We would shut them down.[82] This harsh rhetoric signals that the deans and codirectors perceive their role as active shapers and even arbitrators of CI initiatives rather than as passive recipients.

The response of Ethiopian elites toward China's tangible enticement, therefore, can be understood as a mix of strategic engagement or taking advantage of the offerings for personal and institutional empowerment, as well as selective appropriation and negotiation of China's diplomatic influence. The practical rationale for participation is not surprising given that Chinese actors, whether it's the embassy staff or CI directors, tend to present their initiatives as opportunities for access to experiences and resources. The fluidity and unevenness of China's deployment of tangible diplomacy arguably creates some avenues for appropriation and pushback. Of course, the power dynamics between the Chinese and Ethiopian counterparts are unequal, as the former possess and distribute the resources, and the latter primarily receive them. At the same time, the analysis of Ethiopian engagement demonstrates that Ethiopian counterparts can actively shape and even halt China's initiatives, especially when it comes to the expansion of the Confucius program. Unlike the ideological reasoning that guided the decisions to shut down the institutes in the West, in Ethiopia, it is the pragmatic rationale that shapes this decision-making process.

3.5 CONCLUSION

This chapter examined one of the core mechanisms in China's image-making in Ethiopia – tangible enticement – or the centering of practical

---

[81] Informal discussion and interviews with the author and Ethiopian colleagues, Mekelle, 2018 and 2019.

[82] Informal discussions and interviews with university Deans that host Confucius Institutes, 2018 and 2019.

benefits in China's diplomacy. It demonstrated how providing access to opportunities, resources, and material aspirations is critical to China's efforts at engaging Ethiopian elites (both current and future) and projecting an image of China as a generous "giver." From offering large-scale free trips and educational opportunities to China to subsidizing Chinese language training and linking it to lucrative employment to sponsoring access to media resources to material gifts in the form of public infrastructure, China's diplomacy clearly carries a material appeal.

At the same time, the analysis of distribution of these benefits reveals unevenness as an underlying characteristic. China's tangible enticement is at once methodical and erratic, coherent and inconsistent. In the case of elite training and educational invitations, the Chinese embassy targets core strategic institutions, while leaving room for ad hoc recruitment, and delegating selection to Ethiopian counterparts. In expanding the Confucius Institutes and Classrooms, the Chinese partners target selective universities, as well as adapt to requests from the bottom-up. In recruiting students, individual directors converge in underscoring the material payoffs but diverge in how they promote and facilitate them. In distributing Chinese media content, Chinese state media representatives and diplomats approach strategic Ethiopian news outlets but also improvise in delivering content to places rarely frequented by Ethiopians.

This uneven implementation can be attributed to several factors, including the underlying objectives of different initiatives, as well as their decentralized operations. As for the objectives, the motivation for fulfilling a large-scale training quota might lead Chinese diplomats and educators to resort to various tactics, including strategic targeting, as well as ad hoc and indirect invitations. The more open-ended motivation to expand and localize Chinese language training in Ethiopia, combined with limited resources, can yield a mix of strategic and adaptive expansion of the Confucius Initiative. The looser aspiration of enhancing Chinese media visibility might transpire in a more performative dissemination of content regardless of strategic relevance of the targeted spaces.

The degree of decentralization present across these different initiatives can also fuel inconsistent strategies. The ad hoc participation in training recruitment by non-embassy actors, such as Chinese professors and governance institutes, in addition to the more consistent work of the Chinese embassy, means that invitations can be extended in different forms by different actors at the same time. The decentralized CI operations whereby the directors have little coordination among themselves or with the higher-ups translates into variations in recruitment and employment mentorship strategies pursued by different Confucius Institutes and Classrooms. The engagement of different actors in media distribution, including Chinese embassy, state media outlets, and even Confucius Institutes, can cause coordination problems.

The elasticity of China's tangible "soft power," as evident in the mix of strategic and improvised targeting, creates opportunities for deliberate consumption, as well as for negotiation of Chinese offerings. As discussed in the final section of this chapter, Ethiopian audiences distill the practical gains from China's initiatives, as well as attempt to negotiate or strike a better deal when possible. Acknowledging the large scale of China's training opportunities, for instance, some Ethiopian elites bargain for more chances to visit and study in China. Taking advantage of the loose selection criteria, Ethiopian institutions carry out their own selective nominations that advance the interests of specific elites. Maneuvering the advantageous power dynamics, in the context of Confucius Institutes, Ethiopian codirectors set preconditions to Chinese directors as part of tolerating their presence on university campuses. As such, this chapter illustrated the multidirectional nature of China's tangible enticement as an image-making mechanism, as it gets stretched and reappropriated both by Chinese and Ethiopian actors involved. We now proceed to examining ideational attraction or the varied promotion of Chinese political ideals and values.

4

Ideational Power

Not Exporting a China Model but Legitimizing China's Path

4.1 INTRODUCTION

This chapter shifts from the analysis of China's tangible appeal to *ideational persuasion* or promotion of China's visions, values, and governance practices. While different diplomatic channels, ranging from official speeches to state media reporting and cultural events, can illuminate elements of ideational promotion, this chapter delves into state-sponsored training of African elites – a practice most often associated with the export of the China model in Western policy and media narratives. In her 2016 analysis for the Brookings Institute on China's political party training programs in Africa, for instance, Yun Sun, a China expert at the Stimson Center, described these initiatives as "institutionally systematic" and likely to yield "a profound psychological and political impact over the choices and preferences of African political parties …."[1] In a 2020 testimony at the US-China Economic and Security Commission Hearing on the "China Model," Elizabeth Economy, a Senior Fellow at the Council on Foreign Relations, identified China's capacity building programs with foreign officials as significant for diffusing the China model (both political and economic), with African elites highlighted as especially receptive to China's narratives. "The China model has perhaps found the most adherents in Africa," she writes, giving examples of training seminars provided by the CCP to the Ethiopian People's Revolutionary Democratic Front and the Sudanese

---

[1] Yun Sun, "Political Party Training: China's Ideological Push in Africa?" *Brookings*, July 5, 2016, www.brookings.edu/articles/political-party-training-chinas-ideological-push-in-africa/.

People's Liberation Movements, among other influential political parties in Africa.[2]

In her 2023 investigation, a journalist and writer, Bethany Allen-Ebrahimian, described the Mwalimu Julius Nyerere Leadership School in Tanzania – funded by a generous donation from the CCP's Central Party School and hosting extensive lectures by Chinese visiting professors – as a "training school for authoritarianism."[3] During my engagements in policy discussions in Washington on China's strategic communication in Africa, I observed that American experts and officials even treated the volume of training opportunities provided to African elites – something I discussed in detail in the previous chapter – as indicative of an ideological export.[4]

These direct associations of state-sponsored elite training with deliberate, cohesive, and effective ideological promotion diverge from the more evasive and ambivalent interpretations of these programs by the participants. "There is no coherent China model," claimed a Chinese expert involved in administering lectures to African elites.[5] "We don't like the word model! There is no one model to follow for Ethiopia, we draw lessons from many countries, including from the West," shared an Ethiopian Foreign Ministry official, aggravated by my question on the relevance of the China model for Ethiopia.[6]

This chapter attempts to reconcile these contradictions between outsider and insider perspectives, as well as to transcend the binary debate on whether China is exporting its model by empirically examining the promotion of China's political ideals, values, and governance practices through these training experiences. Drawing on selective training materials shared by Ethiopian officials, scholars, and journalists, observations of training events, as well as on interviews with Chinese lecturers, training organizers, and Ethiopian (as well as other African) participants, this

---

[2] Elizabeth Economy, "Exporting the China Model," *Council on Foreign Relations*, March 13, 2020, www.uscc.gov/sites/default/files/testimonies/USCCTestimony3-13-20%20(Elizabeth%20Economy)_justified.pdf.

[3] Bethany Allen-Ebrahimian, "In Tanzania, Beijing Is Running a Training School for Authoritarianism," *Axios*, August 21, 2023, www.axios.com/2023/08/21/chinese-communist-party-training-school-africa.

[4] This happened on multiple occasions, including as part of a closed-door briefing at the National Endowment for Democracy and a closed-door briefing for officials in security and defense sector where a China–Africa expert challenged my presentation by arguing that the numbers of Chinese trainings speak for themselves.

[5] Interview CHSC08, Beijing, 2019.

[6] Interview ETOF02, Addis Ababa, 2019.

chapter complicates our understanding of China's ideational power diffusion in several ways.

It demonstrates that immersive training experiences attempt to legitimize China's governance and display its accomplishments rather than to export "authoritarianism." Furthermore, this study shows that China's ideational promotion is not a well-oiled, top-down enterprise, but a mix of coherent and disjointed narratives and practices. Presentations of China feature recurrent ideational themes, including its characterization as a distinctly democratic, people-centric governance system, a benevolent partner to Africa, and an impressive cultural power. These trainings also consistently rely on immersive, experiential persuasion, in addition to lectures, with participants directly encountering and witnessing China in its many dimensions. At the same time, when it comes to specific governance domains like journalism, elite trainings tend to draw on a mosaic of success stories and demonstrations that show-off China rather than present a compelling and coherent narrative. Finally, this chapter examines how Ethiopian participants conceive of these trainings, finding a mix of acknowledgement and inspiration, as well as negotiation of Chinese political narratives and persuasion practices.

Overall, this chapter presents an empirical critique of the "China model export" idea circulating in Western policy discussions and demonstrates how Chinese hosts attempt to shift and soften perceptions of Chinese governance (rarely invoking authoritarianism), often through ad hoc promotional efforts, and how African elites are discerning in engaging with these trainings rather than blindly absorbing the "China model." I now proceed to discuss the motivations and the structure of training exchanges, followed by the analysis of consistent ideational themes and practices and the more opportunistic diffusion of the China story, as well as Ethiopian participants' reflections on these narratives and experiences.

4.2 THE WHY AND HOW OF CHINA'S IDEATIONAL PROMOTION

4.2.1 Explaining and Experiencing China: The Fluid Agenda of Training Exercises

China's ideational promotion as part of elite exchanges with Africa dates back to the Mao era when selective African delegations and students were invited to China for training visits and long-term education programs. Under Mao, these exchanges carried an explicit ideological orientation of building transnational anti-imperialist movements and cultivating "the power for the world revolutionaries."[7] Lovell, in her book on global Maoism, presented stories of influential African elites, including Julius Nyerere – an anti-colonial leader and later the first president of Tanzania – visiting China and leaving with a closer ideological alignment with the Chinese Communist Party.[8] In the contemporary period, following Jiang Zemin's Africa tour of 1996,[9] these exchanges have restarted and expanded dramatically, making them highly accessible to African elites, as discussed in the previous chapter. The ideational agenda, as part of these ongoing trainings, however, is more subtle and more focused on explaining China than on building a movement or exporting China's political ideology.

In group discussions and interviews with Chinese officials and educators who implement the training programs for African elites, they tend to denounce the idea of an export of a China model and instead focus on providing exposure to China. Several Chinese interviewees underscored the challenges of diffusing China's governance experience. A China–Africa expert at the Chinese Academy of Social Sciences (CASS), for instance, highlighted China's scale and strong historical foundations for industrialization, among other features, as distinctive and difficult to incorporate for other developing countries.[10] "They are just too different from us!" remarked another Chinese expert on Sino-African relations, when I asked him whether the trainings he conducted with African officials on China's development would materialize into new modes of governance on the ground.[11] He went on to contrast what he perceived as the remarkable work ethic of Chinese companies with the more relaxed work culture in Africa, as well as the strong centralized leadership of the party with the more fragmented and unstable governance in many African countries. Rather than anticipate a direct diffusion of governance techniques, the Chinese trainers articulated their motivations in more modest and ambiguous terms, such as "helping participants understand China"

---

[7] Huajie Jiang, "Lengzhan shiqi zhongguo dui feizhou guojia de yuanzhu yanjiu, 1960–1978" ("A study on Chinese aid to African countries in Cold War era, 1960–1978"), PhD Dissertation, East China Normal University, 2014.

[8] Julia Lovell, *Maoism: A Global History* (Random House: 2019).

[9] Following the tour, twenty agreements were signed on trade, economic, technical, and cultural cooperation. See Ministry of Foreign Affairs of the PRC, "President Jiang Zemin's Visit to Six African Countries," n.d., www.fmprc.gov.cn/mfa_eng/zilia o_665539/3602_665543/3604_665547/t18035.shtml.

[10] Interview CHSC04, Beijing, 2019.

[11] Interview CHSC08, Beijing, 2019.

(*lijie zhongguo*) and "experience China" (*tiyan zhongguo*) – a message also echoed in official reporting of training seminars.[12]

This mix of understanding and experience is captured in trainings' agenda, which includes a series of lectures and visits to selective sites that symbolize China's success stories. The proportion of lectures to visits varies for different programs and delegations. For three-week programs administered by the Chinese Academy of Governance, for instance, lectures take up approximately two out of the three weeks. For long-term programs, like the China–Africa Press Centre journalism fellowship, lectures make up about one-third of the program.[13] Some trainings also fuse lectures with experiences. Ethiopian journalists who went on a three-week training to China, for example, attended lectures and briefings at various media outlets. Immersions into news outlets directly accompanied official presentations. In some cases, Chinese lecturers themselves travel to Africa to deliver presentations to influential think tanks and other entities. In the summer of 2023, for instance, I attended a seminar discussion at the Institute for Peace and Security Studies (IPSS) in Addis Ababa, led by a delegation from the CASS. In such cases, the immersion is more rhetorical, limited to lectures and discussions.

It is also important to note here that the training exchanges are administered by a variety of Chinese institutions, including the Chinese Academy of Governance, the Central Party School, a range of universities, especially those that host African Studies centers, and even provincial governments and news outlets. As explained in the previous chapter, most of the funding and training quotas are provided by China's Ministry of Finance and Commerce, but the actual implementation mobilizes a range of actors, with different experiences and agendas, which can in part explain the variations in content and styles of delivery presented to the participants, discussed further in the chapter. I now proceed to the more cohesive facets of ideational

---

[12] See for instance Qimin Wu, "Zhongguo feizhou jingji guanli yanxiuban kaixue; Wu Yi xiwang ba zhongfei de jingmao hezuo tuixiang xin gaodu" ("China-Africa Economic Management Seminar Has Started; Wu Yi Calls for Advancing China-Africa Economic and Trade Relations to New Heights"), *People's Daily*, August 4, 1998; "Feizhou guanyuan yanzhong de zhongfei hezuo: zhengdang qishi, weilai keqi" ("China-Africa Cooperation in the Eyes of African Officials: The Right Time, A Promising Future"), Shangguan News, April 25, 2025, https://www.shobserver.com/wx/detail .do?id=899057.

[13] The fellowship's duration recently reduced from ten to four months in 2023. See Seepheephe Mahao, "Over 80 Journalists Join CIPCC Exchange Programme in China," *Public Eye*, August 1, 2023, https://publiceyenews.com/2023/08/01/over-80-journalists-join-cipcc-exchange-programme-in-china%EF%BF%BC/.

diffusion by introducing the recurrent themes, followed by discussion of more ad hoc presentations, with a special focus on the media sector.

4.2.2 Legitimizing China: China as a Democratic, Effective Governance Alternative and Benevolent Power in Africa

My analysis of selective training materials shared by Ethiopian officials,[14] as well as interviews with a wide range of participants, book-length memoirs of these trips, and immersive observations,[15] reveal the recurrent and coherent political messaging about China as a democratic and competent political system, and as a benevolent actor in the Global South. Across these themes, China is presented as an exceptional power, with its approaches to governance rooted in China's history and traditional culture.

4.2.2.1 *China's Democratic Features and Accomplishments*

Starting with the overarching theme of China as practicing an alternative democracy, it is communicated both directly and indirectly in lectures and experiential site visits. Chinese lecturers appear to balance the acknowledgment and justification of the one-party rule with depictions of the Chinese political system as harboring democratic features. As for acknowledgment, some introductory lectures I analyzed underscore that China is led by the Chinese Communist Party – the only political entity capable of guiding the Chinese people into an "arduous struggle" and the "realization of China's independence and liberation."[16] In lecture notes on Chinese politics to

---

[14] The author was fortunate to gain access to a series of training materials through Ethiopian interviewees, including a full set of slides from a recurrent ten-day trip to the Chinese Academy of Governance for Ethiopian officials working in civil servants' training academies, as well as a set of journalism training slides from a recurrent short-term program in Hunan, and some partial materials from other short-term media and governance trainings. The author also collected selective materials shared by participants from other training trips, including long-term journalism fellowships in Beijing.

[15] The author took part in a one-week training program at the Shanghai Party School in November 2023. The group of trainees was from the United States, but the content and style of training was similar to those delivered to African participants, according to the trainers who administered this trip. The trainers mentioned that they gave similar seminars and tours to African visitors (only in English). I also attended several Sino-African training sessions, including lectures on media and journalism at the Communication University of China, a South–South Summit in Guangzhou, and an in-depth seminar on Chinese governance in Ethiopia, among other events.

[16] Dong Mingfa, "Leadership Training and Development in China," lecture delivered by the Chinese Academy of Governance to the Ethiopian delegation from Meles Zenawi Academy, Beijing, June 12, 2017, p. 1.

Ethiopian officials at the Chinese Academy of Governance, for instance, the phrase "The PRC is and must be led by the Communist Party of China" appears on multiple slides, as if lecturers are channeling their loyalty to the party through these training seminars or are speaking to the invisible critics of the party's monopoly on power, rather than to their Ethiopian guests. Training participants are also routinely gifted books written by Xi Jinping.

At the same time, Chinese hosts depict China's political system as distinctly democratic based on its consultative and meritocratic features, as well as on its impressive state capacity. Even when not directly referring to China as a democracy, these trainings emphasize the Chinese polity as successfully delivering for its people. As for consultative governance, the lecture materials explain different channels for accountability and inclusion of societal voices. "Rejection of the multi-party system does not mean China does not allow the existence of other parties. There are 8 democratic parties in China, representing views and interests of intellectuals and business circles and overseas Chinese," reads the introductory brief on China's political system, shared with Ethiopian officials during a training visit to the Chinese Academy of Governance.[17] The lecture brief also notes direct elections at the village level, indirect elections within the party (or intra-party democracy), and other consultative mechanisms that allow for expression of public opinion on governance matters. An example of bottom-up consultation provided in the materials was that of the process of adoption of the Chinese constitution involving "nationwide discussions" and multiple revisions to reflect citizens' concerns and interests.[18] The overarching message is that the decision-making processes within the CCP are deliberately inclusive of varied opinions, including from within and outside the party institutions.

The specific terminology used by Chinese lecturers to explain the participatory nature of China's political system has evolved in response to official ideological slogans and pronouncements. For instance, after Xi Jinping invoked the term "whole-process democracy" in 2019,[19] the introduction of China's political system started to echo this terminology. During a one-week training experience at the Shanghai Party School in the fall of 2023, I was exposed to this concept multiple times, with the lecturers and organizers conveying the key characteristic of "whole-

---

[17] "The Chinese Political System," a brief shared with Ethiopian participants as part of a training program with the Chinese Academy of Governance, June 12, 2017.

[18] Ibid.

[19] "Xictionary: Whole-Process People's Democracy," Ministry of Justice of the People's Republic of China, last modified March 5, 2024, http://en.moj.gov.cn/2024-03/05/c_96 7573.htm.

process democracy" as official responsiveness to citizens' demands and grievances at all levels of the system. In the context of the Shanghai training, "whole-process democracy" was demonstrated through the official policy of constructing "people's cities" (*renmin chengshi*) or redeveloping urban areas into more livable and sustainable spaces. A lecturer at the Shanghai Party School gave an example of a redevelopment project that took ten months to secure residents' agreement through intensive negotiation and feedback gathering.[20] Once all frictions were resolved, the residents voted in favor of the city's proposition, according to the speaker.

In addition to presenting Chinese-style democracy as responsive to public input, the trainings also emphasize its meritocracy by explaining the intensive preparation that Chinese party officials endure in their careers. Some lectures, for instance, highlight how cadres at all levels undergo a 550-hour long training every five years, as well as grassroots and hardship rotations as part of their promotion process.[21] In comparing Chinese and Western political promotion systems, a lecture slide from a training at the Chinese Academy of Governance describes the Chinese approach as more rigorous and comprehensive. Whereas Western politicians' competencies include management skills and representing people's will, Chinese officials have "both theoretical knowledge and practical experience," and a mix of general and expert knowledge.[22] The slide also contrasts Western politicians' professional development via elections or rank-based promotion with Chinese officials often undergoing cross-regional and cross-sectoral transfers. In addition to these rotation practices, Ethiopian participants in these trainings recalled learning about Xi Jinping's anti-corruption campaign as an illustration of the leadership's capacity to tackle preexisting governance failures and inspire more dedication among party officials.[23]

Training seminars also promote China's governance efficacy or performance legitimacy, namely the capacity of the political system to deliver development. During the discussion session following a China seminar at IPSS think tank in Addis Ababa University, a young speaker from CASS

---

[20] "China's Comprehensive Democracy," lecture at Shanghai Party School, November 14, 2023.

[21] Mingfa, "Leadership Training and Development in China."

[22] Ibid. This argument about Chinese-style democracy as more meritocratic than the US-style often circulates in Chinese media, often promoted by Western experts. See Don Rechtman, "US vs Chinese-Style Democracy," *Shenzhen Daily*, July 1, 2021, https://szdaily .sznews.com/PC/content/202107/01/content_1054032.html; Daniel Bell, "*The China Model: Political Meritocracy and the Limits of Democracy*," 2015, pp. 179–180.

[23] ITJFG02, Addis Ababa, 2019.

corrected a discussant's comment that China is not a democracy by underscoring its performance record. "China is a democracy, but we define differently what a democracy is. China has been able to overcome underdevelopment in non-central regions because of its political structure," he argued, somewhat impatiently.[24] The speaker didn't specify what he meant by the "political structure," but he signaled that impressive economic outputs should be treated as a measure of democracy. In another lecture on China's modernization and governance at the Chinese Academy of Governance, a presentation slide read that "the very purpose of the CPC in leading the Chinese people in revolution, development and reform is to make the people prosperous and the country strong and rejuvenate the Chinese nation."[25] This quote doesn't directly invoke democracy, but it presents the core political mission of the Chinese party-state as delivering economic welfare for its citizens.

Explaining China's developmental trajectory (often referred to as modernization) is part of most training programs, but the most widely invoked illustration of the Chinese political system's performance legitimacy is its success in poverty alleviation. "Achievements in the past 67 years – what was China like in 1949, lifting hundreds of millions of people out of poverty proves the government is effective and working for the prosperity of the people," reads an excerpt from an introduction to China's political system.[26] More recently, the lecturers have invoked a striking statistic of 700 million people being lifted out of poverty, and since 2021, declaring a "complete victory" over poverty eradication, echoing the words of Xi Jinping.[27] Some Chinese trainers who have personally witnessed both extreme poverty and its eradication in their lifetime convey special pride in this accomplishment. "When I think of my own background coming from rural poor areas, growing up hungry (to this day I have stomach problems because of that), I'm in awe of how far we have come as far as individual empowerment of Chinese people," shared one of the trainers from the Central Party School, his eyes welled up as he spoke about his personal experience.[28] This is the story that he most enjoys sharing in training seminars and discussions with African elites.

---

[24] "Inclusive Development and Sustainable Peace" seminar, IPSS, Addis Ababa, June 15, 2023.
[25] "Modernization and Governance in China," CAG lecture materials, December 6, 2017.
[26] "The Chinese Political System," introductory brief, Chinese Academy of Governance, May 12, 2017.
[27] This formulation was invoked in many interviews and discussions with participants, including those attending the programs post-2021.
[28] Interview CHPD02, Beijing, 2019.

In part due to popular demand from African (including Ethiopian) visitors, poverty alleviation is often discussed in more depth through separate lectures and visits. At the China seminar at the IPSS think tank, for instance, rural development was the leading lecture presented to the participants. The presenter, a professor specializing in China's rural governance, delved into factors behind China's poverty reduction trajectory, including the sustained GDP growth over the years and the expansion of social services, such as medical care, among other policies. As with the Central Party School professor introduced earlier, this lecturer also invoked dramatic comparisons to illustrate China's success story. "Almost 45 years ago, all the population of the country was living in poverty, but now it is near zero," he proclaimed with notable pride.[29] As part of these lectures and other seminars on development, Chinese hosts often emphasize China's distinct, non-Western approach to modernization, though they rarely present a concrete set of practices to imitate, as I discuss in section 4.1.3.

4.2.2.2 *Witnessing China's "Democracy" and Economic Success*

The lectures, statistical tables, and personal stories are accompanied by selective and carefully curated site visits that showcase China's democratic practices and state capacity. Some Ethiopian journalists, for instance, shared that they were exposed to minority parties when attending a Party Congress meeting.[30] During my participation in the training tour in Shanghai, our group visited the Shanghai Municipal People's Congress, as well as a local community center where new technology allows residents to voice complaints and suggestions to local officials and community leaders.[31]

In demonstrating the party's performance in rural governance and poverty alleviation, participants directly experience rural areas. Interviewees described rural sites as "clean and well-organized."[32] Some also shared that their hosts would present development contrasts by showcasing images of a particular village or township from fifty years ago and then taking them directly there to witness the transformation.

---

[29] "Inclusive Development and Sustainable Peace" seminar, IPSS, Addis Ababa, June 15, 2023.

[30] Interview ETJ08, Addis Ababa, 2019. Informal conversation with Ethiopian state media journalists, Addis Ababa, 2018 and 2019.

[31] Shanghai Party School trip, November 20–27, 2023. Both sites, but especially the community centers were also frequented by African visitors, according to the organizers.

[32] Interview ETJ29, June 19, 2023, Addis Ababa.

"Then we saw what they told us," recalled an Ethiopian journalist in his reflections about China's rural development.[33] This persuasion technique of witnessing and directly experiencing the official rhetoric was also notable in the Shanghai Party School training. As part of the visit to a new community center, we were taken on a tour of a photo gallery that juxtaposed the shoddy construction of the past with photos of new buildings, followed by a tour of the new housing compound.

On some trips, the participants had a chance to encounter prescreened members of the community who articulated official narratives in more personal and relatable terms. In his book about his ten-month journalism fellowship experience in China, a Nigerian journalist, Julius Idowu Enehikhuere, for instance, writes about his experience of learning from a farmer about Chinese conceptions of democracy as entwined with material well-being. When he tried to ask the farmer about democracy and human rights, he responded that to him these ideas "are equal to an abundant life, provision of social amenities, infrastructure to the people, and meeting the needs of people like him and the right to good life."[34] The farmer invoked the notion of democracy as rooted in government performance rather than in abstract ideals and values.

Other than traveling through rural areas, the participants immerse in urban landscapes of China's modernity and innovation – another demonstration of the Chinese government's efficacy in rejuvenating its nation. African visitors are taken on tours of Chinese tech companies like Alibaba and industrial park corporations (that also have branches in Ethiopia), as well as on visits to China's impressive infrastructure sites. A former Nigerian journalist who published a book about his experience on a journalism fellowship, for instance, writes about touring "the world's longest sea bridge, which links Hong Kong and Macao to the Chinese mainland."[35] In the book, he notes that the length of the bridge is fifty-five kilometers and that it is "similar to mega projects like the Three Gorges Dam, another symbol of the Chinese government's determination to bend the forces of nature to its will."[36] My experience in the training program in Shanghai also included exposure to striking modernity, including a full day

---

[33] Interview ETJ18, Addis Ababa, 2023.

[34] Julius Idowu Enehikhuere, *China in the Eyes of an African Journalist: Reports on New Strategies and Implementation of China-Africa Economic Cooperation*, (self-published: 2015), p. 16.

[35] Solomon Elusoji, *Traveling with Big Brother: A Reporter's Junket across China* (The Question Marker: Lagos, 2019), p. 97.

[36] Ibid.

visit to the tallest skyscraper in Shanghai. Our group traveled from one floor to another in what was described as the fastest elevator in the world. We even got to see an impressive bookstore on the 122nd floor and an immersive art performance, among other spectacular sites.

While showing off and articulating China's accomplishments in political and economic governance, the training seminars and visits also carry an aspirational tone, underscoring that the Chinese political system is always in the process of adaptation and improvement. Numerous slides from the modernization lecture delivered to Ethiopian officials, for instance, detail the future directions of reform, from improving the modern market system to strengthening government accountability and expanding the culture of volunteerism, among other suggestions.[37] These suggestions signal that China's polity is in a state of self-reflection and reinvention. Though some lectures introduce visitors to China's ongoing challenges, such as that of crisis management, they largely avoid sensitive political topics, and instead, embrace the constructive and optimistic lens of future improvement.[38]

The depiction of China's political system as having democratic characteristics in trainings of Ethiopian elites and other foreign visitors mirrors the larger ideational turn in China's external propaganda that discredits Western associations of China with autocracy by stretching and adjusting the concept of democracy to fit China's political realities. This persuasion effort is notable in official policy pronouncements, forums, and media reports. In 2021, for instance, China's State Council Information Office released a White Paper publicized by the Chinese embassy in the United States among other important entities, titled: "China: Democracy that Works." "Democracy is not a decorative ornament, but an instrument for addressing the issues that concern people," argues the report, emphasizing both the participatory and the performance features of Chinese political system.[39] As part of this persuasion campaign, Chinese authorities have also held high-level international summits on the theme of democracy[40] and diffused global

[37] "Modernization and Governance in China," lecture at China National School of Administration, December 6, 2017.

[38] The constructive tone, of course, is not unique to these training narratives. The author also found constructive tone as a core feature of Chinese journalism in her earlier work.

[39] "China: Democracy That Works," the State Council Information Office of the People's Republic of China, last modified December 4, 2021, http://us.china-embassy.gov.cn/eng/zgyw/202112/t20211204_10462468.htm.

[40] See for instance "Experts Laud Effectiveness of Chinese Democracy, Governance," Xinhua, last modified March 20, 2024, https://english.news.cn/20240320/50d27ecd4a63412bbaebfb771d48cedf/c.html.

media content on this topic.[41] Some of this media production has been disseminated in Africa. "Delivering Democracy" – a Chinese film focused on local Chinese officials' decision-making processes – was screened at a 2024 film festival in Kenya.[42] While the messaging in elite trainings I analyzed was not always as direct as it is in these official statements and media productions, it is still part of the larger push to tell the China story as a democratic alternative and as a system that works for its people.

4.2.2.3 *China as a Benevolent Global Power*

The presentation of China's domestic political governance as inclusive of and responsive to public interests extends into China's positioning of itself as a global power. In introducing China's Global Security Initiative at an IPSS seminar in Addis Ababa, for instance, an expert from CASS underscored China's consultative and equitable approach. "Unlike our Western partners, we don't create criteria from ideological standards . . . instead we try to bring those who disagree with each other to sit by the table and try to persuade them to find a solution," he argued.[43] In contrast to the Western tendency to impose exclusive ideological standards, the Chinese side is open to listening and to creating conditions for dialogue, according to this scholar. This rhetoric of inclusivity is also present in lectures about China's Belt and Road Initiative (BRI) that emphasize mutuality and connectivity as core features, with the Chinese leadership collaborating and cocreating a new vision of shared growth with leaders from the Global South.[44]

Echoing communication about domestic development-centric objectives, Chinese lecturers and officials also frame China's main contribution to Africa as that of fostering development – something also discussed in Chapter 2. In lecture presentations, the BRI project is largely treated as synonymous with growth opportunities for Africa and the Global South. Development is also framed as the centerpiece of conflict resolution. "Chinese people's peace building and peace keeping approach is development-oriented approach, Chinese diplomats and

---

[41] Dan Mattingly, "China's Soft Sell of Autocracy Is Working," Foreign Affairs, September 25, 2024; www.foreignaffairs.com/china/chinas-soft-sell-autocracy-working.

[42] "Documentary on Chinese-Style Democracy Screened at Kenya Film Festival," Xinhua, last modified April 22, 2024, https://english.news.cn/20240422/2c15cfcc06494cad ba99245bedb12678/c.html.

[43] "Inclusive Development and Sustainable Peace," seminar.

[44] Zhao Lei, "Belt & Road: The Public Goods Provided by China during Its Participation in the Global Governance," Institute for International Strategic Studies, Party School of the Central Committee of the CPC; lecture delivered to the Meles Zenawi Academy delegation, February 27, 2019.

scholars all emphasize that without development there will be no peace," stressed the Chinese speaker at the IPSS event.[45] In articulating China's vision for development, some speakers also invoke comparisons with Western approaches, describing them as extractive, in contrast to the needs-based, equitable Chinese practices. In his memoir, Julius Enehikhuere, for instance, quotes a Chinese Foreign Ministry official he encountered during his fellowship as articulating China's role in Africa as exclusively focused on bringing development. "We are not in Africa for selfish reasons nor for oil exploration that are handled by Western countries, we are only offering things that will promote development, especially in areas that Western countries do not care about," shared the Foreign Ministry official.[46] In this remark, the official characterizes China as benevolent and generous, in comparison to the West, but also China as replacing the absent West in assisting Africa. These narratives correspond with the diplomatic visions examined in Chapter 2, whereby China articulates its mission of creating a more equitable world order through Africa. They also echo ideational promotion at the China–Ethiopia book talk described in the introductory chapter, as the embassy official introduced China's intentions of sharing with and engaging Africa, rather than exploiting and lecturing, alluding to the more hierarchical practices of Western powers.

The rhetoric of China's consultative and responsive policy toward Africa goes along with a consistent presentation of China as a developing country and by the impressive hospitality of Chinese hosts. As for the former, in his recollection of lecture series as part of the China–Africa Press Fellowship, Elusoji notes that Chinese lecturers would regularly communicate this message with evidence, such as the major development gaps in Western versus Eastern parts of the country.[47] Some lecture materials dramatically describe China as "the world's largest developing country."[48] In lectures and official remarks, Chinese experts also regularly address their African audience as "our brothers and sisters," signaling equanimity, and treat the trainees as high-level guests.[49] The participants recall being welcomed as dignitaries by volunteers awaiting them at the airport terminal and taken to

---

[45] "Inclusive Development and Sustainable Peace," seminar.

[46] Julius Idowu Enehikhuere, *China in the Eyes of an African Journalist: Reports on New Strategies and Implementation of China-Africa Economic Cooperation*, 2015, pp. 91–2.

[47] Elusoji, *Traveling with Big Brother: A Reporter's Junket across China*, p. 107.

[48] "The Chinese Political System," introductory brief, Chinese Academy of Governance, December 5, 2017.

[49] The author witnessed this during multiple seminars and also heard about this from her interviewees.

luxurious accommodations, typically four or five-star hotels. During an official visit to the Hunan China–Africa Trade Expo in 2019, some African journalists I interacted with jokingly complained about their hotel rooms not being up to standard. They were housed in a four-star hotel costing an average of $100 a night. African visitors on short-term and long-term training programs regularly partake in banquet-style meals with their Chinese hosts and esteemed guests from the government and media circles. The visits tend to conclude with shopping at large clothing and electronic markets, with Chinese hosts accompanying their visitors, helping them bargain and even offering modest "stipends" as gifts for their families and friends back home. Adopting the status of a developing country and demonstrating exuberant hospitality and respect toward African visitors serves to flatten out the hierarchy between China and Africa and to bolster the message that China prioritizes the interests of African countries and sees them as allies and equals – echoing the narrative of "sameness" between China and Africa articulated by Chinese scholars (discussed in Chapter 2).

4.2.2.4 *Rooting China's Governance in Traditional Culture*

As part of conveying China's visions and ideals about its political governance both domestically and globally, the lecturers and organizers tend to invoke China's cultural heritage and values as key markers of and connective tissues of its trajectory. In explaining the workings of meritocracy in Chinese political processes, for instance, the lecturer from the Chinese Academy of Governance emphasized the long-standing tradition of talent cultivation among Chinese officials, linking it back to the imperial examination system under Tang Dynasty that lasted for 1,300 years, as well as to the Confucian thought that prioritizes the values of learning and order.[50] The exposure to China's modernity and innovation is combined and entwined with a narrative of China as a civilizational power, with introductory lectures presenting China's inventions of papermaking, printing, gunpowder, and compass.[51] Visitors also experience China's cultural heritage through trips to historical museums, imperial palaces, and the Great Wall, among other excursions, according to the participants and trainers. Some Ethiopian participants even suggest that the main purpose of the

---

[50] Mingfa, "Leadership Training and Development in China."

[51] Xie Jun, "A Brief Introduction to China," lecture delivered to Ethiopian journalists in Hunan; materials shared by one of the participants. No date provided on the slides, but presentation likely took place between 2017 and 2019 and delivered multiple times to different visitors.

training trips is to introduce Chinese culture, and the memoirs written by other African trainees extensively detail these cultural immersions. Elusoji, in his book, for instance, describes the delegation's visit to the Palace Museum and the National Museum, among other places, and highlights the reverence that Chinese people hold for their historical and cultural past,[52] and Enehikhuere's memoir includes photographs of African journalists in Beijing Opera costumes.[53]

The presentation of China's benevolent power in Africa also draws on cultural and historical constructs. The speaker from CASS introduced earlier, for instance, stressed how China's emphasis on conflict resolution through dialogue aligns with the Chinese cultural tenet of respecting differences between the two sides and trying to find a common solution.[54] The presentations of BRI often invoke historical lineages of this project. A professor with official ties to the Central Committee of the CPC, for instance, in his lecture materials, jumps from the introduction of the Silk Road in the nineteenth century to the launch of the Belt and Road by President Xi in his speech in Kazakhstan in 2013.[55] The professor presents the initiative as rooted in historical legacy, thereby marking China's status as a civilizational power. The participants are also taken to visit the sites of the ancient Silk Route. In her memoir of the China training experience, another Nigerian journalist, Bukola Ogunsina, for instance, dedicates a chapter to Gansu province, titled as: "Gansu, Where the Ancient Silk Route Begins," where she highlights the importance of diverse landscapes and people in centering Gansu on this trade route historically, and today, as part of the BRI.[56]

The infusion of cultural context and experiences into China's legitimation of its own polity also revibrates in major leadership slogans and initiatives like Xi Jinping's Global Civilization Initiative launched in 2023. In this initiative, Xi underscores the importance of China's traditional culture in fueling China's modernization trajectory. He also draws on China's traditional values of mutuality and inclusivity to promote mutual

---

[52] Elusoji, *Traveling with Big Brother: A Reporter's Junket across China.*

[53] Enehikhuere, *China in the Eyes of an African Journalist: Reports on New Strategies and Implementation of China-Africa Economic Cooperation.*

[54] China seminar at IPSS think tank, June 15, 2023.

[55] Zhao Lei, "Belt & Road: The Public Goods Provided by China during Its Participation in the Global Governance," Institute for International Strategic Studies, Party School of the Central Committee of the CPC; lecture delivered to the Meles Zenawi Academy delegation, February 27, 2019.

[56] Bukola Ogunsina, *The Red Lantern* (self-published: 2024).

respect for diversity and cultural differences across civilizational exchange as a backbone for global development.[57] In his major international addresses, Xi makes historical and cultural references to bolster more cooperation. In his 2023 congratulatory letter for the inauguration of the Center of Chinese and Greek Ancient Civilizations, for instance, he noted that "over 2,000 years ago, China and Greece, two civilizations glittering at each end of the Eurasian continent, made groundbreaking contributions to the evolution of human civilization."[58] He further called for stronger partnership in contemporary times. As these cultural and historical references continue to appear in Xi's speeches, they are likely to remain prominent in training seminars and presentations with foreign guests, including African elites.

4.2.3 Showing off China: Disjointed Ideational Promotion

While China's ideational persuasion through elite training programs features a consistent and coherent promotion of selective political ideals and practices, much of the training experience is also a patchwork display of China's success stories. Specifically, when it comes to introducing more specialized governance domains (with the exception of rural governance), these visits often focus on showing off the latest success trends. The demonstrations, moreover, are unsystematic in their content and delivery and disconnected from African realities. When trainings correspond to the interests of the delegations, ironically, they often draw more on Western theories and materials than on China's knowledge production.

The incongruencies in China's storytelling are especially visible in the context of short-term journalist training programs analyzed in this study. When presenting on this topic at Western think tanks and universities, members of the audience tend to ask whether Ethiopian journalists are learning about Chinese theories and practices of propaganda and censorship on these visits. While some programs may deliver this type of content, my extensive interviews with Ethiopian journalists who joined these trips reveal little exposure to political and ideological topics. Most journalists recalled numerous visits to modern Chinese newsrooms but had difficulty

---

[57] "Xi proposes Global Civilization Initiative," CGTN, March, 2023, https://news.cgtn.com/news/2023-03-15/Xi-proposes-Global-Civilization-Initiative-1icgxtDI3Go/index.html.
[58] "Why Global Civilization Initiative Matters to Human Progress," *Global Times*, March 16, 2025, www.globaltimes.cn/page/202503/1330177.shtml.

explaining the workings of Chinese media, beyond its close relationship with the government.

My review of twenty-three lectures from a journalist training program repeatedly carried out in Hunan province, along with interviews with participants in other short-term courses, demonstrates an overwhelming focus on showing off successful commercial and digital media trajectories. None of the lectures provided an in-depth overview of China's media transformation and governance structure, with only one slide noting that Chinese media can be divided into state-owned and commercial outlets. Instead, participants were taken on a journey of Hunan media and publishing outlets that conveyed more surfaced and repetitive messages about the successful evolution of Chinese media in the digital age.

A presentation by the editor-in-chief of *Hunan Times*, for instance, introduced its successful market performance, with the number of sold copies rising from 20,000 in 2004 to nearly 500,000 in 2011, and a presentation of the Hunan Broadcasting System shared its annual earnings of 12 billion yuan ($1.9 billion).[59] Another speaker from Hunan TV noted that the annual revenue of Hunan TV's flagship satellite exceeded 10 billion yuan.[60] A lecture about China's online publishing industry highlighted its annual growth of 29.9 percent.[61]

These lectures also explained how Chinese news outlets overcame the challenge of digitalization by transitioning their content online through Xi Jinping's initiative of media convergence (*meiti ronghe*) or state-sponsored and state-directed journalistic digital transformation.[62] A speaker from Changsha Evening News discussed how their media outlet implemented digital transition by creating a so-called central kitchen – "an all-media newsgathering team" that works efficiently on multimedia content.[63] Another talk stressed that big data can be useful for media

---

[59] Tang Shaonan, "Periodical: No Integration, No Future," no date provided on the slides, but presentation took place in 2018 and was delivered multiple times to different visitors (shared by Ethiopian participants with the author in June 2019).

[60] Wang Piaoyuan, "An Introduction to China's Radio and TV Management System & TV Programs of HNTV under the Initiative of 'The Belt and Road'." No date provided on the slides, but presentation took place in 2018 and likely delivered multiple times to different visitors.

[61] Dequan Yao, "China's Network Publishing Operation and Governance," presentation delivered to visiting Ethiopian delegation in Hunan, October 4, 2018.

[62] Kecheng Fang and Maria Repnikova, "The State-Preneurship Model of Digital Journalism Innovation," *International Journal of Press and Politics* 27 (2) (2021): 497-517.

[63] Liu Xiangen, "How Do Journalists Tell Stories in the Converging Media Age?" No date provided on the slides, but presentation took place in 2018 and delivered multiple times to different visitors (shared by Ethiopian participants with the author in June 2019).

management, including for effective audience analysis.[64] Other lectures explained in detail the emergence and expansion of Chinese mobile media companies, such as Tencent, as well as the growth of self-media (*zi meiti*).[65] The themes of commercial and digital success are overlapping, with digital transformation framed as key to increasing revenue of the Chinese media industry. Participants in other training programs also confirmed that most lectures and visits showed off Chinese media's technological prowess.

These programs, moreover, are notably inconsistent, both in content and in style of delivery. In addition to multiple lectures about different provincial media outlets, the Hunan journalism training program incorporated highly specialized and seemingly ad hoc seminars. A lecture titled "The Plan and Market of Children's Programs," for instance, exclusively focused on art programming for kids.[66] Several lectures introduced the literature and publishing industry, including an entire seminar on Hunan Literature and Art Publishing House.[67] A lecture delivered by a faculty from the Hunan Mass Media College engaged with artistic film production, focusing on the introduction of Akira Kurosawa's "dynamic rhythm of the frame."[68] Some participants also noted the randomness of some of the site visits, with tours of media outlets not accompanied by lectures. In some cases, the participants were unsure why they were taken on a particular site tour to begin with. An Ethiopian journalist who took part in a different short-term media training recalled in an interview that he complained to the training organizer that during a visit to Jiangsu

---

[64] Cheng Juan, "Innovation Will Thrive Forever Create a Future-Oriented Talent Ecosphere in Malanshan." No date provided on the slides, but presentation took place in 2018 and delivered multiple times to different visitors (shared by Ethiopian participants with the author in June 2019).

[65] Jason (肖世峰), "Mobile Internet Media Trend, Observed from Tencent influence," lecture (no date provided on the slides, but presentation took place in 2018 and delivered multiple times to different visitors), shared by Ethiopian participants with the author in June 2019.

[66] Shen Yingjizi, "The Plan and Market of Children's Programs" (no date provided on the slides, but presentation took place in 2018 and delivered multiple times to different visitors), shared by Ethiopian participants with the author in June 2019).

[67] Chen Xinwen, "Brightness and Difficulties in Press Digital Transformation" (no date provided on the slides, but presentation took place in 2018 and delivered multiple times to different visitors), shared by Ethiopian participants with the author in June 2019).

[68] Shen Jianfei, "The Application of Art and Technology in Classic Film and Television Works" (no date provided on the slides, but presentation took place in 2018 and delivered multiple times to different visitors), shared by Ethiopian participants with the author in June 2019).

Broadcasting Corporation they only wandered around the building and left.[69] Similar stories were shared by other trainees from different cohorts.

As for uneven delivery style, most presentations feature an overwhelming number of overcrowded slides, filled with large blocks of text, statistics, graphs, and Chinese concepts. Some presentations I reviewed contain over a hundred slides. Many of the slides are in Chinese, including descriptions of visuals and case study examples. This fusion of Chinese and English was also notable in other specialized trainings, such as that organized by the Chinese Academy of Governance for officials from Ethiopia's civil servants' academies. On some slides shared by participants, there are even handwritten notes asking: "Why in Chinese?" Participants across different training programs also shared frequent translation barriers, with most speakers presenting in Chinese through a translator, inhibiting communication flow.

These cursory and unsystematic presentations on more specialized governance domains are also primarily "supply-driven" or focused on presenting Chinese trends and experiences with limited consideration for the interests and backgrounds of participants. The core theme of digital convergence in the media industry has less relevance to Ethiopia than it does to China. Ethiopia's Internet penetration rate is around 16 percent (one of the lowest in Africa), and Ethiopian public tends to consume the news through the radio.[70] The commercialization of the journalism industry in Ethiopia is also in a dire state, with private outlets barely surviving and other media relying on state funding.[71] None of the presentations surveyed for this project attempted to relate to the reality of Ethiopia or Africa at large when it comes to digital media governance or to apply some lessons from China to Africa about media innovation.

The limited efforts to connect the Chinese context with African realities were also notable in presentations and discussions in other training seminars, including on the popular topic of poverty alleviation. At one such presentation, an expert on rural governance concluded with general

---

[69] Interview ETJ04, Addis Ababa, 2019.

[70] On Internet penetration rate in Ethiopia, see Lishan Adam, Andrew Partridge, and Nawal Omar, "Internet Development in Ethiopia: High-Level Findings from the after Access Survey," in Research ICT Africa, February 5, 2024; on radio as the most common source, see Mulu Teka, "Ethiopians Support Media's Watchdog Role but Want Regulated Access to Internet, Social Media," *Afrobarometer*, May 13, 2021, www.afrobarometer.org/wp-content/uploads/2022/02/ad448-ethiopians_support_media_watchdog_role_but_want_regulated_access_to_internet_and_social_media-afrobarometer-12may21.pdf.

[71] Teka, "Ethiopians Support Media's Watchdog Role."

lessons that China's experience offers to Africa, including the importance of managing and maintaining stable socioeconomic environment and incorporating poverty reduction into long-term development planning. When some participants tried to get more specific recommendations from the speakers, another Chinese expert from the delegation resorted to the popular official line of China not imposing its experiences. "Our presentation doesn't aim to give lessons; our aim is to show what China has done, what China's experience is … we are not your teacher," he stated.[72] Though the comment meant to signal equanimity between Chinese and Ethiopians and to show respect, it also bypassed and deflected concrete engagement about how China's lessons may apply to Ethiopia.

In some cases, as with media trainings, the lecturers also had limited grasp of the knowledge base of their visitors, introducing concepts and practical skills that were elementary and already familiar to them. One journalist participant in a short-term training, for instance, recalls a teaching on how to use photoshop. "They thought Ethiopians couldn't use photoshop at all," he shared and then added that he surprised them by showing off his skills and using photoshop better than the Chinese instructors.[73] Another participant in a long-term journalism training in Beijing noted that one of the practical classes was on the use of social media to promote journalism. He already knew the techniques introduced at the lecture and the only novel content to him was about Chinese social media platforms.[74]

Ironically, in training programs more closely designed with participants' backgrounds, as in the case of CAG trainings of Meles Zenawi Academy officials, the detailed and more practical content largely drew on Western theories and writings. Specifically, the lectures delved into the core training techniques, including group discussion, case study, and simulation methods – all originating in Western academy. The lectures also frequently attributed the invention of specific strategies to Western experts, such as the coinage of the brainstorming technique to A. F. Osborn, an American engineer.[75] Some slides reference specific books, such as *The Fifth Discipline* by Peter M. Senge, *Organizing the Power of Action Learning* by Michael J. Marquardt, and *Facilitation Techniques for Consultants* by Ingrid Bens, among others.[76] In this case, therefore, knowledge production

---

[72] China seminar at IPSS think tank, June 15, 2023.
[73] ETJ04, Addis Ababa, 2019.
[74] ETJFG01, Addis Ababa, 2019.
[75] Luo Guangzong, "The Theory and Practice of Action Learning," June 18, 2017.
[76] Dong Mingfa, "Creatively Solving Problems through Group Discussion," Chinese Academy of Governance seminar, June 27, 2018.

appears to trickle down from the West to China and from China to Africa – a topic discussed in more detail in Chapter 6.

It is also important to note that the content and delivery vary significantly by individual lecturer and organizer of these events. In the context of media seminars, for instance, a professor at the China Communication University has taken a more politicized approach to explaining China's media vision and practice. In her training lecture I attended in Beijing in the summer of 2019, she underscored the Chinese journalistic tradition of focusing on solutions and hopefulness, in contrast to the more crisis-oriented negative reporting of Western media. She also encouraged African participants to tell their own stories, echoing China's approach.[77] I haven't encountered such values-centric media governance promotion in other journalist trainings. The quality of delivery also depends on the skill and language fluency of instructors, with some relying heavily on translations, while others speaking fluent English and even a few phrases of African languages like Amharic and Swahili.

Overall, the Chinese experts who manage the trainings themselves acknowledge that China needs to make these programs more systematic and to tell the China story more coherently across different domains.[78] Part of the challenge in systematizing this persuasion campaign is rooted in the bureaucratic setup. As already noted, many lecturers are recruited by their superiors and are in part presenting China to the African guests, and in part also performing their professional duty to their institutions. A former trainer who now works for an international foundation described it as a "state-led mobilization campaign."[79] He shared that trainers are invited on ad hoc basis to deliver these talks and that they possess little awareness of participants' backgrounds and areas of expertise. They are paid about 2,000 yuan ($313) for a three-hour lecture, which considering the required preparation time is not a powerful incentive.[80] As a result, lecturers tend to prioritize the volume of content over the quality of presentation, which in part explains the seemingly sporadic compilation of materials presented on

---

[77] The author attended this lecture delivered to a delegation of African media scholars and practitioners on July 2, 2019, at the China Communications University. This professor has also regularly given similar lectures to the participants of the China–Africa Press Fellowship and has spoken about the idea of "constructive journalism" directly to African officials during her visits to different African countries, including Ethiopia.

[78] Interview CHSC08, Beijing, 2019.

[79] Interview CHSC10, Beijing, 2019.

[80] This number was quoted in 2019 and may have changed by now.

some topics. We now turn to the analysis of reception, or how Ethiopian and, more broadly, African participants engage with these training experiences, and especially the ideals and stories conveyed by their Chinese hosts.

4.3 RECEPTION: FROM APPRECIATION TO NEGOTIATION OF THE CHINA STORY

China's persuasion efforts through elite training experiences yield complex responses from participants. On the one hand, they appear to soften their perceptions of China's governance and appreciation of its specific features, echoing the training talking points. At the same time, the participant interviewees offer critical reflections and occasionally even directly challenge China's persuasion narratives and practices.

4.3.1 Appreciation and Acknowledgement of China's Trajectory

In their reflections, Ethiopian interviewees often share that through immersive visits to China they discover that China is more democratic, more developed, and more "cultured" than they anticipated. Whereas Chinese lectures and official visits tend to fuse democracy and development, the participants often treat the two as separate governance domains. In discussing China's political system, my interlocutors tend to invoke its meritocratic and consultative features – the core training themes introduced in the previous section. An EPRDF official who participated in multiple China trainings, for instance, highlighted the impressive, rigorous promotion process for Chinese party cadres. He thought that the Chinese party appears to serve public interests and pointed to various institutions in place to channel public input, including the People's Congress, and others.[81] He further acknowledged that the trip has changed his perceptions of China's political system. Before going on the trip, he was influenced by Western media depictions of China as undemocratic and repressive. After returning, he was under the impression that China is more democratic than he anticipated.[82]

In many conversations, interviewees zoom in on either meritocratic facets or on evidence of public input. Officials from the former Meles

---

[81] Informal discussions and site visit, Addis Ababa, 2018 and 2019.
[82] Ibid.

Zenawi Academy, for instance, emphasized meritocracy in their remarks about the Chinese political system, underscoring the CCP's strict recruitment policies and the discipline of party cadres they observed during their training.[83] Some noted that they wish that a similar system existed in the Ethiopian contexts that they described as more loose when it comes to criteria for entering and staying in public service.

Others reflected more on political input from non-official groups and the public at large. Referring to control over the distribution of economic resources, a state media journalist who just returned from a China training trip at the time of our interview positioned China as more equitable than the West. "Concerning democracy, if you see the reality in the West where most of the economy is in the hands of a few rich individuals, in China, many business projects are owned and managed by societal groups like teachers' associations, farmers' cooperatives, and other community organizations. In China, they all talk about democracy, they want to democratize their country," he shared.[84] In presenting this contrast with the West, likely borrowed from training lectures, the journalist suggests that governance is more consultative and inclusive in China, allowing for more bottom-up participation from diverse, less privileged groups.

Another Ethiopian state media journalist reflected on public participation in governance through media channels. His impression from the visit to China was that the media "was not completely closed, as often depicted in the West" and that "people have a loop to express their voices."[85] He didn't elaborate on how people communicate through the media but was convinced that media can facilitate some public expression. A think tank expert who took part in a longer fellowship in China highlighted his experience of witnessing the official turn from Zero-covid policy in response to public pressure as evidence that public matters in political decision-making. "Before going to China, I thought that everything was decided from the top-down. Now, I still think that it's decided from the top-down, but with input from the public," he added.[86]

---

[83] I heard similar remarks in informal discussions and interviews with Meles Zenawi training academy officials in Hawassa, Mekelle, and Jimma in 2018 and 2019.

[84] Interview ETJ20, Addis Ababa, 2023. The idea of people shaping the economy is also invoked in Chinese official writings about its version of democracy. The 2021 White Paper on Chinese democracy, for instance, underscores public ownership as playing an important role in Chinese economy, and describes the economy as being "firmly in the hands of the people." See www.news.cn/english/2021-12/04/c_1310351231.htm.

[85] Interview ETJ18, Addis Ababa, 2023.

[86] Interview ETOF38, Addis Ababa, 2023.

Even training participants who struggled to describe China's political system or comment on its specific characteristics still often resorted to Chinese official talking points. "China is a mixed regime, encompassing some degree of development and democracy," noted a journalist from Ethiopia's major TV network who recently visited China.[87] The Chinese system is a "democracy with Chinese characteristics," articulated another training participant.[88] Drawing on Chinese slogans and articulations, these interviewees inadvertently stretched the concept of democracy to include China or at least to complicate and obfuscate the common characterization of China as an authoritarian system.

Other than softening perceptions about China's political system, the trainees expanded their views about China's development trajectory and cultural confidence. As for development, many interviewees were struck by China's success record in rural development as well as in urbanization and innovation across different sectors. The immersive experience of seeing China and how much it has developed appears to leave the deepest impression. "Seeing is believing," commented an Ethiopian professor with close links to China. "Chinese dynamism is always beyond one's imagination," he added and gave an example of "paying with your fingerprint everywhere."[89] An Addis Ababa University official who traveled to China for a short-term training on international education and Confucius Institutes used a cooking metaphor to describe China's progress in urbanization:

I don't have deep memories of the lectures or the conversations I had at this conference, but I was struck by how modern Chinese cities are. Shanghai is on par with New York, and even the smallest cities in China are enormous and have everything. It is as if China has closed the door and was cooking quietly, and then they opened the door for everyone to witness the feast.[90]

In this reflection, the university administrator places China's metropolis, Shanghai, in the same category of global cities as New York and describes China's urbanization as a spectacle for others to witness. Others commented on specific urban sites that impressed them like the Beijing subway. "Beijing has over 24 million people and we couldn't see so many on

---

[87] Interview ETJ19, Addis Ababa, 2023.
[88] Interview ETJ06, Addis Ababa, 2019.
[89] Interview ETEX08, Addis Ababa, 2023.
[90] Interview ETUAD02, Addis Ababa, 2019. Part of this excerpt previously appeared in "Rethinking China's Soft Power: 'Pragmatic Enticement' of Confucius Institutes in Ethiopia," *The China Quarterly* 250 (2022): 440–63.

the street. So we thought where are they? Then we found them underneath, in the subway," recalled an Ethiopian official in informal group discussion.[91] "Beijing subway is very attractive!" commented a TV show host from the Oromia region who recently traveled to China.[92] Some interviewees also marveled at witnessing innovation firsthand. "Innovation is everywhere, in every sector," exclaimed a think tank expert. He then pulled out a video to show me a restaurant he visited in Guangzhou where robots were serving the dishes. "In China robots can perform many functions, like painting large buildings in a short time," he added.[93]

This appreciation of China's development and innovation at times morphs into inspiration. Visiting China, for many participants, is witnessing what's possible. Reflecting on digitalization of Chinese media – a topic covered in detail in journalist trainings – an Ethiopian media professional remarked that "visiting China is like seeing the future."[94] Some interlocutors directly compared China and Ethiopia's levels of development following their visits. "Before going to China, I thought Ethiopia was quite developed (based on growth statistics), but once I got to see China, I realized we are still far behind, but also if we work hard, we could one day become like China," shared an Ethiopian official who visited China several times for training.[95] For this official, witnessing China's progress fueled a fresh impetus to work toward Ethiopia's developmental goals. China, to him, was a benchmark for success.

Many Ethiopian elites also invoked their changed perspectives on Chinese culture, shaped by affective ties formed with Chinese people during the visit and by cultural visits and lectures. A public relations official for the Ministry of Finance who traveled to China multiple times described Chinese people he met there as "very humble" – a shift from how he used to perceive them in Ethiopia. "My thoughts about China changed after the trip. When you see Chinese people in Ethiopia, you assume they are mostly working people, or how do I put it … uncultured. When I went to China though, I see that they are different in their own country. They are great people!" he exclaimed.[96] Some training

---

[91] Informal group conversation as part of site visit and observation at the leadership academy, Bahir Dar, 2018.
[92] Interview ETJ31, Adama, 2023.
[93] Interview ETOF38, Addis Ababa, 2023.
[94] Interview ETJ31, Adama, 2023.
[95] Interview ETOF13, Addis Ababa, 2019.
[96] Interview ETOF28, Addis Ababa, 2023.

participants also described Chinese people they met through these trips as surprisingly helpful, curious, and compassionate. "One day, I try to walk at night, and I miss my hotel. Chinese take me to my hotel from far area," recalled a journalist from Addis TV about his experience on a short-term fellowship in China.[97] A think tank expert remembered meeting curious Chinese high school students at the Great Wall who insisted on taking pictures together. He expected more hostile reactions but has generally found Chinese people very warm. Another former trainee recalled Chinese hosts displaying emotion at their parting. "They cried when we left them, they cried for our separation," he recalled in surprise.[98] Since Chinese people in Ethiopia mostly live in isolated compounds and adhere to a grueling work schedule with limited contact with Ethiopian society,[99] there is a notable disconnect between Chinese and local communities in Ethiopia. Traveling to China can present the first opportunity for genuine cross-cultural encounters.

Finally, my interlocutors shared their appreciation for what they perceived as expressions of China's cultural pride. An Ethiopian official shared how even the tour guides were positive and proud of their history. He then added that he was impressed by how any Chinese person can tell you the important dates and events in their history and it creates pride in their people.[100] "They think that China is like the world," noted an Ethiopian journalist, referring to Chinese hosts positioning China as a civilizational power – a world in itself.[101] Many also associated trainers' reliance on Chinese language as a signal of cultural confidence – something the participants saw as admirable coming from a country where English is often the working language, especially with foreigners. As part of their travels across China, Ethiopian elites also noticed booming domestic cultural tourism – something that signaled a deep interest in their own culture, as well as in cultural preservation. "It is possible to grow without destroying culture," shared a state media journalist in response to a question about what he learned about China and Chinese people from the training.[102]

---

[97] Interview ETJ21, Addis Ababa, 2023.
[98] Interview ETJ20, Addis Ababa, 2023.
[99] See for instance Miriam Driessen, *Tale of Hope, Tastes of Bitterness: Chinese Road Builders in Ethiopia* (Hong Kong University Press: 2019).
[100] Informal group discussion as part of site visit, 2019.
[101] Interview ETJ31, Adama, 2023.
[102] Interview ETJ21, Addis Ababa, 2023.

4.3.2 Discerning and Negotiating China's Persuasion Narratives and Practices

The softening of perceptions about Chinese politics, development, and culture is accompanied by selective questioning and negotiating of China's official narratives and persuasion practices. The participants I interacted with questioned China's positioning as a democracy by invoking its persisting authoritarian features and challenged China's mutuality claims through experiences of inequitable treatment. Some interviewees also expressed cynicism about the delivery of trainings as one-sided or focused on conveying China's experience. Other than sharing critical reflections privately in our discussions, some participants also voiced their opinions and questions directly to their hosts.

While Ethiopian elites acknowledged China's limited democratic channels for public participation and the relatively meritocratic and rigorous promotion system for party cadres, they also observed the persistence of its autocratic features, mainly manifested in information control. The inability to access Western digital platforms, such as Facebook and Google, is a routine and an inescapable part of the experience that stays with many participants I spoke to. Following my lecture titled "Developmental Communication: Lessons from China" at Meles Zenawi Academy, one of the first questions from the audience concerned China's censorship. "When I was in China, much of the global Internet was blocked, which made it difficult to communicate. Do these strategies hurt China's image and make it more disconnected from the world?" asked one of the audience members who frequently traveled to China.[103] In discussions with journalists trained in China, they associated China's censorship of the Internet with intensive media control and even indoctrination. Some put forward a righteous claim that "Chinese people deserve more media freedom," drawing on their experiences with online information access in China.[104] Some journalist interviewees also presented censorship as a downside of an otherwise efficient system. "China provides peace, stability, and good governance," noted an Ethiopian journalist who spent ten months in China on a training program, "but in turn, they have to 'zip zip,'" he concluded and covered his mouth to illustrate the act of zipping with his face.[105]

---

[103] "Developmental Communication: Lessons from China Lecture," lecture delivered by the author at Meles Zenawi Academy, Addis, 2018.

[104] Focus group ETJFG01, Addis Ababa, 2019.

[105] Focus group ETJFG03, Addis Ababa, 2023.

Most interviewees also scrutinized the narrative of mutuality and China's benevolence toward Africa. "Is it a win-win or a China-win?" asked an Ethiopian official who had recently traveled to China. This question masked a suspicion and concern that China might gain more from its relationship with Africa than vice versa – a sentiment I encountered among past training participants beyond Ethiopia. "They keep talking about the win-win!" an African journalism fellow from Zambia said mockingly at his goodbye party on his last evening in Beijing. "But is it really a win-win?" he added.[106] His three colleagues, also returning home the following morning, asked me whether I thought what China was doing in Africa was really a good thing – a question that was frequently raised in lecture seminars I gave around Ethiopia with officials, journalists, and graduate students, many of whom have been to China on training trips. During an informal discussion at the Oromia Leadership Academy in Adama, for instance, one official framed the question about China's influence in more controversial terms: "Is China involved in modern slavery, exploiting Ethiopian resources and selling very cheap goods to Ethiopia?"[107] Another official quickly jumped in to say that overall China's relationship with Ethiopia is good, but China should sell higher-quality products to Ethiopia, alluding to the popular perception that Chinese goods sent to Africa are deliberately of low quality. In another discussion with journalist trainees from state media outlets, the conversation also shifted to the theme of unequal relations with China. "If we don't repay our loan for the Djibouti Railway and the Light Rail, the Chinese might just take over the train operations!" said one senior editor.[108] These anxieties about debt are further explored in the next chapter on how Ethiopian elites informally subvert China's censorial power.

Ironically, exposure to China through lectures and visits didn't appear to soften these preexisting concerns about China's influence in Ethiopia, but in some cases, even exacerbated them. For instance, after experiencing the ability to purchase high-quality goods in China, a senior editor from a state media outlet became more convinced that China is purposefully selling lower-quality goods to Ethiopia. "Why can't China have stricter

---

[106] Informal conversation as part of the final pre-departure gathering of African officials in Beijing, July 2019.

[107] Oromo Leadership Academy Nation Branding seminar, delivered by the author, April 23, 2019, Adama.

[108] Focus group ETJFG01, Addis Ababa, 2019.

export quality controls?" he remarked. He even raised this issue with officials in Guangzhou during his journalism fellowship in China.[109] The officials promised to investigate this matter, but no substantial change followed the conversation. Other training participants shared their observations on contrasts in the quality of Chinese goods available in China versus Ethiopia.

Encounters with racism and alienation also aggravated the perceptions of hierarchies that underpin this geopolitical relationship. While the interactions with Chinese hosts yielded positive impressions of Chinese people and culture, some unanticipated encounters with authorities and lay citizens at times signaled discrimination and distancing. A former journalism fellow shared that when he landed in Beijing, along with other African journalists, they were taken into interrogation rooms, where they were photographed and asked repetitive questions about the purpose of their visits. White passengers were allowed to pass right through. My interviewee was startled by this treatment but abstained from extensively complaining to his hosts out of fear of compromising the program.[110] Some Ethiopian journalists also recalled being greeted with "Ebola" in public spaces. "A small child was staring me at the subway station," shared another former trainee, "and then his father looked at him and said 'Ebola' turning his son away from me."[111] Other visitors were referred to as "Ebola" in taxis and in grocery stores.

In spontaneous encounters with Chinese citizens, in addition to welcoming sentiments, Ethiopian visitors recounted exotification that bordered on discomfort, including frequent picture-taking and uninvited touch and greetings. In informal conversations, some Ethiopians also shared instances of avoidance when Chinese residents would not take elevators with them or sit together in public transport. These moments of racialization recounted in the interviews took place in the larger context of complicated racial dynamics between Chinese and Africans. In the spring of 2020, for instance, the world witnessed "the Guangzhou incident," when many Africans residing in Guangzhou faced discriminatory treatment.[112] Scholars of Sino-African racial relations also find that

---

[109] Focus group ETJFG03, Addis Ababa, 2023.
[110] Interview ETJ14, Addis Ababa, 2019.
[111] Focus group, ETJFG01, Addis Ababa, 2019.
[112] There was a lot of international media reporting on this "incident," which included evictions of African residents from their homes. See for instance "African Nationals 'Mistreated, Evicted' in China over Coronavirus," AlJazeera, April 12, 2020, www.aljazeera.com/news/2020/4/12/african-nationals-mistreated-evicted-in-china-over-coronavirus.

Chinese perspectives on race reflect both Western superiority and social Darwinist worldview – both positioning Africans at the bottom of racial hierarchies.[113] That said, my Ethiopian interlocutors often dismissed "racist" interpretations of their experiences, and instead blamed what they described as unfortunate encounters on ignorance and limited exposure of Chinese people to other peoples and cultures.

Other than critically reflecting on Chinese official narratives and experiences in China in these interviews and discussions, some training participants also attempted to negotiate them with their hosts. One state media journalist, for instance, recalls asking "why they prohibit social media and other Western media and why they don't allow more freedom of expression" to a Chinese lecturer.[114] Another state media editor shared that he asked "Why China is not progressing as fast in democracy as in economic development."[115] Some participants also openly questioned the win–win narrative. A senior official from Oromia region, for instance, asked his Chinese trainer about environmental degradation as a side effect of the BRI.[116] Following a lecture by Chinese experts at the IPSS think tank in Addis, a member of the audience also directly questioned the negative implications of China's economic and political involvement in Africa. "There are some criticisms, in the Ethiopian case, for instance, about the lack of feasibility studies, corruption, and China working with autocratic leaders. Of course, we admire China working in Africa, but how do you evaluate this?" he asked.[117]

These instances of directly challenging Chinese official persuasion narratives were largely met with a mix of official talking points, ignoring, and even confrontation – tactics that only deepened the concerns of the participants. The response to the question on media freedom, for instance, as the Ethiopian journalist recalls, was that "Chinese follow the development-human rights approach," and that "they have their own social media platforms for their citizens."[118] In engaging with the Oromo official on the thorny issue of environmental degradation associated with Chinese initiatives, the Chinese interlocutor scrutinized the Ethiopian guest. "Are

---

[113] Binxin Zhang, "Africans in China, Western/White Supremacy and the Ambivalence of Chinese Racial Identity," *The China Quarterly* 260 (2024): 932–947.

[114] Interview ETJ20, Addis Ababa, 2023.

[115] Interview ETJ02, Addis Ababa, 2019.

[116] Interview ETOF08, Adama, 2019.

[117] "Inclusive Development and Sustainable Peace" seminar, IPSS, Addis Ababa, June 15, 2023.

[118] Interview ETJ20, Addis Ababa, 2023.

you coming from America? Why do you say negative things about BRI?" the interviewee narrated his Chinese hosts.[119] "I responded that my country is suffering from ecological devastation as part of the BRI projects, and I want to hear the measures the Chinese government is taking to address these problems. The reaction was silence and a change of topic,"[120] he recalled to me in frustration. This interaction left the official with more suspicion and discontent about Chinese influence in Ethiopia. The following chapter delves deeper into silencing and disciplinary practices, but it is important to note here both the efforts of selective participants to directly engage their hosts on sensitive topics and the limited and largely unsatisfying responses they got in return.

In addition to questioning and challenging core persuasion narratives, some Ethiopians also critically reflected on persuasion practices or the information delivery in these trainings. First, most participants describe these programs as China's "show-off exercises" rather than as genuine training or knowledge production exchanges. "They always want to show off China," shared one of the former trainees, a journalist from a state-owned Ethiopian newspaper, with a streak of sarcasm.[121] Most participants struggled to explain or give examples of specific lessons they could implement from these trainings. In discussing lectures, they shared that they remember very little. Some expressed annoyance at limited tangible skills or ideas gained. An official working in technical and vocational education and training in Addis Ababa (TVET), for instance, signaled a clear preference for Germany. He noted that in Germany, you explore culture by yourself, but when you are in an official capacity, you get straight to business. There are no big group tours like there are in China. All the cultural stuff is personal business.[122] Similar comments were shared by journalists who preferred Europe and the United States for training exchanges – a theme developed more in Chapter 6. Ethiopian training participants also described the overwhelming, disjointed, and top-down delivery of content as unsatisfying. An official who took part in a training that included representatives from different African countries, for instance, commented on brief discussion sessions and daunting

---

[119] Interview ETOF08, Adama, 2019.
[120] Ibid.
[121] Focus group discussion with Ethiopian journalists who participated in China trainings, ETJFG01, Addis Ababa, 2019.
[122] Informal conversation with the author and Ethiopian colleagues, Addis Ababa, 2018.

lecture materials leaving everyone bored. "Some of the other African delegates even walked out and skipped some lessons," he shared.[123]

While directly challenging the presentation formats was less common than questioning certain principles or ideas, the trainees still found ways to adapt to and negotiate their circumstances. Though Ethiopian participants didn't dare to directly quit lectures like their other African counterparts, they admitted to often ignoring them, and treating the trips as entertainment and as pathways to see the world – something already discussed in the previous chapter. After describing lectures and interactions with Chinese trainers as stifling and China-centric, a senior editor, for instance, shared that he would still accept another opportunity if granted. "Of course, I would, why wouldn't I want to go to a picnic?" he said, referring to these trips as fun, even if of little professional utility.[124] In rare cases, Ethiopian elites shared their efforts at informing Chinese authorities about certain deficiencies in the programming. A state media journalist from Addis Ababa, for instance, wrote a letter to the Chinese embassy upon his return, asking for improvement in training programs to avoid more superficial visits and to engage in more targeted experience sharing. His efforts were ignored, and eventually he gave up trying.

Overall, Chinese training experience elicited mixed responses from Ethiopian elites. The acknowledgment, and in some cases, appreciation of China's distinct governance trajectory, including in political, economic, and cultural spheres, is combined with selective critiques and negotiation of Chinese ideological narratives and persuasion practices. Participants both privately and publicly question China's limited freedom of expression and its unequal relations with Africa, as well as the top-down and at times overwhelming presentation style of their hosts. Far from entirely absorbing and adapting Chinese political ideals, therefore, Ethiopian elites experience a modest positive shift in perceptions toward China, but also remain discerning and cynical, especially toward narratives that directly concern Ethiopia. As with reception toward China's tangible enticement analyzed in the previous chapter, Ethiopians exposed to China's ideational power selectively appropriate it to their advantage by extracting the inspirational and entertaining facets from the mundane, and by ignoring the content and ideas that they deem less relevant and less convincing. A conversation with an

---

[123] Interview ETOF25, Addis Ababa, 2023.
[124] Interview ETJ02, Addis Ababa, 2019.

Ethiopian official and professor at Addis Ababa University captures this duality well. In reflecting on his experiences in China, he remarked: "I have a lot of admiration for China and what it has accomplished."[125] When asked about lessons he brought back, however, he noted: "I didn't take those too seriously." The official effortlessly combined an acknowledgment and inspiration of the China story with indifference for its relevance for Ethiopia.[126]

4.4 CONCLUSION

This chapter examined China's ideational influence or diffusion of Chinese political ideals, values, and governance practices through elite training programs with Ethiopian (and more broadly African) officials and journalists. The analysis of training materials and experiences demonstrates that while China is not exporting a "model," it attempts to legitimize its domestic and global governance through these persuasion exercises and more broadly, to "show off" China. The consistent themes of China as presenting a non-Western democratic and competent governance alternative, and an equitable partner to Africa are combined with more sporadic and superficial content that illustrates China's successes across different sectors, such as the media. The strategic deployment of coherent persuasion narratives, immersive experiences, and choreographed hospitality coexists with ad hoc and supply-driven content delivery – largely a product of large-scale mobilization of trainers with varied skills and levels of preparation for interacting with African guests.

The engagement with these trainings is also multidirectional, including a notable softening in perceptions about key facets of Chinese governance and society, as well as scrutiny over specific narratives, realities, and practices the participants encounter in China. While critical questioning

---

[125] Interview ETOF22, Addis Ababa, 2023.

[126] It is important to note that whereas training programs and state-sponsored visits that target elites, especially officials, journalists, and policy experts, tend to illicit this dualistic reaction of inspiration and dismissal of China lessons, more technical trainings that are focused on teaching Ethiopians how to operate certain machinery (i.e., the Addis-Djibouti railway), or the training programs that bring Chinese technical experts to Ethiopia, as in the case of the agricultural assistance, illicit different responses – more satisfaction with knowledge transfer, according to my interviews and visits to the Ministry of Agriculture and the Railway Corporation (see Appendix II). Since I was more interested in examining ideational influence in this chapter, and my focus is primarily on Ethiopian elites (current and future), I didn't focus on the study of these programs here, but they deserve more future research.

tends to proceed in private or informal spaces, some trainees also dare to question and challenge their hosts – efforts largely unwelcomed and dismissed. The next chapter turns to China's deployment of silencing and censorial power in detail, with a special focus on how it works in Ethiopian media and public sphere.

5

Defensive Image-Making

Guarding China Narratives

5.1 INTRODUCTION

"Chinese authorities are watchful; they notice all reporting about China. If they aren't happy, they can reach out and give comments," shared a public relations officer at the Ministry of Finance.[1] "You can report on China as much as you like, but it has to be positive," noted a state media journalist, with a hint of sarcasm.[2] The theme of active guarding of China narratives in Ethiopia and the ensuing sensitivity about public expressions about China pierced through most of my fieldwork, especially in encounters with Ethiopian communication professionals at major political institutions and media organizations, but also with journalists and officials who were trained in China. Other than proactive image-making through diffusion of tangible opportunities and ideational appeal, Chinese actors also strive to patrol China's image through indirect and overt acts of censorship.

This chapter delves into the workings of China's censorial power, drawing primarily on experiences of Ethiopian journalists and other elites who report on and communicate about China as part of their jobs. I also discuss how silencing permeates other Sino-Ethiopian encounters, including at Confucius Institutes and as part of elite trainings. Inspired by Roberts' broad conceptualization of censorship as restricting both the "expression of information and access to information,"[3] this chapter illuminates subtle

---

[1] Interview ETOF28, Addis Ababa, 2023.
[2] Focus group ETJFG02, Addis Ababa, 2023.
[3] Margaret E. Roberts, *Censored: Distraction and Diversion inside China's Great Firewall* (Princeton University Press: 2018), p. 38.

control over information flows via inhibiting access, but also at times by repressing certain expressions about China.

Echoing the previous chapters, the analysis demonstrates both systematic and opportunistic disciplinary practices. On the one hand, Chinese diplomats and company representatives routinely and proactively engage in what I describe as "managed publicity," whereby information about Chinese activities and projects is diffused through carefully staged public relations events, and information access is otherwise declined or significantly inhibited for journalists, officials, and researchers. At the same time, some Chinese actors, especially, but not limited to, private company personnel, occasionally deploy enterprising silencing tactics to halt a negative story, including through a mix of co-optation and threats. This range of strategies mirrors China's domestic environment, where the party-state regularly resorts to staged publicity and information withdrawal as part of image management, and officials and company representatives endeavor to contain narratives that can hold them accountable and compromise their professional standing.

As with other influence mechanisms, the responses to China's censorial power in Ethiopia are layered. Ethiopian government institutions work alongside with Chinese entities to spread positive messaging and contain negative stories, while news outlets self-censor their coverage of China. Rather than treating this as merely subjugation to China's pressure, however, Ethiopian elites articulate these practices as serving the national interest – maintaining strong relations with China and spreading a positive image of Ethiopia. Alongside this strategic complicity, Ethiopian elites and broader publics also subvert China's censorial power by crafting alternative narratives in nonofficial contexts and spaces. In doing so, they often draw on sarcasm and rumors. China's censorial power appears to yield public-facing compliance, but also facilitate resentment and push-back, expressed through interpersonal communication. The chapter now continues to examine Chinese censorship practices, starting with more systematic information management in Ethiopia.

5.2 CHINA'S CENSORIAL PRACTICES

5.2.1 Routine Disciplining: Managed Publicity and Information Withdrawal

5.2.1.1 *Strategic Communication in the Media Sphere*

Chinese actors in Ethiopia control the production of China narratives primarily through guarding information access about Chinese activities.

According to Ethiopian officials and journalist interviewees, Chinese companies and officials rely on carefully curated public relations briefings to diffuse positive information and routinely neglect journalists' interview requests. This results in highly managed publicity, with little room for unanticipated questions and encounters.

In sharing information with media and the public, Chinese company and embassy representatives prefer top-down filtering of positive information through organized press conferences. Ethiopian public relations officials and journalists emphasize that these celebratory events tend to mostly mark an initiation of a project. "If there is a loan or another agreement signed, they organize a ceremony. They try to invite as many media representatives as possible. In comparison to other foreign stakeholders, Chinese need more publicity. I don't know why, but they need ceremonies," reflected a public relations official from the Ministry of Finance.[4] This persistent quest for publicity was also noted by other public relations officials across major Ethiopian institutions that engage with China, such as the Investment Commission and the Ethiopian Road Authority, among others. Even the American embassy officials in Addis commented that Chinese embassy excels in branding, with the smallest project or initiative actively promoted and publicized, in contrast to American projects that often go unnoticed.[5]

Other than its distinctive emphasis on scale of promotion, Chinese publicity also differs from that of its counterparts in its more controlled or managed implementation. While all public relations conferences are generally aimed at favorable diffusion of information,[6] Western briefings, according to Ethiopian interviewees, tend to be polished and professionalized, but also interactive and inclusive of participants' questions. The Chinese ceremonies, in contrast, are relatively one-sided, with Chinese actors setting and controlling the agenda. "Chinese press conferences are highly centralized, their information release is event-driven, making it very challenging to ask questions that are off-script or not pre-planned," shared an experienced reporter who attended many of these briefings.[7] "Question time is limited, and all questions are pre-screened," commented a senior editor. "They typically distribute the brochures about

---

4 Interview ETOF28, Addis Ababa, 2023.

5 Informal conversation with US embassy staff in Ethiopia, Addis Ababa, 2023.

6 Mats Ekström and Göran Eriksson, "Press Conferences," in Ruth Wodak and Bernhard Forchtner (editors), *The Routledge Handbook of Language and Politics* (Routledge: 2017), 342–54.

7 Interview ETJ33, Addis Ababa, 2023.

a project or a deal containing information that can be easily found on their websites," he added.[8]

Controlled publicity can also include careful responses to questions but limited access to spontaneous encounters at a project site. An excerpt from an interview with an Ethiopian journalist from a state media outlet about his experience in covering the launch of a new Chinese mining project captures this dynamic:

The Chinese were in control of the agenda, and the story largely followed it. In the opening remarks, the Chinese promised to train and employ Ethiopians. I posed some questions about the number of workers to be employed and about environmental protections and infrastructure development. The Chinese side answered all the questions in broad satisfactory manner, but didn't let us visit the site, keeping us at a designated hotel in the city. It was disappointing, as I wasn't able to talk to Ethiopian workers or to see the actual site for myself to evaluate it independently. Even the local government complained about the lack of access. I encountered similar dynamics in attending a Chinese press conference about a railway project. I was also unable to visit the construction site.[9]

It is striking that a Chinese company and embassy representatives have the capacity to block journalists and local officials from visiting the sites located on foreign territory. It is also ironic that a press conference marking the launch of a project kept journalists away from witnessing the project or from visiting the site as part of the delegation. The journalist covering this event wanted to incorporate more voices into his article and to tell a richer story, but he was limited to using official responses and statements he gathered at these press conferences. In cases where site visits are incorporated into the ceremony, as with launches of new projects at the China-financed Industrial Parks, journalists partake in carefully guided tours with little room for unplanned interviews or conversations.[10]

Outside the press conference or event-driven information diffusion model, access to Chinese activities is heavily and systematically restricted, according to most Ethiopian journalists interviewed for this study. An investigative journalist from a private news outlet describes the contrast between press conferences and their aftermath for reporting on Chinese projects:

Chinese companies and officials are eager to welcome journalists to the launch of a new project, during the MOU signing ceremony. At this festive moment, they explain the future of the project, how many Ethiopians will be hired, etc. Once the

---

[8] Interview ETJ16, Addis Ababa, 2023.
[9] Interview ETJ04, Addis Ababa, 2019.
[10] Interview ETOF35, Addis Ababa, 2023.

project is in progress, however, they tend to avoid all media communication. Even if you want to write a positive story, they will be unwilling to give an interview.[11]

This journalist describes China's information management as a sliding door that opens slightly during major events and remains shut for the remainder of time. This silencing and withholding of information outside the parameters of press conferences was noted by many interviewees. The most frequent response to requests for a site visit or an interview is a mix of silence and rerouting of requests to the Chinese embassy. "Carrying out any in-depth reporting about China in Ethiopia is nearly impossible because all reporting is filtered through the Chinese embassy. If you request a meeting with a company, they will typically go through the embassy," shared an experienced editor at a large state media outlet.[12]

The embassy, however, is also not very responsive, especially to requests from private media. "Chinese company representatives almost never reply to my requests, and the Chinese embassy staff promise to get back to me, but they usually don't," shared a former editor at a large private news outlet.[13] Even in reporting positive stories, aimed at celebrating Chinese initiatives, the companies and officials generally avoid interview requests. A TV journalist at a major regional network, for instance, gave an example of an optimistic story he was hoping to produce about a Chinese company using fertilizer in their production. "We wanted to ask where they got the fertilizer and how they use it, but they closed the door on us," he shared.[14] The embassy also didn't help in facilitating the interview.

This systematic information withdrawal from local media has also been documented in other African contexts. Li's study of China–Africa media encounters in Kenya, for instance, features an interview with the president of the Political Journalists Association in Kenya, who speaks to the apparent limits on information access to Chinese entities:

It is not that we are biased or [that we do] not want Chinese people's voices [to be] heard. [The] problem [is that] we, Kenyan journalists, find it difficult to reach the Chinese. When there is news, we contact them, but they are either very slow to respond to us or do not respond to our questions . . . so we have been actually thinking hard about how to better engage with the Chinese in Kenya, and to make our stories more balanced.[15] (p. 39)

---

[11] Interview ETJ09, Addis Ababa, 2019.
[12] Interview ETJ16, Addis Ababa, 2023.
[13] Interview ETJ33, Addis Ababa, 2023.
[14] Interview ETJ31, Addis Ababa, 2023.
[15] Hangwei Li, "Understanding African Journalistic Agency in China–Africa Media Interactions: The Case of Kenya," *International Communication Gazette* 85(1) (2023): 39.

Ojo's recent study of African journalists' challenges in covering China–Africa relations also points to persisting information constraints. "Getting access to officials from China has been quite challenging. They are not open to the press. A balanced story should have the views of experts from both sides, but when one side (China) keeps sealed lips, it makes the reporting process perilous," shared an interviewee cited in his study.[16]

In my analysis of the Ethiopian context, I found that in rare cases when an interview is granted, according to journalist practitioners, it is typically with the "top boss" who was cleared by the embassy. Access to his subordinates or regular workers is still consistently blocked. An excerpt from an interview with a senior journalist at a major state outlet who often reports about China captures this hierarchical access:

What surprised me the most in covering China projects in Ethiopia is that I could not talk to any ordinary Chinese workers who are part of the project. In the cases of reporting about Addis Rail, for instance, I tried to speak to those driving the trains, but nobody would agree to talk to me with their boss there. We can only speak to the top guy, with the permission of the embassy. Even the ambassador would at times have to get permission from Beijing to do an interview with us...[17]

This journalist articulates the vertical power structures at play within Chinese enterprises and official entities in communicating with Ethiopian media, necessitating permissions or clearances from above. Publicity work is only relegated to higher-ranked personnel, and interviews turn into mini-press briefings for participating journalists. Unanticipated discoveries through conversations with other Chinese actors are strictly off-limits.

Alongside with limiting information access to news outlets, Chinese companies and representatives from the embassy provide preferential access to Chinese state media, namely to the Xinhua News Agency in covering Chinese initiatives in Ethiopia, according to Ethiopian reporters working at Xinhua and at local news outlets. A Xinhua journalist with years of experience boasted that in contrast to challenges encountered by Ethiopian media, Xinhua journalists in Ethiopia have no trouble accessing Chinese sources. "For Chinese companies, they welcome our coverage as they know that they can anticipate positive stories, which boost their recognition and approval. The Chinese embassy also invites us to cover any event that they are hosting," he shared, and further added that the embassy routinely helps them facilitate interviews with Chinese

---

[16] Tokunbo Ojo, "Through Their Eyes: Reporters' Challenges in Covering China–Africa Relations," *Journalism Practice* 14(10) (November 25, 2020): 1186.
[17] Focus group ETJFG03, Addis Ababa, 2023.

stakeholders.[18] Journalists based in Ethiopian media observed similar realities when it comes to Xinhua access. "Chinese embassy prefers filtering information through them, as it knows they will publish what they want," commented a former Ethiopian editor.[19] This preferential access to Xinhua is important, as it makes Ethiopian news media reliant on it for China coverage – something I discuss further in this chapter.

5.2.1.2 *Strategic Silencing in Other Diplomatic Engagements*

The deliberately and consistently guarded information management by Chinese stakeholders extends beyond the Ethiopian media sphere and permeates other diplomatic spaces and engagements. Some Ethiopian faculty at universities that host Confucius Institutes, for instance, were surprised that CI directors and teachers would avoid interactions outside of the official teaching responsibilities and celebrations. A lecturer at Mekelle University unsuccessfully tried to contact local Confucius Classroom teachers several times and invite them to local events. He expressed exasperation with what he interpreted as "secrecy" and doubts over "the real nature of their activities."[20] Confucius Institutes' directors also routinely deny access to research interviews unless preapproved by higher-ups. I experienced this information challenge directly when visiting some local Confucius Classrooms. The Chinese teacher volunteers referred me to their director, and the director asked me to contact the main Confucius Institute in TVETI, Addis Ababa. "The Director isn't here, you better wait for him," cautioned a teacher volunteer in Mekelle. "When is he coming back?" I ask. "He is in China. If you need anything, you need to speak to Addis," he stated firmly and signaled the end of our conversation. The director in Addis, in turn, asked me to speak to Hanban, in Beijing. Though there is also some unpredictability at play here, with openness varying depending on a director in charge (I discuss this more in the methods Appendix I).

In the context of ideational promotion through elite trainings analyzed in the previous chapter, participants highlighted the often one-directional communication flow. Some trainees, on longer journalism fellowships, recalled attending carefully orchestrated press conferences like the ones they observed in Ethiopia. One interviewee shared:

When we were invited to cover a speech by a well-known Chinese official, we would always arrive twenty minutes prior to the start of the press conference so

---

[18] Interview ETJ30, July 1, 2023, Addis Ababa.
[19] Interview ETJ33, Addis Ababa, 2023.
[20] Interview ETEX02, Mekelle, 2019.

that the organizers could screen us and pick the questions selectively. One technique I noted is that of Chinese officials taking many questions at once and then only answering the ones they are comfortable with, while ignoring the rest.[21]

Another technique this journalist highlighted was the flooding of positive narratives about Africa and African people, thereby indirectly pre-empting negative questions or commentaries. "The official in charge of African Affairs that we met in Beijing took most of his time to offer nuanced understanding of African politics. After hearing so many positive comments about Africa, nobody cared to challenge him or ask any difficult questions," he explained.[22]

The controlled, top-down communication also characterized many seminars, as part of training experiences. The Chinese side would deliver elaborate presentations but leave little room for questions and discussion – something already discussed briefly in the previous chapter. "They want us only to listen!" declared a senior government official who took part in multiple trainings.[23] Another official who went to China multiple times and welcomed Chinese delegations to his academy noted that even when he spent time carefully preparing questions in advance, he rarely got satisfying answers. "Most of the time, their response is that they are unable to talk about this issue," he said. "Chinese come with a framework and don't want to go beyond it, they are very restricted," he added.[24] In a Chinese training seminar I attended in Addis Ababa, I observed these dynamics directly, with the lecturers taking up most of the time, and the Q&A session kept relatively short. At one point, the Chinese speaker averted a challenging question from the audience by stating: "we are not here to give you lessons."[25]

Access to non-sanctioned information gathering was also heavily limited during the trainings, especially for journalist fellows. Reflecting on his long stay as a press fellow in China, an Ethiopian journalist shared that a Chinese coordinator insisted on accompanying him on all trips and interviews during his stay, as well as on managing interview requests. On his first visit to Guangzhou, for instance, he wanted to interview some Africans, including Ethiopians, who lived there, about their experiences in China. He sensed that there were grievances they wanted to voice, but they

---

[21] Interview ETJ16, Addis Ababa, 2023.
[22] Interview ETJ14, Addis Ababa, 2019.
[23] Interview ETOF25, Addis Ababa, 2023.
[24] Interview ETOF08, Adama, 2019.
[25] "Inclusive Development and Sustainable Peace" seminar, IPSS, June 15, 2023, Addis Ababa.

shared only positive impressions in front of the Chinese coordinator. On another trip, he wanted to interview the Ethiopian Consul in Guangzhou, but the coordinator insisted on arranging the meeting and later informed the journalist that the Consul is not available. She did not share his phone number – something that the journalist saw as a deliberate act of divergence or silencing on her part.[26]

In addition to experiencing information sanctioning during training experiences, some Ethiopian officials who returned from China enthusiastic about launching new collaborations with Chinese embassy also encountered surprising silencing or avoidance. A young Ethiopian government official who started a new China–Ethiopia youth initiative after traveling to China for a state-organized visit, for instance, expressed frustrations at the embassy's lackluster response to their requests about collaboration. "Chinese embassy barely responds to our emails and requests, they don't take advantage of our initiative," he shared, and went on to draw comparisons to Italian embassy, which responded immediately. "Chinese often go for silence, we don't know what their sensitive zones are, they have to guide us!" he added.[27] In this commentary, the government official appears as willing to comply with Chinese norms, so long as the boundaries are more clearly demarcated. I return to the topic of self-censorship among Ethiopian elites later in the chapter.

Chinese officials, educators, and company representatives' overarching reluctance to engage with media and public inquiry outside of tightly controlled official formats likely stems from an understanding that the risk of negative publicity outweighs the gains of positive coverage and trust-building. This rationale has long persisted in China's domestic context. In March 2024, the Chinese government even halted the annual Premier's news conference – the only platform for journalists to pose questions to top leaders.[28] In the context of operating in Africa, the limited grasp of local media landscape and cultural context, combined with relatively high stakes of negative publicity given China's diplomatic rhetoric about building a positive image and battling Western misconceptions (as discussed in Chapter 2), likely adds to the unease. Though access to Chinese officials and company personnel in Ethiopia on this

---

[26] Interview ETJ14, Addis Ababa, 2019.
[27] BRI Discussion Seminar, April 23, 2019, Addis Ababa.
[28] Li Yuan, "A Window into Chinese Government Has Now Slammed Shut," *The New York Times*, March 6, 2024, www.nytimes.com/2024/03/06/business/china-national-peoples-congress.html.

topic was limited given its sensitivity, scholars like Hangwei Li, who managed to carry out such interviews in other African countries highlight their deliberately risk-averse attitudes toward information disclosure. In response to Li's question about why the Chinese embassy in Kenya ignored Kenyan journalists' proposal for deeper engagement with Chinese community, for instance, a senior embassy official responded: "Our principle is the 'less trouble, the better.' We also prefer to organize things by ourselves, not by others. In that way, we can fully control the agenda."[29] In response to the same query, a senior manager at the China Media Group interviewed by Li shared the potential risks of more openness: "If we want to work with them on these initiatives, it means that we will have to apply for multiple layers of approval. Sometimes the more you do, the more mistakes you make, especially you know the Kenyan organizations have very close relationships with Western media and Western NGOs."[30] These quotes demonstrate how suspicions about local contexts and concerns with negative publicity can translate into a stance that saying and doing less is more secure and productive than more transparent engagement. Fears of being misquoted and misinterpreted by African journalists, foreign researchers, and official visitors can also explain the constrained information sharing as part of CI events and training experiences. We now shift to the discussion of more ad hoc, opportunistic disciplining carried out by selective Chinese actors in Ethiopia.

5.2.2 Opportunistic Disciplining: Combining Ad hoc Co-optation and Threats

In addition to routine, systematic silencing practices, Chinese actors, from company representatives to officials, also engage in more improvised censoring of China-related narratives. Most of these efforts, as documented through the interviews with Ethiopian media practitioners, tend to be reactive, aimed at controlling the narrative or at crisis management, drawing on a mix of co-optation and coercion. These practices are more opportunistic and irregular, often deployed by private company personnel, but are still important to analyze as part of the mosaic of China's censorial power.

---

[29] Li, "Understanding African Journalistic Agency in China–Africa Media Interactions: The Case of Kenya," p. 40.
[30] Ibid, p. 40.

Ethiopian journalists and editors who experienced covering sensitive stories about China shared that they faced a combination of cajoling and threats from Chinese actors. An independent journalist who had previously worked at a large private news outlet recalled investigating a dramatic story about a fire at a Chinese-built stadium, still under construction, burning several Ethiopians to death. The accident, according to Ethiopian witnesses he interviewed, was allegedly caused by a fire that spread from a Chinese worker's kitchen on the site's premises. When he went to the Chinese company's office, he was first greeted with a warm welcome, including a big dinner and an assortment of gifts. He even recalled that they tried to set him up with a beautiful Chinese woman.[31] As he declined the offerings and proceeded with the story, however, the company's tone changed from friendliness to threats. "The government is fine with it, be careful," was the warning the journalist got from a Chinese company representative. While not threatening him directly, the message conveyed that the Ethiopian government was in favor of secrecy and was watching him. I discuss the collusion of Ethiopian officials in controlling the production of China narratives in the next section, but I want to highlight here that the threatening warning came from the Chinese side, signaling that they have both the confidence to attempt to censor Ethiopian media, as well as the protection from the local government.

Another illustration of mixed tools arbitrarily deployed by Chinese actors is a story about media reporting on a Chinese-owned donkey slaughterhouse near Bishoftu – a town close to Addis Ababa. The journalist who covered it was based at a respected private news outlet.[32] While slaughtering donkeys was still legal at the time in Ethiopia, donkeys are revered animals in Ethiopian culture and the news about the slaughterhouse attracted a lot of public criticism. After the article was published, the slaughterhouse manager contacted the journalist and requested a meeting. In contrast to the stadium construction encounter, in this case, the manager started with an accusatory threat. "Who gave you the permission to publish this story?" the journalist recalled the threatening questioning. The manager then handed him a plastic bag full of cash. "I was a young reporter at the time, making a small salary, and I have never seen such money before," he shared with a smile. The journalist refused

---

[31] Interview ETJ27, Addis Ababa, 2023.
[32] Interview ETJ28, Addis Ababa, 2023.

the bribe, and the manager resumed with threats. "I was genuinely afraid that he would hurt me …" my interviewee shared.[33]

In other cases, Ethiopian journalists experienced either co-optive or coercive tactics from Chinese actors trying to halt sensitive stories. One investigative journalist, for instance, talked about Chinese efforts at changing his story about a court hearing on high-level corruption allegations against a major Chinese state-owned company and its Ethiopian business partners. "The day after the court hearing, many Chinese company representatives came to our media office denying everything and offering a different version of the story. 'We just do everything with the government,' they reasoned," shared the journalist.[34] The story, in this case, was published, and the court hearing was still ongoing at the time of the interview.[35] Other journalists noted that the Chinese embassy personnel also frequently reacted and at times attempted to amend their China coverage. In rare cases of negative reporting, they offered a counterresponse or a clarification of their position. While this tactic is not unique to Chinese embassy, the journalists highlighted the distinctly close reading of their articles by the Chinese staff. "They really do read our articles!" exclaimed one of the senior reporters during a group discussion.[36]

At times, Ethiopian journalists also experienced more coercive efforts at delegitimizing their narratives by the Chinese side. An impulsive reaction of a high-level Chinese official to his apparent information mismanagement with local media captures this dynamic. According to the journalist present at the scene, the Chinese Ambassador to the African Union said on record that China would provide troops to a disputed territory between Eritrea and Djibouti if asked by both parties.[37] The journalist recalled that all reporters at the scene had their recorders out and the official never mentioned that his comments were off the record. Once the story came out, however, the diplomat publicly refuted his remarks, and directly scolded the journalists for misrepresenting him, according to the interviewee.[38] In this case, the official improvised

---

[33] Ibid.

[34] Interview ETJ09, Addis Ababa, 2019.

[35] On court cases and the legal sphere as a channel for contestation of Chinese power in Ethiopia, see Miriam Driessen, *Immunity on Trial: Ethiopian Courts, Chinese Corporations, and Contestations over Sovereignty* (UC Press: 2026).

[36] Interview ETJFG03, Addis Ababa, 2023.

[37] Interview ETJ01, Addis Ababa, 2019.

[38] Ibid.

a coercive communication response to control for sensitive messaging that he had previously disseminated to the media.

Another reporter at a private news outlet shared a dramatic case of covering a story about an intoxicated director of a Chinese company in Ethiopia (with close ties to the Chinese government) allegedly running over and killing an elderly Ethiopian man. The journalist happened to be near the scene and took a photo of the license plate and all the surrounding evidence and later wrote a report about it. The following day, the journalist remembers Chinese company representatives storming into his office and denying that his boss was even in the country.[39] The company then accused the newspaper of defamation. The court dropped all the charges against both the company and the newspaper, according to the journalist.[40]

While most of these ad hoc disciplinary acts are deployed in the aftermath of a publication or investigation, in some cases, Ethiopian journalists also shared that Chinese company representatives would attempt to shape a China-related story through spontaneous preemptive bribery. An editor at a large news outlet in Addis discussed an unusual case of a Chinese company approaching him to offer a lead on a China-related story.[41] The editor agreed and said that his news outlet would do their best to examine the story comprehensively and objectively. Not long after that meeting, the Chinese contact offered a payment directly to him, signaling an interest in a certain framing. The editor refused. To his surprise, the contact persisted, and after a short while scheduled another meeting. This time, he handed him an envelope. When the editor opened it, he discovered a blank gift card to a large supermarket. Again, he sternly refused and continued with his story. In retelling this incident, the editor was seemingly more offended by the obtuse efforts of the Chinese counterpart than by the act of bribing itself. The editor felt disrespected by an assumption that a supermarket gift card would sway the ethical standards of a well-regarded media professional. If offered to a lower-ranking or to a less ethically minded journalist, however, this strategy may have worked in shaping a pro-China media narrative.

As with more systematic information management, these irregular practices mirror the domestic Chinese media context. In my past research

---

[39] According to this journalist, the Chinese side tilted the story by substituting the photo of their boss with another Chinese man and sending their boss out of the country.

[40] Interview ETJ09, Addis Ababa, 2019.

[41] Interview ETJ25, Addis Ababa, 2023.

on Chinese investigative journalism, I found that journalists frequently experience ad hoc co-optive and coercive silencing from Chinese officials and company managers, especially at the local level. One striking example I came across was that of a local official following a journalist to the train station, and then sitting next to him on the train and incessantly staring at him as an act of intimidation.[42] Another incident I documented in my first book is that of officials placing red envelopes with cash under the hotel door of investigative journalists and the following morning sending police to arrest them on account of corruption.[43] Given how influential Chinese actors deploy arbitrary censorship practices in China, it is not surprising that they would resort to some of them when operating abroad.

The overzealous initiatives at information management whereby some officials, and especially company managers, might over-perform their responsibilities may also reflect the phenomenon of "low-level reds" (*diji hong*) or expressions of mindless patriotism that can hinder the actual policies and visions of the country.[44] The phrase made it into the party discourse in 2024, as the General Office of the Central Committee released an influential document guiding Party Committees to guard against both "high-level blackmails" (using exaggerated praise as a form of sarcasm) and "low-level reds" or self-defeating nationalism.[45] The excessive (and at times coercive) silencing by Chinese actors has also at times been met with indirect criticism and distancing from Beijing. Chinese officials, for instance, often blame inexperienced company representatives for smearing China's image in Africa by being insensitive to local media and political context.[46] In some cases, even Chinese diplomats can get criticized for their disproportionate reactions to negative local media coverage. In one instance I encountered in my fieldwork, a high-ranking Chinese embassy official in Ethiopia criticized a Chinese researcher for Ethiopian media's

---

[42] Maria Repnikova, *Media Politics in China: Improvising Power under Authoritarianism* (Cambridge University Press: 2017).

[43] Ibid.

[44] This phrase became popularized in 2018 after a competitive race of a Chinese long-distance runner was disrupted by a volunteer trying to force a flag into her hands. See https://u.osu.edu/mclc/2019/03/18/low-level-red-and-other-concerns/.

[45] Zhonggong zhongyang yinfa "tongzhi," Zai quandang kaizhan dangji xuexi jiaoyu ("The Central Committee of the Chinese Communist Party releases a 'Notice': Conducting party discipline education within the party"). The State Council Information Office of the People's Republic of China. April 7, 2024, www.scio.gov.cn /zdgz/jj/202404/t20240408_841566.html.

[46] I often heard such comments in informal conversations with Chinese officials and experts as part of my fieldwork in Ethiopia and China. Chinese companies were described as crude and incapable of successful PR and community outreach.

misrepresentation of Chinese enterprise strategy and closed off much of international research access to Chinese companies. A well-known professor in Beijing, involved in this research project, in turn, wrote a letter to the Ministry of Commerce, criticizing the embassy official, referring to her behavior as an act of *diji hong*.[47] More studies into these emerging frictions across bureaucratic levels as part of China's global censorial power are necessary to further illuminate the diverse, often conflicting interests at play in China's image-making.

The arbitrary efforts to derail or change the ongoing negative coverage and public narratives about China in Ethiopia, however, are rarer than more routine practices of managed publicity and information withdrawal. This is in part because few Ethiopian journalists dare to publish a negative story in the first place, as will be discussed more in the next section. At the same time, the ad hoc attempts to co-opt or coerce journalists into silence are important to acknowledge as they demonstrate the dynamic and at times bottom-up efforts by Chinese actors to engage in image management. Several illustrations introduced in this section involve private Chinese companies. Though they aren't directly responsible for state-led image-making, their efforts still impact how it is constructed by Ethiopian elite communicators, and therefore was worthy of including here. Resonant with other forms of image-making analyzed in this book, the implementation is multidirectional and at times even surprising and messy, as in the case of the awkward bribery attempt with the supermarket gift card.

5.3 ENGAGING WITH CHINA'S CENSORIAL POWER

In responding to and managing these varied information restrictions, Ethiopian elites deploy a mix of strategic complicity and subtle contestation. Ethiopian public relations and media regulating officials actively take part in and augment China's censorial power by promoting positive narratives and disincentivizing negative ones as part of safeguarding Ethiopia's economic benefits. Ethiopian media professionals, especially at influential state media outlets, deliberately self-censor in response to Chinese and Ethiopian information climate and journalists' own strategic motivations to promote Ethiopian interests. We also see similar patterns among elite training participants. Finally, outside of the official, performative realm, Ethiopian elites and lay citizens engage in stretching and remaking narratives about China,

---

[47] Informal online conversation with one of the witnesses in this incident, July 2023.

often drawing on rumors and humor as rhetorical devices. We now turn to co-disciplinary practices of Ethiopian officials.

5.3.1 Strategic Complicity

5.3.1.1 Ethiopian Institutions as Co-disciplining China Narratives
Interviews with public relations officials at the Ministry of Finance, the Investment Commission, the Industrial Park Corporation, the Ethiopian Road Authority, and the Ministry of Foreign Affairs, among others, directly involved in Chinese initiatives and projects, reveal a proactive effort at promoting and protecting China's image in Ethiopia. The officials interviewed shared an awareness of China's quest for controlled publicity and appeared to largely abet and expand on China's censorial efforts through a mix of targeted and controlled promotion and silencing – similar techniques deployed by their Chinese counterparts. In justifying this work, Ethiopian officials tend to highlight China's importance for Ethiopia and the value of this strategic partnership. Several interviewees noted that while their offices also manage information flows about other foreign companies and initiatives, "they give special attention to China" in large part because of China's influence across major sectors of Ethiopian economy and society.[48]

In terms of promotional efforts, most of these institutions help organize public relations conferences and briefings with Chinese embassy and company representatives, as well as regularly disseminate public relations announcements about Chinese initiatives, and take Ethiopian media on organized tours of various Chinese projects. In discussing the joint work on press conferences, Ethiopian officials noted that they regularly engage with Chinese embassy's proposals to host public events and assist the embassy with organizing, including in targeting specific journalists and news outlets to attend the gatherings. Ethiopian institutions also carry out their own publicity of China–Ethiopia projects. An Ethiopian Road Authority official, for instance, shared that he organized nearly thirty tours per year for media representatives to witness Chinese construction sites.[49] The Industrial Park Corporation also regularly brings journalists to learn about the latest developments and to visit select Chinese companies through organized tours.[50] Ethiopian government communication

---

[48] Interview ETOF29; ETOF28; ETOF28, Addis Ababa, 2023.
[49] Interview ETOF09, Addis Ababa, 2019.
[50] Interview ETOF35, Addis Ababa, 2023.

practitioners also give positive comments to Chinese state media as part of publicity collaboration. In a 2020 interview with Xinhua, for instance, a spokesperson for the Ethiopian Foreign Ministry spoke glowingly about his country's relationship with China, describing it as an epitome of Africa–China cooperation.[51] Even a Xinhua news journalist admitted that while getting Ethiopian elites to respond to interview requests is relatively easy, they tend to be so positive in their remarks that the Chinese editors question their authenticity.[52]

When receiving contentious queries about China, Ethiopian officials engage in routine silencing practices. A public relations official from the Ministry of Finance, for instance, shared that other than diffusing positive and reassuring information about China, his office opts for a "no response" policy in case of rare, sensitive questions from the media. "No response is also a type of response," he noted.[53] When asked whether this strategy works, he asserted its effectiveness: "They can publish that they asked us, but they didn't get a response. The issue then dies out over time."[54] Other public relations officers confirmed their use of this silencing tactic – not only in response to sensitive China queries but also in engaging with sensitive information requests more broadly. Some public relations officials also shared that they attempt to diffuse China-related frictions before they even get to the media. An official from the Ethiopian Road Authority, for instance, noted that there are occasional public concerns about Chinese-funded and constructed road projects, and that his office responds to them promptly to preempt the public from contacting the media.[55]

Ethiopian public relations offices also use information access in punitive ways. A private media editor, for instance, shared his outlet's frictions with the government following a publication of an article about a Chinese company leaving the Hawassa Industrial Park.[56] When the editor asked the Commission to provide more information on this issue, an official

---

[51] "Interview: Ethiopia-China Relations a Good Example of Cooperation – Official," *Xinhua*, October 23, 2020, https://govt.chinadaily.com.cn/s/202010/23/WS5f924 e15498eaba5051bc12c/interview-ethiopia-china-relations-a-good-example-of-cooperation-official.html; "Interview: China Plays Rising Role in Ethiopia's Renewable Energy Dev't: Official," *Xinhua*, April 14, 2022, https://english.news.cn/20220413/aoe eb850d65c44edb2006a44dcb1a32e/c.html.
[52] ETJ30, Addis Ababa, 2023.
[53] Interview ETOF28, Addis Ababa, 2023.
[54] Ibid.
[55] Interview ETOF25, June 20, 2023, Addis Ababa.
[56] Interview ETJ28, Addis Ababa, 2023.

representative agreed to help but only if they could read a pre-publication version. The paper refused and noted in an article that the Commission declined their information request, which led to the Commission blocking further information access to this outlet on other stories, including banning it from attending press conferences. The same editor also noted that their paper faced similar retribution from the Ministry of Finance and from the Planning Commission, not only in response to China stories but also to any alternative framings of Ethiopia's economic governance. As a result, the outlet resorted to relying on public Parliamentary briefings and insider connections for information gathering.

Ethiopian media regulating institutions, namely the Government Communication Ministry at the state level and the Media Authority at the party level, complement the co-disciplinary efforts of public relations government offices, as they encourage positive coverage of what they refer to as Ethiopia's "important partners." When asked about media guidance on China stories, an official from the Communication Service Ministry answered in broad strokes, avoiding mentioning China directly: "If a country and its companies do good for our people, we direct our media to give them coverage." The Ministry holds weekly briefings with top media outlets to guide their editorial agenda. If coverage is deemed as countering the government agenda, the Ministry interferes and "asks media for correction."[57]

The Media Authority engages in what its top official described as "post-facto, soft regulation" over news outlets' adherence to "national interest" described vaguely as "anything of national concern and priority."[58] Maintaining good relations with key economic and political partners like China falls under this broad category. The official regulatory practices include advice to the media on altering coverage, followed by verbal and written warnings. The Media Authority official also abstained from directly invoking China as a topic of interest but rather referred to monitoring all media coverage about international partnerships and foreign actors in Ethiopia.[59] The official shared that in his experience, China coverage thus far has not necessitated regulatory action. In the past, however, under the leadership of EPRDF, party officials regulating the media deployed coercive tactics against journalists critical of China. An Ethiopian journalist working for Western media, for instance, recalls

---

[57] Interview ETOF39, Addis Ababa, 2023.
[58] Interview ETHOF32, July 4, 2023, Addis Ababa.
[59] Ibid.

nearly losing his reporting license after publishing a negative story about Huajian – a large shoe-manufacturing company with a major factory in Ethiopia. The article depicted violent treatment of Ethiopian workers at the factory, including beatings and payment withholdings from Chinese managers. When the journalist showed up to renew his license, he was told that it was cancelled for creating unfavorable work environment for China.[60] His license later got renewed under the new leadership that initially promised more press freedom.

The analysis of co-disciplinary efforts by major Ethiopian institutions underscores that Chinese censorship does not take place in a vacuum but rather works in conjunction with local official interests. Ethiopian officials serving in public relations and information management roles are savvy about sensitivities of Chinese actors, but they distance themselves from the role of simply serving or responding to China's directives. Instead, they position themselves as working for Ethiopia's future, which includes promoting important international relationships. Whereas PR officers are more explicit about prioritizing China, media regulating officials avoid highlighting it and instead offer general endorsement of positive coverage of Ethiopia's major international partners. Ethiopia's government collaboration with China in shaping China–Ethiopia narratives, therefore, is strategic and deliberate, seen as part of a larger national objective. We now shift to the discussion of self-censorship practiced by Ethiopian media practitioners.

5.3.1.2 *Journalistic Self-censorship or Deliberate Avoidance of Sensitive Edges*

While some private news outlets and independent journalists occasionally push the boundaries and pursue alternative coverage of China, most media, especially influential state news outlets, opt for a cautious, diplomatic stance. In a focus group discussion, a senior journalist at a major state outlet remarked with irony that even Chinese media seems more critical or engaged in sensitive issues on China–Ethiopia relations than Ethiopian media.[61] He gave an example of Chinese journalists on official delegation from the China Journalism Association visiting a number of Chinese construction sites and inquiring about delays on projects – something that their Ethiopian counterparts were unable to question.

---

[60] Interview ETJ01, Addis Ababa, 2019.
[61] Focus group ETJFG01, Addis Ababa, 2019.

Studies of Ethiopian media coverage of China confirm this overarching positive framing. Skjerdal and Gusu's analysis of the framing of Sino-Ethiopian relations in state-owned Ethiopian Herald and privately owned Ethiopian Reporter reveals the dominance of positive themes about China as an altruistic partner in the former, and the presence of only mild occasional criticism of China in the private paper.[62] My analysis of more recent coverage of China by the Ethiopian News Agency (ENA) and Ethiopian Reporter also finds a largely affirmative framing, with many articles drawing on public relations announcements, with occasional frictions presented as manageable.[63] A 2018 Ethiopian Reporter article on a new $230 million loan from the Chinese government, for instance, is titled as: "The loan pressure is not beyond Ethiopia's capacity."[64] The journalist acknowledges the increasing national dependency on China but concludes on a reassuring note about the Chinese government lowering its interest rate to facilitate future repayments. During recent fieldwork trips, Ethiopian media practitioners also shared about their increasing reliance on Chinese sources, like Xinhua and CGTN for China coverage, further reinforcing a predominantly positive China framing.[65]

Ethiopian media's careful and largely positive China coverage reflects both Chinese and domestic censorship practices, as well as journalists' own aspirations for China storytelling. As for absorbing and responding to China's information management, some journalist interviewees acknowledged the swift adaptation to Chinese communication norms. Referring to constrained public relations conference format and limited space for questions, for instance, an editor at a major state media outlet reflected on inevitable adjustments made by Ethiopian media. "After

---

[62] Terje Skjerdal and Fufa Gusu, "Positive Portrayal of Sino-African Relations in the Ethiopian Press," in Xiaoling Zhang, Herman Wasserman and Winston Mano (editors), *China's Media and Soft Power: Promotion and Perceptions* (Palgrave Macmillan: 2009), 149–63.

[63] My sample year was 2018 and 2019 for ENA and 2017 and 2018 for Ethiopian Reporter. The reason for these specific dates was the availability of archives for these outlets. A total of forty-nine stories that featured China were uncovered in ENA, and a total of forty-two in Ethiopian Reporter. The majority of stories were positive, and the ones exploring the tensions (primarily in the private news outlet) carried a constructive tone.

[64] "K'China Yetegegnew Bider Chana K'ageritu Y'mekifele akem gar temetatagn new tebale" (The Loan Pressure from China Is Not beyond Ethiopia's Repayment Capacity), *Ethiopian Reporter*, December 28, 2018, www.ethiopianreporter.com/index.php/con tent/ከቻይና-የተገኘው-ብድር-ጫና-ከአገሪቱ-የመክፈል-አቅም-ጋር-ተመጣጣኝ-ነው-ተባለ.

[65] Most journalists interviewed shared that they regularly rely on Xinhua and CGTN for China coverage, including journalists in private media outlets.

a while, all Ethiopian media got used to it and they no longer probe or ask for interviews," he commented.[66] "It is not worth the effort, as information is completely limited," noted another editor.[67] "We don't even conceive of reporting in-depth stories about China," shared another state media reporter.[68] Some journalists also shared that they take advantage of Chinese public relations conferences to mingle with officials and get easy news coverage.[69] Similar practices of socialization into and absorption of China's communication modalities emerged in interviews with training participants. Many shared that after receiving silent treatment from their hosts in response to more sensitive questions, they opted for avoiding the triggers and even passed on their acquired knowledge to future participants.

At the same time, Ethiopian media practitioners also acknowledged internal editorial policies that caution against negative coverage of Ethiopia's major partners – mirroring the directives from media regulating institutions and public relations offices discussed in the previous section. A producer at the national broadcaster, ETV, for instance, noted the cautiousness of reporting on Ethiopia's major partners – a practice he attributed to the guidelines from the Communication Service Ministry. "Generally, when it comes to the countries we have close relations with, our policy is to minimize negative coverage; if negative stories come, we have to decide if they have sufficient news value for our audiences," he explained.[70] "Bad news about China are not appropriate for our media, we take care of the Chinese," he added. "We tend to focus on inauguration of Chinese projects, when the story turns out more negative, the Ethiopian side tends to take responsibility for any problems with China deals," shared another state media employee.[71] "I will cover the story if it comes to me," shared another interviewee, meaning that he wouldn't initiate a negative China coverage, but only follow the lead.[72]

While acknowledging their adjustments to systematic restrictions and editorial pressures, Ethiopian editors and journalists also often justify self-censorship on China as strategic in materially and symbolically elevating Ethiopia. As for material elevation, a former journalist from a private

<hr>

[66] Interview ETJ16, Addis Ababa, 2023.
[67] Focus group ETJFG03, Addis Ababa, 2023.
[68] Focus Group ETJFG02, Addis Ababa, 2019.
[69] Focus Group ETJFG03, Addis Ababa, 2023.
[70] Interview ETJ19, Addis Ababa, 2023.
[71] Interview ETJ02, Addis Ababa, 2019.
[72] ETJ19, Addis Ababa, 2023.

news outlet recalled proposing a story that would advocate for some construction contracts in Ethiopia to be granted to local companies rather than the majority of them allocated to Chinese firms.[73] Their editor opposed the idea and reminded journalists that Chinese companies are the only ones capable of constructing mega projects at fast speed. Indirectly questioning China, therefore, would impede on national economic objectives – a rationale that echoes Ethiopia's long-standing tradition of developmental journalism, whereby media aspire to fostering development.[74]

Ethiopian media professionals also rationalize their engagement and co-optation of China-related publicity as helping boost Ethiopia's image (alongside with China). A state media editor, for instance, shared that he prioritizes China stories that highlight the latest deals signed with China, and joint projects launched and completed, while avoiding reprinting Chinese embassy briefings that solely promote China's positions, such as its narratives about Xinjiang, Tibet, and other sensitive domestic issues.[75] A TV producer for a regional network also shared that they tend to deliberately engage with and promote Chinese companies' publicity to improve Ethiopia's image as attractive for foreign investment. "Highlighting the positive image of Chinese companies by focusing on practices like tech transfer and local employment, among others, also makes Ethiopia look good – the two are interconnected," he shared.[76] The same rationale of Ethiopia promotion applied to state media journalists relying on Xinhua news coverage of China. As noted in section 5.1, Xinhua tends to get preferential access to Chinese officials, deemed as a reliable source. In reprinting Xinhua articles, editors shared that they pick stories that tend to celebrate bilateral success and present Ethiopia as following a hopeful economic and political trajectory, not solely promote China. For example, a 2019 ENA report repurposed a Xinhua story about how Chinese assistance is helping develop the bamboo industry in East Africa, including in Ethiopia;[77] another repurposed Xinhua story highlighted the ongoing construction

---

[73] Interview ETJ27, Addis Ababa, 2023.

[74] Terje Skjerdal, "Development Journalism Revived: The Case of Ethiopia," *Ecquid Novi: African Journalism Studies* 32(2) (2011): 58–74, https://doi.org/10.1080/02560054.2011.578879.

[75] Interview ETJ16, Addis Ababa, 2023.

[76] Interview ETJ31, Adama, 2023.

[77] "Expert Hails Chinese Assistance to Bamboo Industry Dev't in East Africa," *Ethiopian News Agency*, December 13, 2019, www.ena.et/web/eng/w/en_11286.

of a Chinese-funded cement factory, which was framed as boosting Ethiopia's manufacturing capacity.[78]

A similar reasoning of promoting Ethiopia's national interests and image was also invoked in journalists' discussions of self-censorship in the context of Chinese training programs. Several participants noted that while they consciously communicate positive things about China to their hosts, they also try to promote a good image of Ethiopia. "I tried to show my appreciation for China, but also be a good cultural representative for Ethiopia and take an effort to explain Ethiopia and communicate with local people," shared a former journalist fellow who spent a year in Beijing.[79] "We know these trips are primarily about public diplomacy, so we try our best to be good diplomats for Ethiopia as part of these exchanges," noted another media fellowship participant.[80]

It is also important to note here that self-censorship has direct material implications for Ethiopian elites partaking in co-shaping China narratives. As analyzed in the chapter on tangible enticement, Ethiopian state media benefit from Chinese material assistance, including access to free trips to China and other educational opportunities, as well as ad revenues and media infrastructure. Ethiopian media, including private news outlets, are also severely underfunded, lacking resources for long-term China investigations. Beyond China coverage, scholars of Ethiopian media find that it heavily outsources much of its reporting to public relations offices in a model described by Jemal Mohammed as public relations-driven journalism.[81] For these outlets, therefore, self-censorship can be a cost-effective strategy, especially considering the challenges in accessing Chinese and Ethiopian sources. Some might argue that exposure to China's ideational power as part of the organized trips analyzed in the previous chapter and other experiences with China also fuels self-censorship. Though Ethiopian reporters tend to produce some positive stories about their experiences in China, given their critical questioning of China's presentation of its win–win narrative, it is unlikely that their choice to largely avoid challenging China is rooted in genuine absorption of China's official narratives. The public-facing self-censorship, moreover,

---

[78] "Lemi Nat'l Cement Factory Set to Boost Ethiopia's Annual Production Capacity by 8 Mil Metric Ton," *Ethiopian News Agency*, November 28, 2023, www.ena.et/web/eng/w/ eng_3646132.

[79] Focus group ETJFG01, Addis Ababa, 2019.

[80] Ibid.

[81] Jemal Mohammed, "PR-Driven Model: The Case of Ethiopia," *African Journalism Studies* 42(1) (2021): 108–27.

coexists with more private criticisms and sarcastic expressions about China among officials and journalists, as discussed in the following section.

5.3.2 Bypassing Censorial Power: Crafting and Sharing Subversive China Narratives

Alongside strategically participating in and augmenting China's censorial efforts to promote positive publicity and contain negative stories, Ethiopian elites, and more broadly Ethiopian publics, also communicate alternative, often unfavorable views about Chinese influence in Ethiopia. Most of this communication takes place in informal, private realms, including in-person conversations and social media platforms, and deploys rumors and humor as rhetorical devices. This section explores these communication practices, drawing on the author's group discussions with Ethiopian elites (between 2018 and 2023),[82] including journalists, public relations officials, and other government workers, as well as on selective social media commentaries about China in Amharic.[83] The analysis demonstrates that ironically the secrecy surrounding Chinese activities in Ethiopia and beyond, in part empowered through Ethiopian elites and institutions, also backfires in fueling suspicion and resentment toward it. Specifically, Ethiopian elites often interpret China as an exploitative partner, as they emphasize its manipulation of unresolved debt, as well as deployment of what they perceive as prison labor and low-quality product-dumping. Some of these themes overlap with critical reflections about China experienced by elites who participated in training programs (as discussed in Chapter 4).

The anxiety about indebtedness to China overshadows most conversations about Chinese influence in Ethiopia. Ethiopian elites tend to raise the question of debt burden and management of loans in seminars about China I conducted throughout the country, as well as invoke it informally in focus group discussions. There is a widespread understanding that Ethiopia owes excessive debt to China. The concerns over the repercussions of

---

[82] The author gave many seminars across the country on China–Africa relations between 2018 and 2023, which elucidated active debates, questions, and more personal reflections about Chinese influence in Ethiopia. She also conducted extensive focus groups on this topic (please see the Appendix II for more details).

[83] The social media post examples in this section draw from a project carried out with Global Voices on BRI perceptions in receiving countries as part of the Civic Media observatory. With the help of an Ethiopian researcher, the author examined social media posts on Facebook in Amharic that invoked China between 2018 and 2021. For more details on this, see https://globalvoices.org/special/observatory/ and https://global voices.org/special/belt-and-road-observatory/.

non-repayment are often communicated with a mix of satire and rumors. A senior Ethiopian state media editor shared that he overheard his older kid debate whether financial dependence on China is a form of neocolonialism and then added his own conspiratorial take on future scenarios. "If we don't repay the loan for the China-Djibouti Railway or for the Light Rail project, then the Chinese might take over the train!" he exclaimed.[84] At times, commentaries allude to other African cases of asset take over as a window into Ethiopia's future. One journalist, for instance, brought up Somalia, where he alleged China took over water-storage facilities as punishment. "I wouldn't be surprised if China would take over Ethiopian Airlines if we don't pay back the loans," he added.[85] Other focus group discussion participants pointed to the Uganda airport already being run by the Chinese, and the airlines taken over by Chinese companies in Congo, among other examples. Some of these rumors are also shared online. A popular 2019 Facebook post that attracted 100 reactions and 11 commentaries, for instance, noted that the Zambian International Airport has already been taken over by China due to loan non-repayment, and that the Ethiopian railway that links Addis Ababa and Djibouti is likely to face a similar fate.[86] One of the comments under this post reads: "What about Ethiopia Airlines? Is it China free?" "China planted modern slavery," notes another. When asked to provide more details or links to stories about China asset takeover during in-person conversations, most of my interlocutors struggled with specificity, but expressed conviction about catastrophic implications of Ethiopia's dependency on China. At times, the comments were exaggerated for dramatic effect, and accompanied with laughter, further fusing the imaginary with reality.

Another common elite narrative about Chinese activities concerns the operating practices of Chinese companies in Ethiopia, including allegations of their use of prison labor. In most discussions I led with Ethiopian elites, they depict Chinese operations as self-sufficient and one-sided. "Chinese come here with big projects, but often bring their own labor, allowing for very limited knowledge and skill transfer," commented an audience member in a China–Ethiopia seminar I held at the Civil Servants University in 2019 who often works on and publicly promotes Chinese projects. "Their own labor," however, is further associated with a popular rumor about Chinese

---

[84] Focus group ETJFG01, Addis Ababa, 2019.

[85] Ibid.

[86] www.facebook.com/abel.gebrekidan.33/posts/2184836015163753. Originally cited in: "China in Ethiopia: Between a Savior and an Exploiter," Global Voices, September 24, 2021; https://globalvoices.org/2021/09/24/china-in-ethiopia-between-a-savior-and-an-exploiter/

prison labor coming to Ethiopia. Whether or not Chinese workers are prisoners, transported from China to pay their dues on construction sites was one of the most common questions posed to me during various seminars I held with Ethiopian government officials and journalists. This stereotype, of course, extends much beyond Ethiopia. Hairong and Sautman, for instance, show that rumors about the export of Chinese convict labor have been widespread in many developing countries, often originating from the grassroots but at times also amplified by elites who promote anti-China agenda.[87] In Ethiopia, these rumors rarely spill into the official public discourse, but unofficially, even politicians who frequently travel to China and publicly speak in favor of it, still contend that the presence of Chinese prisoners in Ethiopia is an undisputable reality. These perceptions are reinforced by distant observations of the regimented employment of Chinese workers in Ethiopia, who live in isolated communes and work extremely long hours, including on weekends[88] – something perceived as alien and associated with involuntary labor.

Finally, the associations of China with low quality also percolated in my discussions with Ethiopian elites, as they often satirically commented on what they perceive as subpar quality of Chinese goods (and projects). In one of my early trips to Ethiopia, a media professional at a private news outlet generally favorable toward China shared the following joke in discussing Chinese image: An Ethiopian woman gives birth to a Chinese baby, and the baby is dying in a hospital – the response of her family is that 'what were you thinking, Chinese goods don't last long.'[89] The editor conveyed the joke with roaring laughter. These critiques of Chinese product quality veiled in humor are also present on social media. A popular online commentary, for instance, ridicules Chinese makeup products by posting two photos of a couple: before and after the kiss. In the after photo, the man's face is smudged in makeup. The posting adds an advisory note: "women who use China-made make-up should be careful when they kiss."[90] Other sarcastic jokes poke at made-in-China mobile phones as having a short battery life, and television sets as turning on and off involuntarily.

---

[87] Yan Hairong and Barry Sautman, "Chasing Ghosts: Rumours and Representations of the Export of Chinese Convict Labour to Developing Countries," *The China Quarterly* 210 (2012): 398–418.

[88] On the lifestyle Chinese works in Ethiopia, see Miriam Driessen, *Tales of Hope, Tastes of Bitterness: Chinese Road Builders in Ethiopia* (Hong Kong University Press: 2019).

[89] Informal conversation and site visit with the author, Addis Ababa, 2018. Variations of this joke were retold by other interlocutors.

[90] www.facebook.com/groups/689588931876708/posts/791334428368824/.

In conversations and on social media, Ethiopians also scrutinize the quality of China-built infrastructure, and share potential explanations behind it, often linking quality deficiency directly to China's responsibility and intent. While infrastructure projects like the Light Rail (the over-ground metro system in Addis built by a Chinese company) tend to be comanaged and supervised by Ethiopian institutions, some discussion participants allude to China's intentional export or "dumping" of low-quality goods to Africa, including construction materials. "It was built by low quality," argued a graduate student at the New Generation University who is also a government official, in reference to the Light Rail.[91] Some also suggest that China-inflicted corruption further compounds the quality issue, as the Ethiopian side is co-opted and thereby only loosely monitors China's practices. "They are involved in corruption here, and that corrodes the quality," argued another Ethiopian official.[92] Even officials at institutions like the Road Authority were critical of the quality of Chinese projects, as I discuss more in Chapter 6. Overall, the trope of China as a low-quality exporter and producer is widespread and often channeled through satire or unverified rumors about the operations of Chinese companies in Ethiopia.

The themes analyzed in this section are not exhaustive when it comes to negative depictions of China by Ethiopian elites in more private communication spaces. Other themes I came across in my research include the portrayal of China as a cultural threat, especially in reference to a growing but isolated Chinese community in Ethiopia; China as a resource exploiter in different parts of Africa; and China as a bolsterer of dictators. I am unable to develop all these themes due to space constraints, but I hope the discussion of the dominant critical narratives presented here showcases the dynamic and contested depictions of China's influence, including by the same elites who tend to contain criticisms about it in public. While they comply with and expand China's censorial power in their daily work, these elites also privately bypass it and resort to devices like rumor and satire to express more contentious sentiments – tactics commonly used in communicating subversive narratives in other authoritarian contexts, including in China itself.[93]

---

[91] ETSTFOC12, Addis Ababa, 2023.
[92] Ibid.
[93] Guobin Yang and Min Jiang, "The Networked Practice of Online Political Satire in China: Between Ritual and Resistance," *International Communication Gazette* 77(3) (2015): 215–31, https://doi.org/10.1177/1748048514568757; Luwei Rose Luqiu, "The Cost of Humour: Political Satire on Social Media and Censorship in China," *Global Media and Communication* 13(2) (2017): 123–38, https://doi.org/10.1177/1742766517704471.

5.4 CONCLUSION

This chapter examined the workings of China's defensive image-making or what I referred to as censorial power. It analyzed how Chinese actors in Ethiopia, including embassy personnel and company representatives, but also educators and training hosts, routinely guard the production and dissemination of China narratives through contained public relations spectacles and systematic information withdrawal, as well as spontaneously try to block negative stories through a mix of coercion and co-optation. These information management practices are rooted in China's domestic context, where more openness is often associated with higher reputational risks. The limited understanding of local media and public sphere by Chinese actors in Ethiopia further exacerbates concerns about potential trouble sparked through more unscripted interactions.

The chapter also presented the complex engagement with China's censorial power by Ethiopian elites. Challenging a binary tale of coercion and resistance, with Chinese actors representing the censors and Ethiopians the victims of oppression, the perspectives from Ethiopian officials and journalists reveal their strategic complicity with China's disciplinary efforts, as well as ambiguity and subtle resistance. As for deliberate complicity, Ethiopian officials help contain negative narratives about China and justify safeguarding China's image as part of protecting Ethiopia's economic interests. Ethiopian journalists practice self-censorship – in part as a resigned response to information withdrawals from both Chinese and Ethiopian officials, but also as part of a larger developmental journalism mission and an effort to boost Ethiopia's image through positive coverage of China–Ethiopia relations.

These strategic official and journalistic collaborations with Chinese censorial efforts are also accompanied by subtle and less visible contestation through private remaking of China narratives. Some of the same officials and journalists who publicly promote China in Ethiopia rely on humor and rumor to depict China as an exploitative actor, deliberately amassing debt in Ethiopia, importing its own prison labor, and dumping cheap, low-quality products and infrastructure. As with Ethiopian responses to other China's image-making strategies discussed in previous chapters, therefore, the reception or engagement with China's censorial power is uneven and somewhat unpredictable. The next chapter delves into another dimension of this unevenness – the shared pull toward the West by Chinese and Ethiopian interlocutors.

PART III

TRANSNATIONAL AND COMPARATIVE PERSPECTIVES

6

Unintended Synergies

The Shared Longing for the West

6.1 INTRODUCTION

"China is OK, but I prefer America or Europe," shared a biology teacher at a boarding school in Adama – one of the few high schools in the country that teaches Mandarin with the help of Confucius Institute volunteers. On my first visit to the school in the summer of 2019, I struck up a conversation about China with teachers I spotted on their lunch break. Several of them have heard of Chinese scholarship and training opportunities, but expressed muted excitement, quickly jumping to questions about getting a PhD in the United States. This was one of many encounters that revealed a preference or aspiration for studying in the United States, Canada, Europe, and other parts of the West, in contrast to a more subdued sentiment about China. Similar hierarchical positioning of China versus the West also appeared in discussions of China's other tangible offerings, including media content and infrastructure (discussed in Chapter 3), as well as in the ideational domain of aspirational political values and visions (see Chapter 4).

Ironically, the shadow of the West also featured in interviews and interactions with many Chinese public diplomacy practitioners. Whereas China attempts to distinguish its image from the West and emphasize the unique importance of its relationship with Africa, Western standards still linger in China's diplomatic practices, and individuals who shape this relationship often perceive Africa (and in this case Ethiopia) as a transitory destination in their global professional journeys. In particular, Chinese journalists, educators, and diplomats I met in the field describe Ethiopia posts as professional immersive opportunities that

155

would serve as steppingstones toward more desired locations. In the hierarchy of global postings, the United States and Europe have been placed at the top, and African countries at the bottom.

In this chapter, I explore these parallel realities of China's image-making project whereby the West continues to linger in the Sino-Ethiopian "soft power" encounter. Taking a step back from analyzing the workings of China's major image-making mechanisms, this chapter draws on perspectives of individual participants and on individual trajectories that make up China's diplomacy. For Ethiopian elites, the West remains the benchmark through which China's offerings and practices are accepted and evaluated, and for many Chinese practitioners, the West is still an aspirational standard and a professional destination. In distilling this shared pull toward the West, this chapter treats the West as an imagined entity rather than a fixed geographic region or a geopolitical constellation. Though the United States is often associated with the West in these discussions, it is also often invoked in more expansive and amorphous terms, not limited to a specific country or political entity. The analysis that follows illustrates the varied visions and interpretations of the "West" by Ethiopian and Chinese participants, as well as the conflicting perceptions and sentiments, including a mix of aspiration and resentment. I proceed next to the discussion of how these visions shape the engagement with Chinese diplomatic initiatives in Ethiopia.

6.2 ETHIOPIAN PARTICIPANTS: CHINA IN THE SHADOW OF THE WEST

In informal conversations, interviews, and focus groups, Ethiopian participants often incorporate comparisons with the West in evaluating China. In the context of tangible offerings and opportunities, China is treated as a secondary, albeit a more accessible option, with some interviewees also using China as a passageway to Western countries and experiences. In the ideational realm, aspirations toward Western-style democracy and values tend to overshadow the enticement toward China's visions and ideals. Even when Western ideological stances are critiqued, China is appreciated in juxtaposition with the West, rather than on its own terms.

6.2.1 China's Offerings Standing in for Western Desires

Starting with tangible opportunities, my Ethiopian interlocutors often invoked the West as the primary choice, and China as a choice of necessity in the context of education and training, but also in discussions of media content and infrastructure projects. As for education, officials, journalists, and students identified the United States, Europe, and Canada as the top choices,[1] and used the opportunity of our encounter to inquire about Western scholarships. Most focus groups, for instance, concluded with questions about studying in the West, with many interviewees following up with additional inquiries. While my positionality as a US-based professor has likely contributed to curiosity and strategic networking about the American education system (something I talk about more in Appendix I), these subtle preferences are rooted in long-standing perceptions of quality of Western education as superior.

In discussing the increasing availability of Chinese scholarships and training exchanges for university faculty and students, for instance, the former president of Jimma University, who also served as the founding codirector of the Confucius Classroom there, confided that a graduate degree from a Western university is still seen as more valuable for job placement than a diploma from China.[2] A high-ranking official from the Ethiopian Ministry of Education similarly reflected on widespread perceptions of the West as more attractive for education experiences in part because of its high standards, but also because of the aspirational lifestyle associated with earning high income and even settling abroad.[3] He described Western scholarships and exchanges as potentially "changing lives," in contrast to mere exposure and training provided by China.

Going to China, for some Ethiopian elites, in turn, followed elaborate, but in the end, unsuccessful attempts at enrolling in programs in Western institutions. The experience of an Ethiopian professor who ended up pursuing a PhD in Economics in China is illustrative of how accepting China invitations can be a result of complicated circumstances rather than an innate interest in Chinese higher education. The following excerpt from our email exchange details the professor's complex journey from the United States to China:

I had a plan to pursue the PhD in the States essentially because I believed in the quality of graduate programs out there. And I applied for and got academic

---

[1] This was a choice that featured strongly across all focus group discussions with elites and students in Ethiopia (please see the appendix II for more details on focus groups). The participants were asked about their top preferences for training and education abroad as one of the questions. This question was also asked in interviews with elites who traveled to China for trainings.

[2] Interview ETUAD04, Addis Ababa, 2019.

[3] Interview ETOF24, Addis Ababa, 2023.

admission to the PhD program in Applied Economics . . . for fall of 2017. Except a suggestive remark about funding that the department will get in contact with me when funding becomes available, I did not get the offer for one of the positions typical in the US graduate schools – teaching and/or research assistant . . . I applied again in 2018. In the meantime, I work hard, become frugal . . . and saved some money contemplating that they may offer me at least tuition waver. The outcome turned out same academic admission without funding offers. By then, I was here in China on an official visit to promote the research and training partnership between University X and the Southwest University of Finance and Economics I motivated back in 2015. By the time I finished reading the email from WMU, I jumped into another email to the College of International Education at SWUFE. I applied for admission to the PhD programs in Economics . . . I won the Chinese government scholarship in July 2018. And the choice to accept/decline it was like a knife-edge. . . . Finally, I opted to keep myself at a distance and see if I can make the best out of it.[4]

In his longer correspondence, the professor explained his concerns about political instability in Ethiopia as creating additional pressure or what he called the "knife-edge" sensation. At the time of our email exchange, ethnic tensions were already rising in parts of the country that later spilled over into civil war between the Tigray People's Liberation Front (TPLF) and the federal government. Safety and what he described as the possibility of "distance" have also played a role in his eventual choice to let go of American dreams and to opt for China. Overall, his decision to go to China was in part a serendipitous one: The offer came right when the route to the United States was blocked, and Ethiopia itself started to descend into chaos. The decision was also a compromise: The most practical option in the context of limited possibilities and disillusion with persistent yet in the end failed efforts at enrolling into a US graduate program.

Parallel stories of unfulfilled dreams of studying in America (and in some cases in Europe and Canada) as driving them toward China were shared by other interlocutors. Some individuals have similarly invested significant time into applying, while others gave up sooner, once they realized there were no official scholarship programs in the United States. In a conversation about Chinese versus American education programs, one Ethiopian interviewee recalled his close friend dreaming of attending graduate school in Michigan, but when he learned that the Ministry of Education only had formal agreements with India and China, he ended up in China, a world away from Michigan.[5] In educational sessions I led at

4 Interview via email correspondence, March 2019.
5 Interview ETJ08, Addis Ababa, 2019.

American Corners across Ethiopia as part of my field research, I also noticed that the interest of attendants would begin to dwindle as I explained the lack of centralized scholarship programs and the efforts required of the applicants to individually identify the programs and funding streams.[6] Some participants directly noted that going to China is much easier. The scarcity of US opportunities as an impetus for engaging with China was also expressed in the context of short-term training. "We tried many many times, but your door is very narrow," shared an official at the Oromo Leadership Academy who has visited China for trainings.[7] He went on to explain how the short-term fellowships to the United States are limited and just like the applications for university scholarships require more effort and skill from the applicants.

Other than prioritizing opportunities in the West, those who end up accepting Chinese educational and training invitations at times treat them as direct and indirect channels toward Western exposure. As for direct passageways, many interviewees regarded China's training and education programs as opportunities to build up credentials and experiences for applying to programs in Western countries. Some Chinese experts I have interviewed have also shared with slight frustration that many students on scholarships in China end up later going to the West.[8] This notion of aspired transiting via China to other destinations is also reflected in the works on African migrants in China. In her interview-based research about the Nigerian community in Guangzhou, for instance, Haugen found that while some of her interviewees chose to go to China due to perceived trade opportunities, most were primarily driven by the relative accessibility of China. "China was sometimes seen as a springboard toward more desirable destinations, including Japan, Australia and Europe," she writes.[9] She quotes one of her Nigerian informants as saying: "I'm just here on my way to Ireland."[10] While educational journeys don't directly mirror migration ones, there is some overlap in treating China as a transition or a compromise.

Some participants in Chinese education initiatives also sought out Western exposure while in China. An engineering student from

---

[6] In 2019, I gave lectures about education in America at the American Corner library in Addis Ababa, Bahir Dar, and Jimma.

[7] Interview ETOF08, Adama, 2019.

[8] Interview CHSC05, Beijing, 2019.

[9] Heidi Østbø Haugen, "Nigerians in China: A Second State of Immobility," *International Migration* 50(2) (2012): 71.

[10] Ibid.

Ethiopia, for instance, shared that one of her most memorable experiences in China was interning for an American company in Beijing. She described her time at the company as "enriching" and as a rare opportunity to learn practical skills through careful guidance from her supervisors.[11] A public relations official from Ethiopia's Ministry of Trade and Investment who was pursuing a master's degree in International Communication in Beijing when we met brought up attending an international translation conference that included representatives from US entertainment companies as one of his highlights.[12] Ironically, this official applied to study translation on a Chinese government scholarship, but when he arrived to China, he was told he would need Chinese language skills to be part of that program, and was registered for the international communication degree instead. His exposure to translation work – his main passion – came from international conferences that have also afforded this encounter with the United States. A technology expert at a major Ethiopian media company who spent a year in southern China on a master's scholarship met American missionaries, attended religious ceremonies, and traveled to rural China with them to teach English and to introduce the Bible to Chinese kids – something he recalled with warmth and enthusiasm.[13] Considering that China is now a global hub for business, diplomatic, knowledge, and even limited religious exchange, it is not surprising that some of the participants in Chinese diplomatic engagements end up with Western exposure in China, especially if they deliberately pursue it, as in the case of this Ethiopian official, the engineering student, and the media professional.

Other than in discussions on education and training, the prioritization of the West and the designation of China as a secondary choice were also invoked in the context of media and public infrastructure. As for exposure and consumption of international news content, my Ethiopian interlocutors tended to prefer major Western news outlets and Al Jazeera to Chinese media outlets like CGTN, Xinhua News, or China Daily, despite the latter often being more accessible. In seminars I carried out about China and Chinese diplomacy with Ethiopian elites and students, few participants could recall a single Chinese news outlet, in contrast to a widespread familiarity with Western news outlets (and Al Jazeera). Journalists I have interviewed shared that they follow and rely on

---

[11] Interview ETHST01, Beijing, 2019.
[12] Interview ETHST04, Beijing, 2019.
[13] Interview ETJ26, Addis Ababa, 2023.

Western sources, including BBC and CNN, more closely when they cover international events, and draw on Chinese coverage mainly in reporting on China–Ethiopia stories. Some Ethiopian editors also acknowledged that they occasionally rely on Chinese media databases for international news out of necessity, as they are free of charge in contrast to subscription-based services of Reuters and AP, among others (as discussed in Chapter 3).[14] Others drew a more ideational contrast in quality, with Western media content described as entertaining and more objective, and Chinese content as more positive, but boring.[15] The relative preferences for Western media sources by African journalists go beyond Ethiopia. In Wasserman's survey of over 100 journalists in South Africa, for instance, he found that they perceived Chinese outlets as less credible and less engaging.[16]

The hierarchical positioning of the West above China also transpired in conversations about public infrastructure projects. An official from the Ethiopian Road Authority, for instance, at first praised China's contribution to Ethiopian infrastructure but then offered criticisms of these projects, including what he described as "mediocre quality of the work," corruption, and even occasional usage of fake equipment.[17] He attributed Ethiopia's collaboration with Chinese companies to its underdeveloped status. "We are poor, so we go to the Chinese. If we could, we would go to Western companies, but since we don't have a choice, we go to China," he concluded. In focus groups with students and government officials, Chinese infrastructure projects were similarly often described as "low quality" and "corrupt." "The roads are not durable, they won't last long, maybe they are doing this on purpose, so we can keep depending on them," commented one of the participants.[18] In the end, however, these interlocutors acknowledged that Chinese companies are most engaged in Ethiopian infrastructure. This sentiment of resigning to China for infrastructure needs was echoed in many interviews and group discussions, whereby Western companies were deemed unaffordable, but desirable, and China seen as the only feasible option.

---

[14] Focus group ETJFG03, Addis Ababa, 2023.
[15] Ibid; Focus group ETJFG01, Addis Ababa, 2019.
[16] Herman Wasserman, "China's 'Soft Power' and Its Influence on Editorial Agendas in South Africa," *Chinese Journal of Communication* 9(1) (2016): 8–20.
[17] Interview ETOF25, Addis Ababa, 2023.
[18] Focus group ETSTFOC06, Addis Ababa, 2023.

6.2.2 The Ideational Shadows of the West

My Ethiopian interlocutors also expressed ideational affinities with the West, manifested in intrigue with US politics and attraction toward democratic practices and values, and treated the West as a reference point for evaluating China's political principles. In contrast to the topic of Chinese political system that I typically had to raise and direct toward my interlocutors, American politics came up organically and elucidated more dynamic and nuanced opinions. Whereas in discussions of China, focus group participants often invoked political restrictions and, in some cases, limited forms of political participation, in the context of the United States, they passionately debated different political candidates and policies. In a memorable discussion in the summer of 2019, for instance, one journalist immediately proclaimed himself a Bernie fan, noting that he followed his statements and policies on social media.[19] This comment sparked a lively debate about Bernie's potential for electoral success in America, and whether he presented a realistic candidate against the then president Trump. Throughout the discussion, it was notable how well-versed Ethiopian journalists were in American politics, arguably more so than some of their counterparts in the United States. They could readily transition from the analysis of local politics to national politics and foreign policy. In immersing themselves so deeply into American political culture, these media professionals also appeared to indirectly partake in US political processes by picking sides and advocating for their favorite candidates.

The visibility of American politics to Ethiopian elites through widespread and relatively open international media coverage might make it more inviting for indirect participation, in contrast to more controlled and opaque political coverage in China that rarely exposes foreign audiences to internal debates and frictions. The US openness, of course, also reveals the cracks in its political system and leaders. And yet even these weaknesses or aberrations can become objects of fascination, as was the case with Trump's first presidency which was often the prime topic of conversation in Ethiopia during my trips in 2018 and 2019. Some interlocutors admired Trump's decisiveness and vigor, and others lamented him hurting American democracy. "America doesn't deserve Trump, he is ruining America's image in the world," shared an Ethiopian editor with deep ties to the United States.[20]

---

[19] Focus group ETJFG02, Addis Ababa, 2019.
[20] Informal discussion with the author and Ethiopian colleagues, Addis Ababa, 2019.

Beyond playful curiosity and deeper immersion in American politics, in discussions about Ethiopia's political visions, elites and students underscored their aspirations toward a democratic future, with some calling Ethiopia an "imperfect democracy." Whereas China also presents itself as a democracy, and some of its successes are acknowledged by Ethiopian officials, as discussed in Chapter 4, in envisioning Ethiopia's political trajectory, my interlocutors tended to gaze more toward the West. Some mentioned the United States, but many also invoked Scandinavian countries as aspirational democratic systems to learn from. A high-level official at the Prosperity Party outlined the shift from EPRDF to Prosperity Party as that from a Communist orientation toward a more pro-Western aspiration. He stated:

EPRDF was ideologically closer to Communism, the Prosperity Party is more ideologically hybrid. Under the Prosperity Party, the ideological position of the party is less clear, but there is a deliberate effort to tilt toward the West, with democratic principles advocated by the Party. We don't have an exact ideology, but we are not Communist. We try to focus on Western countries, especially on Scandinavian countries. We want to learn from Western political parties, how they operate, how democracy works there.[21]

At times this ideational tilt toward the West was communicated indirectly in discussions about the China model. "China is definitely not a model" exclaimed a high-level official in charge of media regulation, adding that Ethiopia is on a path towards democracy.[22] While he didn't specify Western-style democracy, it was clear that he saw China's political ideals as oppositional to Ethiopia's.

Ironically, as with other engagements, in the ideational domain, while Ethiopian elites can indirectly consume Western politics through the media, direct learning and cooperation with Western political parties is less feasible, leaving China (and Russia) as the alternative option. The Prosperity Party official who emphasized the hybrid orientation of his party, for instance, discussed his party's unsuccessful efforts at engaging Western counterparts. He noted:

When we held our first Prosperity Party Congress, we invited many party representatives from Western countries, but not a single one came. Most of them sent congratulatory letters but they didn't send representatives to attend the Congress. Nobody from the West came, so we again, shifted to China and Russia. They are the only ones who sent representatives, other than political parties from Africa.[23]

---

[21] Interview ETOF37, Addis Ababa, 2023.
[22] Interview ETOF32, Addis Ababa, 2023.
[23] Interview ETOF37, Addis Ababa, 2023.

This official further acknowledged that Ethiopia's ideological "hybridity" is challenging for the West and that Ethiopia is still not seen as a democratic country.[24] When asked whether China is concerned about Ethiopia's courtship of Western partners, the official remarked: "Chinese don't worry about our interest in the West. They always try to be our friends."[25] In this reflection about the Prosperity Party's efforts at engaging the West, it is striking how the desire for recognition and learning is directed more toward Western political parties, but the muted response from them leads Ethiopian party officials back to China.

When Ethiopian elites articulated Chinese political values as attractive and preferable, they still evaluated them through comparisons with the West. This was notable in discussions of China's policy of noninterference in Ethiopian domestic affairs. My interlocutors often expressed their appreciation for China's hands-off approach through grievances with Western interference. Following presentations by Chinese speakers at the IPSS think tank, for instance, one of the Ethiopians in attendance expressed his gratitude for China's support for Ethiopia during the civil war in 2020–22: "Thank you, China, Chinese people, we know what you did for us, for Ethiopia. The West took the Ethiopian internal conflict to the United Nations, and China played a critical role in blocking sanctions for Ethiopia."[26] In these heated remarks that were followed by clapping and supportive nods from the audience and the Chinese participants, China's contribution was illuminated in contrast to perceived destructive intrusion by the West, and especially by the United States that accused the Abiy regime of war crimes in Tigray.[27] In an interview with an Ethiopian

---

[24] In 2023, Freedom House designated Ethiopia as "not free," citing electoral malpractices, corruption, and human rights abuses. In 2021, US Secretary of State, Anthony Blinken, criticized the violence that shaped the June 21 elections in Ethiopia, describing the process as not free or fair. For details, see "Ethiopia," Freedom House, accessed July 22, 2024, https://freedomhouse.org/country/ethiopia/freedom-world/2024; "Building a Stronger Democracy in Ethiopia," US Embassy in Ethiopia, accessed July 22, 2024, https://et .usembassy.gov/building-a-stronger-democracy-in-ethiopia/.

[25] Interview ETOF37, Addis Ababa, 2023.

[26] "Inclusive Development and Sustainable Peace," Seminar, IPSS, Addis Ababa, June 15, 2023.

[27] In March 2023, the US stated that all sides, including the Abiy regime, involved in the years-long conflict in Tigray had committed war crimes. In response, the Ethiopian government accused the United States of being partisan. The war, which killed up to 600,000 people, soured relations between Ethiopia and the United States. For more, see Giulia Paravicini, "Ethiopia Calls US Accusations of War Crimes 'Inflammatory'," *Reuters*, March 21, 2023, www.reuters.com/world/africa/ethiopia-calls-us-accusations-war-crimes-inflammatory-2023-03-21/; David Pilling and Andres Schipani, "War in

journalist working for Xinhua News Agency, he similarly articulated the renewed appreciation of China's proclaimed principles of mutuality and noninterference as a product of disappointment with the West. "People at times prefer China out of grievances with the West . . . the West 'forces us to obey,'" he explained.[28] "People are bored with the West, especially during the recent conflict, when Western countries were intrusive, judgmental and abandoning Ethiopia during a difficult time . . . this also made China's principles stand out as attractive," shared an Ethiopian professor and think tank expert and a frequent commentator on China–Ethiopia relations.[29] China's principles of noninterference and "win-win," therefore, were at times appreciated and interpreted through the lens of Western actions rather than on their own terms. We now shift toward the discussion of the positioning of the West in practices and aspirations of Chinese public diplomacy practitioners.

6.3 CHINESE SOFT POWER PRACTITIONERS: THE WEST AS A STANDARD AND A DESTINATION

The shadow of the West is also notable in Chinese diplomatic practices and visions. More broadly, as discussed in Chapter 2, the perceived strength of the West in public diplomacy, as well as the threat it poses to China's image in the Global South, motivates China to expand and refine its image-making in Africa. China's image-making practices are also often mediated through Western standards, and many soft power practitioners aspire toward the West as a final destination and a marker of career recognition.

6.3.1 The West as a Standard in China's Image-Making

While China attempts to project a distinctive image in Africa and to challenge the perceived Western discursive dominance on the continent through an array of sophisticated image-making mechanisms examined in this book, Western standards still shape China's diplomatic practices. Specifically, English language, Western education, and Western political

Tigray May Have Killed 600,000 People, Peace Mediator Says," *Financial Times*, January 15, 2023, www.ft.com/content/2f385e95-0899-403a-9e3b-ed8c24adf4e7<color_Yellow>
[28] Interview ETJ30, Addis Ababa, 2023.
[29] Interview ETEX08, Addis Ababa, 2023.

ideologies mediate China's encounters with Ethiopian elites. As for the English language, though Ethiopians are encouraged to learn Chinese through the Confucius Institutes and Classrooms, most communication between Chinese and Ethiopians is conducted in English either directly or through a translator. In fact, one of the requirements for getting a scholarship to a Chinese university or short-term training is English language proficiency.[30] Chinese experts involved in diplomacy in Africa treat this reliance on English with a mix of frustration and resignation. One expert in China–Africa relations in Beijing interpreted the prevalence of English as Africans' limited commitment to learning Chinese – something he perceived as a major relationship-building barrier. "Chinese is a foundation of learning about China," he noted and compared the enthusiastic embrace of English and other foreign languages by Chinese people with a more relaxed attitude toward the study of Chinese by Africans.[31] His comment, however, still points to the relative importance of English fluency as a valued skill in China. Another interviewee, a director of a major Confucius Institute in Addis, had a more accepting attitude toward the dominance of the English language. "English will remain the language of the future," he said and stressed that young Chinese people are still working hard to master their English language skills. "Teaching Chinese is not aimed at replacing English, but rather at facilitating mutual understanding and cultural exchange," he shared.[32] In this comment, the Chinese educator acknowledges global linguistic hierarchies positioning English at the top, and articulated the role of Chinese in more modest terms, not as the language of global communication, but rather as a language that mediates specific cultural encounters.

Western education also plays into China's image-making. Chinese educators and hosts who receive African visitors are largely members of Western educated elite – something observed directly by Ethiopian elites I have spoken to about their time in China. Many noted that their professors are primarily educated in the West and that they send their kids to Western universities – something that further reinforces Ethiopians' perceptions of education quality discussed in the first part of the chapter. "If professors are sending their own kids to the West, then what does this say

---

[30] English language proficiency is noted in calls for scholarship applicants distributed to Ethiopian institutions. The author was able to access these calls with the help of Ethiopian colleagues.

[31] Interview CHSC05, Beijing, 2019.

[32] Interview CI09, Addis Ababa, 2023.

about the Chinese education system," wondered a senior Ethiopian journalist who witnessed this phenomenon while studying in China.[33]

The curricula taught to African students in programs like international communication and public policy, according to both Chinese and Ethiopian interviewees, also incorporates a significant share of Western materials, including academic articles and textbooks. Even in short-term training programs, the examples, citations, and even techniques conveyed to Ethiopian visitors were often derived from American textbooks, as already discussed in Chapter 4 in the context of civil servants' trainings by the Chinese Academy of Governance. The infusion of Western educational experiences and materials in Sino-Ethiopian diplomatic engagements is not surprising given the long-standing internationalization of the Chinese higher education system. Some experts specifically point to "Western dominance" in this process, including in the area of curricula development, with education standards mimicking the West, and Chinese students internalizing the superiority of Western knowledge above local knowledge production.[34] Even in domestic teachings of relatively sensitive subjects like journalism, Chinese university professors (many of whom are Western-educated) often incorporate Western teaching materials, and students tend to aspire to Western journalistic practices.[35] When it comes to education standards, both Ethiopian and Chinese interlocutors appear to hold the "West" in higher regard.

Finally, in the ideational realm, as discussed in Chapter 4, Chinese educators and officials present China as a distinctive democracy that can outperform Western-style democratic systems. While attempting to distinguish China's political values, however, Chinese practitioners indirectly appear to legitimize democracy as the aspirational system of governance. By adopting and redefining this concept in promoting China, Chinese elites are competing in Western-centered ideational spaces rather than creating their own. In some contexts, this competition takes on a defensive form, as illustrated with an example from Chapter 4 about a Chinese educator in Ethiopia pushing back on an audience remark that China is not a democratic system.[36] The mix of contestation and mimicry

---

[33] Focus group discussion ETJFG01, Addis Ababa, 2019.

[34] Yan Guo, Shibao Guo, and Xiaoli Liu, "Internationalization of Chinese Higher Education: Is It Westernization?" *Journal of Studies in International Education* 26(4) (2021).

[35] Maria Repnikova, "Thought Work Contested: Ideology and Journalism Education in China," *The China Quarterly* 230 (2017): 399–419.

[36] "Inclusive Development and Sustainable Peace," Seminar, IPSS, Addis Ababa, June 15, 2023.

of Western democratic values is also notable in China's hosting of an international forum on democracy immediately following the Summit for Democracy held in Washington.[37] Echoing the writings on hybridity in global communication studies, whereby countries in the Global South often adopt and remake Western cultural products and narratives but don't entirely challenge them,[38] China critically engages with Western political values and then readapts them to suit its objectives while abstaining from proposing radically new or subversive ideals.

In presenting itself as an equitable partner to Africa, not interfering in domestic political affairs, China appears to carve out a starker ideational contrast with the West, but it still tends to rely on comparisons with Western countries to explain and legitimize its agenda. Like Ethiopian participants who often evaluate China's ideational stances through the lens of the West, Chinese practitioners tend to invoke the West as an undesirable alternative that China aspires to counter. At the Chinese governance seminar at IPSS think tank, for instance, the Chinese expert articulated the Chinese approach in opposition to the West. "The West wants to decide who is right and who is wrong and ask for urgent political transformation. Our understanding is focused on developmental cooperation," he argued, contrasting the impulsive and disruptive approach of Western powers with the more constructive and inclusive approach of China toward Africa.[39] Similar arguments are made in Chinese media commentaries, portraying the West as disruptive and China as prioritizing African development.[40] Even in the opening vignette of this book, a senior Chinese diplomat presents China as disinterested in geopolitics, passively drawing a contrast to the more geopolitically motivated and profit-hungry West. Chinese officials, diplomats, and educators, therefore, tactically deploy the shadow of the West to articulate China's distinct stance toward

---

[37] Shi Jiangtao, "As China Lashes Out at US Democracy Summit, Analysts Warn of More Division," *South China Morning Post*, March 27, 2023, www.scmp.com/news/china/diplomacy/article/3215020/china-lashes-out-us-democracy-summit-analysts-warn-more-division.

[38] On a critical review of hybridity in global communication context, see Marwan M. Kraidy, "Hybridity in Cultural Globalization," *Communication Theory* 12(3) (2006): 316–39.

[39] "Inclusive Development and Sustainable Peace," Seminar, IPSS, Addis Ababa, June 15, 2023.

[40] Zhu Shaobin, "Xinhua Commentary: Africa Should Not Be a Battleground for a Great Power Rivalry," Xinhuanet, January 29, 2023, https://english.news.cn/20230129/2c2edc4b550d495f8bb1f20a21d6f17e/c.html; Liu Youmin and Yang Jun, "World Insights: Key Facts U.S. Deliberately Ignores about African Debt," Xinhuanet, February 7, 2023, https://english.news.cn/20230207/2e2f36625525400f90b8ea4993ffa4d6/c.html.

Africa. We now shift to more immediate considerations of the West as an aspiration in China's image-making through the lens of Chinese practitioners.

6.3.2 Chinese Soft Power Practitioners: Africa as a Step on the Global Ladder

Echoing the opportunistic attitudes of their Ethiopian counterparts vis-à-vis China, my Chinese interviewees, including Confucius Institute directors and volunteers, as well as journalists working for state media outlets, and diplomats, treat their work in Ethiopia and in Africa more broadly as an experience-building opportunity, and for many as a transitory destination en route to more desirable postings in the West.

When learning about their decisions to choose Ethiopia or other African countries for long-term job postings, I was struck by the relatively dispassionate explanations, featuring a mix of duty and necessity. My interlocutors were either sent there by their agencies or institutions or volunteered to gain firsthand work experience and international exposure. Some practitioners like Confucius Institute directors described their stay in Ethiopia as a professional obligation. Confucius Institutes and Classrooms in Ethiopia have an institutional relationship with Tianjin University of Technology and Education, which sends directors and volunteers to Ethiopia. When asked why he came to Ethiopia, a former director of a Confucius Classroom in Jimma, for instance, simply said, "My department sent me," and then further explained that he saw it as his turn to "volunteer" to teach in Ethiopia.[41] Foreign correspondent postings for Chinese state media journalists (and diplomats) are also assigned by their agencies, and while journalists can present their top choices, the agency makes the final determination.

Those educators and journalists who volunteered to come to Africa were generally younger and seeking international professional experiences that would advance their careers. Africa, and especially Ethiopia, presented a timely (and at times the only) opportunity for international exposure. The following excerpt from an interview with a CI volunteer at Addis Ababa University encapsulates the pragmatic decision to come to Ethiopia:

Most of us, volunteers, are graduates of Chinese as a foreign language major. For us, it's the first work experience, the first chance to apply our skills in a classroom.

---

[41] Interview CI03, Jimma, Addis Ababa, 2019.

Our university has a partnership with Ethiopia, and our teachers encouraged us to go, so I signed up. The decision to come here for most of us, is a practical one. It has little to do with interest in Africa or in Ethiopia in particular. If I were told to go elsewhere, I similarly wouldn't hesitate.[42]

This reflection is revealing of how the experience in Ethiopia can play an initiation role into larger global journeys for Chinese volunteers, whether it means teaching Chinese to foreigners in other countries or in China. At the same time, it is notable how this volunteer presents Ethiopia as an interchangeable destination. She found it accessible because of university connections but didn't depict it as particularly desirable or even distinctive from other locations that offer these professional experiences. Similar sentiments and reflections appeared in conversations with other Chinese volunteers stationed at Confucius Institutes and Classrooms across Ethiopia. Some, including the CI director whose first extensive international stay was Ethiopia, highlighted the motivation to practice and improve their English language skills as part of professional advancement. Some interviewees shared their ease in making mistakes in Ethiopia, in comparison to the West where they would feel self-conscious about practicing with native speakers. This mirrors the discussion on English language dominance in overshadowing China–Africa encounters.

Chinese foreign correspondents working for state media outlets like Xinhua News Agency also appeared to treat Africa as an experience-building opportunity. A television producer at Xinhua News Agency previously stationed in Nairobi described Chinese journalists in Africa as "relatively young." "This can be an upside," she shared, "as they are open-minded, curious, and passionate, but the downside can be the lack of experience."[43] Many Xinhua journalists I corresponded with came from the External Propaganda Bureau in Beijing (*duiwai xuanchuan bumen*) and have an academic background in foreign languages. Africa postings presented their first immersion into international reporting. This experimental attitude is also echoed in larger strategic plans for Chinese media expansion in Africa, whereby Africa is portrayed as an important context for innovating Chinese persuasion strategies or "a place to pilot Chinese media's international products and learn."[44]

---

[42] CI04, Addis Ababa, 2019. This quote was originally included in the author's article on Confucius Institutes. See Maria Repnikova, "Rethinking China's Soft Power: 'Pragmatic Enticement' of Confucius Institutes in Ethiopia," *The China Quarterly* 250 (2022): 440–63.

[43] Interview CHJ03, Beijing, July 30, 2019.

[44] Pál Nyíri, *Reporting for China: How Chinese Correspondents Work with the World* (University of Washington Press: 2017), p. 21.

Other than offering professional experience via international exposure, it is also worth noting that African countries are considered hardship destinations (*jianku diqu*) and come with financial bonuses. Confucius Institute volunteer teachers in Ethiopia, for instance, received an $820 monthly bonus payment or hardship subsidy, in addition to regular salaries, as Ethiopia fell into tier 3 of hardship destinations.[45] While in contrast to temporary Chinese labor migrants in Ethiopia primarily motivated by material quests or desires to "fix the mortgage problem,"[46] Chinese soft power practitioners didn't position material gains as their core objective for going to Ethiopia, but they still acknowledged the financial perks as enticing.

Treating them as professionally and materially advantageous, my interlocutors also saw these postings as transitory or as career-building blocks toward other, more attractive destinations. While some soft power practitioners, like CI volunteers, returned to China for further graduate education and job pursuits, others, including CI directors and media professionals, aspired toward more international careers. "After going to Africa, you can request other postings," shared an editor at Xinhua Agency.[47] When asked about their most desired locations, these Chinese professionals generally invoked Europe or the United States. They further elaborated that Western countries symbolized more prestige and professional growth, as well as safety and comfort. In an informal discussion, a Xinhua editor in Addis shared that everyone strives to go to the United States, but very few get to go. He added bitterly that getting a posting to America requires a mix of skill and connections (*guanxi*).[48] The Xinhua producers I met in Beijing who had previously spent time in Kenya noted that "the best talent gets sent to Europe and the United States," and associated the West with the most professional growth.[49] Journalist interviewees further shared that China–Africa stories carry relatively lower stakes with their superiors in Beijing than stories about America and

[45] The bonus payment has likely increased since the official allocation was publicized in 2011. See "Caijing bu yu jiaoyu bu guanyu yinfa 'guojia gongpai chuguo jiaoshisheng shenghuo daiyu guanli guiding' de tongzhi," (The Ministry of Finance and the Ministry of Education with regard to the distribution of "the guiding stipulations about the livelihood and treatment of teachers sent abroad by the state," July 7, 2011.

[46] Miriam Driessen, "Migrating for the Bank: Housing and Chinese Labour Migration to Ethiopia," *The China Quarterly*, 221: 143–60.

[47] Interview CHJ03, Beijing, 2019.

[48] Informal discussion with the author, Addis Ababa, 2018 and 2019.

[49] Interview CHJ02, Beijing, 2019.

Europe that are more scrutinized by domestic publics and elites.[50] This puts more pressure on professional performance.

Chinese soft power practitioners I encountered also perceived Western countries as generally safer and more comfortable. A Xinhua journalist with extensive experience in covering Africa from Nairobi described his stay as interesting and stimulating, but he didn't hesitate to state his preference for Western countries, pointing to safety as the key factor. He recounted his life at the Xinhua compound in Nairobi as highly constrained by security precautions: "Every day, we have to be back at the compound by 5:00 pm. I wasn't allowed to exit past that hour without official permission from the boss."[51] He also added that his family back in China was very worried about him.

Discussions with Confucius Institute volunteers and directors similarly revealed their aspirations for more comfort and freedom of movement, and safety as a major concern and limitation of their stay. Volunteers stationed in Africa highlighted high-security precautions practiced by directors in the field, like those instituted at the Xinhua News Agency. A female Confucius Classroom volunteer based in the southern Ethiopian city of Hawassa shared how she was not allowed to wander off the compound after 5 pm, and that her life in Ethiopia generally consisted of work, communal meals with other volunteers and the director, and walks from dormitory to the classroom.[52] Ironically, while one of the premises of Chinese diplomacy in Africa is to carve out a more positive story about Africa, these associations of Africa with instability and crime echo Western media coverage of the continent.[53] Former Hanban officials even linked the perceptions of Africa as a dangerous destination with meek interest toward it among potential volunteers.[54] As the security situation in Ethiopia deteriorated starting in 2020, some volunteers and directors temporarily left the country. Whether or not the staffing returned to normal was unclear on my last visit.

[50] Interview CHJ06 & 07, Beijing, 2019.

[51] Interview CHJ02, Beijing, July 30, 2019.

[52] Informal discussion with Chinese volunteers at Hawassa Confucius Classroom, Hawassa, May 10, 2019.

[53] Caroline Kimeu, "Negative Stereotypes in International Media Cost Africa £3.2 Billion a Year – Report," *The Guardian*, October 17, 2024, www.theguardian.com/global-development/2024/oct/17/media-stereotypes-africa-higher-interest-report-payments-on-sovereign-debt.

[54] Interview CHPD03, Beijing, 2019.

These reflections on safety also featured sentiments of boredom and exasperation with what appears as a monotonous lifestyle – something vividly depicted in other studies on Chinese workers stationed in Africa. Schmitz, in her evocative analysis of Chinese managers and workers in Angola, for instance, documents their varied attempts at "passing time," from playing video games to taking Portuguese lessons. Life in Angola, for these Chinese workers, was almost placed on hold, in slow anticipation of restarting it again in China.[55] In contrast to Chinese managers and workers in Angola, Chinese soft power practitioners, including journalists and volunteers, envisioned an eventual transit to other, safer, and more thrilling foreign destinations, like Europe and North America.

As part of sharing aspirations for professional postings in the West, some Chinese interlocutors (like the Ethiopian ones) attempted to take advantage of our encounters to gather more information about America, and in some cases make connections to create opportunities there, not necessarily related to their current careers. Curiosity about the United States transpired in many of my fieldwork conversations with Chinese diplomacy practitioners in Ethiopia. In a discussion about Chinese media reporting of Africa, my interlocutor, a journalist at the Xinhua News Agency in Ethiopia, attempted to divert the conversation from China to life in the United States. In doing so, he threw a series of questions at me, one after another: What are the current housing prices in Atlanta? What's the average salary? How much does a professor like you make? What are the monthly healthcare costs and what's included in medical coverage? What are the pollution levels these days? What are the requirements for getting into a PhD program at your university? My responses were disappointing to this editor. I kept qualifying almost every answer with "well, it depends …" and presented some generalities. He kept pushing back, asking for approximate facts, numbers, and personal details about my American life. In an informal chat with a former CI director in Jimma, he brought up the topic of visiting academic fellowships and living conditions in Atlanta. Like the Xinhua editor, he asked detailed factual questions that spoke to both an attempt to indirectly measure China against the United States, as well as to envision a possible life there. Curiosity about America also pierced through spontaneous encounters with members of Chinese migrant community in Ethiopia. A Chinese company employee I met

---

55 Cheryl Mei-Ting Schmitz, "Doing Time, Making Money at a Chinese State Firm in Angola," *Made in China*, January 25, 2021, https://madeinchinajournal.com/2021/01/2 5/doing-time-making-money-at-a-chinese-state-firm-in-angola/.

while exploring different rice produce at a Chinese grocery shop greeted me enthusiastically after learning that I come from America: "You are the first American I have ever met. America is a great country! So honored to meet you," he said, quickly offering me a ride home, followed by a dinner invitation. It is intriguing how these positive and curious reactions to America persist despite the framework of Great Power Competition adopted by both the United States and the Chinese leadership that positions the two countries as hostile competitors.

In some cases, similarly to my Ethiopian contacts, the Chinese professionals also attempted to build more opportunistic connections. Some, like the Xinhua editor, brought this up jokingly: if I move to a famous school, he would come study as my PhD student and then he could get a job as a professor at Beijing University. If he gets a PhD at Beijing University, he can only teach at smaller, second-tier schools in China. This journalist's commentary illuminates his association of education in the United States with prestigious opportunities back in China, although he does appear to differentiate between so-called famous schools and less famous public universities, where I am currently based as an associate professor. Other interlocutors, like the Confucius Institute director in Addis Ababa, would sprinkle friendly remarks such as "I will come visit you in America" or "You should invite me there" into our conversations about China and Africa. Some, like the team of Chinese doctors I met who work for the Beijing hospital outside Addis Ababa, made direct practical propositions. After hearing how expensive acupuncture and other traditional medicine treatments are in the United States, these doctors suggested I set up a company and hire them to work with me. These remarks, of course, are more wistful and playful than realistic, not typically materializing in extensive follow-ups (see the Methods Appendix 1 for more reflections on this). It is as if these Chinese practitioners allowed themselves to get lost in thought or withdraw from their current realities and imagine fun alternative paths or even temporary stopovers in America.

Even while being based in Ethiopia, some of these Chinese diplomatic representatives sought out more Western exposure (as have Ethiopians residing in China). Confucius Institute directors and volunteers talked about watching Hollywood films and listening to American music in their spare time. Like Ethiopian journalists and educators, they primarily consumed Western media and cultural content. Consumption of Ethiopian culture was more related to work, including journalistic coverage or relationship building, than to leisure. Chinese diplomats also shared that they send their kids to an American school in Addis Ababa. In a rare moment of informal frankness during a simple lunch at a Chinese construction company headquarters in the outskirts of Jimma, a young diplomat expressed slight frustration with what he saw as the inevitable Westernization of his kids. "We Chinese need to set up such schools as well!" he noted. For now, this idea has not materialized, and for his next posting, in Eastern Europe, the diplomat has already enrolled his son in another American school.

This analysis of motivations and aspirations of Chinese soft power practitioners in Ethiopia illuminates their strategic perspectives on Ethiopia and more broadly on Africa postings. They see them more as initiation rituals into their longer international careers and visions that culminate in Western countries. Their desires for the West are also expressed in curiosity and in consumption of Western culture and education, though it is also mixed with resentment about the weak Chinese alternatives. Whereas officially Chinese diplomats, educators, and journalists are in Ethiopia to fulfill the larger mission of improving and solidifying Sino-Ethiopian ties, unofficially they appear to pursue their agendas of individual empowerment or forging their paths on the "upward" journey from the Global South to the Global North.

6.4 CONCLUSIONS AND IMPLICATIONS

This chapter illustrated the shared synergies toward the West among the Ethiopians and Chinese partaking in China's image-making encounters. While Ethiopian elites evaluate China's diplomacy through the comparative benchmark of the West and often prioritize Western engagement, Chinese soft power practitioners still draw on Western standards and ideas and aspire to building their careers in the West. Of course, there are exceptions to these patterns. In rare instances, I have observed alternative routes or pathways from the West to China and Ethiopia. Two Ethiopian translators I interviewed who work for Chinese enterprises, for instance, revealed that they initially learned Chinese from an American Jehovah's witness couple doing missionary work in Ethiopia. The translators recalled that the couple was fluent in Mandarin and skilled in teaching the language. As part of immersing into the religious practices, these two young men also acquired a high-level fluency in Mandarin that they now use to earn their living. Neither of them had prior encounters with Chinese culture or Chinese communities, and yet their daily lives are now intricately connected to them.

Some of my Chinese interlocutors have also come to Ethiopia via the West. A Chinese entrepreneur I met in Addis who runs a tourism agency serving Chinese visitors, including Chinese officials and businesspeople, has moved to Ethiopia from the United States. After a decade in America, he decided to try out Ethiopia as an adventure, and as potentially an easier place to make a living, compared to what he described as grueling work culture in the United States. His efforts have thus far paid off, and he doesn't seem to miss the comforts of American life, though he does intend to retire in China. For some Chinese practitioners, like company representatives involved in guarding China's image, moreover, the West was rarely an option given that their work, largely in construction sector, is more suited for the Global South. While these exceptional and distinct trajectories are noteworthy, most of my Ethiopian and Chinese contacts treated their interactions as transitory pathways in Western-dominated global hierarchies and relied on the West as a standard-setter.

The presence of this lingering shadow of the West, and especially of the United States, in the story of Chinese image-making in Ethiopia further deromanticizes the notion of South–South solidarity. It is increasingly popular to position the Global South as a potential alternative to neoliberalism or as an emancipatory force against the structures of the Global North.[56] The analysis in this chapter, however, shows that Global South encounters are still in part conditioned by the Global North. This does not dismantle the ambitious project of China's image-making analyzed in this book but rather reinforces and expands our understanding of its multi-directionality. The already dynamic and often contested bilateral encounter examined in previous chapters is further complicated by the comparative and intersecting context of the West.

It is also worth acknowledging that the shadow of the West is not all-encompassing, nor stagnant. In some image-making domains like censorial power, the West appears as less visible, in large part because Western presence is limited in Ethiopia, as is the coverage of Western activities by Ethiopian media. Ethiopian interlocutors occasionally referred to Western public relations as more skillful, but they generally discussed China on its own terms. The practices of censoring narratives about China are also arguably more rooted in China's domestic environment than in learning from the West.

---

[56] Martin Müller, "In Search of the Global East: Thinking between North and South," *Geopolitics* 25(3) (2020): 734–55.

The attractiveness of the United States as part of Sino-Ethiopian engagements might also weaken over time across all domains if the West becomes more removed from daily realities and imaginaries of Chinese and Ethiopians. In China, some shifts are already happening in de-Westernizing of Chinese culture and education system. Under Xi Jinping's rule, "Western values" are now banned in university education and the use of English is officially limited in some elementary schools.[57] At the same time, America (and liberal democracies at large) has become less open to Chinese students, officials, and journalists, as anti-China sentiment has spiraled in recent years, especially during the coronavirus pandemic. The anti-China policies and narratives have only deepened since Trump's reelection and his renewed trade war with China. Whether or not the United States and the West more broadly remain a top destination for Chinese soft power practitioners is now uncertain. A mix of cultural protectionism, nationalism, and resentment toward the West might translate into less enthusiasm for seeking recognition from it.

In Ethiopia, as discussed in this chapter, officials and lay citizens have critiqued the United States for barging into Ethiopia's ethnic conflict. Some Ethiopian officials and commentators have also reacted sharply to Western media for what they perceived as biased coverage favoring the TPLF.[58] The exasperation with the United States' alleged interference in Ethiopian domestic affairs is also mixed with a growing resentment about its absence in providing infrastructure and education opportunities. Ethiopian educators, officials, and journalists often invoked the disconnect between the US official narratives of competing with China in Africa, and the limited resources dedicated to this so-called competition. "Americans? Where are they?" was one of the questions I often heard during my fieldwork. "America gets angry, but it doesn't compete ...," argued the former president of the Meles Zenawi Academy.[59]

This questioning of the US absence was a pervasive theme in my fieldwork, signaling the growing cynicism and disappointment along with an invitation to engage. This cynicism is likely to only escalate in the coming years under Trump's second administration. The destruction of USAID, the VOA, and the shrinkage of CDC – all active in Ethiopia,

---

[57] "China Says No Room for 'Western Values' in University Education," *The Guardian*, January 30, 2015.

[58] See, for instance, the negative reactions to the tweet about the war crimes committed in Tigray published *The New Humanitarian* magazine, https://twitter.com/newhumanitar ian/status/1470056095238479879.

[59] Interview ETOF07, Addis Ababa, 2019.

along with new program cuts at the State Department and complications in student and international scholar visa processing, position the United States as ever more disengaged from and unwelcoming to Ethiopia and to Africa at large.[60] If the United States continues to be seen as at once a political agitator and an absent competitor, especially in the realm of diplomacy, the reach for America may eventually fade in favor of a deeper appreciation of China and Chinese offerings. The evolution of these dynamics requires continuous observation and grounded fieldwork in both China and Ethiopia. For now, an interest to partake in Western-centric globalization is still strong at the individual level. Over time, however, the desire for the West might morph into more explicit anti-Western sentiments and more profound Sino-Ethiopian solidarities.

[60] For more on the impact of US foreign aid withdrawal in Africa, see Majd Al-Waheidi, Reena Advani, and Michel Martin. "'You Can Now Die': The Human Cost of America's Foreign aid Cuts in Africa," *NPR*, March 19, 2025, www.npr.org/2025/03/13/nx-s1-53 16282/usaid-aid-funds-economy-africa; Desmond Thompson, "US aid Freeze Threatens Higher Education Alliances in Africa," *University World News*, February 6, 2025, www .universityworldnews.com/post.php?story=20250205163446916; Abdi Latif Dahir, China's Quiet Win: Outmaneuvering U.S. for Africa's Future Leaders, *The New York Times*, June 7, 2025, www.nytimes.com/2025/06/07/world/africa/africa-universities-us-china-trump-visas.html.

7

Conclusions and New Research Directions

Through in-depth, multi-sited fieldwork in China and Ethiopia this book endeavored to parse out China's dynamic image-making in Africa, focusing primarily on state-directed outreach to Ethiopian elites. While it is tempting to assess China's image promotion through the lens of "soft power" or "sharp power," on-the-ground realities challenge the utility of this binary. I find that Chinese actors, including state and state-affiliated individuals and groups (as well as some private entities), partake in both promotional and obstructive strategies – at once inviting and guarding engagement with China. Specifically, in this book, I identified and analyzed three core mechanisms: *tangible enticement, ideational persuasion, and censorial power.*

In Chapter 3, I showed how offering tangible benefits and opportunities is central to China's elite diplomacy, including a vast distribution of educational and training scholarships, the paid-for and accessible Chinese language teaching through Confucius Institutes that also link students to jobs, and allocation of media resources. In Chapter 4, I examined ideational promotion through the prism of elite training programs often associated with the export of a China model in popular and policy writings. I argued that there is no coherent export, but there are extensive efforts to legitimize China. This endeavor to showcase China's strengths goes along with censorship or guarding China's image that I analyze in Chapter 5. In this chapter, I explored how Ethiopian communication professionals face controlled publicity, silencing, and coercion from

Chinese state and non-state actors as they try to publicly write and ask about China and its activities in Ethiopia. While the three strategies were analyzed separately for analytical clarity, in practice, of course, they tend to overlap and intersect across different initiatives.

Foregoing the pursuit of linear outcomes, this book prioritized illuminating the complex practices of implementation and reception in these different arenas. Across the chapters, I demonstrated how China's image-making is characterized by unevenness from within, as well as in Ethiopians' layered engagement with China, and a continuous pull of the West for both Chinese and Ethiopian interlocutors. As for internal disjointedness, across the chapters, I showcased a mix of deliberate, consistent image-making practices, alongside more improvised and ad hoc tactics. In distributing and promoting tangible opportunities, for instance, Chinese embassy officials, educators, and media outlets are at once methodical in who they target and how, as well as spontaneous, reactive, and even selectively disengaged, as in the case of delegating training selection criteria to Ethiopian counterparts. In diffusing China's ideals and values, Chinese educators and training organizers promote certain coherent narratives of China as a successful democracy and benevolent power in Africa, but also present patchy, one-sided accounts of critical governance domains like journalism, and generally overflood visitors with information. In guarding the production of China narratives, Chinese embassy and company representatives consistently limit the contours of access to Chinese projects and sensitive topics through contrived press briefings and information withdrawal, as well as react to perceived threats on-the-spot through selective acts of coercion and co-optation. Mirroring China's domestic governance, China's global reach features strategic visions and consistent implementation, but also widespread improvisation or haphazard adaptation to on-the-ground realities.

This study also demonstrated the multifaceted responses by Ethiopian elites that challenge the labels of "success" or "failure" in evaluating the effects of China's image-making. On the one hand, China's efforts and initiatives are impactful in engaging Ethiopians as recipients, sympathizers, and co-guardians of China's image. Ethiopian elites readily accept China's tangible offerings, thereby legitimizing China's projection of itself as a generous power. They acknowledge and appreciate some of China's ideational narratives, including that of China as a distinctive democracy (that suits China), as well as an innovative and cultured rising power. Ethiopian officials and journalists also proactively take part in China's censorial effort by co-disciplining and self-censoring the production and dissemination of public narratives about China in Ethiopia.

At the same time, this engagement should not be mistaken for mere reactiveness and acquiescence to China. Throughout this book, I demonstrated how Ethiopian elites also act as proactive initiators and negotiators of Chinese influence. The initiating is especially notable in the context of tangible enticement, with Ethiopian elites frequently requesting more opportunities and resources, such as trainings and Confucius Institutes. In participating in censorial power, Ethiopian officials and editors work to preempt China's sensitive responses by deluding and homogenizing representation of China in local media. Even in responding to ideational power, Ethiopians at times request specific topics for engagement, such as poverty alleviation trainings.

Ethiopian elites also routinely negotiate Chinese outreach. They place conditionality on accepting Chinese gifts, as in the case of Confucius Institutes, privately (and occasionally publicly) critique some Chinese official political rhetoric, self-censor selectively to promote Ethiopia along with China, and disseminate alternative, critical narratives about China in informal contexts. At times, negotiation can also mean ignoring and poking fun at Chinese influence, such as by not taking the training content seriously or by disseminating rumors about China that derail the official accounts of unbreakable friendship. Overall, the study of reception in this book suggests that Chinese influence is at best partial, as it is deployed disjointedly, and is actively reappropriated, contested, and even neglected by target audiences.

The uneven Sino-Ethiopian encounter is further stretched by the looming presence of Western hierarchies or shared aspirations toward the West, as examined in Chapter 6. While Chinese officials and scholars aspire toward transgressing Western influence and redefining China's image through Africa, as discussed in Chapter 2, many Chinese "soft power" practitioners adhere to Western standards, and work toward careers in the West, with Africa treated as a steppingstone. Ethiopian elites, in turn, while welcoming, engaging and negotiating with China, also evaluate this relationship through the comparative prism of the West by treating it as a quality benchmark, and as the more desirable destination. This transnational layer of the West adds to the multidirectionality of China's image-making project, as it continues to speak to and from the West while being directed at Africa.

The China–Ethiopia and the China–Africa story, of course, is a fast moving one. While this book attempted to theorize and empirically grapple with China's image-making in Ethiopia, it is still limited to a particular period. As noted in the previous chapter and discussed further in this conclusion, the appeal of the West, and especially of the United States, in Africa may transform because of the demise of the American diplomacy (and democracy) under Trump's leadership. And China's attractiveness might become less ambiguous and less guarded because of waning competition with the United States. Ethiopia itself is undergoing a lot of changes. Even in the duration of my fieldwork, I found affinities toward China change among certain groups. Tigray officials, for instance, used to be very pro-China, but following the devastating war in Tigray, with China standing on the sidelines, some became more skeptical and recalcitrant in talking about China–Ethiopia relations. And Chinese teachers and CI volunteers who treated Ethiopia as a relatively safe destination within Africa also started to shift their perspectives with an ongoing security crisis following the war. COVID-19 pandemic is another encapsulation of unpredictable shifts – Chinese diplomacy focused on assistance to Africa, including Ethiopia, but years after the pandemic, this assistance was rarely talked about, and neither was the pandemic.

These uncertain trajectories are present in the larger Sino-Ethiopian relationship – something captured beautifully in the recent widely acclaimed documentary film, *Made in Ethiopia*, which traces the expansion of China's ambitious industrial park project through the lens of its many characters.[1] The expansion stalled through COVID-19 and security tensions in Ethiopia. By the end of the film, some major participants entirely change directions. An Ethiopian manufacturing worker, Beti, went back to school (though she joined another Chinese company later), and the flamboyant Chinese factory boss abandoned the industrial park for a new coffee export business. The anti-climactic ending symbolizes the complexity of China in Ethiopia (and China in Africa more broadly) – against all speculation, this relationship is dynamic and amorphous. It is swayed by larger political currents, but also made up of individual characters with their own impulses and trajectories. Like the film, this book doesn't claim to prescribe the future of China's image-making in Ethiopia or in Africa at large, but it attempted to capture a slice of these dynamic realities, to make sense of the "chaos," and to offer new ways of thinking about China's efforts to promote its image that can also apply to other contexts. I turn to this next.

---

[1] For a free viewing of the film, see www.pbs.org/pov/films/madeinethiopia/.

7.2 SHIFTING BEYOND ETHIOPIA: CHINA'S UNEVEN IMAGE-MAKING IN THE GLOBAL SOUTH

Though the Ethiopian context carries some distinctive and arguably unique characteristics, such as its lack of colonial experience, its diplomatic significance to the rest of Africa, and it's extensive economic and political ties with China, this case renders visible the possibilities and the limitations of China's image-making. The closeness of this relationship and its importance to China reveals the scope of China's state-led image efforts. At the same time, Ethiopia's history with hedging against different foreign partners helps illuminate the varied responses to Chinese influence, and the types of negotiations possible even in cases that appear to lean "pro-China."

The analytical framework from the study of China and Ethiopia can also apply to other cases. Shifting from the more ideologically loaded and polarizing concepts of soft and sharp power and instead focusing on specific image mechanisms allows for capturing the complexity of China's efforts at building (and guarding) sympathies across the Global South. A cursory look at secondary sources suggests that the three core strategies identified in this study play out in different forms on a larger scale. *Tangible enticement*, or the material underbelly of Chinese "soft power," for instance, is on display in other African countries, as well as in other regions in the Global South. At the 2024 FOCAC Meeting, the Chinese government has pledged 60,000 new training opportunities for Africans,[2] in addition to 10,000 scholarships allocated annually "along the Belt and Road,"[3] and new scholarship programs launched in Latin America and the Caribbean.[4] Confucius Institutes and Classrooms also continue to operate and, in some cases, grow in the Global South,[5] tying Chinese language offerings to practical benefits, often adjusted to the local context. A CI at the University of Sierra Leone, for

---

[2] "Forum on China-Africa Cooperation: Beijing Action Plan (2025–2027)," Ministry of Foreign Affairs: The People's Republic of China, September 5, 2024, www.mfa.gov.cn/eng/xw/zyxw/202409/t20240905_11485719.html.

[3] "Full Text: Action Plan on the Belt and Road Initiative," The State Council, March 30, 2015, https://english.www.gov.cn/archive/publications/2015/03/30/content_281475080249035.htm.

[4] Margaret Myers, "China's Education Diplomacy in Latin America," *Wilson Center*, March 15, 2024, www.wilsoncenter.org/blog-post/chinas-education-diplomacy-latin-america.

[5] In 2023 alone, higher education institutes in Brazil, Botswana, and Djibouti inaugurated new Confucius Institutes. For more on the growth of Confucius Institutes in the Global South, see Rachel Cheung, "China's Confucius Institutes Go South," *The Wire China*, October 1, 2023, www.thewirechina.com/2023/10/01/chinas-confucius-institutes-go-south/; Elaine Chan, "China's Confucius Institutes Flourish in ASEAN after West's

instance, promotes Chinese medicine by first introducing Chinese language training at local hospitals, and then setting up medical collaborations there.[6] A CI at Egerton University in Kenya offers regular courses on environmental governance and agriculture technology for the Nakuru County government, in addition to regular Chinese language classes.[7] Meanwhile, across the Global South, China is setting up Luban workshops, offering different types of vocational training at universities.[8]

Chinese government also widely provides logistical support to major news outlets. In May 2024, the Chinese Ambassador to Seychelles, for instance, presented technical equipment for the new headquarters of the Seychelles Broadcasting Corporation. The construction of the headquarters was also financed through a Chinese government grant.[9] China has financed similar projects in South Sudan,[10] Equatorial Guinea,[11] and Antigua and Barbuda,[12] among other places. Xinhua News Agency signed over 3,600 content sharing agreements with media outlets around the world;[13] most of its partner agencies are in developing countries.

Freeze-out," *Nikkei Asia*, May 12, 2024, https://asia.nikkei.com/Business/Education/ China-s-Confucius-Institutes-flourish-in-ASEAN-after-West-s-freeze-out.

[6] "Confucius Institutes in Africa Teach Chinese Outside Schools," Haiwainet, June 8, 2018, http://news.haiwainet.cn/n/2018/0608/c3541083-31330800.html?nojump=1.

[7] "Confucius Institute's "Chinese +' Model: Customized Chinese Vocational Training Courses for Local People," *People's Daily Overseas Edition*, October 19, 2018, www .chinaqw.com/hwjy/2018/10-19/205558.shtml.

[8] Coy Li, "Why China Is Looking to Vocational Training to Build Bridges with the Global South," *South China Morning Post*, August 18, 2024, www.scmp.com/news/china/diplo macy/article/3274892/why-china-looking-vocational-training-build-bridges-global-south; Jian Li and Eryong Xue, "Luban Workshop Development in China," in *Opening Education to the Outside World: Rethinking International Education in China During Post COVID-19* (Singapore: Springer Nature: 2022), 57–71.

[9] Sedrick Nicette, "Seychelles Broadcasting Corporation's Nearly Completed HQ Gets New Equipment from China," *Seychelles News Agency*, May 17, 2024, www .seychellesnewsagency.com/articles/20579/Seychelles+Broadcasting+Corporation%27s+ nearly+completed+HQ+gets+new+equipment+from+China.

[10] "China to Build $100 Million TV, Radio Broadcast Station in Juba," *CGTN Africa*, June 15, 2023, https://africa.cgtn.com/china-to-build-100-million-tv-radio-broadcast-station-in-juba/.

[11] Cobus van Staden, "Equatorial Guinea Media Donation Highlights a Key Chinese Soft Power Strategy," *China Global South Project*, April 13, 2022, https://chinaglobalsouth.com/2022/ 04/13/equatorial-guinea-media-donation-highlights-a-key-chinese-soft-power-strategy/.

[12] "Media Cooperation: China's CMG Donates Media Equipment to Antigua and Barbuda Broadcasting Service," *CGTN*, May 29, 2024, https://news.cgtn.com/news/2024-05-29/ VHJhbnNjcmlwdDc5MDEw/index.html.

[13] "Xinhua Signs Agreements with Foreign Media Outlets, Institutions to Deepen Cooperation," *Xinhua*, December 2, 2023, https://english.news.cn/20231202/f2b5 b6179da94b07814ffab014228083/c.html.

Other than tangible empowerment, China's efforts at promoting its ideals and values reverberate on a macroscale. Chinese officials frequently stress the importance of better understanding China and correcting for unfair Western stereotypes to their Global South audiences. For example, during a visit to Mombasa, Kenya, in 2022, the Chinese foreign minister, Wang Yi, criticized the popularized debt trap narrative and told local journalists at the press briefing that China was only interested in helping Africa speed up its development.[14] While comprehensive analyses of elite training materials and experiences are limited, a new dataset of MOFCOM descriptions of its training programs and exchanges with the Global South suggests that promoting Chinese governance (both political and economic) is central to the agenda.[15] A recent study of Chinese state media's external propaganda also finds the focus on efficacy of China's governance system, including its responsive institutions and successful economic development[16] – the central themes in elite training seminars with Ethiopians (Chapter 4). At major summits and in important writings on Chinese diplomacy in the Global South, Chinese officials underscore the importance of promoting an equitable world order, and China as the "equalizer"[17] – another core theme analyzed in Ethiopia–China exchanges. In cultural diplomatic events like the Chinese Bridge competition, similarly to elite training exchanges, Chinese hosts promote China as a civilizational power, with admirable ancient history and culture.[18]

Finally, China's censorial power often referred to as coercion and censorship in reports and academic writings is widely documented. As noted in Chapter 5, journalists in Kenya, and in other African countries, similarly to their Ethiopian counterparts, struggle with gaining access to Chinese sources outside the public relations realm. In Brazil, there are indications that the Chinese embassy monitors and responds to

---

[14] "Chinese FM Refutes 'Debt Trap' Allegation in China–Africa Cooperation," *People's Daily*, January 6, 2022, http://en.people.cn/n3/2022/0107/c90000-9942192.html.

[15] Reid Standish, "Is China Exporting Its Political Model to the World? A New Report Says Yes," Radio Free Europe, June 13, 2024.

[16] Daniel Mattingly et al., "Chinese State Media Persuades a Global Audience that the 'China Model' Is Superior: Evidence from a 19-Country Experiment," *American Journal of Political Science* 69 (3) (2024): 1029–1046.

[17] See for instance Liu Jianchao, "Riding the Tide of History: Working Together to Boost Solidarity and Cooperation among the Global South," Qiushi, June 2024, http://en.qstheory.cn/2024-07/08/c_1001807.htm.

[18] "'Chinese Bridge:' A Bridge for the World to China," China Daily, October 14, 2024, www.chinadaily.com.cn/a/202410/14/WS670ca87ba310f1265a1c7734.html.

media commentary about China. In one case, such monitoring apparently led to the early closure of a Falun Gong exhibit in Brasília in March 2019.[19] In Chile, a journalist reported self-censorship attitudes among public opinion leaders largely due to fears of economic backlash from China,[20] and in the Philippines, independent journalists are often excluded from Chinese embassy briefings and face intimidation from Chinese officials and state-aligned Internet trolls.[21]

The uneven deployment of and reception toward China's image-making can also be observed and studied in many places. Chinese soft power practitioners I spoke to in Beijing acknowledged the often-disjointed implementation as a feature of their work. A former CI director who was stationed in Botswana, for instance, shared that the recruitment and promotion efforts of Confucius Institutes in Africa fluctuate based on individual directors' motivations and commitment.[22] He was very enthusiastic about his role, but admitted that some colleagues felt lethargic about their Africa missions. Officials and experts who give lectures to Global South visitors noted that these learning experiences need more coherence and consistency and that the instructors are often limited in time and resources to adjust their presentations to different groups. In the context of broader ideational propaganda, Chinese officials themselves often stress that Chinese practitioners, especially Chinese journalists, still need to work harder to tell China stories.[23] While censorial power was rarely discussed by Chinese interviewees, ad hoc acts of censorship to halt negative stories, in addition to the overarching climate of limited information access, have been recorded by Global South journalists. An Indonesian journalist, Bayu Hermawan, for instance, reported receiving a WhatsApp message from a Chinese official who expressed displeasure at Hermawan's account of a 2019 Beijing-organized tour to

[19] Ellie Young, Sarah Cook, and anonymous, "Brazil: Beijing's Global Media Influence 2022 Country Report," *Freedom House*, accessed August 24, 2022, https://freedom house.org/country/brazil/beijings-global-media-influence/2022#footnoteref52_miyont4.

[20] BC Han and Sascha Hannig, "Chile: Beijing's Global Media Influence 2022 Country Report," *Freedom House*, accessed August 24, 2022, https://freedomhouse.org/country/chile/beijings-global-media-influence/2022#footnoteref62_ioud9gc.

[21] BC Han and Camille Elemia, "Philippines: Beijing's Global Media Influence 2022 Country Report," *Freedom House*, accessed August 24, 2022, https://freedomhouse.org/country/philippines/beijings-global-media-influence/2022#footnoteref49_k51uwmz.

[22] Interview CI06, Shanghai, 2019.

[23] Ben Westcott, "Beijing Calls for Chinese Journalists to 'Arm Their Minds' with Xi Jinping Thought," CNN, December 17, 2019, www.cnn.com/2019/12/17/asia/china-journalist-code-intl-hnk/index.html.

Xinjiang.[24] And in Nigeria, the Chinese embassy paid journalists not to cover negative stories about China, according to an editor at a major online publication.[25] Even in Western contexts, there is evidence of improvised censorial diplomacy. In their book on Global China, for instance, Franceschini and Loubere recall a soft bribery offer by a Chinese CI codirector at a European university – funding for translation with a precondition of not researching politically sensitive subjects.[26]

The reception toward China's image-making efforts in other parts of the Global South echoes the dynamic and discerning strategies of Ethiopian elites. In discussing the growing number of Confucius Institutes in Latin America, for instance, an expert from the region described this development as "very much a two-way street." "This is not only China pushing for greater engagement. This is also the Latin American side wanting a larger Chinese participation within the hemisphere," he noted.[27] A recent study on Confucius Institutes in Africa also found proactive initiation efforts from African university officials.[28] The Chinese authorities originally focused on convincing elite African universities to join the CI network, creating a promotional effect that prompted other African universities to take note. According to one CI director from Southern Africa quoted in the study, seeing the best university in their country partner with a Confucius Institute convinced his own institution to make the initial approach.[29] In the ideational realm, Global South elites, and especially journalists, who travel to China often publicize positive reflections about China,[30] but also

---

[24] Jon Emont, "How China Persuaded One Muslim Nation to Keep Silent on Xinjiang Camps," *The Wall Street Journal*, December 11, 2019, www.wsj.com/articles/how-china-persuaded-one-muslim-nation-to-keep-silent-on-xinjiang-camps-11576090976.

[25] Angeli Datt and Emeka Umejei, "Nigeria: Beijing's Global Media Influence 2022 Country Report," *Freedom House*, accessed August 24, 2022, https://freedomhouse.org/country/nigeria/beijings-global-media-influence/2022#footnoteref68_at35brt.

[26] Franceschini and Loubere, *Global China as a Method*.

[27] Rachel Cheung, "China's Confucius Institutes Go South," The Wire China, October 1, 2023, www.thewirechina.com/2023/10/01/chinas-confucius-institutes-go-south/.

[28] Siyuan Li, "China's Confucius Institute in Africa: A Different Story?" *International Journal of Comparative Education and Development* 23(4) (October 1, 2021): 353–66. https://doi.org/10.1108/IJCED-02-2021-0014.

[29] Ibid.

[30] Shelton Indika Bandara, "Asian Journalists Praise the New Development Drive in China," *China Daily*, August 30, 2018, www.chinadaily.com.cn/a/201808/30/WS5b87b116a310add14f388b64.html; Lei Li, "World Reporters Gain Insights at Two Sessions," *China Daily*, March 12, 2024, www.chinadaily.com.cn/a/202403/12/WS65ef8e7da31082fc043bbfff.html.

critique and push back on some aspects of Chinese governance. After visiting China, for instance, an Argentinian journalist was critical of China's imprisonment of someone for "writing about homosexuality" and a Kenyan journalist described China Daily as a "crazy newspaper" that never prints negative stories.[31] Studies on Chinese media propaganda also find mixed resonance, with Global South audiences questioning the objectivity and interests of Chinese state media.[32] In responding to China's censorial power, while self-censorship has been documented in other contexts,[33] so have the many pushbacks. In more openly democratic societies in Africa like Kenya, Nigeria, and South Africa, for instance, private news outlets have publicized damaging narratives about China. In 2023, a Nigerian newspaper, *The Cable*, citing a British publication, reported on how Chinese entities are funding terrorist groups to gain access to mineral reserves in Nigeria.[34] The newspaper has also published opinion pieces linking Chinese influence to a new type of colonialism.[35] In South Africa, an independent newspaper, *Daily Maverick*, also published articles critical of Chinese influence in the country. In a 2023 editorial, for instance, the authors described South Africa's relations with China as a "cheap date," and criticized the government for pursuing closer ties with China.[36]

Finally, the shadow of the West looms over Chinese image-making across the Global South. The latest Afrobarometer surveys on preferences

---

[31] Andrew McCormick, "Even if You Don't Think You Have a Relationship with China, China Has a Big Relationship with You," *Columbia Journalism Review*, June 20, 2019, www.cjr.org/special_report/china-foreign-journalists-oral-history.php.

[32] Herman Wasserman and Dani Madrid-Morales, "How Influential Are Chinese Media in Africa? An Audience Analysis in Kenya and South Africa," *International Journal of Communication* 12 (2018): 2212–2231.

[33] Freedom House has extensively documented cases of self-censorship triggered by Chinese influence around the world. See Sarah Cook, "Beijing's Global Media Influence 2022," *Freedom House*, 2022, https://freedomhouse.org/report/beijing-global-media-influence/2022/authoritarian-expansion-power-democratic-resilience.

[34] Samad Uthman, "Report: How Chinese Are Funding Terrorist Groups to Gain Access to Mineral Reserves in Nigeria," *The Cable*, April 15, 2023, www.thecable.ng/report-how-chinese-are-funding-terrorist-groups-to-gain-access-to-mineral-reserves-in-nigeria/.

[35] Benedict Peters, "Beware of China's New Colonialism," The Cable, May 19, 2019, www.thecable.ng/beware-of-chinas-new-colonialism/; Adeola Akinremi, "China's Weird Way with Africa," *The Cable*, April 21, 2020, www.thecable.ng/chinas-weird-way-with-africa/; Fredrick Nwabufo, "Nigeria's Abusive Marriage with China and Slave Agreements," *The Cable*, July 30, 2020, www.thecable.ng/nigerias-abusive-marriage-with-china-and-slave-agreements/.

[36] Greg Mills and Ray Hartley, "South Africa's Strange Obsession with China Is Proof that It's a Cheap Date," *Daily Maverick*, August 27, 2023, www.dailymaverick.co.za/article/2023-08-27-south-africas-strange-obsession-with-china-is-proof-that-its-a-cheap-date/.

for the United States versus China's developmental model (conducted in 2021), show that the United States still comes on top, though affinities toward China are increasing over the years.[37] In Southeast Asia, while the US favorability has dropped, 49.5 percent of respondents in a 2024 poll conducted by ISEAS-Yusof Ishak Institute said they would still pick the United States over China if they were "forced to align itself with one of the strategic rivals."[38] In Latin America, China has made major gains in countries such as Brazil and Argentina, but many citizens still have favorable views of the United States.[39] According to a 2021 Gallup poll, the United States, Canada, Germany, Spain, France, and the United Kingdom are the top five most desired destinations for millions of migrants in sub-Saharan Africa, Latin America, and parts of Asia.[40] The United States also ranked as the number one destination for international migrants in a 2024 World Migration Report.[41] Of course, these metrics may change if the US diplomacy and democracy continue to shrink under Trump's leadership. In a Pew public opinion survey published in June 2025, President Trump received largely negative ratings across twenty-four countries that participated in the polling, while ratings of the United States have declined in fifteen countries.[42] As of summer 2025, the US political trajectory is tumultuous and unpredictable, but regardless of its attractiveness, China is likely to still be evaluated through the comparative perspective of the United States (and the West at large).

Chinese public diplomacy also continues to draw on and reinvent Western ideals like democracy, as discussed in Chapter 6, but also to

---

[37] Thomas P. Sheehy and Joseph Asunka, "Countering China on the Continent: A Look at African Views," *United States Institute of Peace*, June 23, 2021, www.usip.org/publications/2021/06/countering-china-continent-look-african-views.

[38] David Hutt, "No, Southeast Asians Do Not Now Prefer China over the US," *Radio Free Asia*, April 20, 2024, www.rfa.org/english/commentaries/asean-usa-china-04202024093133.html.

[39] Laura Silver, Christine Huang, Laura Clancy, et al., "Comparing Views of the U.S. and China in 24 Countries," *Pew Research Center*, November 6, 2023, www.pewresearch.org/global/2023/11/06/comparing-views-of-the-us-and-china-in-24-countries/.

[40] Anita Pugliese and Julie Ray, "Nearly 900 Million Worldwide Wanted to Migrate in 2021," *Gallup*, January 24, 2023, https://news.gallup.com/poll/468218/nearly-900-million-worldwide-wanted-migrate-2021.aspx.

[41] "World Migration Report 2024," *IOM World Migration Report*. Bloomfield: United Nations Research Institute for Social Development, 2024, https://publications.iom.int/books/world-migration-report-2024.

[42] Richard Wike, Jacob Poushter, Laura Silver, and Janell Fetterolf, "U.S. Image Declines in Many Nations Amid Low Confidence in Trump," Pew Research Center, June 11, 2025, www.pewresearch.org/global/2025/06/11/us-image-declines-in-many-nations-amid-low-confidence-in-trump/.

engage with the West through the Global South. A recent empirical study of the roles that INGOs play in China's "going out" campaign by Farid and Li finds that INGOs offer a range of support to Chinese stakeholders, including tangible and symbolic resources, as China expands its developmental footprint.[43] Studies of China's Twitter diplomacy in Africa found that Chinese embassy and diplomat accounts often invoke the West (in a critical way) in their outreach to African audiences.[44] Though more empirical research is needed on the aspired destinations for Chinese soft power practitioners in other parts of the Global South, the fact that major country diplomacy remains the priority in China's diplomatic speeches suggests that there is still more prestige and professional reward associated with Western destinations (though it is worth nothing that major country diplomacy also includes Russia).

7.3 FUTURE RESEARCH DIRECTIONS

7.3.1 Cross-Regional Comparisons

While there are parallels in dynamics of China's outreach to and reception in Ethiopia with that in other parts of the Global South, we need more systematic empirical research and comparisons across the region to better grasp the consistencies and variations in China's image-making. Comparisons across political regime types, levels of economic interconnectedness, and cultural proximity would be especially enriching. The political regime comparison, such as that between China's image-making in more democratic versus authoritarian contexts, could reveal both whether and how the Chinese authorities cater their outreach to different political systems, as well as the varied forms of collaboration, negotiation, and contestation they may encounter. As for the former, some studies already showcase the divergent strategies Chinese actors take in their image-making and communication across political contexts. A recent detailed article by Hangwei Li and Yuan Wang, for instance, found that Chinese companies in Kenya, an African country with a pluralistic and relatively free media, had more robust public relations

---

[43] May Farid and Hui Li, "International NGOs as Intermediaries in China's 'Going Out' Strategy," *International Affairs* 97(6) (2021): 1945–62.

[44] Maria Repnikova and Keyu Alexander Chen, "Asymmetrical Discursive Competition: China–United States Digital Diplomacy in Africa." *International Communication Gazette* 85(1) (2023): 15–31. https://doi.org/10.1177/17480485221139460.

strategies compared to those in Ethiopia. In Ethiopia, they did not bother to develop their corporate communications toolkit as they operated in a less hostile media environment.[45] Iginio Gagliardone's insightful book-length comparative study of China's Internet infrastructure projects in Ghana, Rwanda, Ethiopia, and Kenya highlighted China's adaptability to African needs and political environments.[46] In more democratic Ghana and Kenya, the Chinese government and Chinese companies collaborated with private actors to develop a relatively decentralized ICT sector. Meanwhile, in Ethiopia, the Chinese worked with the national government to implement a centrally controlled ICT sector, displaying an ability to adapt to local, political conditions. As for negotiations and pushbacks to China, as mentioned in the previous section, in the context of media censorship, news outlets in more democratic African countries tend to self-censor their China reporting less in contrast to more cautious outlets and journalists in more autocratic media systems like Ethiopia. Civil society actors also tend to push back on Chinese initiatives more actively and publicly in democracies.[47]

Economic relationship variations in levels of investments from and trade with China may help delineate the extent to which China's commitment to image-making varies based on economic relevance of the recipient country. It would be interesting to determine, for instance, whether China picks the "star countries" for its image-making – that is, major economic and political partners. In conversations with officials and scholars in Beijing, they often pointed to this idea of prioritizing certain important countries that could in turn help influence other countries in the region. The extent of economic dependency on China may also shape the responses to China's image-making, especially toward diffusion of censorship.

45 Hangwei Li and Yuan Wang. "African Media Cultures and Chinese Public Relations Strategies in Kenya and Ethiopia," *Carnegie Endowment for International Peace*, February 27, 2023, https://carnegieendowment.org/research/2023/02/african-media-cultures-and-chinese-public-relations-strategies-in-kenya-and-ethiopia?lang=en.

46 Iginio Gagliardone, *China, Africa, and the Future of the Internet* (Zed: 2019).

47 For examples, see Isuma Mark, "Chinese Companies May Seize Nigerian Assets Over MOU with Enugu State, Group Warns," *The Whistler*, September 25, 2024, https://the whistler.ng/chinese-companies-may-seize-nigerian-assets-over-mou-with-enugu-state-group-warns/; Eric Olander, "While Ghana's Governing Elites Call for Deeper Economic Engagement with China, Civil Society Groups Fume," *China Global South Project*, May 3, 2021, https://chinaglobalsouth.com/2021/05/03/while-ghanas-governing-elites-call-for-deeper-economic-engagement-with-china-civil-society-groups-fume/.

The cultural proximity contrast, such as between China's outreach to Southeast Asia versus Africa, can showcase whether and how cultural closeness shapes the approaches and perspectives of Chinese and local stakeholders. In Southeast Asia, for instance, some studies show that Chinese diasporic communities have bolstered China's image, including by expanding economic and political networks for Chinese official stakeholders.[48] Some Chinese cultural exports like TV series and video games have also made their way into the Southeast Asian markets.[49] In Africa, Chinese migrant communities often operate as separately from official entities,[50] and Chinese popular culture still has a less extensive reach (though this might be changing, as I discuss further on).

7.3.2 Comparing China to Other Global South Influencers

Other than cross-case comparisons of China's image-making, studies that place China's efforts in juxtaposition to those of other major geopolitical actors, including Western countries like the United States, but also rising non-Western powers like Russia and Turkey, would help illuminate the distinctive, as well as the more generalizable, characteristics of China's image-making. In my limited research into the US soft power in Ethiopia and US policy discussions of China in Africa, I found that the US approach centers more on ideational persuasion, combined with some tangible enticement, and only occasional (more rarely deployed) censorial power. The in-person and online US diplomatic activities I observed in Ethiopia emphasized the attractiveness of American values and culture, from diversity to freedom of expression and democracy. In one in-person public event I attended at the embassy, an official from the Public Affairs section

---

[48] Na Ren and Hong Liu. "Southeast Asian Chinese Engage a Rising China: Business Associations, Institutionalised Transnationalism, and the Networked State," *Journal of Ethnic and Migration Studies* 48(4) (March 12, 2022): 873–93. https://doi.org/10.1080/1369183X.2021.1983952.

[49] Li Xuanmin and Hao Shuangyan, "Chinese TV Series 'Make Big Splash' in Southeast Asian Countries," *Global Times*, August 17, 2023, www.globaltimes.cn/page/202308/1296472.shtml; Lakeisha Leo, "China Power: C-drama Fever Sweeps Southeast Asia, with Shows Dominating Screens and Hearts," *CNA*, April 17, 2025, www.channelnewsasia.com/east-asia/china-c-dramas-soft-power-boom-southeast-asia-tourism-5056776; Tao Xing, "China's New Cultural Exports Reach Global Shores," *Beijing Review*, September 29, 2024, www.bjreview.com/China/202409/t20240929_800379043.html.

[50] Yan Hairong, Barry Sautman, and Yao Lu, "Chinese and 'Self-Segregation' in Africa," in Obert Hodzi (editor), *Chinese in Africa: 'Chineseness' and the Complexities of Identities*, 1st ed. (Routledge: 2020). https://doi.org/10.4324/9780367815714.

played "This is America" by Childish Gambino – a powerful commentary and critique on racism and violence faced by the Black community in America. The Public Affairs official noted to the Ethiopian youth in the audience that the ability to talk about these issues in America showcases an openness and willingness to evolve as a country. In this case, the pervasive racialization of American society was co-opted into the narrative of democracy and transparency, presented by a White man.

As part of the US training and elite visiting programs like the Yali fellowship and the International Visitor Leadership Program, selected participants get to walk the "corridors" of American democracy by visiting local state houses, as well as various political and civic institutions in Washington.[51] The social media account of US embassy in Ethiopia often features "model" American citizens – many of African and specifically Ethiopian origins. For example, on May 19, 2025, the embassy spotlighted Baalu Girma on its Twitter account.[52] Baalu is an Ethiopian journalist and novelist who received his training in the United States. The account described Girma as a visionary who spoke truth to power. Also, on June 2, 2025, the embassy focused on a Black American writer and journalist, Alex Haley.[53] The account praised Haley for his deep exploration of African-American history and identity.

The US elite diplomatic outreach also includes some tangible benefits like fellowships, internships, and college-application workshops, but as discussed in Chapters 3 and 6, these opportunities are significantly more competitive and scarce in comparison to Chinese offerings. In contrast to the Chinese embassy that tends to distribute fellowship "quota" to many Ethiopian institutions, the US embassy, except for some selective fellowships, tends to educate about American universities and delegate the effort to the applicants. At one such educational session I attended, an Ethiopian

[51] For more details on the IVLP, see International Visitor Leadership Program, US State Department, https://exchanges.state.gov/files/exchanges/ivlp_onepager_-_2025.pdf. Accessed on July 29, 2025.

For an account from an IVLP participant, see Ibrahim al-Tayeb, Photos: Al-Masry Al-Youm captures scenes from America's heartlands in a tour across several states, Egypt Independent, July 2, 2024, https://egyptindependent.com/photos-al-masry-al-youm-captures-scenes-from-americas-heartlands-in-a-tour-across-several-states/.

[52] U.S. Embassy Addis (@USEmbassyAddis). 2025. "This Monday, We Draw Inspiration from the Remarkable Life of Baalu Girma," X, May 19, 2025, https://x.com/USEmbassyAddis/status/1924372854436491406.

[53] U.S. Embassy Addis (@USEmbassyAddis). 2025. "#MondayInspiration: Alex Haley Was an American Writer, Journalist, and Producer Best Known for the Autobiography of Malcolm X," X, June 2, 2025, https://x.com/USEmbassyAddis/status/1929425247645937782.

embassy staff even cautioned Ethiopian participants not to write to the embassy with specific scholarship requests, but to do their own research and apply directly to universities. Though it is also worth noting that if we look at US public diplomacy more broadly, then until recently, humanitarian aid through USAID was a major component of it – an arena where China was less competitive.[54]

In contrast to Chinese routine use of censorial power, the US diplomacy includes cautious information management, such as via relationship building with local news outlets and press conference style information delivery, but there is more openness and space for spontaneous interactions, and more transparency about the US initiatives, according to Ethiopian interlocutors (something I also touched upon in the previous chapter).

When it comes to major rising powers like Russia in the Global South, the existing research, including my analysis of Russia's diplomacy in Ethiopia, suggests that they are using some similar strategies as China, but thus far their outreach is more circumscribed. Russia, for instance, offers tangible opportunities, as part of its diplomacy in Ethiopia, including selective scholarships, and more recently, content-sharing agreements with Sputnik, Russia's state-owned news agency (signed with ENA),[55] but the scale is nowhere close to China. The Russian embassy provides approximately thirty higher-education scholarships a year, and they must be cosponsored by the Ethiopian government.[56] Russian soft power practitioners shared that competition with China is unrealistic. In the words of a former Pushkin Center Director in Addis: "We all know that China is the leader here and acts as one."[57] Russia also engages in ideational outreach through varied mediums, but again, the persuasion is narrower – more focused on building nostalgic ties with Ethiopian Russian-speaking community. On one occasion, for instance, in the spring of 2019, I attended a World War II commemoration gathering at the Pushkin Cultural Center where the main guests were Ethiopian alumni of Soviet universities. They

[54] Samantha Custer, Bryan Burgess, and Narayani Sritharan. "Into the Breach: Will China Step Up as the U.S. Retreats from Global Development?" Williamsburg, VA: AidData at William & Mary, 2025. https://docs.aiddata.org/ad4/pdfs/Into_the_Breach.pdf.

[55] "Ethiopian, Russian News Agencies Sign Memorandum of Understanding," ENA, October 6, 2022, www.ena.et/web/eng/w/en_38875.

[56] Informal discussion at the Russian cultural centre (Pushkin) Addis Ababa, 2018.

[57] Informal discussion at the Russian cultural centre (Puskin), Addis Ababa, 2019. The comparisons with China as being more active and influential in Africa in terms of soft power were also presented in some academic studies. See Samuel Ramani, "Russia and China in Africa: Prospective Partners or Asymmetric Rivals?" South African Institute of International Affairs, 2021. www.jstor.org/stable/resrep38659.

were older, professionally established, and fluent in Russian. They were emotionally connected to Russian history and narratives, as some teared up at the sight of the military at the Red Square glaring on the big screen. There were noticeably almost no young people in this audience, and on most of my visits, Pushkin center was eerily quiet and empty. At the same time, it is important to consider that Russia may not be as invested in image-making as it is more committed to disrupting the reputation of the West through sophisticated disinformation campaigns, including in Africa.[58] According to the Africa Center for Strategic Studies, Russia is the single largest sponsor of disinformation campaigns in Africa. These campaigns typically consist of paying African influencers to parrot Russian-inspired narratives and the use of digital avatars to spread misleading information.[59] More systematic comparative research would help highlight whether these distinctions apply to the United States and Russia's image-making in other Global South contexts. Future research should also engage with other rising powers like Turkey, which has recently deployed its state-run media, such as TRT World, and cultural diplomacy through organizations like the Turkish Cooperation and Coordination Agency (TIKA) to foster connections in Africa, Latin America, and Asia.[60] Turkish state organs, such as TRT, TRT World, and the Anadolu Agency, have also initiated journalist training programs targeting media practitioners from the Middle East, Central Asia, Africa, and the Balkans.[61]

7.3.3 Non-state Image-Making

Finally, while this book focused primarily on state-led image-making efforts, non-state image-making deserves more attention, including how it may overlap with and contradict state-led initiatives. Whereas

---

[58] Rida Liammouri and Youssef Eddazi, "Russian Interference in Africa: Disinformation and Mercenaries," Policy Center for the New South Policy Brief, June 2020, www.policycenter.ma/sites/default/files/2021-01/PB_20-60_Lyammouri.pdf.

[59] "Mapping a Surge of Disinformation in Africa," *The Africa Center for Strategic Studies*, March 13, 2024, https://africacenter.org/spotlight/mapping-a-surge-of-disinformation-in-africa/.

[60] Yunus Turhan, "Turkey's Public Diplomacy: The Role of Turkish Non-governmental Organisations," *Diplomacy & Statecraft* 34(2) (April 3, 2023): 325–42. https://doi.org/10.1080/09592296.2023.2213078; Yeşil Bilge, *Talking Back to the West: How Turkey Uses Counter-Hegemony to Reshape the Global Communication Order.* The Geopolitics of Information (University of Illinois Press: 2024).

[61] Yeşil Bilge, *Talking Back to the West: How Turkey Uses Counter-Hegemony to Reshape the Global Communication Order.*

state-led efforts often target elites, non-state initiatives might have a broader societal reach. One important example of non-state image-making is ideational and tangible outreach via corporate social responsibility initiatives. In recent years, for instance, Chinese companies, such as Huawei and China Railway Construction Corporation (CRCC), have increased their investment in community outreach across the Global South, focusing on infrastructure projects, healthcare, and education.[62] Another productive research direction is the growing expansion of Chinese NGOs. While some of these are state-affiliated organizations, others are more informal, smaller-scale, and farther removed from the state. These Chinese NGOs often focus on issues such as environmental conservation, poverty alleviation, and education, contributing to China's state-directed image-making.[63] Ideational outreach via non-state entertainment channels and venues is also an important new research domain. On my last trip to Ethiopia (in the summer of 2023), a Chinese entrepreneur just launched a Chinese TV station that would largely broadcast film and show content. Platforms like StarTimes, a Chinese-owned digital TV service, also disseminate Chinese content widely across Africa, contributing to China's cultural diplomacy.[64] Chinese video games like Wukong and the animation film *Ne Zha 2*, drawing on Chinese ancient mythology, have recently bolstered China's cultural influence globally.[65] Specifically in Africa, in July 2025, the BBC has reported that Chinese mini-dramas are going viral.[66] Some Western news headlines even started to attribute

[62] For one example of such schemes, see "Huawei, Digital Economy Ministry Launch Scholarship Programme For Nigeria's ICT Talent Development," *Independent*, December 27, 2023, https://independent.ng/huawei-digital-economy-ministry-launch-scholarship-programme-for-nigerias-ict-talent-development/.

[63] Ying Wang, "Going Global: The International Endeavours of Chinese NGOs," *The People's Map of Global China*, June 1, 2021, https://thepeoplesmap.net/2021/06/01/going-global-the-international-endeavours-of-chinese-ngos/.

[64] "China's StarTimes Boosts Soft Power with Popular Shows and Football in Africa," *The Express Tribune*, September 4, 2024, https://tribune.com.pk/story/2493520/China%27s-StarTimes-boosts-soft-power-with-popular-shows-and-football-in-Africa.

[65] Ryan M. Allen, "'Black Myth: Wukong' Shows China's Cultural Soft Power Is No Myth," *The Diplomat*, August 23, 2024, https://thediplomat.com/2024/08/black-myth-wukong-shows-chinas-cultural-soft-power-is-no-myth/. Derrick Bryson Taylor, "'Ne Zha 2,' Blockbuster Chinese Animated Film, Will Get English Version," *The New York Times*, July 9, 2025, www.nytimes.com/2025/07/09/movies/ne-zha-2-english-us-theaters.html.

[66] For example, the BBC has reported on how Chinese mini-dramas are going viral in Africa. See The Chinese minidramas going viral in Africa and worldwide – BBC Africa, Youtube, accessed on July 31, 2025, www.youtube.com/watch?v=rSAMF11l20M.

"coolness" to China as result of these cultural exports.[67] How this cultural content appeals to local audiences, and what ideals and values it conveys, will be fascinating to examine.

7.4 IMPLICATIONS FOR WESTERN IMAGE-MAKING IN THE GLOBAL SOUTH

I conclude with some implications for Western policymakers in thinking about their diplomatic engagements with Africa and more broadly with the Global South. Specifically, the case of China highlights the importance of expanding the scale of tangible offerings in public diplomacy, sharpening ideational pull, and enhancing transparency-building initiatives. As for tangible offerings, the China–Ethiopia study clearly demonstrated China's centering of practical benefits in its diplomacy, and Ethiopians' engagement with them as filtered through a Western comparison. China was often not the first choice, but the only available choice (see Chapter 6). Expanding opportunities for scholarships, exchanges, and media resources would significantly increase the visibility and accessibility of the West to Global South publics, especially for elites who are still eager to engage with, learn from, and experience Western liberal democracies. In my conversations with US public diplomacy practitioners, there was generally an agreement that China is ahead of the United States in providing these tangible opportunities, but also often a sense of entitlement that "the right people" would still manage to access the United States. Such diplomatic vision is narrow and passive, and it makes the United States appear as more distant and less competitive than the more accessible China. As I'm writing the conclusion to this book, the US diplomacy appears to veer into the opposite direction of drastically thinning out tangible diplomatic benefits. Within the first six months, the Trump administration has shrunk the State Department, shut down USAID, and cut down on many CDC programs operating in Africa, among other radical transformations. My hope is that this direction is temporary and can be reversed in the years to come, but also that other Western governments, including European countries and Canada, can take advantage of the US decline and offer new competing benefits to African countries and publics. In some ways, this is already happening. For example, in March 2025, as

---

[67] "How China Became Cool," *The Economist*, May 20, 2025, www.economist.com/china/2025/05/20/how-china-became-cool.

the United States pulled aid from South Africa, the EU announced $5.1 billion in investments in the African country while agreeing to start discussions on new trade deals.[68] Also, in March 2025, Canada launched an Africa Strategy designed to promote "economic prosperity, security and fairness" for both Canadians and Africans.[69] While these are largely economic programs, they provide some assurance that, unlike the United States, both the EU and Canada are not actively pulling away from the continent.

Other than expanding the material reach of Western public diplomacy, it is timely to sharpen the ideational pull – in terms of both narratives and persuasion practices. The core narrative of the battle between democracies and autocracies (or the good versus evil) has dominated the US (and at times more broadly Western) diplomatic discourse in its competition with China. While this dramatic binary may serve the function of alerting policymakers about the importance of investing in public diplomacy,[70] it has a limited appeal to Global South audiences. The elites I spoke to in Ethiopia aspire to Western democratic standards but are also cynical of the United States as representing an idealized form of democracy, as they are aware of its democratic backsliding and routine support for autocratic regimes. This is especially the case in the current moment of the US domestic autocratic turn on display.

China's promotion of its own efficiency-based democratic vision further muddles the democratic-authoritarian contrast, especially for elites who traveled and experienced China (as discussed in Chapter 4). The United States and more broadly Western promotion of democracy would be more compelling if it incorporated acknowledgments of domestic democratic

---

[68] "EU Announces a $5 Billion Investment in South Africa as the Tariffs War with Trump Escalates," *Associated Press*, March 13, 2025, www.usnews.com/news/business/articles/2025-03-13/south-africa-eu-summit-centers-on-boosting-trade-and-diplomatic-ties-as-both-feel-trumps-impact.

[69] 'Canada Launches Its First Global Africa Strategy: A Partnership for Shared Prosperity and Security," *Government of Canada*, March 6, 2025, www.canada.ca/en/global-affairs/news/2025/03/canada-launches-its-first-global-africa-strategy-a-partnership-for-shared-prosperity-and-security.html.

[70] Competing with China is often used as a narrative to expand public diplomacy funding. For example, see David O. Shullman, "China Pairs Actions with Messaging in Latin America. The United States Should Do the Same," *Atlantic Council*, February 12, 2024, www.atlanticcouncil.org/in-depth-research-reports/issue-brief/china-pairs-actions-with-messaging-in-latin-america-the-united-states-should-do-the-same/; Joshua Eisenman, "China's Media Propaganda in Africa: A Strategic Assessment," *United States Institute of Peace*, March 16, 2023, www.usip.org/publications/2023/03/chinas-media-propaganda-africa-strategic-assessment.

struggles, as well as a clearer message about what a Western liberal democracy can accomplish in comparison to a China-style "democracy." For instance, the US political and economic system is arguably more adaptive to crises and allows for more creativity and entrepreneurship, and some Western liberal democracies have reacted to Trump's win by electing more progressive and left-leaning politicians.[71] In the moment of a large-scale authoritarian expansion across the globe,[72] simply asserting the superiority of democracy will not suffice. The narratives must delve into its resiliency and practical outputs for citizens and leaders still straddling the lines between democracy and autocracy. The ideational pull is also tied to more tangible investments in public diplomacy, as more exposure to the West and more accessibility to Western education system would deepen an understanding of liberal democratic values.

Considering the guarded information management of Chinese officials and companies, enhancing and highlighting transparency would also help distinguish and elevate Western stakeholders. While Western embassies, companies, and organizations tend to be more transparent in their operations in the Global South, Ethiopian journalists I interviewed shared that access to Western stakeholders can still be challenging, as they also tend to opt for public relations model of information diffusion (albeit a more open one than that practiced by China). These constraints are notable in research access as well. As I write in detail in my ethnographic reflection appendix I, when carrying out fieldwork on American Corners and other US public diplomacy instruments, I often faced suspicion and restrictions akin to those from Chinese entities. Rather than restrain access (to journalists and academics), US diplomatic bureaucracies should deliberately make themselves more visible, accessible, and interactive.

Western stakeholders can also provide more capacity building to Global South civil society and media to equip them with tools to better grapple with, investigate, and report on major initiatives from foreign partners, including (but not exclusive) to China.[73] In carrying out this

---

[71] Leyland Cecco, "Trump Wanted to Break Us," says Carney as Liberals triumph in Canadian election, *The Guardian*, April 25, 2025, www.theguardian.com/world/2025/apr/29/canada-election-result-liberal-win-mark-carney-anti-trump.

[72] See for instance "Freedom in the World 2025," Freedom House Report, https://freedomhouse.org/sites/default/files/2025-03/FITW_World2025digitalN.pdf.

[73] The Presidential Initiative for Democratic Renewal (PIDR) is a good example of this type of work (see "The Presidential Initiative for Democratic Renewal (PIDR) Fact Sheet," USAID, accessed on October 18, 2024, www.usaid.gov/democracy/pidr/factsheet/pidr-factsheet-2024).

capacity building work, Western organizations should include state-owned and state-affiliated media and civil society organizations. In my experience in Ethiopia, they were often excluded in favor of non-state actors, despite being influential and eager to engage. Providing funding for independent local knowledge production about China is also critical. In Ethiopia, I met many talented researchers who are eager to study China–Ethiopia relations but lack funding to pursue empirical work. Modest funding can go a long way in equipping them to collect data and build networks with other Africa–China researchers across the continent.

China's image-making efforts in the Global South are not going away. Instead, they are expanding and becoming more innovative, albeit still disjointed and only partially effective in building allegiances and sympathies on the ground. If the West takes competition with China in the Global South seriously, it needs to move beyond alarming rhetoric about China taking over the region and exporting authoritarianism. Instead, it should carve out a comprehensive and innovative diplomatic toolkit for offering a complimentary alternative to China in terms of practical gains, political and moral values, and transparent engagements. Despite the growing South–South synergies, the West still matters in the Global South. It should take advantage of its persisting relevance before it fades into a distant memory.

Studying China's Image-Making: Fieldwork Reflection and Guide

My journey toward China's "soft power" in Africa has followed a circuitous route. I first encountered this topic nearly fifteen years ago at a workshop I co-organized with Nicole Stremlau and Iginio Gagliardone at the University of Oxford, where I was a graduate student. We brought together participants from China, Africa, and Europe to discuss the modes, the scope and the implications of China's media engagements on the continent.[1] Chinese communication outreach to Africa was already expansive at that time – from Internet infrastructure investments to state media expansion and journalist trainings. Yet the outcomes were mixed. At this workshop I learned that China was more successful with material media projects than with discursive and symbolic engagements – something that in part still holds today as I showed in this book.

Nearly a decade later, after publishing my first book on China's domestic media politics, several journeys and conversations brought me back to the China–Africa encounter. In 2017–18, while doing fieldwork in Beijing on a smaller project on China's external propaganda, I again witnessed the importance of Africa in China's global diplomacy. The editors and journalists I spoke to from the Xinhua News Agency's External Propaganda Bureau (*duiwai xuanchuanbu*) invoked the continent as an experimental terrain for China's media and diplomatic influence. Theoretically, around the same time I also became intrigued with the emerging interdisciplinary approach to studying "Global China,"

---

[1] See the workshop report here: "China in Africa: A New Approach to Media Development?" The Programme in Comparative Media Law and Policy, University of Oxford, 2010, https://repository.upenn.edu/server/api/core/bitstreams/6e9f7de4-5963-43 01-86c1-fec88300e1b9/content.

pioneered by Ching Kwan Lee and her book on the varieties of Chinese capital in Zambia.[2] When I presented my *Media Politics in China* book at UCLA in 2017, CK was in the audience. Not surprisingly, she asked hard questions and at dinner probed my next research direction. Our conversation inspired me to pursue a Global China book on China's media and diplomatic engagements, and to carefully select a rich field site that could capture the variations of China's activities and reception toward them.

My specific turn toward Ethiopia and the larger topic of "image-making" emerged from initial exploratory fieldwork. In 2018, I was awarded an SSRC Transregional Junior Research Fellowship to study how the China "model" was promoted and appropriated in three authoritarian countries: Ethiopia, Russia, and Kazakhstan. This project focused on China's diplomacy and media narratives, with an emphasis on "China model" diffusion. My first trip was to Ethiopia where I was astounded by the scope of Chinese diplomatic influence that cuts across different governance sectors. I visited vibrant Confucius Institutes and Classrooms, met government and party officials who frequently traveled to China for trainings, attended China-led publicity events, and held seminars at universities about China, among other activities. It quickly became clear to me that Chinese media is not the main channel for shaping perceptions on the ground, and that focusing solely on the "China model" would be too narrow.

During this first trip, I was already struck by dynamic perceptions of China by Ethiopians. China was an easy conversation topic – everyone, from taxi drivers to hotel workers and government officials had something to say about it. "Oh, it's a China road," commented my driver on the way from the airport. "It looks good, but it floods in the summers," he added with some disgruntlement. When I complained about my TV turning on and off in the hotel room in the middle of the night, the hotel worker laughed and said: "It's a China TV," as if that automatically explains its unruliness. In more serious in-depth conversations, as I illustrated in earlier chapters, China was often treated with a mix of enthusiasm and caution, skepticism and engagement.

My first visit to Ethiopia in 2018 also coincided with a very exciting political moment in the country, as the young, popular politician at the time, Abiy Ahmed, became prime minister, promising democracy and the demise of tight grip on power by the Tigray-led political coalition.[3] This

---

[2] Lee, *The Specter of Global China.*

[3] Yohannes Gedamu, "The Many Promises of Prime Minister Abiy Ahmed," *The National Interest,* November 13, 2019, https://nationalinterest.org/blog/buzz/many-promises-prime-minister-abiy-ahmed-95836.

made access to Ethiopian institutions relatively smooth in the first stages of my research. Though I still made a field visit to Russia the following year to consider pursuing the comparison, I was pulled back toward Ethiopia where the richness and the contrasts of Chinese diplomatic influence were more pronounced, but also often puzzling and at times difficult to decipher. Having completed all my requirements for tenure, I prioritized depth over breadth and dug deeper into China in Ethiopia.

The actual fieldwork that proceeded over the course of multiple trips between 2018 and 2023, including a multi-month stay in China, was enriching, but also at times turbulent, stretching my ethnographic skills and testing my patience and imagination for what's possible. In this brief methodological essay, I discuss the challenges and opportunities of access to contextual data and records, as well as to Chinese, Ethiopian, and other stakeholders. I further offer some reflections about my identity – as a multinational researcher, but also as a woman navigating new field sites often dominated by men. I then turn to temporalities, and how I managed the dynamic, asynchronous pace of research, including the micro tensions of waiting, but also the more macro-level socioeconomic and political change. As the studies of soft power and public diplomacy (not exclusive to China) often prioritize a top-down approach of examining official and media narratives, this appendix offers an alternative empirical route. It may also serve as an additional guide to carrying out Global China research, inspired by the detailed and instructive methodological appendix that CK Lee included in her book on China in Zambia, but also by an ethnographic reflection in Andrea Pollio's book on China's tech entrepreneurship in Kenya.[4]

A.1 NAVIGATING ACCESS

A.1.1 Mapping the Contours of the Field

As with my past fieldwork in China and Russia, I traveled to Ethiopia (and later again to China) with a list of initial contacts that I gathered carefully with the help of colleagues and friends, including Ethiopian scholars with linkages to the United States. Johannes Gedamu, a graduate of Georgia State PhD program in political science, and a prolific commentator on Ethiopian politics, was especially helpful in making my first forays into the

---

[4] Andrea Pollio, *Silicon Elsewhere: Nairobi, Global China, and the Promise of Techno Capital* (University of California Press: 2026).

FIGURE AI.1 Author with Amharic teacher at Addis Ababa University.

field. As part of my preparation, I also read extensively on Ethiopian history and politics and started studying Amharic, which I continued to learn on-and-off with mixed results over the years, including at Addis Ababa University (see Figure AI.1 of me with my Amharic teacher). Unfortunately, I never reached the level of fluency to carry out interviews in Amharic, but my very beginner abilities to exchange greetings with Ethiopian interlocutors helped establish rapport. Since English language is prominent in Ethiopian higher education, many of my contacts spoke it fluently, but language barriers were still present – a limitation of my research that I mitigated in part with the help of research assistants who spoke multiple Ethiopian languages.

Throughout my visits I established affiliations with Addis Ababa University, first at the School of Journalism and later with the Department of Political Science – both of which provided official introduction letters and helped navigate Ethiopian bureaucracies, as well as connected me to wonderful research assistants and collaborators. In Beijing, where I conducted part of the research for this book, I received immense support from Chinese colleagues, including scholars at Beijing University and at the Communication University of China.

My mapping of the "field" proceeded alongside with reaching various participants in China's image-making engagements and observing different practices. Echoing Andrea Pollio's reflection on the fluid and experimental nature of his fieldwork on China's techno-optimism in Kenya,[5] my research also didn't take a linear shape but rather encompassed a collection of disparate, but interconnected elements of China's diplomacy on the ground. I started by charting the contours or the thick strokes of Chinese influence by focusing on several core diplomatic initiatives associated with Chinese soft power in Africa (i.e., elite trainings (and more broadly education diplomacy), Confucius Institutes, media diplomacy, public relations and strategic communication by state and state-affiliated actors). At the same time, I also stayed open to and curious about practices and strategies I spontaneously came across on the ground.

One of the first challenges I encountered was grasping the scope of Chinese initiatives due to limited record-keeping. In her ethnography appendix, CK Lee writes about her difficulties accessing reliable and systematic official records in Zambia. She describes her experience at the National Archive of Zambia, where no files were kept from 1980s onward, and the frustrating visits to government offices, where she witnessed "chaotic or, more often, nonexistent paper filing system."[6] In my research in Ethiopia, I experienced similar struggles. Public records were sparse if not nonexistent on both Ethiopian and Chinese sides.

In examining elite training and educational exchanges, for instance, the best record I could retrieve was from the Ministry of Finance – a simple table of approximate numbers of trainings given up to date across different government sectors in Ethiopia. It was not clear whether the table included all short-term exchanges and if it accounted for the fellowships offered or accepted or both. When I posed additional questions to the official in charge of China relations at the time, he didn't have further information and said that he got the table from the

---

[5] Ibid. He discusses his fluid and improvised fieldwork in a very instructive final chapter titled "Ethnographies of techno-optimism."

[6] Lee, *The Specter of Global China*, p. 170.

Chinese embassy. Chinese official statements tend to release the aggregate numbers of trainings for the continent (typically disclosed during FOCAC meetings) but rarely break them down by countries and sectors – this is in part because so many of these initiatives are carried out in a decentralized manner, with various institutions in China loosely keeping records.

The actual number of Confucius Classrooms is also not widely nor accurately publicized. Many Ethiopian officials I spoke to, including at the Ministry of Education, were learning about them for the first time from me. Accessing enrollment and graduation data was also complicated. During one of my trips, an administrator at the Addis Ababa University scribbled some general enrollment numbers for me on a piece of paper. During a follow-up trip, my research assistant struggled to access these numbers – they required more approvals from the higher-ups. I faced similar difficulties in other sectors, including Chinese infrastructure projects (especially the loan-free ones) and capacity building programs in Ethiopia (i.e., trainings that take place in-country).

I partially mitigated limited records by doing my own mapping from the ground-up. For training diplomacy, for instance, I visited most major government offices, media organizations, top universities, and think tanks and asked about their people-to-people engagements with China. In many cases, these institutions still couldn't provide specific numbers, but they gave me approximations and the departments that get prioritized for China trips. I was surprised to discover that even regional media outlets like the Oromia Television Network, as well as private media like The Reporter newspaper, received China invitations, in addition to state-owned media. This ground-up mapping is laborious, but important for grasping the scope of initiatives not captured in the sparse tables I received from the Ministry of Finance.

For information on Confucius Classrooms, I asked Chinese directors and volunteers at the two Confucius Institutes in Addis, as well as Ethiopian officials in different regions. In Oromia region, for instance, Chinese language was taught at a boarding school by Confucius Institute volunteers, but there was no official Confucius Classroom – something I learned during my visit to the Oromia Leadership Academy where several interlocutors closely tracked China activities in their region. I came across other important contextual information on Chinese diplomacy in similarly serendipitous ways. While interviewing journalists and editors at the *Ethiopian Herald*, a famous state-owned media outlet, for instance, some of them shared casually that Xinhua News has repeatedly placed an advert in their newspaper – something that the former Xinhua bureau chief in Addis neglected to mention. This insight led me to explore whether other major news outlets have established similar agreements. It turned out, The Reporter, a private outlet, had a placement agreement with *China Daily*. During a chat with a Confucius Institute volunteer in Addis, I also learned that CI volunteers deliver copies of the newspaper to top university leadership offices – again, an anticipated insight that emerged in an unrelated chat about Chinese language teachings. I learned about the extensive public relations exercises and the efforts to "guard" China's image that I discussed in Chapter 6 from Ethiopian communication professionals, including public relations officers and journalists.

Some of this context mapping transpired from physical observations of public spaces. Driving on Bole Road one day – a large Chinese-built road that leads all the way to the airport – I spotted a sign for China–Ethiopia Trade Fair and decided to attend (see Figure AI.2 of the sign). At the event, I met and talked to a range of high-ranking officials from Hunan province who sponsored the gathering and learned about the importance of China's provincial diplomacy in Ethiopia. In my routine visits to government offices, media outlets, hotels, sports centers, and universities, I also

FIGURE AI.2 Poster advertising China trade week in Ethiopia.

observed television screens and print media on public display. I noticed the rare appearance of Chinese media – CNN and Al Jazeera were more visible, as were Turkish TV dramas. I also rarely spotted Chinese print media, with an exception for hotels and some government offices. This taught me that the uptake in Chinese media is limited in comparison to its competitors, and that focusing on Chinese media narratives is less informative for my study.

*

A.2 ACCESSING THE INFORMANTS: TOP-DOWN, BOTTOM-UP, AND HORIZONTAL NETWORKING

As with most fieldwork, the actual conversations and engagements with different stakeholders in China's image-making project involved navigating various power dynamics: top-down, bottom-up, and horizontal. Initially, I assumed that distance from Beijing would make it more straightforward to access Chinese interlocutors, but it proved to be the bigger challenge. In securing access, I faced two possibilities: try my luck with the Chinese embassy or big bureaucracies like Hanban and Xinhua headquarters in Beijing or tackle the different outposts one-by-one without the prior high-level authorization. Going with the high-level approach is risky. If connections are strong, then many doors can quickly open, especially given the vertical power structures at most Chinese bureaucracies. At the same time, the higher-ups can shut down access by issuing a warning not to talk to a foreign researcher.

I decided to go for the more localized strategy but utilize my connections with Ethiopian contacts in high-level leadership positions to get the initial introductions. For instance, in studying Confucius Institutes and Classrooms, once I mapped out their locations, I traveled to most of them and engaged them through local university deans. This approach yielded mixed results. A US-based researcher showing up at relatively obscure sites like remote Confucius Classrooms drew a mix of curiosity and suspicion. Some Confucius Classroom directors welcomed me with warmth and enthusiasm, eager to hear more about my findings and how they can apply them, as well as to learn more about life and educational opportunities in the United States. One director in particular, whom I met in Jimma, kept asking me about what they could do better and spoke frankly about the limited resources they had on the ground.

Others found my presence puzzling and even threatening. I reflect more on my identity further in this piece. In cases of severe suspicion, high-level Ethiopian contacts were rarely able to help. During my second visit to a Confucius Classroom at Hawassa University in 2019, for instance, the Dean of the Humanities confidently led me there. When we arrived, the Chinese director recognized me from the year before, asked why I am back again, and then escorted the Ethiopian dean into the hallway. According to the dean, the Chinese director sternly warned him: "Don't make me talk to her! Don't make me talk to Americans!" He then walked out and slammed the door, clearly signaling that I am not welcome. Interestingly, this experience also illustrated the unequal power dynamics in Chinese diplomacy in Ethiopia – a Chinese director dared to tell off his Ethiopian colleague, a respected dean, not fearing repercussion. He was more concerned with his reputation with Chinese higher-ups. In other instances of difficult access, I was told to contact Hanban in Beijing and only come back when I have an official permission. I experienced similar inconsistencies with accessing Chinese state media personnel. In 2018 and 2019, a regional chief of Xinhua readily agreed to meet me, but in 2023, a new head was much more suspicious, asking to read my publications in advance. He was especially displeased when he learned that I spoke to some of his Ethiopian employees prior to getting his permission.

Despite these frictions, I still managed to gather rich data by largely avoiding the "top," and embracing serendipity. Even the unpleasant meeting with the Chinese director in Hawassa was not entirely fruitless. Once the director left, the Chinese volunteers gathered around me and spontaneously shared their stories. I kept looking at the clock on the wall, worried that the director might come up and still find me there, but the volunteers mentioned he is off to teach a class and continued to chat. The tense encounter with the Chinese director also brought me closer with the Ethiopian dean who was more eager to share his experience with me during my visit.

Other than grasping micro moments of opportunity during otherwise disappointing experiences, the advantage of multiyear fieldwork that proceeded in shorter-term increments – an approach that Günel and Watanabe described as "patchwork ethnography"[7] – was the possibility of witnessing personnel changes and getting another chance at gaining access. In 2023, for example, a new director of the same Confucius

---

[7] Gökçe Günel and Chika Watanabe, "Patchwork Ethnography," *American Ethnologist*, 51(1) (2024): 131–9.

Institute that refused access in 2019 welcomed me to his office and warmly introduced the workings of his institute. He came from a more academic background and spent nearly a decade teaching robotics and other subjects at the local university. In fact, I met him by chance when visiting the robotics showroom (funded by Luban workshop) where he did his trainings. He was surprised that I could speak Chinese and excited about the opportunity to talk about his experience in his language. I also managed to mitigate some access challenges in Ethiopia by tracing and engaging Chinese contacts in China. To my surprise, a lot of the Chinese stakeholders were more accessible in their own environment. In the summer of 2019, in Beijing, I interviewed Chinese experts and trainers, journalists, and CI directors and observed interesting Sino-African encounters.

In part due to the access difficulties with interviewing Chinese soft power practitioners, a larger proportion of my interviews and focus groups involved Ethiopian interlocutors. Learning about China through Ethiopia, for me, went beyond studying reception, but also grasping the workings of Chinese power, as in the case of censorship. This approach mirrors what Stern and O'Brien described as the "state reflected in society" approach or studying the Chinese state from the bottom-up.[8] In my case, I was often studying Chinese diplomacy through the lens of Ethiopian participants and observers.

In communicating with Ethiopian contacts, I learned that bottom-up and horizontal networks were just as important as vertical ones. Showing up at government offices and media outlets with just a letter of introduction brought unexpected results. I was at first suspicious of this strategy when one of my research assistants recommended just coming to major government offices and making an appointment with the secretary. I was used to relying on networks and relationships (*guanxi*) in doing research in China. The long waits at various offices, however, paid off, and sometimes I managed to meet with high-level officials without prior introductions. Of course, part of my success at access had to do with my foreigner, white female privilege – something I discuss further – but my research assistants also often secured meetings by surviving the arduous wait times in long grey corridors.

Horizontal networking through individuals of the same or similar rank and background was also productive. On several occasions, for instance, a journalist interviewee in a newsroom would quickly introduce me to

---

[8] Rachel E. Stern and Kevin J. O'Brien, "Politics at the Boundary: Mixed Signals and the Chinese State," *Modern China* 38(2) (2011): 174–98.

colleagues as potential future interviewees. At times they even jumped into conversations spontaneously if the interview took place on site. The most insightful conversations and interviews were focus groups with professionals from similar ranks and establishments discussing their challenges and opportunities in engaging with China. In this relatively equitable, open, and dynamic environment, I could gauge not just individual opinions but also debates, frictions, and the ways of making sense of China's presence.

As part of my fieldwork, I also endeavored to create horizontal networks of knowledge production and exchange by volunteering to deliver lectures on China and China's diplomacy in Africa to a range of audiences, including university faculty and students, government ministries, civil servant training academies, and influential think tanks. I delivered these talks across the country (see an example of a talk advertisement in Figure AI.3), encouraging questions, comments, and critiques. This research approach is in line with what Asiamah, Awal, and MacLean conceptualized as "collaborative methodologies," whereby research projects in the field are "(1) salient for those studied,

FIGURE AI.3 Poster advertising the author's public lecture at Oromia State University.

(2) informed by those studied, and (3) beneficial for those studied" (p. 549).[9] I can't claim direct benefits of my research, but the topic did attract large and engaged audiences and informed my study. During the Q&A discussions, Ethiopian participants often challenged my assumptions and arguments. At one talk, for instance, a think tank expert responded to my comment on China's material soft power as competitive vis-à-vis the US influence by noting that most Ethiopians he knows still aspire to American lifestyle and to moving to or studying in the United States. At another presentation, an Ethiopian government official noted that I omitted a discussion of Chinese censorship and asked me directly how such closed information and political system could lead the world. At some talks, my audiences also asked me poignant questions about China's motives in Africa and then raised more philosophical questions about whether China's involvement is a "win-win or a China-win," something I discussed in detail in Chapter 4.

A.3 NAVIGATING MULTILAYERED IDENTITY

A.3.1 Multinational and Racial Privilege and Limitations

As I already alluded to in this essay, throughout my fieldwork, the question of identity came up in direct and subtle ways. As a Russian-American, US-based, white female researcher and professor, my identities both privileged me and transpired in frictions and misunderstandings. Going back to those wait lines at government offices, at times I got quicker responses, with officials ushering me in front of others. Local researchers often commented that they would be unable to study China–Ethiopia relations in a way that I did because government officials and journalists would not treat them in as high of a regard. One Ethiopian-American scholar also emphasized my racial privilege. When I asked him about his access at local institutions, he grabbed my arm and pinched my skin, and then said something along the lines of: "I don't have this." That moment was a little unnerving, but still instructive of the hierarchies of privilege and power, and my place in them. My Whiteness and my Western belonging were likely entwined in how I was perceived in the field.

[9] Gildfred B. Asiamah, Mohammed S. Awal, and Lauren MacLean, "Collaboration for Designing, Conceptualizing, and (Possibly) Decolonizing Research in African Politics," Profession Symposium, American Political Science Association, July 2021.

My Russian roots often deepened the connection, as Russian culture and Russian government are very popular in Ethiopia. The Orthodox faith shared by both Russia and Ethiopia created an instant affinity (even though I don't claim to be religious and I'm also Jewish). I would also often hear statements like "I love Putin! He is a great leader!" or "Russia is a great country." These comments were emotionally hard to bear at times, especially during my visit in 2023, a year into Russia's invasion of Ukraine – something that my Ethiopian interlocutors often voiced support for. At times, I tried to explain my anti-war position, but often I chose to ignore or shift from this topic in order to maintain the focus on our research questions. My Russianness also fostered trust for my informants (both Ethiopian and Chinese) to discuss the United States more critically – I was seen as part of multiple places, with my loyalties not squarely set with America. I was also treated as a helpful insider on the US immigration experience – a topic of interest to both Chinese and Ethiopians.

It is also worth noting that perceptions of my identity in Ethiopia were at times comical and surprising. Outside of elite encounters, Ethiopian market vendors and street dwellers often called out to me as "China China!" China's ubiquitous presence means that all foreigners were often taken for Chinese – something that Miriam Driessen also discusses in her first book. "Much to my surprise, however, I was seen as Chinese by many young Ethiopians, despite my white skin and blonde hair," she writes.[10] For me, these associations with "Chineseness" gave me a broader context on China's influence and occasionally sparked spontaneous conversations about China and its presence in Ethiopia.

My identity privileges (namely, my Western background and affiliation), however, also came with high expectations and suspicions. As an American professor, during many site visits and interviews, I was asked for tangible resources – library books for a boarding school, PhD scholarships and training opportunities for government officials, and university agreements for civil servant academies. At times, I was pointedly asked broad questions like: "What can you do for us?" China's material enticement that I discussed in Chapter 3 has arguably conditioned my Ethiopian interlocutors to directly ask for support and to measure commitment and goodwill in material terms. To preempt these requests, I learned to say in Amharic that I am not a US embassy employee (*"Eneye ye America Embassye serategna ayedelehum"*). This only helped

---

[10] Miriam Driessen, *Tales of Hope, Tastes of Bitterness: Chinese Road Builders in Ethiopia* (Hong Kong University Press: 2019).

somewhat. After interviews and focus groups, I still received practical requests. In the spirit of collaborative research, I put together information packets about fellowships and scholarships in the United States for journalists and officials, shared the requirements for PhD acceptance at my university, answered many questions about studying in America, and directed my interviewees to resources and information sessions at the US embassy.

My Chinese interviewees and contacts also asked for information and proposed some whimsical plans about collaborations in the United States – from starting acupuncture clinics together to applying for research grants. One of my favorite lines from a Chinese media practitioner was: "When you get to a famous university, I will come study with you!" Coming to America wasn't enough, it must be a status-elevating experience. Both Ethiopians and Chinese expressed fascination with the United States (and the West more broadly) – something I discussed in detail in Chapter 6.

As for suspicions, in contrast to Andrea Pollio's description of himself as an outsider from what he describes as a "peripheral country" (Italy) privileging his access,[11] my outside position was inevitably entwined with geopolitical competition and hierarchies. "Why are you studying this? What is your motivation?" were the frequent questions from my Ethiopian audiences following my presentations. At times, the follow-up was whether I work for the US embassy. As an academic trained to give dispassionate explanations of the intellectual and scientific merits of my work, I was initially unprepared for such raw and direct questioning of my intentions. I reflected on how I would address these queries in my hotel room on stormy summer nights, and eventually went for a simple answer: "I am here to learn from you, to understand this complex relationship from all perspectives, I am here as a student, a researcher, not an official or a journalist, thank you for sharing your insights and questions with me." My acknowledgment of the question helped build connection with the audience, even if some chose to remain guarded.

On the Chinese side, as noted in the previous section, a US-based professor showing up at Chinese sites and events often triggered concern, as well as exclusion. In contrast to Miriam Driessen's experience of geopolitics rarely permeating her fieldwork on Chinese construction sites in Ethiopia,[12] international politics were often present, even if implicitly in my conversations and visits with Chinese

---

[11] Pollio, *Silicon Elsewhere*.
[12] Driessen, *Tales of Hope, Tastes of Bitterness: Chinese Road Builders in Ethiopia*.

soft power practitioners. This was also the case in doing research in China. While I had some luck tracing Chinese contacts and initiatives, I also struggled with entering Sino-African spaces. When I tried to attend China–Africa events and summits, I was often told that it is for Chinese and Africans only. Returning to the opening vignette of this book, my identity quickly became worrisome for Chinese officials.

These bilateral, exclusive knowledge production practices also transpired in digital spaces. During my China fieldwork in 2019, a friendly think tank expert in Beijing invited me to join a China–Africa WeChat group. I was excited about the possibility of learning and witnessing these online interactions, but my excitement was short-lived. The same day, I got another message from the same expert informing me that a co-organizer of the group, a famous Chinese professor, blocked the request, alluding to my nationality and professional affiliation. In other encounters, Chinese academic colleagues asked me directly: "Why don't you study China-Russia relations instead?" Given the deep-seated concerns with Western narratives about China in Africa that I discussed in Chapter 2, it is not surprising that a Western researcher would be deemed a threat. The close linkages between state interests and academic agendas in China also informed attitudes toward me, as my interlocutors often presumed that I am funded by the US government, and as such represent its interests. As with Ethiopian colleagues, I tried my best to explain the US academic system, to be transparent about my funding sources, and about my interests in studying this topic. Some, especially more academically inclined contacts, found this convincing. Others maintained distance.

My academic presentations on China–Africa relations to both Ethiopian and Chinese audiences often helped disarm these preexisting assumptions about my stance and motivations. "When I saw that an American professor is going to talk about China, I expected something very negative, but I was surprised that you were so balanced," shared a senior official at the Meles Zenawi civil servants training academy in Addis after I presented on China's approach to media development in the spring of 2018. I received similar remarks after my talks in China. Following my presentation on Chinese Confucius Institutes at a large Global South summit in Guangzhou in 2019, several Chinese academics and officials approached me with relief and appreciation. When they saw the topic of presentation and my affiliation, they anticipated a takedown of Confucius Institutes. What they heard instead was an empirical account of their opportunities and challenges in Ethiopia.

It is important to add here that learning about other major powers' engagement in Ethiopia and in Africa more broadly was also sensitive. The suspicion was not unique to Chinese and Ethiopian contacts. My interactions with US embassy personnel, for instance, were in part friendly, but also uneasy and restrictive. One diplomat directly asked about my Russian last name and how long I have been in the United States. Another US official working at the African Union was convinced that I was a spy and that my academic job is simply a cover for something more sinister. Others tested my loyalty by demanding a thesis of my research in advance. I had to explain to one pushy diplomat that qualitative, ethnographic research should not start with a thesis, and if it does, that would be a flawed research design. He shrugged and continued to respond vaguely to my questions. Most US officials insisted on speaking on background, even on seemingly innocuous topics like American Corners – modest study and educational spaces hosted by local libraries across the country (see an image of me lecturing at an American Corner in Figure AI.4).

FIGURE AI.4 Author giving a talk at American Corner in Ethiopia as part of her fieldwork on US soft power.

A.3.2 Navigating Gender Dynamics and Ambiguities

My gender also both facilitated and challenged my presence in the field. As a female researcher, I was deemed as less threatening, more approachable, and relatable to my informants. Conversations often shifted into a more personal terrain, and the power hierarchies seemed to temporarily melt away between us. The common associations of women with naivete also meant that my informants would overexplain things to me, which could help clarify context, but also slow down the interview and allow me to process and improvise further questions.

Conducting research with mostly male interlocutors in Ethiopia, however, was at times emotionally taxing. The lines between warmth and flirtation were often blurry, and I occasionally struggled to interpret and uphold them. Many men asked about my marriage and family status, bemused at the idea of an unmarried woman existing in the world. Some proposed to meet in more intimate spaces, like small restaurants in the evenings, or even hotel rooms and their homes. Others took it upon themselves to become my guardians and would text or call repeatedly to check on me. Sometimes the initial texts would follow with more flirtatious references. On one occasion, for instance, two hours after our interview meeting, a journalist wrote: "Are you fine, Maria?" He then called me "honey" in Amharic followed by a giant smiley emoji. "Do you know what this word means?" he asked, proud of his mischief. "Yes, it means honey." "Have you tried our local honey?" he continued with the innuendo. Sometimes even months after our meetings, the men would message and ask personal questions – most of which I ignored, but they still felt intrusive – a reminder of loose boundaries I experienced in the field.

In rare instances, I also felt unsafe. Following a haphazard interview with a well-known, boisterous Ethiopian journalist, he offered me a ride to my hotel, saying he was going in the same direction. I ended up in a car packed with four of his male friends, listening to loud provocative music. The journalist who drove the car at one point looked straight in the mirror at me and said that next time we should meet at a night club, and that he finds me quite attractive. Rationally, I knew that I should be safe, but emotionally, I felt uncertain and anxious until I finally saw the signs for my hotel. I never met this reporter again.

There were a lot more women among my Chinese interlocutors, including CI directors, volunteers, scholars, and diplomats, though gender dynamics still occasionally crept into my encounters. In one instance, I met with a male Chinese entrepreneur who was doing some media work in Ethiopia. I didn't anticipate this meeting to become a fancy dinner that he insisted on paying for. Throughout the meeting, he rarely touched upon my questions of interest and talked about dating and masculinity instead. In this case, I didn't feel in danger but certainly felt a sense of unease and anticipation for this encounter to be over.

My experiences with gender dynamics, of course, are not unique to China and Ethiopia. I have faced harsher research environments in Russia when I was much younger and less experienced. As a Fulbright Scholar studying Chinese labor migration to Russia in 2006–07, I traveled across the Sino-Russian border to trace Chinese communities there. In one memorable moment, driving across endless forests in the Russian Far East, my Russian male interlocutor who was bringing me to visit Chinese farming sites put his hand on my leg and wouldn't let go. The drive lasted about an hour but felt like a lifetime. He only released his hand when we got out of the car, and I started speaking Chinese – a skill he found useful for his own work as an NGO director dealing with Chinese labor. On the way back, he did not touch me, and we drove in silence. I never reflected on this in my writings or spoke about the incident with my advisors at the time.

As a more "seasoned" researcher, I tried to anticipate and plan out my interactions more thoroughly, meet in public spaces during the day, and mostly travel with my research assistants (who also happened to be male). I also befriended wonderful women in the field, including a brilliant PhD candidate at AAU political science department (the only female student in her department), Meseret, and an experienced professor and ethnographer, Meron – both shared their stories in managing gender relations, but also humor and warmth that soothed my journey.

That said, the subtleties of gender hierarchies and sexual harassment are hard to premeditate and are still little talked about in ethnographic reflections. In her recent article on this topic, Chevalier, an ethnographer of urban spaces, writes about the marginalization of this topic in the academic domain in part because discussions of positionality can put into question the validity of scholarly work.[13] In her earlier, poignant reflection about the traumatic experience of being raped by one of her fieldwork interlocutors, Mingwei Huang writes that some of her male colleagues questioned her motives for revealing this story, and whether it

---

[13] Danielle Chevalier, "Close Encounters with a Third Leg: Including Fieldwork Experiences of Sexual Harassment as Research Data," *Ethnography* (2025).

was a careerist move on her part.[14] This same colleague consoled her that her work is high quality, so she doesn't need to bring this story into light until later, as if publishing it would somehow eclipse her reputation. Huang also mentions the role of the institutional review boards in the inherent neglect of the vulnerability of the researcher, especially in studying sensitive contexts. The protection is overwhelmingly placed on the interviewees, even if they are not the ones in need of protection. The experiences I discussed here, of course, are not nearly as traumatic or disturbing as Huang's, but I hope my reflection adds to the growing conversation of the positionality of female researchers in the field and the often-invisible power dynamics and emotional labor associated with it.

A.4 NAVIGATING TEMPORALITIES: FROM MICRO-WAITS TO MACRO-TRIBULATIONS

My entry into the Ethiopian research context as a novice and my "patchwork" approach to data collection also meant grappling with distinct temporalities – slower and uncertain daily rhythms combined with macro-scale unpredictability. The contrast in pacing of life and research is something that CK Lee also writes about in her appendix about working in Zambia versus China. She compares the nearly twenty-four-hour fieldwork rush in China with more tempered work style in Zambia where interviewees were typically late and at times wouldn't show at all. I have experienced a similar contrast. Even Chinese interlocutors were more mercurial and harder to pin down in Ethiopia. Interview meetings proceeded, but often with delays. Some delays were also linked to infrastructure challenges. During big rainstorms in the summers, for instance, the roads quickly flooded and all movement across the city came to a halt.

When I shared my struggles to adjust to these slowdowns and what to me felt like "gaps" in fieldworks schedule, a dear friend who works across many cultural contexts, Filip Noubel, advised me to use such moments to read or to notice and speak to people around me. Instead of worrying about my next meeting, I embraced a longer lunch with calming sounds of rain around me. When I ate alone, I also looked around and started

---

[14] Mingwei Huang, "Vulnerable Observers: Notes on Fieldwork and Rape," *The Chronicle of Higher Education*, October 12, 2026, www.chronicle.com/article/vulnerable-observers -notes-on-fieldwork-and-rape/?resetPassword=true&email=mrepnikova%40gsu.edu &success=true&bc_nonce=7hs3xzri4p3oxbleoagztb.

conversations with strangers – often other faculty or students waiting out the rain over multiple tiny cups of *buna*. China quickly came up as a topic, with insights and arguments shared organically across the table. Like CK, I came to appreciate the slower pace. It left more time for spontaneous encounters, but also to observe, reflect, and feel through my experience, not solely collect and record the data (see Figure AI.5 of a spontaneous research break, eating watermelon with my research assistant, en route to Hawassa).

My research also faced some tribulations due to major macro events that affected both countries. Between 2020 and 2022, the world, starting with China, has witnessed COVID-19 pandemic. This event disrupted many people's lives, including my own. After intensive research in Beijing in 2019, I nearly secured an affiliation at the Chinese Academy of Social

FIGURE AI.5 Author with her research assistant, on the road trip to Hawassa.

Sciences (Africa unit) for the spring or summer of 2020 and planned to return to China for a follow-up visit and then spend more time in Ethiopia on my sabbatical. These plans, of course, were entirely shattered. I was locked away in Scotland and then Washington, DC, scrutinizing my existing data and living day-by-day like everyone else.

When I finally returned to my field sites in 2023, both countries have changed significantly. On my last field trip to Ethiopia in 2023, it was just emerging from a devastating two-year war between Ethiopia's federal forces and the Tigray People's Liberation Front (TPLF) in the north. According to reputable estimates, the war claimed 600,000 lives and displaced over three million people.[15] Both sides were accused of war crimes, though the former faced much harsher Western scrutiny of "ethnic cleansing," including mass rape and other war crimes.[16] During my visit, the atmosphere was more solemn and challenging for fieldwork. Though the war officially ended, ethnic conflicts still broke out in other places, and much of the country was deemed inaccessible for research. My Ethiopian colleagues spoke with fear of kidnappings, and even in Addis Ababa, the security atmosphere significantly deteriorated. I witnessed more police car checks during my trips across the city and was warned not to go out at night alone. Sharper ethnic divides also permeated my interview encounters. Some interlocutors asked me directly which ethnic group I support and why. Others inquired whether I'm learning any Ethiopian languages and then expressed offense at me choosing the official national language, Amharic, instead of Oromo – another Ethiopian language spoken by the largest ethnic group. Ethiopian Prime Minister Abiy descended from this group. The tensions and instability also affected China's presence in Ethiopia – something I discussed in earlier chapters, with many companies and individuals choosing to leave out of safety concerns.

In China, post-COVID-19, I found the research environment more politically sensitive. Foreign scholars and their sponsoring institutions faced more scrutiny in participation at conferences and conducting interviews. The Chinese scholars at the Social Sciences Academy who used to interact relatively freely in 2019 now talked about having to

---

[15] "Conflict in Ethiopia," Center for Preventive Action, Council on Foreign Relations, Updated on March 20, 2025, www.cfr.org/global-conflict-tracker/conflict/conflict-ethiopia.

[16] Alexis Okeowo, "Ethiopia's Agony: 'I have Never Seen This Kind of Cruelty in My Life," *The New York Times Magazine*, December 5, 2024, www.nytimes.com/2024/12/05/magazine/ethiopia-civil-war-crimes.html.

write reports about their meetings with foreign researchers. In a telling occurrence, when I asked an old contact about whether I can follow-up with some questions after reading a book she just gifted me, she looked at me directly and said: "It is best not to ask," and then quickly walked away. Of course, access still varies by institution and individual connections. Toward the end of my brief trip in 2023, I was invited to attend an interesting Global South conference. The timing didn't work out, but the invitation was still noteworthy.

As with any fieldwork experience, one faces a sense of constantly catching up with and trying to capture and document the latest shifts in the contexts we study. I was surprised and a little relieved to find that in Ethiopia, despite all the changes, China's diplomatic outreach bounced back in 2023, and the topic of China still resonated widely. As I am doing my final revisions of this book in August 2025, two years have already passed since my last field trip to Ethiopia and over a year since the last visit to China. "Isn't your book already outdated?" asked my sharp, ninety-seven-year-old grandmother on one of my recent calls with her. This book certainly does not claim to be "up to date," or compete with journalistic writings on timeliness, but that is not the point of academic research. There is a moment in data collection process when a researcher decides that it is time to make sense of things or to capture the "chaos." I hope my efforts accounted for the complexity and fluidity of the places I studied and did justice to the many people who trusted my process. I also hope more scholars will join me on the messy, delightful pursuit of fieldwork in studying Global China, "soft power," and Sino-African relations. In the high-speed age of automation, it is precisely this close-to-the ground, and dare I say, risky practice of learning and documenting human experiences that is especially valuable. It allows us to capture what's invisible in large-scale trends – the contradictions and negotiations that make up most encounters with power and that shape the uneven terrains of geopolitical change.

APPENDIX II

List of Interviews and Focus Groups[1]

ETHIOPIAN INTERVIEWEES

Journalists

ETJ01, February 26, 2019, journalist, Western media outlet

ETJ02, March 19, 2019, editor, *Ethiopian Herald*

ETJ03, March 19, 2019, editor, Ethiopian News Agency (ENA)

ETJ04, March 20, 2019, journalist, *Addis Zemen*

ETJ05, March 20, 2019, media management executive, Walta

ETJ06, March 20, 2019, journalist, Walta

ETJ07, March 20, 2019, editor, Walta

ETJ08, March 20, 2019, journalist, Walta

ETJ09, April 1, 2019, journalist, Reporter

ETJ10, April 2, 2019, editor, private media

ETJ11, April 9, 2019, editor, Ethiopian News Agency

ETJ12, May 10, 2019, editor, Ethiopian News Agency

ETJ13, May 10, 2019, senior media professional, Ethiopian News Agency

[1] While all the names are made anonymous per ethical standards, the anonymity levels vary depending on the interviewees' preferences. Some interviewees preferred not listing their news outlet or organization. In this case, I use generic references to a type of media or a type of organization. The author also draws on informal discussions and site visits, including during an exploratory fieldwork trip to Ethiopia in 2018. These are not included as formal interviews but occasionally introduced in the text. In addition to discussions, interviews and focus groups, the research also involved participant observation of various events, including author-led seminars. Many of the informal encounters and discussions in this book from these events are included in the chapters. They inform much of the analysis, especially the interactions with Chinese soft power practitioners.

ETJ14, May 10, 2019, journalist and editor at state media

ETJ15, June 22, 2019, journalist, Ethiopian News Agency

ETJ16, May 31, 2023, editor, state media

ETJ17, June 4, 2023, senior staff, Ethiopian Broadcasting Corporation

ETJ18, June 15, 2023, journalist, Ethiopian News Agency

ETJ19, June 16, 2023, producer, ETV

ETJ20, June 19, 2023, journalist and editor, Fana

ETJ21, June 19, 2023, journalists, Addis TV

ETJ22, June 20, 2023, journalist and editor, state media

ETJ23, June 20, 2023, journalist, Walta media

ETJ24, June 26, 2023, production staff, Oromia Media Network

ETJ25, June 26, 2023, editor, private newspaper

ETJ26, June 27, 2023, journalist, Oromo TV (part of Fana)

ETJ27, June 28, 2023, former private media journalist, now an independent reporter, Addis Ababa

ETJ28, June 29, 2023, editor, private newspaper, Addis Ababa

ETJ29, June 29, 2023, columnist, private newspaper, Addis Ababa

ETJ30, July 1, 2023, Ethiopian journalist working for Chinese state media

ETJ31, July 2, 2023, journalist, Oromia Network

ETJ32, July 13, 2023, veteran journalist and head of Ethiopia's journalist association

ETJ33, July 8, 2023, journalist with experience in several private media

ETJ34, July 14, 2023, journalist with extensive experience in private media

Party and Government Officials (Including Former Officials)

ETOF01, February 21, 2019, official, Foreign Affairs Ministry

ETOF02, February 21, 2019, official, Foreign Affairs Ministry

ETOF03, February 21, 2019, official, Meles Zenawi Academy (federal office)

ETOF04, February 24, 2019, official, Ministry of Women's Affairs

ETOF05, February 24, 2019, official, Ministry of Children's Affairs

ETOF06, February 26, 2019, official, Ministry of Education

ETOF07, February 26, 2019, high-level official, Meles Zenawi Academy

ETOF08, March 4, 2019, senior official at the Oromia Leadership Academy, Adama

ETOF09, March 10, 2019, official, Ethiopian Road Authority

ETOF10, March 18, 2019, former official, Communications Ministry

ETOF11, March 18, 2019, vice-head of a state-owned media

ETOF12, March 20, 2019, official, Railway Corporation

ETOF13, March 21, 2019, party official, EPRDF

ETOF14, March 27, 2019, official Meles Zenawi Academy (Mekelle)

ETOF15, April 10, 2019, official, Ministry of Finance, China–Ethiopia Development Office

ETOF16, April 15, 2019, official, Ministry of Agriculture

ETOF17, April 15, 2019, official, Ministry of Agriculture

ETOF18, April 16, 2019, official, Ministry of Culture

ETOF19, May 10, 2019, official, Ministry of Education

ETOF20, July 4, 2019, official, Ministry of Trade and Investment

ETOF21, July 31, 2019, diplomat, Ethiopian Embassy in Beijing

ETOF22, May 30, 2023, official and professor

ETOF23, May 31, 2023, official, the Ministry of Defense

ETOF24, June 8, 2023, official, Ministry of Education

ETOF25, June 20, 2023, official, Ethiopian Road Authority

ETOF26, June 31, 2023, public relations officer, Ministry of Planning Commission

ETOF27, July 3, 2023, Ethio-China Department Director, Ministry of Finance

ETOF28, July 3, 2023, public relations official, Ministry of Finance

ETOF29, July 3, 2023, public relations official, Ministry of Planning Commission

ETOF30, July 3, 2023, former official, Ethio-China Department, Ministry of Finance

ETOF31, July 4, 2023, General Director of the Ethiopian Technical University (TVETI)

ETOF32, July 4, 2023, senior official, Media Authority

ETOF33, July 5, 2023, public relations official, Investment Commission

ETOF34, July 6, 2023, official, Ministry of Labor and Skill

ETOF35, July 7, 2023, public relations official, Industrial Park Corporation

ETOF36, July 8, 2023, official, Mayor's office, Addis Ababa City Administration

ETOF37, July 14, 2023, official, Prosperity Party, International Relations department

ETOF38, July 18, 2023, former government official, now graduate student

ETOF39, July 19, 2023, official, Government Communication Service

University Administrators (Deans and Presidents)

ETUAD01, February 19, 2019, former dean, School of Journalism, Addis Ababa University

ETUAD02, February 24, 2019, former dean of Humanities, Addis Ababa University

ETUAD03, February 25, 2019, former dean of Humanities, Addis Ababa University

ETUAD04, February 25, 2019, former Jimma University president, founding director of Jimma University Confucius Institute

ETUAD05, February 29, 2019, former dean, Arba Minch University

ETUAD06, March 4, 2019, vice-principal, Adama Boarding School

ETUAD07, April 2, 2019, external relations official, Jimma University

ETUAD08, April 4, 2019, dean of Arts and Sciences, Jimma University

ETUAD09, May 10, 2019, dean, Hawassa University

ETUAD10, May 14, 2019, dean of Humanities, Addis Ababa University

ETUAD11, June 19, 2023, former dean of the Ethio-China College (founding director of Confucius Institute there)

ACADEMICS AND THINK TANK EXPERTS

ETEX01, March 9, 2019, former vice-president of Arba Minch University

ETEX02, March 26, 2019, professor, Mekelle University

ETEX03, March 27, 2019, professor, Mekelle University

ETEX04, June 1, 2023, think tank expert, Institute of Foreign Affairs

ETEX05, June 5, 2023, senior think tank expert, Institute of Foreign Affairs

ETEX06, June 20, 2023, think tank expert, Policy Institute

ETEX07, June 27, 2023, think tank director

ETEX08, July 4, 2023, expert and editor, Policy Institute, and Professor at AAU

ETEX09, July 7, 2023, independent scholar and NGO practitioner

Technical Experts

ETTCH01, engineering department expert, Ethiopian Road Authority,
   March 10, 2019
ETTCH02, design expert, Ethiopian Road Authority, March 10, 2019
ETTCH03, engineering consultant, Ethiopian Road Authority,
   March 10, 2019

Current and Former Confucius Institute/Classroom Students

CIST01, March 7, 2019, Confucius Institute graduate, now
   a translator for a Chinese company
CIST02, March 21, 2019, Confucius Classroom graduate, now
   a translator for a Chinese company
CIST03, March 29, 2019, Confucius Institute graduate, now a director
   of a Chinese language school
CIST04, April 10, 2019, Confucius Institute graduate, now a translator
CIST05, May 15, 2019, Confucius Classroom graduate, now
   a translator
CIST06, July 7, 2023, Confucius Classroom graduate, now a Chinese
   language teacher

Ethiopian Students (Current and Former) in China

ETST01, July 1, 2019, former engineering student and communica-
   tions officer for Ethiopian student organization
ETST02, July 10, 2019, post-doc in stem field, PhD graduate from
   a Chinese university
ETST03, July 13, 2019, recent graduate, a long-term resident in Beijing
ETST04, July 10, 2019, current international communication MA
   student and translator
ETST05, July 14, 2019, engineering Ma students

Focus Groups

Focus Groups with University Students (Social Science Majors)

ETSTFOC01, group discussion with five political science undergraduate students, Addis Ababa, June 12, 2023
ETSTFOC02, group discussion with five graduate students in political
   science, Addis Ababa, June 14, 2023

ETSTFOC03, group discussion with six undergraduate political science students, Addis Ababa, June 16, 2023

ETSTFOC04, group discussion with four undergraduate political science students, Addis Ababa, June 30, 2023

ETSTFOC05, group discussion with four graduate students in policy and security studies, Addis Ababa, July 7, 2023

ETSTFOC06, group discussion with five graduate students in social sciences, Addis Ababa, July 7, 2023

ETSTFOC07, group discussion with four first-year undergraduate students in social sciences, July 12, 2023

ETSTFOC08, group discussion with four first-year undergraduate students in social sciences, July 12, 2023

ETSTFOC09, group discussion with four undergraduate students in political science, July 13, 2023

ETHSTFOC10, group discussion with six MA students in political science (now government officials), July 17, 2023

ETHSTFOC11, group discussion with seven MA students in political science (now government officials), July 18, 2019

ETHSTFOC12, group discussion with four MA students in political science, Addis Ababa, June 5, 2023

Focus Groups with Confucius Classroom Students and Graduates (Now Translators at Chinese Companies)

ETCIFOC01, group discussion with three current CI students, March 1, 2019, Mekelle University

ETCIFOC02, group discussion with three former CI students, March 21, 2023, Addis Ababa

ETCIFOC3, group discussion with three current CI students, June 5, 2023, Addis Ababa

Focus Groups with Journalists (Three to Four Participants Each from Different State Media)

ETJFG01, March 18, 2019, state media journalists who participated in trainings in China

ETJFG02, March 19, 2019, state media journalists who participated in trainings in China

ETJFG03, June 14, 2023, senior journalist, journalist and editor, state media (two out of three trained in China)

CHINESE INTERVIEWEES

Journalists

CHJ01, June 23, 2019, former journalist for *China Daily*

CHJ02, July 30, 2019, former documentary producer in Nairobi

CHJ03, July 30, 2019, Xinhua international news editor

CHJ04, July 30, 2019, Xinhua News journalist

CHJ05, July 30, 2019, Xinhua News journalist

CHJ06, August 4, 2019, *China Daily* editor

CHJ07, August 7, 2019, former *China Daily* reporter and editor

Chinese Experts and Scholars Engaged in China–Africa Issues[2]

CHSC01, April 10, 2019, professor and expert in African studies

CHSC02, April 28, 2019, instructor and coordinator for the Ethiopia's Ministry of Agriculture

CHSC03, June 17, 2019, professor, Chinese Academy of Social Sciences (Shanghai branch)

CHSC04, July 9, 2019, China–Africa expert, the Chinese Academy of Social Sciences (Beijing branch)

CHSC05, July 9, China–Africa expert, the Chinese Academy of Social Sciences (Beijing branch)

CHSC06, July 15, 2019, China–Africa researcher, Tianjin Zhiye Daxue

CHSC07, July 15, 2019, China–Africa researcher, Tianjin Zhiye Daxue

CHSC08, July 17, 2019, China–Africa experts, China Institute of International Studies

CHSC09, July 26, 2019, communication professor

CHSC10, July 31, 2019, poverty alleviation expert (lectured to African visitors)

CHSC11, August 1, 2019, cultural studies and Confucius Institutes expert, works with African students, Jinan University

CHSC12, August 5, 2019, Chaoyang finance institute, expert on international relations

---

[2] The author also held discussions on China–Africa relations with faculty and students at Shanghai Shifan University, Fudan University, and Beijing University in June 2019.

Officials and Administrators Involved in Public Diplomacy in Africa

CHPD01, July 8, 2019, training management department official, Chinese Academy of Governance

CHPD02, July 13, 2019, diplomacy expert, Central Party School

CHPD03, August 10, 2019, Hanban official

Confucius Institute/Classroom Directors and Volunteers

CI01, March 4, 2019, CI volunteer, Adama Boarding School

CI02, April 4, 2019, Jimma Confucius Classroom director

CI03, April 4, 2019, Jimma Confucius Classroom teacher/volunteer

CI04, April 20, teacher/volunteer, Confucius Institute Addis Ababa

CI05, May 10, 2019, teacher/volunteer, Mekelle University

CI06, June 20, 2019 (Shanghai), former Confucius Institute director in Botswana

CI07, July 2019, former director of Addis Ababa CI (email interview)

CI08, June 21, 2019, former Chinese language volunteer at a boarding school in Adama

CI09, July 4, 2023, Director of TVETI Confucius Institute

Other (Non-official Actors)

CHNOF01, February 20, 2019, tourism company owner and manager

CHNOF02, April 20, 2019, agriculture expert and instructor with the Ministry of Agriculture in Ethiopia

CHNOF03, April 25, 2019, short-term employee UNESCO

CHNOF04, June 19, 2019, former translator and manager at a Chinese construction company in Congo

CHNOF05, July 5, 2023, entrepreneur and consultant

CHNOF06, July 7, 2023, entrepreneur

Author's Lectures and Seminars in Ethiopia[3]

2018

Confucius Classroom, Mekelle University
Civil Servants University

---

[3] These seminars were carried out as part of participatory and collaborative fieldwork methodology that I discuss in my ethnography appendix.

Meles Zenawi Academy (Addis)
American Corner, Bahir Dar

2019

Civil Servants University
China–Ethiopia Friendship Association
Oromo Leadership Academy
Foreign Affairs Ministry
Meles Zenawi Leadership Academy (Addis Ababa)
Mekelle University, political science department
American Corner, Jimma
Beijing University
Fudan University

2023

Institute of Foreign Affairs
Addis Ababa University, political science department
Oromia State University (transformed from Oromia Leadership
    Academy)
Boarding School (Adama)

Bibliography

"1984 nian, 6 yue, 4 ri, deng xiaoping zai zhongyang junwei kuoda huiyi shang" ("June 4, 1985 Deng Xiaoping at the Expanded Meeting of the Central Military Commission"). *People's Daily Online.* May 5, 2016. http://cpc.people.com.cn/BIG5/n1/2016/0505/c69113-28326613.html.

"2021 nian zhongguo waijiao: bingchi tianxia xionghuai, jianxing weiguo weimin" ("China's Diplomacy in 2021: Embracing a Global Vision and Serving the Nation and Its People"). The Ministry of Foreign Affairs of the People's Republic of China, December 20, 2021. www.fmprc.gov.cn/web/wjbzhd/202112/t20211220_10471837.shtml.

"A New State of Lending: Chinese Loans to Africa." *Global Development Policy Center Report,* September 18, 2023. www.bu.edu/gdp/2023/09/18/a-new-state-of-lending-chinese-loans-to-africa.

Adam, Lishan, Esubalew Alemneh, Andrew Partridge, and Nawal Omar. Internet Development in Ethiopia: High-Level Findings from the after Access Survey. *Research ICT Africa,* February 5, 2024. https://researchictafrica.net/research/internet-development-in-ethiopia-high-level-findings-from-the-after-access-survey/.

"African Nationals 'Mistreated, Evicted' in China over Coronavirus." *AlJazeera,* April 12, 2020. www.aljazeera.com/news/2020/4/12/african-nationals-mistreated-evicted-in-china-over-coronavirus.

"African Union Opens Chinese-Funded HQ in Ethiopia." *BBC,* January 28, 2012. www.bbc.com/news/world-africa-16770932.

Akinremi, Adeola. "China's Weird Way with Africa." *The Cable,* April 21, 2020. www.thecable.ng/chinas-weird-way-with-africa.

"Al-Masry Al-Youm Captures Scenes from America's Heartlands in a Tour across Several States." *Egypt Independent,* July 2, 2024. https://egyptindependent.com/photos-al-masry-al-youm-captures-scenes-from-americas-heartlands-in-a-tour-across-several-states.

Al-Waheidi, Majd, Reena Advani, and Michel Martin. "'You Can Now Die': The Human Cost of America's Foreign Aid Cuts in Africa." *NPR,* March 19, 2025. www.npr.org/2025/03/13/nx-s1-5316282/usaid-aid-funds-economy-africa.

Alden, Chris. "The Global South and Russia's Invasion of Ukraine." *LSE Public Policy Review* 3, no. 1 (2023): 1–8.

Allen-Ebrahimian, Bethany. "In Tanzania, Beijing Is Running a Training School for Authoritarianism." *Axios*, August 21, 2023. www.axios.com/2023/08/21/chinese-communist-party-training-school-africa.

Allen, Ryan M. "'Black Myth: Wukong' Shows China's Cultural Soft Power Is No Myth." *The Diplomat*, August 23, 2024. https://thediplomat.com/2024/08/black-myth-wukong-shows-chinas-cultural-soft-power-is-no-myth.

Ang, Yuen Yuen. *How China Escaped the Poverty Trap*. Cornell Studies in Political Economy. Ithaca: Cornell University Press, 2016.

Anthony, Ross. "China's R370bn 'Gift' Demands Scrutiny." *Mail and Guardian*, September 17, 2018. https://mg.co.za/article/2018-09-17-chinas-r370bn-gift-demands-scrutiny.

Asiamah, Gildfred B., Mohammed S. Awal, and Lauren MacLean. "Collaboration for Designing, Conceptualizing, and (Possibly) Decolonizing Research in African Politics." Professional Symposium, American Political Science Association, July 2021.

Bailard, Catie Snow. "China in Africa: An Analysis of the Effect of Chinese Media Expansion on African Public Opinion." *The International Journal of Press/Politics* 21, no. 4 (2016): 446–71. https://doi.org/10.1177/1940161216646733.

Bandara, Shelton Indika. "Asian Journalists Praise the New Development Drive in China." *China Daily*, August 30, 2018. www.chinadaily.com.cn/a/201808/30/WS5b87b116a310add14f388b64.html.

Baykurt, Burcu, and Victoria De Grazia, eds. *Soft-Power Internationalism: Competing for Cultural Influence in the 21st-Century Global Order*. New York: Columbia University Press, 2021.

Bell, Daniel. *The China Model: Political Meritocracy and the Limits of Democracy*. Princeton: Princeton University Press, 2015.

Benabdallah, Lina. *Shaping the Future of Power: Knowledge Production and Network-Building in China-Africa Relations*. Ann Arbor: University of Michigan Press, 2020.

Brautigam, Deborah. *Will Africa Feed China?* Oxford; New York: Oxford University Press, 2015.

— "A Critical Look at Chinese 'Debt-Trap Diplomacy': The Rise of a Meme." *Area Development and Policy* 5, no. 1 (January 2, 2020): 1–14. https://doi.org/10.1080/23792949.2019.1689828.

Brautigam, Deborah, and Meg Rithmire. "The Chinese 'Debt Trap' Is a Myth." *The Atlantic*, February 6, 2021. www.theatlantic.com/international/archive/2021/02/china-debt-trap-diplomacy/617953/.

Brazinsky, Gregg. *Winning the Third World: Sino-American Rivalry during the Cold War*. Chapel Hill: The University of North Carolina Press, 2017.

"Building a Stronger Democracy in Ethiopia." *US Embassy in Ethiopia*, June 25, 2021. https://et.usembassy.gov/building-a-stronger-democracy-in-ethiopia.

Burke, Jason. "'These Changes Are Unprecedented': How Abiy Is Upending Ethiopian Politics." *The Guardian*, July 8, 2018. www.theguardian.com/world/2018/jul/08/abiy-ahmed-upending-ethiopian-politics.

"Can Ethiopia Become a Manufacturing Powerhouse?" UNDP Working Paper Series, December 2023. www.undp.org/sites/g/files/zskgke326/files/2023-12/undp_ethiopia-_working_paper_series_4_2023_online_version_finanl.pdf.

"Canada Launches Its First Global Africa Strategy: A Partnership for Shared Prosperity and Security." *Government of Canada*, March 6, 2025. www.canada.ca/en/global-affairs /news/2025/03/canada-launches-its-rst-global-africa-strategy-a-partnership-for-shared -prosperity-and-security.html.

Carney, Richard W. *China's Chance to Lead: Acquiring Global Influence via Infrastructure Development and Digitalization*. Cambridge: Cambridge University Press, 2024.

Carrai, Maria Adele. "Is America Losing the Global South? Assessing the Dynamics of Sino-American Rivalry in Infrastructure Diplomacy." *Orbis* 67, no. 4 (2023): 524–43. https://doi.org/10.1016/j.orbis.2023.08.004.

Carrozza, Ilaria, and Lina Benabdallah. "South–South Knowledge Production and Hegemony: Searching for Africa in Chinese Theories of IR." *International Studies Review* 24, no. 1 (2022) . https://doi.org/10.1093/isr/viab063.

Cecco, Leyland. "'Trump Wanted to Break Us,' says Carney as Liberals Triumph in Canadian election." *The Guardian*, April 25, 2025. www.theguardian.com/world/2025/apr/29/canada-election-result-liberal-win-mark-carney-anti-trump.

Chadha, Kalyani, and Anandam Kavoori. "Media Imperialism Revisited: Some Findings from the Asian Case." *Media, Culture & Society* 22, no. 4 (2000): 415–32. https://doi.org/10.1177/016344300022004003.

Chan, Elaine. "China's Confucius Institutes Flourish in ASEAN after West's Freeze-out." *Nikkei Asia*, May 12, 2024. https://asia.nikkei.com/Business/Education/ China-s-Confucius-Institutes- ourish-in-ASEAN-after-West-s-freeze-out.

Cheng Weihua, Liu Aijun, and Dong Weichun. "Zhongguo jiaoyu yuanzhu feizhou xiangmu youxiaoxing yanjiu" ("Study of Effectiveness of China's Educational Aid Programs in Africa"). *Gaodeng Nongye Jiaoyu (Higher Agricultural Education)* no. 3 (2015): 29–32.

Cheung, Rachel. "China's Confucius Institutes Go South." *The Wire China*, October 1, 2023. www.thewirechina.com/2023/10/01/chinas-confucius-institutes-go-south/.

Chevalier, Danielle. "Close Encounters with a Third Leg: Including Fieldwork Experiences of Sexual Harassment as Research Data." *Ethnography*, April 11, 2025. https://doi.org/10.1177/14661381251332456.

"China: Democracy That Works." The State Council Information Office of the People's Republic of China, December 4, 2021. http://us.china-embassy.gov.cn/eng/zgyw/202112/t20211204_10462468.htm.

"China-Africa: Mutual Gains, Not One-Sided Aid." The State Council Information Office, September 7, 2023. http://english.scio.gov.cn/videos/2023-09/07/content_113357168.htm.

"China Built Dam Heralds End to Water Supply Challenges in Mauritius." *Ethiopian Herald*, October 19, 2018.

"China: Democracy That Works." The State Council Information Office of the People's Republic of China, December 4, 2024. https://web.archive.org/web/20211204023733/http://www.news.cn/english/2021-12/04/c_1310351231.htm.

"China in Africa: A New Approach to Media Development?" The Programme in Comparative Media Law and Policy, University of Oxford, 2010. https://reposi tory.upenn.edu/server/api/core/bitstreams/6e9f7de4-5963-4301-86c1-fec88300e1b9/content.

"China in Africa: The New Colonialism?" Hearing before the Subcommittee on Africa, Global Health, Global Human Rights, and International Organizations of the Committee on Foreign Affairs House, House of Representatives, March 7, 2018. www.govinfo.gov/content/pkg/CHRG-115hhrg28876/pdf/CHRG-115hhrg28876.pdf.

"China Remains Africa's Largest Trading Partner, Key Contributor to dev't: Officials." *Xinhua*, April 17, 2025. https://english.news.cn/20250417/2a10d6 dbda13437ba2370395076f24a0/c.html.

"China Says No Room for 'Western Values' in University Education." *The Guardian*, January 30, 2015. www.theguardian.com/world/2015/jan/30/china-says-no-room-for-western-values-in-university-education.

"China to Build \$100 Million TV, Radio Broadcast Station in Juba." *CGTN Africa*, June 15, 2023. https://africa.cgtn.com/china-to-build-100-million-tv-ra dio-broadcast- station-in-juba.

"China's StarTimes Boosts Soft Power with Popular Shows and Football in Africa." *The Express Tribune*, September 4, 2024. https://tribune.com.pk/stor y/2493520/China%27s-StarTimes-boosts-soft-power-with-popular-shows-an d-football-in-Africa.

"Chinese-Aided Project Transforms Heart of Ethiopia's Capital." *Xinhua*, August 12, 2021. www.xinhuanet.com/english/2021-08/12/c_1310123458 .htm.

"'Chinese Bridge': A Bridge for the World to China." *China Daily*, October 14, 2024. http://chinadaily.com.cn/a/202410/14/WS670ca87ba310f1265a1c7734 .html.

"Chinese-Built Industrial Parks Drive Ethiopia's Ambition in Manufacturing Sector, Job Creation." *Xinhuanet*, August 30, 2019. www.xinhuanet.com/english/2019-08/30/c_138351330.htm.

"Chinese FM Refutes 'Debt Trap' Allegation in China–Africa Cooperation." *People' s Daily*, January 6, 2022. http://en.people.cn/n3/2022/0107/c90000-9 942192.html.

"Chinese Medical Center Pledges Support to Ethiopia's Efforts to Become Regional Medical Tourism Hub." *Fana*, September 22, 2024. www.fanamc.com/english/chinese-medical-center-pledges-support-to-ethiopias-efforts-to-become-regional-medical-tourism-hub/.

"Conflict in Ethiopia." Center for Preventive Action, Council on Foreign Relations. March 20, 2025. www.cfr.org/global-conflict-tracker/conflict/conflict-ethiopia.

"Confucius Institutes in Africa Teach Chinese Outside Schools." *Haiwainet*, June 8, 2018. http://news.haiwainet.cn/n/2018/0608/c3541083-31330800.html?nojump=1.

"Confucius Institute's 'Chinese +' Model: Customized Chinese Vocational Training Courses for Local People." *People's Daily Overseas Edition*, October 19, 2018. http://chinaqw.com/hwjy/2018/10-19/205558.shtml.

Cook, Sarah. "Beijing's Global Media Influence 2022." *Freedom House*, accessed August 24, 2022. https://freedomhouse.org/report/beijing-global-media-influence/2022/authoritarian-expansion-power-democratic-resilience.

"Countering China in Africa." *The Economist*, May 20, 2022. www.economist.com/special-report/2022/05/20/countering-china-in-africa.

Cowen, Tyler. "Ethiopia Already Is the 'China of Africa'." *Bloomberg*, May 29, 2018. www.bloomberg.com/view/articles/2018-05-29/ethiopia-already-is-the-china-of-africa?embedded-checkout=true.

Cull, Nicholas. 'Public Diplomacy and the Road to Reputational Security: Analogue Lessons from US History for a Digital Age.' Background Research. Gates Forum I, November 2022.

Cunningham, Fiona S. *Under the Nuclear Shadow: China's Information-Age Weapons in International Security*. Princeton: Princeton University Press, 2025.

Custer, Samantha, Bryan Burgess, and Narayani Sritharan. "Into the Breach: Will China Step up as the U.S. Retreats from Global Development?" *AidData at William & Mary*, 2025. https://docs.aiddata.org/ad4/pdfs/Into_the_Breach.pdf.

Dahir, Abdi Latif. "China 'Gifted' the African Union a Headquarters Building and Then Allegedly Bugged It for State Secrets." *Quartz*, January 30, 2018. https://qz.com/africa/1192493/china-spied-on-african-union-headquarters-for-five-years.

— "China's Quiet Win: Outmaneuvering U.S. for Africa's Future Leaders." *New York Times*, June 7, 2025. www.nytimes.com/2025/06/07/world/africa/africa-universities-us-china-trump-visas.html.

Dai Changzheng. "Zhongguo tese daguo waijiao de neihan yu jiazhi" ("Connotation and Value of Major-Country Diplomacy with Chinese Characteristics"). *China's Diplomacy in the New Era*, April 29, 2022. http://cn.chinadiplomacy.org.cn/2022-04/29/content_78193494.shtml.

Daka, Tsegab Kebebew. "Understanding the Shift in Ethiopia's 'Developmental State' Trajectory: A Political Settlement Perspective." Master's Thesis, CERIS-ULB Diplomatic School of Brussels, January 2021. www.ceris.be/wp-content/uploads/2021/11/Understanding-the-Shift-in-Ethiopias-DS-trajectory.pdf.

"Data: Chinese Investment in Africa, 2003–2022." *China Africa Research Initiative*, accessed on August 28, 2025. www.sais-cari.org/chinese-investment-in-africa.

Datt, Angeli, and Emeka Umejei. "Nigeria: Beijing's Global Media In uence 2022 Country Report." *Freedom House*, accessed August 24, 2022. https://freedomhouse.org/country/ nigeria/beijings-global-media-in uence/2022#footnoteref68_at35brt.

"Defense High-Tech Hospital Receives $18mln Worth of Medical Equipment Assistance From China." *Fana News*, November 12, 2022. www.fanamc.com/english/defense-high-tech-hospital-receives-18mln-worth-of-medical-equipment-assistance-from-china/.

DeLisle, Jacques, and Avery Goldstein, eds. *China's Global Engagement: Cooperation, Competition, and Influence in the 21st Century*. Washington, DC: Brookings Institution Press, 2017.

Deng, Yong. *China's Struggle for Status: The Realignment of International Relations*. Cambridge, England; New York: Cambridge University Press, 2008.

Diamond, Larry, and Orville Schell (editors). "China's Influence & American Interests: Promoting Constructive Vigilance." *Report of the Working Group on Chinese Influence Activities in the United States*, Hoover Institution Press, 2019. www.hoover.org/research/chinas-influence-american-interests-promoting-constructive-vigilance.

DiCarlo, Jessica, and Meredith DeBoom. "Six Paths of Global China: A Genealogy of a Contested Geographical Imaginary." *Dialogues in Human Geography* (2025): 1–23. https://doi.org/10.1177/20438206251345563.

"Documentary on Chinese-Style Democracy Screened at Kenya Film Festival." *Xinhua*, April 22, 2024. https://english.news.cn/20240422/2c15cfcc06494cad ba99245bedb12678/c.html.

Doyle, Laura. "Inter-Imperiality: Dialectics in a Postcolonial World History." *Interventions* 16, no. 2 (March 4, 2014): 159–96. https://doi.org/10.1080/ 1369801X.2013.776244.

Driessen, Miriam. *Immunity on Trial: Ethiopian Courts, Chinese Corporations, and Contesations over Sovereignty*. Oakland: UC Press: 2026.

— "Migrating for the Bank: Housing and Chinese Labour Migration to Ethiopia." *The China Quarterly* 221 (2015): 143–60. https://doi.org/10.1017 /S030574101400157X.

— *Tales of Hope, Tastes of Bitterness: Chinese Road Builders in Ethiopia*. Hong Kong: HKU Press, 2019.

Dukalskis, Alexander. *Making the World Safe for Dictatorship*. New York: Oxford University Press, 2021.

Economy, Elizabeth. "Exporting the China Model." Council on Foreign Relations, March 13, 2020. www.uscc.gov/sites/default/files/testimonies/ USCCTestimony3-13-20%20(Elizabeth%20Economy)_justified.pdf.

Eisenman, Joshua. "China's Media Propaganda in Africa: A Strategic Assessment." US Institute of Peace, 2023. www.jstor.org/stable/resrep48506.

Eisenman, Joshua. "China's Relational Power in Africa: Beijing's 'new type of party-to-party relations.'" *Third World Quarterly* 44, no. 12 (2023): 2441-2461.

Ekström, Mats, and Göran Eriksson. "Press Conferences." In *The Routledge Handbook of Language and Politics*, edited by Ruth Wodak and Bernhard Forchtner. Routledge Handbooks in Linguistics. London: Routledge, 2017, 342–354.

Elusoji, Solomon. *Traveling with Big Brother: A Reporter's Junket across China*. Independently Published, 2019.

Emont, Jon. "How China Persuaded One Muslim Nation to Keep Silent on Xinjiang Camps." *The Wall Street Journal*, December 11, 2019. www.wsj.co m/articles/how-china- persuaded-one-muslim-nation-to-keep-silent-on-xin jiang-camps-11576090976.

Enehikhuere, Julius Idowu. *China in the Eyes of an African Journalist: Reports on New Strategies and Implementation of China-Africa Economic Cooperation*. Self-published: 2015.

"Ethiopia, China Enjoy Strong Cooperation on Human Resource Dev't: Officials." *Xinhua*, March 31, 2018. www.xinhuanet.com/english/2019-10/27 /c_138505711.htm.

"Ethiopia-China Ties Set for Further Boost: official." *Xinhua*, October 26, 2019. www.xinhuanet.com/english/2019-10/26/c_138503431.htm.

"Ethiopia." *Freedom House*, accessed on August 28, 2025. https://freedomhouse .org/country/ethiopia/freedom-world/2024.

"Ethiopian PM Inaugurates China-Supported Military Hospital." *Xinhua*, May 19, 2024. https://english.news.cn/20240519/158f522b50e7430c a08282135eb1b71a/c.html.

"Ethiopian, Russian News Agencies Sign Memorandum of Understanding." *ENA*, October 6, 2022. www.ena.et/web/eng/w/en_38875.

"Ethiopian Scholar Highlights Deepening China–Africa Ties in New Book." *Xinhua*, July 17, 2023. https://english.news.cn/20230716/cec63013e41947ccb f68285285dcdd14/c.html.

"EU Announces a \$5 Billion Investment in South Africa as the Tariffs War with Trump Escalates," *Associated Press*, March 13, 2025. www.usnews.com/news/ business/articles/2025-03-13/south-africa-eu-summit-centers-on-boosting-trad e-and-diplomatic-ties-as-both-feel-trumps-impact.

"Expert Hails Chinese Assistance to Bamboo Industry Dev't in East Africa." *Ethiopian News Agency*, December 13, 2019. www.ena.et/web/eng/w/ en_11286.

"Experts Commend China's Role in Advancing Quality Education in Africa." *Xinhua*, May 18, 2024. https://english.news.cn/20240518/822ed216d11 d49939704fc55301996b3/c.html.

"Experts Laud Effectiveness of Chinese Democracy, Governance." *Xinhua*, March 20, 2024. https://english.news.cn/20240320/50d27ecd4a63412b baebfb771d48cedf/c.html.

Fang, Kecheng, and Maria Repnikova. "The State-Preneurship Model of Digital Journalism Innovation: Cases from China." *The International Journal of Press/ Politics* 27, no. 2 (2022): 497–517. https://doi.org/10.1177/1940161221991779.

Farid, May, and Hui Li. "International NGOs as Intermediaries in China's 'Going Out' Strategy." *International Affairs* 97, no 6 (2021): 1945–62.

"Feature: China-Aided Science Museum Wins Hearts of Science-Enthusiast Ethiopians." *Xinhua*, November 19, 2022. https://english.news.cn/20221119/ 20306acce7ce4d0a90aed208c65311b3/c.html.

Feng Tianyu. "Ruanshili chuyi" ("On Soft Power"). *Wenhua Ruanshili Yanjiu (Studies on Cultural Soft Power)* 1, no. 1 (2016): 11–13. https://doi.org/10 .19468/j.cnki.2096-1987.2016.01.003.

Feng Weijiang. "Xinshidai zhongguo tese daguo waijiao: kexue neihan zhanlue buju yu shijian yaoqiu" ("On Major Country Diplomacy with Chinese Characteristics in a New Era: Vision, Planning, and Practice"). *Guoji Zhanwang (Global Review)* 10, no. 3 (2018): 13–28.

"Forum on China-Africa Cooperation: Beijing Action Plan (2025–2027)." *Ministry of Foreign Affairs: The People's Republic of China*, September 5, 2024. www.mfa.gov.cn/eng/xw/zyxw/202409/t20240905_11485719.html.

Fourie, Elsje. "China's Example for Meles' Ethiopia: When Development 'Models Land'." *The Journal of Modern African Studies* 53, no. 3 (2015): 289–316. https://doi.org/10.1017/S0022278X15000397.

Franceschini, Ivan, and Nicholas Loubere. *Global China as Method.* 1st ed. Cambridge: Cambridge University Press, 2022. https://doi.org/10.1017/9781108999472.

Fravel, M. Taylor. *Active Defense: China's Military Strategy since 1949.* Princeton: Princeton University Press, 2019.

"Freedom in the World 2024: Ethiopia." *Freedom House.* Accessed on August 16, 2025. https://freedomhouse.org/country/ethiopia/freedom-world/2024.

"Freedom in the World 2025." *Freedom House Report.* https://freedomhouse.org/sites/default/les/2025-03/FITW_World2025digitalN.pdf.

French, Howard. "Why Ukraine Is Not a Priority for the Global South." *Foreign Policy*, September 19, 2023. https://foreignpolicy.com/2023/09/19/unga-ukraine-zelensky-speech-russia-global-south-support.

"Full Text of Chinese President Xi Jinping's Speech at Opening Ceremony of 2018 FOCAC Beijing Summit." *Xinhua*, September 3, 2018, www.xinhuanet.com/english/2018-09/03/c_129946189.htm.

"Full Text of Xi Jinping's Keynote Speech at 3rd Belt and Road Forum for Int'l Cooperation." *Xinhua*, October 18, 2023. https://english.news.cn/20231018/7bfc16ac51d443c6a7a00ce25c972104/c.html.

"Full Text: Action Plan on the Belt and Road Initiative." *The State Council*, March 30, 2015. https://english.www.gov.cn/archive/publications/2015/03/30/content_281475080249035.htm.

"Full Text: Keynote Address by Chinese President Xi Jinping at Opening Ceremony of 2024 FOCAC Summit." *China Daily*, September 5, 2024. www.chinadaily.com.cn/a/202409/05/WS66d95a04a3108f29c1fca5c0.html.

Fuller, Hacrourt. *Building the Ghanaian Nation-State: Kwame Nkrumah's Symbolic Nationalism.* New York: Palgrave Macmillan, 2014.

Gagliardone, Iginio. *China, Africa, and the Future of the Internet.* London: Zed Press, 2019.

Gagliardone, Iginio, and Nyíri Pál. "Freer but Not Free Enough? Chinese Journalists Finding Their Feet in Africa." *Journalism* 18, no. 8 (2017): 1049–63.

Gamso, Jonas. "Is China Worsening the Developing World's Environmental Crisis?" *The Conversation*, August 22, 2018. https://theconversation.com/is-china-worsening-the-developing-worlds-environmental-crisis-100284.

Gebrekidan, Fikru. "From Adwa to OAU: Ethiopia and the Politics of Pan-Africanism, 1896–1963." *International Journal of Ethiopian Studies* 6 no. 1/2 (2012): 71–86.

Gedamu, Yohannes. "The Many Promises of Prime Minister Abiy Ahmed." *The National Interest*, November 13, 2019. https://nationalinterest.org/blog/buzz/many-promises-prime-minister-abiy-ahmed-95836.

Gedeon, Joseph. "Trump Administration Orders US Embassies to Stop Student Visa Interviews." *The Guardian*, May 27, 2025. www.theguardian.com/us-news/2025/may/27/international-student-visa-trump.

Ghai, Yash Pal. "Is Kenya a Beneficiary or Victim of Chinese Belt and Road Initiative?" *The Star*, April 28, 2019. www.the-star.co.ke/siasa/2019-04-28-is-kenya-a-beneficiary-or-victim-of-chinese-belt-and-road-initiative.

Girard, Bonnie. "The Rise and Fall of Confucius Institutes in the US." *The Diplomat*, November 28, 2023. https://thediplomat.com/2023/11/the-rise-and-fall-of-confucius-institutes-in-the-us.

Glasius, Marlies. "Extraterritorial Authoritarian Practices: A Framework." *Globalizations* 15, no. 2 (February 23, 2018): 179–97. https://doi.org/10.1080/14747731.2017.1403781.

Guan, Hai, and Wei Lu. "'Low-Level Red'" and Other Concerns." MCLC Resource Center, Ohio State University, March 18, 2019. https://u.osu.edu/mclc/2019/03/18/low-level-red-and-other-concerns.

Günel, Gökçe, and Chika Watanabe. "Patchwork Ethnography." *American Ethnologist* 51, no. 1 (2024): 131–9. https://doi.org/10.1111/amet.13243.

Guo Hongwei. "Zou heping fazhan daolu: zhongguoshi xiandaihua daguo waijiao de hexin luoji" ("Pursuing a Path of Peaceful Development: The Core Logic of Great Power Diplomacy with Chinese Characteristics"). *Lilun Yanjiu (Theoretical Research)* no. 1 (2024): 7–14.

Guo, Yan, Shibao Guo, Lorin Yochim, and Xiaoli Liu. "Internationalization of Chinese Higher Education: Is It Westernization?" *Journal of Studies in International Education* 26, no. 4 (2022): 436–53. https://doi.org/10.1177/10283153211990745.

Hackenesch, Christine, and Julia Bader. "The Struggle for Minds and Influence: The Chinese Communist Party's Global Outreach." *International Studies Quarterly* 64, no. 3 (September 1, 2020): 723–33. https://doi.org/10.1093/isq/sqaa028.

Hairong, Yan, and Barry Sautman. "Chasing Ghosts: Rumours and Representations of the Export of Chinese Convict Labour to Developing Countries." *The China Quarterly* 210 (2012): 398–418. https://doi.org/10.1017/S0305741012000422.

— "China, Ethiopia and the Significance of the Belt and Road Initiative." *The China Quarterly* 257 (2024): 222–47. https://doi.org/10.1017/S0305741023000966.

Han, BC, and Camille Elemia. "Philippines: Beijing's Global Media Influence 2022 Country Report." *Freedom House*, accessed on August 24, 2022. https://freedomhouse.org/country/philippines/beijings-global-media-inuence/2022#footnoteref49_k51uwmz.

Han, BC, and Sascha Hannig. "Chile: Beijing's Global Media Influence 2022 Country Report." *Freedom House*, accessed on August 24, 2022. https://freedomhouse.org/country/chile/beijings-global-media-inuence/2022#footnoteref62_ioud9gc.

"How China Became Cool." *The Economist*, May 20, 2025. www.economist.com/china/2025/05/20/how-china-became-cool.

"Hu jintao zai quanguo xuanchuan sixiang gongzuo huiyi shang fabiao zhongyao jianghua" ("Hu Jintao Delivers Important Speech at the National Propaganda Thought Work Meeting"). *Sina News*, December 9, 2003. https://news.sina.com.cn/o/2003-12-09/21411299177s.shtml.

"Hu jintao guanyu wenhua jianshe he wenhua tizhi gaige de zhongda lilun guandian" ("Hu Jintao's Major Theoretical Views on Cultural Development and Cultural System Reform"). *China Daily*, October 21, 2011. www .chinadaily.com.cn/dfpd/17jlzqh/2011-10/21/content_13949506_2.htm.

"Huawei, Digital Economy Ministry Launch Scholarship Programme for Nigeria's ICT Talent Development." *Independent*, December 27, 2023. http s://independent.ng/huawei-digital-economy-ministry-launch-scholarship-pro gramme-for-nigerias-ict-talent-development.

Hao Yuanyuan, and Shuang Chuanxue. "Renlei mingyun gongtongti shiyu xia de guojia wenhua ruanshili jianshe" ("National Cultural Soft Power Construction from the Perspective of Shared Destiny of the Mankind"). *Zhongguo Tese Shehui Zhuyi Yanjiu (Study of Socialism with Chinese Characteristics)* no. 6 (2017): 65–71.

Haugen, Heidi Østbø. "Nigerians in China: A Second State of Immobility." *International Migration* 50, no. 2 (2012): 65–80. https://doi.org/10.1111/j .1468-2435.2011.00713.x.

He Wenping. "Tuidao gaoqiang lun zhongfei guanxi zhong de ruanshili jianshe" ("To Pull down the Wall: Building Soft Power in China–African Relations"). *Xiya Feizhou (West Asia and Africa)* no. 7 (2009): 5–12, 79.

Heilmann, Sebastian. "Policy Experimentation in China's Economic Rise." *Studies in Comparative International Development* 43, no. 1 (2008): 1–26. https://doi.org/10.1007/s12116-007-9014-4.

Heine, Jorge. "International Reaction to Gaza Siege Has Exposed the Growing Rift between the West and the Global South." *The Conversation*, November 8, 2023. https://theconversation.com/international-reaction-to-gaza-siege-has-exposed-the-growing-rift-between-the-west-and-the-global-south-216938.

Hellyer, H. A. "The West Is Losing the Global South over Gaza." *Time Magazine*, November 3, 2023. https://time.com/6330746/global-south-ukraine-israel-gaza.

Ho, Selina. "Infrastructure and Chinese Power." *International Affairs* 96, no. 6 (2020): 1461–85. https://doi.org/10.1093/ia/iiaa171.

Ho, Selina, and Terence Lee. "Elite Perceptions of a China-Led Regional Order in Southeast Asia." *Journal of Current Southeast Asian Affairs* 44, no. 1 (2025): 148–73. https://doi.org/10.1177/18681034241294093.

Hogan, Erica, and Stewart Patrick, "A Closer Look at the Global South." Carnegie Endowment for International Peace, May 20, 2024. https://carnegieendowment .org/research/2024/05/global-south-colonialism-imperialism?lang=en.

Hu Dengquan, and Liping Wang. "Feizhou kongzi xueyuan yanjiu shuping 2006–2019 nian" ("Review of Chinese Research on Confucius Institutes in Africa (2006–2019)"). *Zhongguo Feizhou Xuekan (China-Africa Studies)*, 2 no. 1 (2021): 134–53.

Hu Jian. "'Yidai yilu' yu zhongguo ruanshili de tisheng" ("'Belt and Road' and the Improvement of Chinese Soft Power"). *Shehui Kexue (Social Sciences)* no. 3 (2020): 3–18.

"Hu jintao guanyu wenhua jianshe he wenhua tizhi gaige de zhongda lilun guandian" ("Hu Jintao's Major Theoretical Views on Cultural Development and Cultural System Reform"). *China Daily*. October 21, 2011. www .chinadaily.com.cn/dfpd/17jlzqh/2011-10/21/content_13949506_2.htm.

"Hu jintao zai quanguo xuanchuan sixiang gongzuo huiyi shang fabiao zhongyao jianghua" ("Hu Jintao Delivers Important Speech at the National Propaganda Thought Work Meeting"). *Sina News*. December 9, 2003. https://news.sina.com.cn/o/2003-12-09/214112991773s.shtml.

Hu Nan. "Zhongguo dui feizhou ruanshili yanjiu: zhanlue fenxi yu duice jianyi" ("On China's Soft Power in Africa: Strategic Analysis and Policy Recommendations"). Changchun Shiwei Dangxiao Xuebao (*Journal of the Party School of CCP Changchun Municipal Committee*) no. 4 (2011): 67–71.

Hu Zongshan. "Zhongguo guoji huayuquan chuyi" ("On China's International Discourse Power: Realistic Challenges and Ability's Enhancement"). *Shehui Zhuyi Yanjiu (Socialism Studies)* no. 5 (2014): 127–35.

Huang, Mingwei. *Reconfiguring Racial Capitalism: South Africa in the Chinese Century*. Durham: Duke University Press, 2024.

— "Vulnerable Observers: Notes on Fieldwork and Rape." *The Chronicle of Higher Education*. October 12, 2016; www.chronicle.com/article/vulnerable-observers-notes-on-fieldwork-and-rape/?resetPassword=true&email=mrepnikova%40gsu.edu&success=true&bc_nonce=7hs3xzri4p30xbleoagztb.

Hubbert, Jennifer Ann. *China in the World: An Anthropology of Confucius Institutes, Soft Power, and Globalization*. Honolulu: University of Hawai'i Press, 2020.

Hutt, David. "No, Southeast Asians Do Not Now Prefer China over the US." *Radio Free Asia*, April 20, 2024. www.rfa.org/english/commentaries/asean-usa-china-04202024093133.html.

"Interview: China Plays Rising Role in Ethiopia's Renewable Energy dev't: Official." *Xinhua*, April 14, 2022. https://english.news.cn/20220413/a0eeb850d65c44edb2006a44dcb1a32e/c.html

"Interview: Ethiopia-China Relations a Good Example of Cooperation – Official." *Xinhua*, October 23, 2020. https://govt.chinadaily.com.cn/s/202010/23/WS5f924e15498eaba5051bc12c/interview-ethiopia-china-relations-a-good-example-of-cooperation-official.html.

Jardine, Bradley, and Edward Lemon. *Backlash: China's Struggle for Influence in Central Asia*. Oxford, New York: Oxford University Press, 2025.

"Jiaqiang guoji chuanbo nengli jianshe, cujin wenming jiaoliu hujian" ("Strengthen International Communication Capability, Promote Mutual Learning and Exchange among Civilizations"). *Xinhua*, December 27, 2023. www.xinhuanet.com/politics/20231227/c21a7e5c88404d1cb86a4515b5da5815/c.html.

Jiang Changjian. "Bodong zhong de ruanshili yu xin gonggong waijiao" ("Soft Power and New Public Diplomacy amid Changes"). *Xiandai Chuanbo (Zhongguo Chuanmei Daxue Xuebao) (Modern Communication, Journal of Communication University of China)* 8 (2011): 55–60.

"Jiang Zemin zai quanguo duiwai xuanchuan gongzuo huiyi shang qiangdiao, zhanzai genggao qidian shang ba waixuan gonguo zuo de genghao" ("Jiang Zemin Emphasizes at Conference on External Propaganda Work, Strive for Greater Success from a Higher Starting Point"). *People's Daily*. February 27, 1999. https://cn.govopendata.com/renminribao/1999/2/27/1/.

"Jianghao zhongguo gushi rang shijie geng liaojie zhongguo" ("Tell China Stories Well, Let the World to Better Understand China"). *Xinhua*, September 2, 2018. www.xinhuanet.com/politics/2018-09/02/c_1123367300.htm.

Jiang Huajie. "Lengzhan shiqi zhongguo dui feizhou guojia de yuanzhu yanjiu, 1960–1978 (A Study on Chinese aid to African Countries in Cold War Era, 1960–1978)." PhD Dissertation. East China Normal University, 2014.

"Jiang zemin zai quanguo duiwai xuanchuan gongzuo huiyi shang qiangdiao, zhanzai genggao qidian shang ba waixuan gonguo zuo de genghao" ("Jiang Zemin Emphasizes at Conference on External Propaganda Work, Strive for Greater Success from a Higher Starting Point"). *People's Daily*. February 27, 1999. https://cn.govopendata.com/renminribao/1999/2/27/1/

Jianwei Wang. "Xi Jinping's 'Major Country Diplomacy:' A Paradigm Shift?" *Journal of Contemporary China* 28 no. 115 (2018): 15–30.

Jirik, John. "Shift or Stasis‖ CCTV News and Soft Power." *International Journal of Communication* 10, July 19, 2016: 3537. https://ijoc.org/index.php/ijoc/article/view/4811.

"Ju qizhi ju minxin yu xinren xing wenhua zhan xingxiang genghao wancheng xinxingshi xia xuanchuan sixiang gongzuo shiming renwu" ("Raise the Banner, Gather the people, Cultivate New Talents, Develop Culture, and Promote the National Image: Better Fulfilling the Mission of Propaganda and Ideological Work in the New Situation"). *People's Daily Online*, August 23, 2018. http://media.people.com.cn/n1/2018/0823/c40606-30245183.html.

"K'China Yetegegnew Bider Chana K'ageritu Y'mekifele akem gar temetatagn new tebale" ("The Loan Pressure from China Is Not beyond Ethiopia's Repayment Capacity"). *The Ethiopian Reporter*, December 28, 2018. www.ethiopianreporter.com/index.php/content/ከቻይና-የተገኘው-ብድር-ጫና-ከአገሪቱ-የመክፈል-አቅም-ጋር-ተመጣጣኝ-ነው-ተባለ.

Kastner, Scott L., Chad Rector, and Margaret M. Pearson. *China's Strategic Multilateralism: Investing in Global Governance*. Cambridge; New York: Cambridge University Press, 2019.

"Keynote Speech by Chinese President Xi Jinping at Opening Ceremony of 8th FOCAC Ministerial Conference." Forum on China-Africa Cooperation, December 2, 2021. www.focac.org/eng/gdtp/202112/t20211202_10461080.htm.

Kimeu, Caroline. "Negative Stereotypes in International Media Cost Africa £3.2 Billion a Year– Report." *The Guardian*, October 17, 2024. www.theguardian.com/global-development/2024/oct/17/media-stereotypes-africa-higher-interest-report-payments-on-sovereign-debt.

King, Kenneth. *China's Aid and Soft Power in Africa: The Case of Education and Training*. Boydell & Brewer: Suffolk, UK, 2013.

Klobucista, Claire. "Ethiopia: East Africa's Emerging Giant." *Council on Foreign Relations*, November 4, 2020. www.cfr.org/backgrounder/ethiopia-east-africas-emerging-giant.

Kraidy, Marwan M. "Hybridity in Cultural Globalization." *Communication Theory* 12, no. 3 (2002): 316–39. https://doi.org/10.1111/j.1468-2885.2002.tb00272.x.

Krings, Matthias, and Onookome Okome, eds. *Global Nollywood: The Transnational Dimensions of an African Video Film Industry.* African Expressive Cultures. Bloomington: Indiana University Press, 2013.

Kuo, Lily. "Beijing Is Cultivating the Next Generation of African Elites by Training them in China." *Quartz*, December 14, 2017. https://qz.com/africa/1119447/china-is-training-africas-next-generation-of-leaders.

Kurlantzick, Joshua. *Beijing's Global Media Offensive: China's Uneven Campaign to Influence Asia and the World.* Oxford: Oxford University Press, 2023.

Lampton, David M., Selina Ho, and Cheng-Chwee Kuik. *Rivers of Iron: Railroads and Chinese Power in Southeast Asia.* Oakland: University of California Press, 2020.

Landay, Jonathan. "U.S. Imposes New Rules on State-Owned Chinese Media over Propaganda Concerns." *Reuters*, February 19, 2020. www.reuters.com/article/us-usa-china-media/u-s-imposes-new-rules-on-state-owned-chinese-media-over-propaganda-concerns-idUSKBN20C2G1.

Large, Daniel. "Beyond 'Dragon in the Bush': The Study of China Africa Relations." *African Affairs* 107, no. 426 (2007): 45–61. https://doi.org/10.1093/afraf/adm069.

Lee, Ching Kwan. *The Specter of Global China: Politics, Labor, and Foreign Investment in Africa.* Chicago: The University of Chicago Press, 2017.

Leo, Lakeisha. "China Power: C-drama Fever Sweeps Southeast Asia, with Shows Dominating Screens and Hearts." *CNA*, April 17, 2025. www.channelnewsasia.com/east-asia/china-c-dramas-soft-power-boom-southeast-asia-tourism-5056776.

"Lemi Nat'l Cement Factory Set to Boost Ethiopia's Annual Production Capacity by 8 Mil Metric Ton." *Ethiopian News Agency*, November 28, 2023. www.ena.et/web/eng/w/eng_3646132.

Lewis, Simon, Humeyra Pamuk, and Jonathan Landay. "State Dept Overhaul Will Cut Thousands of Jobs, Push 'Western Values'." *Reuters*, May 29, 2025. www.reuters.com/world/us/state-dept-broad-reorganization-plan-submitted-congress-2025-05-29.

Liammouri, Rida, and Youssef Eddazi. "Russian Interference in Africa: Disinformation and Mercenaries." *Policy Center for the New South Policy Brief*, June 2020. www.policycenter.ma/sites/default/les/2021-01/PB_20-60_Lyammouri.pdf.

Li Anshan. "Wei zhongguo zhengming: zhongguo de feizhou zhanlue yu guojia xingxiang" ("In Defense of China: China's Africa Strategy and State Image"). *Shijie Jingji Yu Zhengzhi (World Economics and Politics)* no. 4 (2008): 6–15, 3.

Li Boyi. "Zhongguo huoban waijiao de bianhua" ("Changes in China's Partner Diplomacy.") *Zhanlue Juece Yanjiu* (Journal of Strategy and Decision Making) 12, no. 3 (2021): 36–66, 102.

Li, Coy. "Why China Is Looking to Vocational Training to Build Bridges with the Global South." *South China Morning Post*, August 18, 2024. www.scmp.com/news/china/diplomacy/article/3274892/why-china-looking-vocational-training-build-bridges-global-south.

Li, Hangwei. "Understanding African Journalistic Agency in China–Africa Media Interactions: The Case of Kenya." *International Communication Gazette* 85, no. 1 (2023): 32–47. https://doi.org/10.1177/17480485221139463.

Li, Hangwei, and Yuan Wang. "African Media Cultures and Chinese Public Relations Strategies in Kenya and Ethiopia." *Carnegie Endowment for International Peace*, February 27, 2023. https://carnegieendowment.org/research/2023/02/african-media-cultures-and-chinese-public-relations-strategies-in-kenya-and-ethiopia.

Li Hongfeng. "Zhongguo guojia xingxiang zai feizhou de goujian yu chuanbo: tiaozhan yu yingdui" ("The Construction and Dissemination of China's National Image in Africa: Challenges and Responses"). *Duiwai Chuanbo (International Communications)* 3 (2021): 27–31.

Li, Jian, and Eryong Xue. "Luban Workshop Development in China." In *Opening Education to the Outside World: Rethinking International Education in China During Post COVID-19*, Singapore: Springer Nature, 2022, 57–71. https://doi.org/10.1007/978-981-19-4880-0.

Li, Lei. "World Reporters Gain Insights at Two Sessions." *China Daily*, March 12, 2024. www.chinadaily.com.cn/a/202403/12/WS65ef8e7da31082fc043bbfff.html.

Li, Mingjiang. *Soft Power: China's Emerging Strategy in International Politics.* Lanham: Lexington Books, 2009.

Li Nan. "Daguo jingzheng xia meiguo dui feizhou zhengce de tezheng yu zouxiang" ("The Characteristics and the Prospect of US Policy towards Africa under the 'Great Power Competition'"). *Meiguo Yanjiu (The Chinese Journal of American Studies)* 36 no. 3 (2022): 9–24.

Li, Shubo. *Mediatized China-Africa Relations: How Media Discourses Negotiate the Shifting of Global Order.* Singapore: Palgrave Macmillan, 2017.

Li, Siyuan. "China's Confucius Institute in Africa: A Different Story?" *International Journal of Comparative Education and Development* 23(4) (October 1, 2021): 353–66. https://doi.org/10.1108/IJCED-02-2021-0014.

Li Xinfeng, and Li Yujie. "Xinmiankong yu xinbiange: zhongguo meiti gaibian feizhou chuanmei geju" ("China's Media Engagement in Africa: Influences and Changes"). *Hunan Shifan Daxue Shehui Kexue Xuebao (Journal of Social Science of Hunan Normal University)* 47 no. 3 (2018): 131–40.

Li, Xuanmin, and Hao Shuangyan. "Chinese TV Series 'Make Big Splash' in Southeast Asian Countries." *Global Times*, August 17, 2023. www.globaltimes.cn/page/202308/1296472.shtml.

Li, Yuan. "A Window into Chinese Government Has Now Slammed Shut." *The New York Times*, March 6, 2024. www.nytimes.com/2024/03/06/business/china-national-peoples-congress.html.

Liu Hongwu. "Xifang zhengzhi jingji lilun fansi yu yafei zhishi huayuquan chongjian" ("Retrospections on Western Political and Economic Theories and the Reconstruction of Power of Discourse in Asian-African Knowledge"). *Xiya Feizhou (West Asia and Africa)* no. 1 (2011): 11–16, 79.

Liu, Jianchao. "Riding the Tide of History: Working Together to Boost Solidarity and Cooperation among the Global South." *Qiushi*, June 2024. http://qstheory.cn/2024-07/08/c_1001807.htm.

Liu Qianqian, Zhu Jiming, and Wang Xiaolin. "Zhongguo weisheng ruanyuanzhu shijian wenti yu duice-yi duiwai weisheng renli ziyuan hezuo weili" ("China's Soft Aid for Health: Practices, Issues and Implications: A Case of Health Human Resource Cooperation"). *Zhongguo Weisheng Zhengli Yanjiu (Chinese Journal of Health Policy)* 7 no. 3 (2014): 58–63.

Liu Youmin, and Yang Jun. "World Insights: Key Facts U.S. Deliberately Ignores about African Debt." *Xinhuanet*, February 7, 2023. https://english.news.cn/20230207/2e2f36625525400f90b8ea4993ffa4d6/c.html.

Liu Yumei. "Ruanshili yu zhongfei guanxi de fazhan" ("Soft Power and Development of Sino-African Relations"). *Guoji Wenti Yanjiu (China International Studies)* no. 3 (2007): 16–21.

Liu Zaiqi and Wang Manli. "Yidai yilu zhanlue yu zhongguo canyu quanqiu zhili yanjiu yi huayu quan he huayu tixi wei shijiao" ("Study of 'Belt and Road' Strategy and China's Engagement in Global Governance–from a Perspective of Discourse Power and Discourse System"). *Xuexi Yu Shijian (Study and Practice)* no. 4 (2016): 68–74.

Logan, Carolyn, and Josephine Appiah-Nyamekye Sanny. "China Has Invested Deeply in Africa. We Checked to See Whether That Is Undermining Democracy." *The Washington Post*, October 29, 2021. www.washingtonpost.com/politics/2021/10/29/china-has-invested-deeply-africa-we-checked-see-whether-that-is-undermining-democracy.

Long Xiaonong. "Cong xiongdi dao mingyun gongtongti zhongguo jiangou dui feizhou huayu tixi de linian yu shijian" ("From Brothers to a Community with a Shared Future for Mankind-Principles and Practices of China's Discourse Construction towards Africa"). *Xiandai Chuanbo (Modern Communication)* 38, no. 1 (2016): 75–81.

— "waijiao gouxiangli yu zhongguo zai feizhou guoji huayuquan de tisheng" ("The Ability of Conceptualizing Diplomacy and the Improvement of China's International Discourse Power in Africa"). *Xiandai Chuanbo (Modern Communication)* 36, no. 3 (2014): 56–60.

Lovell, Julia. *Maoism: A Global History*. New York: Alfred A. Knopf, 2019.

Luo Chen, and Wang Yirong. "Meijie jiechu jiazhiguan yu zhongguo zai feizhou yingxiangli pingjia" ("Media Exposure, World Values, and Evaluation of China's Influence in Africa"). *Quanqiu Chuanmei Xuekan (Global Media Journal)* 7, no. 4 (2020): 24–38.

Luo Jianbo. "Ruhe tuijin zhongguo duifei duobian waijiao" ("How to Advance China's Multilateral Diplomacy towards Africa"). *Xiandai Guoji Guanxi (Contemporary International Relations)* 11 (2006): 24–9.

— "Tisheng zhongguo duifei huayuquan de xinjiyu yu xinsikao" ("Promote New Opportunities and New Thinking of China's Discourse Power toward Africa"). *Guoji Chuanbo (International Communications)* 4 (2017): 32–5.

— "Youhua zhongguo zai feizhou de ruanshili" ("Optimizing China's Soft Power in Africa"). *Yafei Zongheng (Asia & Africa Review)* 6 (2007): 18–24, 63.

— "Zhongguo tese daguo waijiao xinlinian xinzhanlue yu xintese" ("Major-Country Diplomacy with Chinese Characteristics: New Concepts, Strategy and Characteristics"). *Xiya Feizhou (West Asia and Africa)* 4 (2017): 28–49.

Luo, Shanshan. "China Remains Africa's Largest Trading Partner for 9 Consecutive Years." *People's Daily*, August 31, 2018. http://en.people.cn/n3/2018/0831/c90000-9495973.html.

Luqiu, Luwei Rose. "The Cost of Humour: Political Satire on Social Media and Censorship in China." *Global Media and Communication* 13, no. 2 (2017): 123–38. https://doi.org/10.1177/1742766517704471.

Maa Hanzhi, and Yu Jiang. "Lun goujian gaoshuiping zhongfei mingyun gongtongti" ("On Building a High-Level China–Africa Community with a Shared Future"). *Guoji Guancha (International Review)* no. 3 (2024): 1-28.

Ma Jianchun. "Ershida yihou de zhongfei jingmao hezuo: xingshi yu jianyi" ("China-Africa Economic and Trade Cooperation After 20th Party Congress of Communist Party of China: New Circumstances and Suggestions"). *Guoji Jingji Hezuo (Journal of International Economic Cooperation)* 39, no. 6 (2023): 1–8.

Madden, Payce. "Figure of the Week: Foreign Direct Investment in Africa." Brookings, October 9, 2019. www.brookings.edu/blog/africa-in-focus/2019/10/09/figure-of-the-week-foreign-direct-investment-in-africa.

Madrid-Morales, Dani. "China's Digital Public Diplomacy towards Africa: Actors, Messages and Audiences." In *China-Africa Relations: Building Images through Cultural Cooperation, Media Representation and Communication*, edited by Kathryn Batchelor and Xiaoling Zhang, 129–46. London: Routledge, 2017.

Madrid-Morales, Dani, and Herman Wasserman. "How Effective Are Chinese Media in Shaping Audiences' Attitudes towards China? A Survey Analysis in Kenya, Nigeria, and South Africa." *Online Media and Global Communication* (December 13, 2022). https://doi.org/10.1515/omgc-2022-0047.

Mahao, Seepheephe. "Over 80 Journalists Join CIPCC Exchange Programme in China." *Public Eye*, August 1, 2023. https://publiceyenews.com/2023/08/01/over-80-journalists-join-cipcc-exchange-programme-in-china%EF%BF%BC.

"Mapping a Surge of Disinformation in Africa." *The Africa Center for Strategic Studies*, March 13, 2024. https://africacenter.org/spotlight/mapping-a-surge-of-disinformation-in-africa.

Mark, Isuma. "Chinese Companies May Seize Nigerian Assets over MOU with Enugu State, Group Warns." *The Whistler*, September 25, 2024. https://thewhistler.ng/chinese-companies-may-seize-nigerian-assets-over-mou-with-enugu-state-group-warns.

Marks, Simon. "How an African State Learned to Play the West off China for Billions." *Politico*, February 7, 2020. www.politico.com/news/2020/02/07/xethiopia-china-west-power-competition-110766.

Marsh, Vivien. *Seeking Truth in International TV News: China, CGTN and the BBC*. London: Routledge, 2023.

Mastro, Oriana Skylar. *Upstart: How China Became a Great Power*. New York: Oxford University Press, 2024.

Mattern, Janice Bially. "Why 'Soft Power' Isn't So Soft: Representational Force and the Sociolinguistic Construction of Attraction in World Politics." *Millennium: Journal of International Studies* 33, no. 3 (2005): 583–612. https://doi.org/10.1177/03058298050330031601.

Mattingly, Daniel, Trevor Incerti, Changwook Ju et al. "Chinese State Media Persuades a Global Audience That the 'China Model' Is Superior: Evidence from a 19-Country Experiment." *American Journal of Political Science*, July 20, 2024. https://doi.org/10.1111/ajps.12887.

Mattingly, Daniel. "China's Soft Sell of Autocracy Is Working." *Foreign Affairs*, September 25, 2024. www.foreignaffairs.com/china/chinas-soft-sell-autocracy-working.

"Media Cooperation: China's CMG Donates Media Equipment to Antigua and Barbuda Broadcasting Service." *CGTN*, May 29, 2024. https://news.cgtn.com/news/2024-05-29/VHJhbnNjcmlwdDc5MDEw/index.html.

Meisel, Collin, Jonathan Moyer, and Mathew J. Burrows. "The US Is Losing the Global South: How to Reverse Course." *The Hill*, June 13, 2023. https://thehill.com/opinion/international/4046182-the-us-is-losing-the-global-south-how-to-reverse-course.

Melaku, Mulualem K. *Africa-China Relations: Ethiopia as a Case Study*. Addis Ababa: Melaku Mulualem K., 2023.

Men Honghua. "Goujian mianxiang weilai de zhongguo waijiao zhanlue xin buju" ("Building a New Layout of China's Diplomatic Strategy for the Future"). *Tansuo Yu Zhengming (Exploration and Free View)* no. 1 (2022): 43–50, 77.

Miladi, Noureddine. "Al Jazeera Network and the Transformations in the Global Communication Flow." In *Routledge Handbook on Arab Media*, edited by Nūr al-Dīn Mīlādī and Noha Mellor, 313–23. London; New York: Routledge, Taylor & Francis Group, 2021.

Mills, Greg, and Ray Hartley. "South Africa's Strange Obsession with China Is Proof that It's a Cheap Date." *Daily Maverick*, August 27, 2023. www.dailymaverick.co.za/article/2023-08-27-south-africas-strange-obsession-with-china-is-proof-that-its-a-cheap-date.

Mohammed, Jemal. "PR-Driven Journalism Model: The Case of Ethiopia." *African Journalism Studies* 42, no. 1 (January 2, 2021): 108–27. https://doi.org/10.1080/23743670.2021.1888138.

Moss, Dana M., and Saipira Furstenberg, eds. *Transnational Repression in the Age of Globalisation*. Edinburgh Studies on Diasporas and Transnationalism. Edinburgh: Edinburgh University Press, 2024.

Müller, Martin. "In Search of the Global East: Thinking between North and South." *Geopolitics* 25, no. 3 (2020): 734–55. https://doi.org/10.1080/14650045.2018.1477757.

Mulugeta, Daniel. "Pan-Africanism and the Affective Charges of the African Union Building in Addis Ababa." *Journal of African Cultural Studies* 33, no. 4 (October 2, 2021): 521–37. https://doi.org/10.1080/13696815.2021.1884971.

Murphy, Dawn C. *China's Rise in the Global South: The Middle East, Africa, and Beijing's Alternative World Order*. Stanford: Stanford University Press, 2022.

Myers, Margaret. "China's Education Diplomacy in Latin America." *Wilson Center*, March 15, 2024. www.wilsoncenter.org/blog-post/chinas-education-diplomacy-latin-america.

Na, Ren, and Hong Liu. "Southeast Asian Chinese Engage a Rising China: Business Associations, Institutionalised Transnationalism, and the Networked

State." *Journal of Ethnic and Migration Studies* 48, no. 4 (2022): 873–93. https://doi.org/10.1080/1369183X.2021.1983952.

Nicette, Sedrick. "Seychelles Broadcasting Corporation's Nearly Completed HQ Gets New Equipment from China." *Seychelles News Agency*, May 17, 2024. www.seychellesnewsagency.com/articles/20579/Seychelles+Broadcasting+Corporation%27s+nearly+completed+HQ+gets+new+equipment+from+China.

Niewenhuis, Lucas. "The 'Debt-Trap Diplomacy' Debate: Are China's Loans Predatory?" *SupChina*, September 18, 2019. https://signal.supchina.com/the-debt-trap-diplomacy-debate-are-chinas-loans-predatory/.

Niu Changsong. "Kongzi xueyuan yu zhongguo duifei yuyan wenhua waijiao" ("Confucius Institutes and China's Language and Cultural Diplomacy in Africa"). *Xiya Feizhou (West Asia and Africa)*, no. 1 (2014): 64–77.

Nkonde, Kalima. "How China Slowly Colonizing Zambian Economy." *Lusaka Times*, July 27, 2018. www.lusakatimes.com/2018/07/27/how-china-slowly-colonizing-zambian-economy.

Nwabufo, Fredrick. "Nigeria's Abusive Marriage with China and Slave Agreements." *The Cable*, July 30, 2020. www.thecable.ng/nigerias-abusive-marriage-with-china-and-slave-agreements.

Nyabiage, Jevans. "China Votes 'No' on Tigray Abuses Probe by UN Team, Calls It Interference in Ethiopia's Affairs." *South China Morning Post*, December 19, 2021. www.scmp.com/news/china/diplomacy/article/3160246/china-votes-no-tigray-abuses-probe-un-team-calls-it.

Nye, Joseph S. *Soft Power: The Means to Success in World Politics*. New York: Public Affairs, 2005.

Nye, Joseph. "Trump Is Liquidating America's Reserves of Soft Power: The United States Can't Beat China with Hard Power alone." *The Washington Post*, March 25, 2025. www.washingtonpost.com/opinions/2025/03/25/soft-power-trump-china.

Nyíri, Pál. *Reporting for China: How Chinese Correspondents Work with the World*. Seattle: University of Washington Press, 2017.

Ofosu, George, and David Sarpong. "China in Africa: On the Competing Perspectives of the Value of Sino-Africa Business Relationships." *Journal of Economic Issues* 56, no. 1 (January 2, 2022): 137–57. https://doi.org/10.1080/00213624.2022.2020025.

Ogunsina, Bukola. *The Red Lantern*. Self-published: 2024.

Ojo, Tokunbo. "Through Their Eyes: Reporters' Challenges in Covering China–Africa Relations." *Journalism Practice* 14, no. 10 (November 25, 2020): 1179–92. https://doi.org/10.1080/17512786.2019.1692689.

Okeowo, Alexis. "Ethiopia's Agony: 'I have Never Seen This Kind of Cruelty in My Life'." *The New York Times Magazine*, December 5, 2024. www.nytimes.com/2024/12/05/magazine/ethiopia-civil-war-crimes.html.

Olander, Eric. "While Ghana's Governing Elites Call for Deeper Economic Engagement with China, Civil Society Groups Fume." *China Global South Project*, May 3, 2021. https://chinaglobalsouth.com/2021/05/03/while-ghanas-governing-elites-call-for-deeper-economic-engagement-with-china-civil-society-groups-fume.

Osnos, Evan. "The Future of America's Contest with China." *The New Yorker*, January 6, 2020. www.newyorker.com/magazine/2020/01/13/the-future-of-americas-contest-with-china.

Oya, Carlos, and Florian Schaefer. "Chinese Firms and Employment Dynamics in Africa: A Comparative Analysis." *IDCEA Research Synthesis Report* (SOAS, University of London: 2019).

Pan, Chengxin, Benjamin Isakhan, and Zim Nwokora. "Othering as Soft-Power Discursive Practice: China Daily's Construction of Trump's America in the 2016 Presidential Election." *Politics* 40, no. 1 (2020): 54–69. https://doi.org/10.1177/0263395719843219.

Paravicini, Giulia. "Ethiopia Calls US Accusations of War Crimes 'Inflammatory'." *Reuters*, March 21, 2023. www.reuters.com/world/africa/ethiopia-calls-us-accusations-war-crimes-inflammatory-2023-03-21/.

Pearson, Margaret M., Meg Rithmire, and Kellee S. Tsai. "China's Party-State Capitalism and International Backlash: From Interdependence to Insecurity." *International Security* 47, no. 2 (October 1, 2022): 135–76. https://doi.org/10.1162/isec_a_00447.

Peralta, Eyder. "A New Chinese-Funded Railway in Kenya Sparks Debt-Trap Fears." *All Things Considered, NPR*, October 8, 2018. www.npr.org/2018/10/08/641625157/a-new-chinese-funded-railway-in-kenya-sparks-debt-trap-fears.

Peters, Benedict. "Beware of China's New Colonialism." *The Cable*, May 19, 2019. http://www.thecable.ng/beware-of-chinas-new-colonialism/

Pilling, David, and Andres Schipani. "War in Tigray May Have Killed 600,000 People, Peace Mediator Says." *Financial Times*, January 15, 2023. www.ft.com/content/2f385e95-0899-403a-9e3b-ed8c24adf4e7.

Pollio, Andrea. *Silicon Elsewhere: Nairobi, Global China, and the Promise of Techno-Capital*. Oakland: University of California Press, 2026.

Prashad, Vijay. *The Poorer Nations: A Possible History of the Global South*. London: Verso, 2012.

"President Jiang Zemin's Visit to Six African Countries." *Ministry of Foreign Affairs of the People's Republic of China*, accessed via Internet Archive [February 1, 2018] on August 28, 2025. www.fmprc.gov.cn/mfa_eng/ziliao_665539/3602_665543/3604_665547/t18035.shtml.

"The Presidential Initiative for Democratic Renewal (PIDR) Fact Sheet." *USAID*, accessed on October 18, 2024. www.usaid.gov/democracy/pidr/factsheet/pidr-factsheet-2024.

Procopio, Maddalena. "The Effectiveness of Confucius Institutes as a Tool of China's Soft Power in South Africa." *African East-Asian Affairs*, no. 1–2 (July 1, 2015). https://doi.org/10.7552/0-1-2-155.

Pu, Xiaoyu. *Rebranding China: Contested Status Signaling in the Changing Global Order*. Studies in Asian Security. Stanford: Stanford University Press, 2019.

Pugliese, Anita, and Julie Ray. "Nearly 900 Million Worldwide Wanted to Migrate in 2021." *Gallup*, January 24, 2023. https://news.gallup.com/poll/468218/nearly-900-million-worldwide-wanted-migrate-2021.aspx.

Punathambekar, Aswin. *From Bombay to Bollywood: The Making of a Global Media Industry*. New York: New York University Press, 2013.

Qing Ying. "Aisabiya: cankao zhongguo moshi de 'feizhoubanzhongguo' zouleduoyuan" ('Ethiopia: Relying on China Model, How Far the African Version of China Has Gone'). *Caixin*, August 18, 2017. https://pit.ifeng.com/a/20170818/51675993_0.shtml.

Ramani, Samuel. "Russia and China in Africa: Prospective Partners or Asymmetric Rivals?" *South African Institute of International Affairs*, 2021. www.http://jstor.org/stable/resrep38659.

Ratigan, Kerry. "Are Peruvians Enticed by the 'China Model'? Chinese Investment and Public Opinion in Peru." *Studies in Comparative International Development* 56, no. 1 (2021): 87–111. https://doi.org/10.1007/s12116-021-09321-0.

Rechtman, Don. "US vs Chinese-Style Democracy." *Shenzhen Daily*, July 1, 2021. https://szdaily.sznews.com/PC/content/202107/01/content_1054032.html.

Repnikova, Maria. *Chinese Soft Power*. Cambridge: Cambridge University Press (Global China Element Series), 2022.

— *Media Politics in China: Improvising Power under Authoritarianism*. Cambridge: Cambridge University Press, 2017.

— "Rethinking China's Soft Power: 'Pragmatic Enticement' of Confucius Institutes in Ethiopia." *The China Quarterly* 250 (2022): 440–63. https://doi.org/10.1017/S0305741022000340.

Repnikova, Maria, and Keyu Alexander Chen. "Asymmetrical Discursive Competition: China–United States Digital Diplomacy in Africa." *International Communication Gazette* 85, no. 1 (2023): 15–31. https://doi.org/10.1177/17480485221139460.

Richard, Wike, Jacob Poushter, Laura Silver, and Janell Fetterolf, "U.S. Image Declines in Many Nations Amid Low Con dence in Trump." *Pew Research Center*, June 11, 2025, www.pewresearch.org/global/2025/06/11/us-image-declines-in-many-nations-amid-low-condence-in-trump.

Roberts, Margaret E. *Censored: Distraction and Diversion inside China's Great Firewall*. Princeton: Princeton University Press, 2018.

Rofel, Lisa, and Carlos Rojas. *New World Orderings: China and the Global South*. Durham: Duke University Press, 2023.

Rolland, Nadège. "China's Southern Strategy: Beijing Is Using the Global South to Constrain America." *Foreign Affairs*, June 2, 2022. www.foreignaffairs.com/articles/china/2022-06-09/chinas-southern-strategy

Sapienza, Zachary S., Narayanan Iyer, and Aaron S. Veenstra. "Reading Lasswell's Model of Communication Backward: Three Scholarly Misconceptions." *Mass Communication and Society* 18, no. 5 (2015): 599–622. https://doi.org/10.1080/15205436.2015.1063666.

Schatz, Edward, and Rachel Silvey, eds. *Seeing China's Belt and Road*. New York: Oxford University Press, 2025.

Schmitz, Cheryl Mei-Ting. "Doing Time, Making Money at a Chinese State Firm in Angola." *Made in China*, January 25, 2021. https://madeinchinajournal.com/2021/01/25/doing-time-making-money-at-a-chinese-state-firm-in-angola.

"Shanghai Import Expo to Promote Egypt's Exports to China: Egyptian Businessman." *Ethiopian Herald,* July 27, 2018.

Sheehy, Thomas P., and Joseph Asunka. "Countering China on the Continent: A Look at African Views." *United States Institute of Peace*, June 23, 2021. www.usip.org/publications/2021/06/countering-china-continent-look-african-views.

Shi Anbin. "Xinshidai guoji chuanbo nengli jianse de xin silu xin zuowei" ("New Strategies and Innovations in Building International Communication Capabilities in the New Era"). *Guoji Chuanbo (Global Communication)* no. 1 (2018): 8–15.

Shi Anbin, and Yang Sheng. "Tanjiu xinshidai guoji chuanbo de fangfalun chuangxin: jiyu quanqiu zhongguo de gainian toushi" ("Innovating China's International Communication Theory and Methodology in the New Era: A Conceptualizing Analysis Based on the Global China"). *Xinwen Yu Chuanbo Pinglun (Journalism & Communication Review)* 74 no. 3 (2021): 005–013.

Shi, Jiangtao. "As China Lashes out at US Democracy Summit, Analysts Warn of More Division." *South China Morning Post*, March 27, 2023. www.scmp.com/news/china/diplomacy/article/3215020/china-lashes-out-us-democracy-summit-analysts-warn-more-division.

Shinn, David H. "China–Africa Ties in Historical Context." In *China-Africa and an Economic Transformation*, edited by Arkebe Oqubay and Justin Yifu Lin, 61–83. Oxford: Oxford University Press, 2019. https://doi.org/10.1093/oso/9780198830504.003.0004.

Shue, Vivienne, and Patricia M. Thornton, eds. *To Govern China: Evolving Practices of Power*. Cambridge: Cambridge University Press, 2017.

Shullman, David O. "Protect the Party: China's Growing Influence in the Developing World." Brookings, January 22, 2019. www.brookings.edu/articles/protect-the-party-chinas-growing-influence-in-the-developing-world.

Silver, Laura, Christine Huang, Laura Clancy et al. "Comparing Views of the U.S. and China in 24 Countries." *Pew Research Center*, November 6, 2023. www.pewresearch.org/global/2023/11/06/comparing-views-of-the-us-and-china-in-24-countries.

Shullman, David O. "China Pairs Actions with Messaging in Latin America: The United States Should Do the Same." *Atlantic Council*, February 12, 2024. www.atlanticcouncil.org/in-depth-research-reports/issue-brief/china-pairs-actions-with-messaging-in-latin-america-the-united-states-should-do-the-same.

Skjerdal, Terje S. "Development Journalism Revived: The Case of Ethiopia." *Ecquid Novi: African Journalism Studies* 32, no. 2 (2011): 58–74. https://doi.org/10.1080/02560054.2011.578879.

Skjerdal, Terje, and Fufa Gusu. "Positive Portrayal of Sino-African Relations in the Ethiopian Press." In *China's Media and Soft Power in Africa*, edited by Xiaoling Zhang, Herman Wasserman, and Winston Mano, 149–61. New York: Palgrave Macmillan US, 2016. https://doi.org/10.1057/9781137539670_11.

"Speech of the Federal Democratic Republic of Ethiopia (FDRE); H.E. Dr. Abiy Ahmed." *African Union*, February 18, 2023. https://au.int/ar/node/42610.

"Statement by President Xi Jinping at the General Debate of the 76th Session of the United Nations General Assembly." Permanent Mission of the People's

Republic of China to the UN, September 21, 2021. http://un.china-mission.gov.cn/eng/zt/20210921/202109/t20210922_10410004.htm.

Standish, Reid. "Is China Exporting Its Political Model to the World? A New Report Says Yes." *Radio Free Europe*, June 13, 2024

Stern, E. Rachel, and Kevin J. O'Brien, "Politics at the Boundary: Mixed Signals and the Chinese State." *Modern China* 38, no. 2 (2011): 174–98.

Sun, Yun. "Political Party Training: China's Ideological Push in Africa?" Brookings, July 5, 2016. www.brookings.edu/articles/political-party-training-chinas-ideological-push-in-africa/.

— "FOCAC 2021: China's Retrenchment from Africa?" Brookings, December 6, 2021. www.brookings.edu/articles/focac-2021-chinas-retrenchment-from-africa/

Szondi, Gyorgy. "From Image Management to Relationship Building: A Public Relations Approach to Nation Branding." *Place Branding and Public Diplomacy* 6, no. 4 (2010): 333–43. https://doi.org/10.1057/pb.2010.32.

Tang Jia. "Tisheng guoji huayu quan, zhongguo xuyao zheyang zuo" ("Improve China's International Discourse, China Needs to Do Like This"). *People's Daily*, June 7, 2021. www.people.com.cn/n1/2021/0607/c437595-32124020.html.

Tao Xing. "China's New Cultural Exports Reach Global Shores." *Beijing Review*, September 29, 2024. www.bjreview.com/China/202409/t20240929_8003790 43.html.

Taylor, Derrick Bryson. "'Ne Zha 2,' Blockbuster Chinese Animated Film, Will Get English Version." *The New York Times*, July 9, 2025. www.nytimes.com/2025/07/09/movies/ne-zha-2-english-us-theaters.html.

Taylor, Ian. *The Forum on China-Africa Cooperation*. Routledge Global Institutions 48. Milton Park, Abingdon, Oxon; New York: Routledge, 2011.

Teka, Mulu. "Ethiopians Support Media's Watchdog Role but Want Regulated access to Internet, Social Media." *Afrobarometer*, May 13, 2021. www .afrobarometer.org/wp-content/uploads/2022/02/ad448-ethiopians_support_media_watchdog_role_but_want_regulated_access_to_internet_and_social_media-afrobarometer-12may21.pdf.

"Ten Years on, Concept of Community with Shared Future for Mankind Injects New Impetus into World." *CGTN*, March 15, 2023. https://news.cgtn.com/news/2023-03-15/Concept-of-community-with-shared-future-injects-new-impetus-into-world-1ibrNlsemoU/index.html.

"The UN Police Is Happy with China's Peacekeeping." *Ethiopian Herald*, June 29, 2018.

Thompson, Desmond. "US aid Freeze Threatens Higher Education Alliances in Africa." *University World News*, February 6, 2025. www.universityworldnews .com/post.php?story=20250205163446916.

Thussu, Daya Kishan. "Contra-Flow in Global Media: An Asian Perspective." *Media Asia* 33, no. 3-4 (2006): 123–9. https://doi.org/10.1080/01296612 .2006.11726823.

Tiffert, Glenn, and Oliver McPherson-Smith. "China's Sharp Power in Africa: A Handbook for Building National Resilience." Hoover Institution, March 21, 2022. www.hoover.org/research/chinas-sharp-power-africa-handbook-building-national-resilience.

Tsourapas, Gerasimos. "Global Autocracies: Strategies of Transnational Repression, Legitimation, and Co-Optation in World Politics." *International Studies Review* 23, no. 3 (August 16, 2021): 616–44. https://doi.org/10.1093/isr/viaa061.

"Tuidong goujian xinxing guoji guanxi shenhua tuozhan quanqiu huoban guanxi" ('Advancing the Building of a New Type of International Relations and Deepening Global Partnerships'). *Global Times*, December 12, 2022. https://baijiahao.baidu.com/s?id=1752012131036694262&wfr=spider&for=pc.

Turhan, Yunus. "Turkey's Public Diplomacy: The Role of Turkish Non-governmental Organisations." *Diplomacy & Statecraft* 34, no. 2 (April 3, 2023): 325–42. https://doi.org/10.1080/09592296.2023.2213078.

Umejei, Emeka. *Chinese Media in Africa: Perception, Performance, and Paradox.* Lanham: Lexington Books, 2020.

Uthman, Samad. "Report: How Chinese Are Funding Terrorist Groups to Gain Access to Mineral Reserves in Nigeria." *The Cable*, April 15, 2023. www.thecable.ng/report-how-chinese-are-funding-terrorist-groups-to-gain-access-to-mineral-reserves-in-nigeria.

Usman, Zainab. "What Do We Know about Chinese Lending in Africa?" *Carnegie Endowment for International Peace*, June 2, 2021. https://carnegieendowment.org/research/2021/06/what-do-we-know-about-chinese-lending-in-africa?lang=en.

Van Staden, Cobus. "Equatorial Guinea Media Donation Highlights a Key Chinese Soft Power Strategy." *China Global South Project*, April 13, 2022. https://chinaglobalsouth.com/2022/04/13/equatorial-guinea-media-donation-highlights-a-key-chinese-soft-power-strategy.

"Waijiao buzhang qingang jiu zhongguo waijiao zhengce he duiwai guanxi huida zhongwai jizhe tiwen" ("Foreign Minister Qin Gang Answers Questions from Chinese and Foreign Journalists on China's Foreign Policy and International Relations"). *Ministry of Foreign Affairs of the People's Republic of China*, March 7, 2023. www.fmprc.gov.cn/web/wjdt_674879/wjbxw_674885/202303/t20230307_11037046.shtml.

Walker, Christopher, Shanthi Kalathil, and Jessica Ludwig. "Forget Hearts and Minds." *Foreign Policy*, September 14, 2018. https://foreignpolicy.com/2018/09/14/forget-hearts-and-minds-sharp-power.

Wang Fan. "Zhongguo tese daguo waijiao: xietiao, biange yu wanshan" ("Big Country Diplomacy with Chinese Characteristics: Coordination, Change and Perfection"). *Tansuo Yu Zhengming (Exploration and Free View)*, no. 1 (2022): 12–15.

Wang Hongyi. "Shilun zhongguo weixie lun" ("On China Threat Theory"). *Xiya Feizhou (West Asia and Africa)*, no. 8 (2006): 28–32.

Wang Lijuan. "Ershiyi shiji zhongguo duifei yuanzhu de biyaoxing ji duice" ("The Necessity of China's Foreign Aid in Africa and Solutions in the 21st Century"). *Dangdai Shijie Yu Shehui Zhuyi (Contemporary World and Socialism)*, no. 3 (2014): 88–92.

"Wang yi guowu weiyuan jian waizhang jiu 2021 nian guoji xingshi he waijiao gongzhuo jieshou xinhuashe he zhongyang guangbo dianshi zongtai lianhe caifang" ("State Councilor and Foreign Minister Wang Yi Gives Interview to

Xinhua News Agency and China Media Group on International Situation and China's diplomacy in 2021"). *Ministry of Foreign Affairs of the People's Republic of China*, December 30, 2021. www.fmprc.gov.cn/web/wjbz_673089/ zyjh_673099/202112/t20211230_10477288.shtml

Wang Yi. "Gaoju renlei mingyun gongtongti qizhi kuobu qianxing" ("Striding Forward Holding High the Banner of Building a Community with a Shared Future for Mankind"). *The Central Government of the People's Republic of China*, January 2, 2022. www.gov.cn/guowuyuan/2022-01/02/content_5666074 .htm.

"Wang Yi Chairs the Coordinators' Meeting on the Implementation of the Follow-up Actions of the Eighth Ministerial Conference of the Forum on China-Africa Cooperation." *Ministry of Foreign Affairs of the People's Republic of China.* August 18, 2022. www.fmprc.gov.cn/mfa_eng/wjb_663304/wjbz_663308/ activities_663312/202208/t20220822_10748826.html.

"Wang Yi: zhongfei lingdaoren jiang zaici jushou beijing, gongshang weilai fazhan daji" ("Wang Yi: China-Africa Leaders to Reunite in Beijing to Discuss Future Development Cooperation"). *Xinhua*, March 7, 2024. www.xinhuanet.com/ politics/20240307/dcc8b436a56b44cf884222a6fe4e476b/c.html.

"Wang Yi: zhongfei youhao yidinghui jixu chengwei nannan hezuo de jiliang, guoji guanxi de dianfan" ("Wang Yi: China-Africa Friendship Will Continue to Be the Backbone in South-South Cooperation and a Fine Example in International Relations"). *Ministry of Foreign Affairs of the People's Republic of China.* August 18, 2022. https://www.fmprc.gov.cn/web/wjb_673085/zzj g_673183/xws_674681/xgxw_674683/202208/t20220818_10745566.shtml.

Wang, Ying. "Going Global: The International Endeavours of Chinese NGOs." *The People's Map of Global China*, June 1, 2021. https://thepeoplesmap.net/2 021/06/01/going-global-the-international-endeavours-of-chinese-ngos.

Wang Yingying. "Feizhou xin xingshi yu zhongfei guanxi" ("New Situation in Africa and China-Africa Relations"). *Guoji Wenti Yanjiu (International Studies)*, no. 2 (2004): 14–18.

Wang Yiwei. "Ruhe kefu zhongguo gonggong waijiao beilun" ("How to Deal with the Paradox of China's Public Diplomacy?"). *Dongbeiya Luntan (Northeast Asia Forum)* 23 no. 3 (2014): 42–50.

Wang Zhimin, and Chen Zonghua. "Goujian renlei mingyun gongtongti: lilun tanyuan, shidai yihan yu shijian jinlu" ("Constructing a Community with a Shared Future for Mankind: Theoretical Origin, Time Implication and Practical Approach"). *Guizhousheng Dangxiao Xuebao (Journal of Guizhou Provincial Party School)* no. 4 (2022): 5–12.

Wasserman, Herman. "China's 'Soft Power' and Its Influence on Editorial Agendas in South Africa." *Chinese Journal of Communication* 9, no. 1 (January 2, 2016): 8–20. https://doi.org/10.1080/17544750.2015.1049953.

Wasserman, Herman, and Dani Madrid-Morales. "How Influential Are Chinese Media in Africa? An Audience Analysis in Kenya and South Africa." *International Journal of Communication* 12 (2018): 2212–31. https://scholars .cityu.edu.hk/en/publications/publication(294db6f2-07e3-4f6d-97cd-27b497 b23140).html.

Wei Xuemei. "Zhongguo yuanzhu feizhou yu tisheng zhongguo ruanshili" ("China's aid to Africa and Improvement of China's Soft Power"). *Guoji Guanxi Xueyuan Xuebao (Journal of University of International Relations)* no. 1 (2011): 31–36.

Weiss, Jessica Chen. "A World Safe for Autocracy? China's Rise and the Future of Global Politics." *Foreign Affairs* (July/August 2019).

Wekesa, Bob. "China Global Television Network's Debate Show, 'Talk Africa': Conflict, Economics, and Geopolitics." In *The Future of Television in the Global South*, edited by George Ogola, 107–28. Cham: Palgrave MacMillan, 2023. https://doi.org/10.1007/978-3-031-18833-6_7.

Westcott, Ben. "Beijing Calls for Chinese Journalists to 'Arm Their Minds' with Xi Jinping Thought." *CNN*, December 17, 2019. www.cnn.com/2019/12/17/asia/china-journalist-code-intl-hnk/index.html.

"What Is the Youth Unemployment Rate in Ethiopia?" *Ethiopian Statistics Service*, 2022. https://web.archive.org/web/20240901140007/https://www.statsethiopia.gov.et/wp-content/uploads/2024/02/Abstract-3-2.pdf.

Wheeler, Anita. "Cultural Diplomacy, Language Planning, and the Case of the University of Nairobi Confucius Institute." *Journal of Asian and African Studies* 49, no. 1 (2014): 49–63. https://doi.org/10.1177/0021909613477834.

"Who Lost China." *Harry S. Truman Library Museum, National Archives*, accessed on August 28, 2025. www.trumanlibrary.gov/education/presidential-inquiries/who-lost-china.

Willems, Wendy. "Beyond Normative Dewesternization: Examining Media Culture from the Vantage Point of the Global South." *The Global South* 8, no. 1 (2014): 7–23. https://doi.org/10.2979/globalsouth.8.1.7.

"World Migration Report 2024." *United Nations Research Institute for Social Development*, 2024. https://publications.iom.int/books/world-migration-report-2024.

Wu Chuanhua, Jia Guo, and Yujie Li. 2018. *Zhongfei renwen jiaoliu yu hezuo (China–Africa People-to-People and Cultural Exchanges and Cooperation)*. Beijing: China Social Science Press, 2018.

Wu Qimin. "Zhongguo feizhou jingji guanli yanxiuban kaixue" ("China-Africa Economic Management Seminar Has Started"). *People's Daily*, August 4, 1998.

Wu Zhicheng, and Li Jiaxuan. "Xi jinping waijiao sixiang zhong de zhengque yiliguan" ("The Pursuit of Shared Interests and Common Good in Xi Jinping Thought on Diplomacy"). *Guoji Wenti Yanjiu (International Studies)* no. 3 (2021): 23–46.

"Why China Is Rebooting the Belt and Road Initiative." *The United States Institute of Peace Report*, October 26, 2023. www.usip.org/publications/2023/10/why-china-rebooting-belt-and-road-initiative.

"Why Global Civilization Initiative Matters to Human Progress." *Global Times*, March 16, 2025. www.globaltimes.cn/page/202503/1330177.shtml.

"Xi Jinping: juesheng quanmian jiancheng xiaokang shehui, duoqu xinshidai zhongguo tese shehui zhuyi weida shengli-zai zhongguo gongchandang di shijiu ci quanguo daibiao dahui shang de baogao" ("Xi Jinping: Secure a Decisive Victory in Building a Moderately Prosperous Society in All Respects and Strive for the Great Success of Socialism with Chinese

Characteristics for the New Era-Report at the 19th National Congress of the Communist Party of China"). *Xinhua*, October 27, 2017. www.xinhuanet.com /politics/leaders/2017-10/27/c_1121867529.htm.

"Xi Jinping: jianshe shehuizhuyi wenhua qiangguo, zhuoli tigao guojia wenhua ruanshili" ("Xi Jinping: Build a Socialist Cultural Powerhouse, Enhance Cultural Soft Power"). *Xinhua*, December 31, 2013. www.xinhuanet.com/pol itics/2013-12/31/c_118788013.htm.

"Xiandaihua daolu shang xieshou xiangqian, gongzhu gao shuiping zhongfei mingyun gongtongti: xi jinping zhuxi xiang di 37 jie feizhou lianmeng fenghui zhi hedian zai feizhou yinfa qianglie fanxiang" ("Jointly Advancing on the Path of Modernization to Build a High-Level China-Africa Community of Shared Future: President Xi Jinping's Congratulatory Message to the 37th African Union Summit Receives Warm Response in Africa"). *People's Daily Online*, February 19, 2024. http://politics.people.com.cn/n1/2024/0219/c1001-40178 907.html.

"Xictionary: Whole-Process People's Democracy." *Ministry of Justice of the People's Republic of China*, March 5, 2024. http://en.moj.gov.cn/2024-03/05/ c_967573.htm.

"Xi proposes Global Civilization Initiative." *CGTN*, March 22, 2023. https://ne ws.cgtn.com/news/2023-03-15/Xi-proposes-Global-Civilization-Initiative-1icg xtDI3Go/index.html.

"Xinhua Signs Agreements with Foreign Media Outlets, Institutions to Deepen Cooperation." *Xinhua*, December 2, 2023. https://english.news.cn/20231202/ f2b5b6179da94b07814ffab014228083/c.html.

Yalew, Mesafint Tarekegn. "Development of Relations between Ethiopia and China during Emperor Haile Selassie: A Product of Timing or the Leadership?" *Cogent Social Sciences* 10, no. 1 (2024).

Yalew, Mesafint Tarekegn. "Development of Relations between Ethiopia and China during Emperor Haile Selassie: A Product of Timing or the Leadership?" *Cogent Social Sciences* 10, no. 1 (December 31, 2024). https://doi .org/10.1080/23311886.2024.2333082.

Yan, Hairong, Barry Sautman, and Yao Lu. "Chinese and 'Self-Segregation' in Africa." In *Chinese in Africa: 'Chineseness' and the Complexities of Identities*, 1st ed., edited by Obert Hodzi. London: Routledge, 2020. https://doi.org/10.4 324/9780367815714.

Yan Xiaoxiao. "Yingdui zhongguo ruishili shuo waijiao shijiao xia zhongguo de ruanshili yunyong yu guoji xingxiang suzao" ("'To Refute that 'China Is a Sharp Power': China's Soft Power Application and International Image Construction from the Perspective of Culture Diplomacy"). *Zhongnan Daxue Xuebao (Journal of Central South University)* 26, no. 5 (2020): 167–176.

Yan Xuetong. "Zhongguo jueqi de shili diwei" ("The Rise of China and its Power Status"). *Guoji Zhengzhi Kexue (Quarterly Journal of International Politics)* no. 2 (2005): 1–25.

Yan Xuetong, and Xu Jin. "Zhongmei ruanshili bijiao" ("A Comparative Study of Chinese and American Soft Power"). *Xiandai Guoji Guanxi (Contemporary International Relations)* no. 1 (2008): 24–29.

Yang, Guobin, and Min Jiang. "The Networked Practice of Online Political Satire in China: Between Ritual and Resistance." *International Communication Gazette* 77, no. 3 (2015): 215–31. https://doi.org/10.1177/1748048514568757.

Yang Jiechi. "Shenru xuexi guanche xi Jjnping waijiao sixiang jinyibu kaituo duiwai gongzuo xin jumian" ("Studying and Implementing Xi Jinping Thought on Diplomacy in a Deep-going Way and Opening up New Horizons in China's External Work"). *People's Daily*, May 16, 2022. http://politics.people.com.cn/n1/2022/0516/c1001-32422054.html.

Yang Jinwei. "Zhongguo tese daguo waijiao de lilun chuangxin he shijian jinlu" ("The Theoretical Innovation and Practical Approach of Great Power Diplomacy with Chinese Characteristics"). *Dong Yue Luntan (Dong Yue Tribune)* 44, no. 3 (2023): 5–12.

Yang, Mayfair Mei-hui. *Gifts, Favors, and Banquets: The Art of Social Relationships in China*. Ithaca: Cornell University Press, 1994.

Yang Wei, Fengjie Zhai, Hong Guo, and Juan Su. "Feizhou kongzi xueyuan de yuyan wenhua chuanbo xiaoguo yanjiu" ("Effect of the Chinese Language and Cultural Communication in Africa's Confucius Institutes"). *Xiya Feizhou (West Asia and Africa)*, no. 3 (2018): 140–60.

Yao Yao. "Zhongfei mingyun gongtongti de lishi yiyi yu lilun jiazhi" ("Historical Significance and Theoretical Value of China – Africa Community with a Shared Future"). *Zhongguo Feizhou Xuekan (Journal of China-Africa Studies)* 2, no. 1 (2021): 3–23, 154.

Yau, Niva. "A Global South with Chinese characteristics." *Atlantic Council*, June 13, 2024. www.atlanticcouncil.org/in-depth-research-reports/report/a-global-south-with-chinese-characteristics.

Ye, Min. "Fragmentation and Mobilization: Domestic Politics of the Belt and Road in China." *Journal of Contemporary China* 28, no. 119 (September 3, 2019): 696–711. https://doi.org/10.1080/10670564.2019.1580428.

— *The Belt Road and beyond: State-Mobilized Globalization in China: 1998–2018*. Cambridge: Cambridge University Press, 2020.

Ye Shulan. "Zhongguo guojia xingxiang de xianshi tiaozhan yu youhua celue" ("Practical Challenges and Optimization Strategies of China's National Image"). *Xueshu Qianyan (Academic Frontiers)* no. 24 (2023): 15–23.

Ye, Wei. *China's Education Aid to Africa: Fragmented Soft Power*. London: Routledge, 2023.

Yesil, Bilge. *Talking Back to the West: How Turkey Uses Counter-Hegemony to Reshape the Global Communication Order*. Urbana: University of Illinois Press, 2024.

Yin Yue. "Wang yi xinnian shoufang tuxian feizhou zhanlue zhongyaoxing" ("Wang Yi's First Visit in the New Year Highlights Africa's Strategic Importance"). *China-Africa Friendly Economic and Trade Development Foundation*, January 22, 2018. www.cnafrica.org/cn/zfxw/14707.html.

You Guolong. "Ruanshili de pinggu lujing yu zhongguo ruanshili de xiyinli" ("Evaluation Paths of Soft Power and Attraction of Chinese Soft Power"). *Xiandai Guoji Guanxi (Modern International Relations)* no. 9 (2017): 18–26.

Youmans, William Lafi. *An Unlikely Audience: Al Jazeera's Struggle in America*. Oxford: Oxford University Press USA – OSO, 2017.

Young, Ellie, Sarah Cook, and anonymous. "Brazil: Beijing's Global Media Influence 2022 Country Report." *Freedom House*, accessed August 24, 2022. https://freedomhouse.org/country/brazil/beijings-global-media-inuence/2022#footnoteref52_miyont4.

Yu Jiang. "Zai duojihua jincheng zhong gongzhu gaoshuiping zhongfei mingyun gongtongti" ("On Building a High-Level China-Africa Community of a Shared Future in the Process of Multipolarization"). *Guoji Guanxi Yu Diqu Qushi (International Relations and Regional Situation)* no. 2 (2024): 50–5.

"Zambia: Workers Detail Abuse in Chinese-Owned Mines." Human Rights Watch, November 3, 2011. www.hrw.org/news/2011/11/03/zambia-workers-detail-abuse-chinese-owned-mines.

Záhořík, Jan, Aleksi Ylönen, and Jonah Lego. "Multiple Layers of Pan-Africanism and Pan-Ethiopianism in Current Debates on Nationalism and Ethnicity in Ethiopia." *Nationalities Papers*, February 10, 2025, 1–16. https://doi.org/10.1017/nps.2024.108.

Zappone, Tanina. "Reinventing Soft Power: The Strong Impact of China's Soft Power 'Shortcomings' on the Global South." *IAI Papers* 23, July 19, 2023. www.iai.it/en/pubblicazioni/co3/reinventing-soft-power-strong-impact-chinas-soft-power-shortcomings-global-south.

Zhang, Binxin. "Africans in China, Western/White Supremacy and the Ambivalence of Chinese Racial Identity." *The China Quarterly* 260 (2024): 932–47.

Zhang Hongming. "Bai deng zhengfu de feizhou zhengce: youxian shixiang yu benzhi neihan" ("The Biden Administration's Africa Policy: Priorities and Essential Implications"). *Xiya Feizhou (West Asia and Africa)* no. 4 (2022): 67–94, 157-158.

Zhang, Xiaoling, Herman Wasserman, and Winston Mano, eds. *China's Media and Soft Power in Africa.* New York: Palgrave Macmillan US, 2016. https://doi.org/10.1057/9781137539670.

Zhang Xinping, and Zhuang Hongtao. "Zhongguo guoji huayuquan: licheng, tiaozhan ji tisheng celue" ("China's International Discourse Power: History, Challenges and Promotion Strategies"). *Nankai Xuebao: Zhexue Shehui Kexue Ban (Nankai Journal: Philosophy & Social Sciences)* no. 6 (2017): 1–10.

Zhang Yongpeng. "Xifang dui feizhou yingxiang shenhua yu kuoda xin taishi zhongfei guanxi mianlin de xin tiaozhan" ("New Situation of Deepening and Expansion of the Influence of the West on Africa – New Challenges for China–Africa Relations"). *Institute of West-Asian and African Studies, Chinese Academy of Social Sciences*, 2013. www.focac.org/lhyj/yjcg/201304/t20130416_7877479.htm.

Zhao Kejin. "Zhongguoshi xiandaihua de waijiao luoji: jiyu shengtai zhidu zhuyi zhengzhixue de fenxi" ("The Diplomatic Logic of Chinese Modernization: An Analysis Based on the Politics of Eco-Institutionalism"). *Guoji Zhanwang (Global Review)* 16 no. 4 (2024): 1–20, 165.

Zhao, Qizheng. *How China Communicates: Public Diplomacy in a Global Age* (Beijing: Foreign Language Press, 2012).

Zhao Yating, "Goujian xinxing nan nan hezuo: quanqiu fazhan changyi yu '2063 nian yicheng' quanmian duijie" ("Constructing a New Model of South-South

Cooperation: Aligning Global Development Initiatives with Agenda 2063.") *Zhongguo Feizhou Xuekan (Journal of China-Africa Studies)* 4, no. 3 (2023): 24–44, 155–6.

Zheng Yongnian and Zhang Chi. "Guoji zhengzhi zhong de ruanliliang yiji dui ruanliliang de guancha" ("Soft Power in International Politics and the Implications for China"). *Shijie Jingji Yu Zheng Zhi (World Economics and Politics)*, no. 7 (July 14, 2007): 6–12.

"Zhonggong zhongyang zhengzhiju weiyuan, waijiao buzhang wang yi jiu zhongguo waijiao zhengce he duiwai guanxi huida zhongwai jizhe tiwen" ("Politburo Member and Foreign Minister Wang Yi Answers Questions from Chinese and Foreign Journalists on China's Foreign Policy and International Relations"). Ministry of Foreign Affairs of the People's Republic of China, March 7, 2024. www.mfa.gov.cn/web/ziliao_674904/zyjh_674906/202403/t20240307_11255225.shtml.

Zhou Shuqing. "Zhongguo zai feizhou de liyi jiqi weihu zhanlue" ("Chinese Interests and the Safeguard Strategies"). *Guoji Guancha (International Review)* no. 2 (2009): 21–28.

Zhou Yuyuan, "Dabianju shidai zhongfei hezuo de xinzhengcheng yu xinsikao" ("China-Africa Cooperation in the Era of Global Changes: New Journey and New Thinking"), *Xiya Feizhou (West Asia and Africa)* no. 3 (2023): 3–25, 155.

Zhu, Shaobin. "Xinhua Commentary: Africa Should Not Be a Battleground for a Great Power Rivalry." *Xinhuanet*, January 29, 2023. https://english.news.cn/20230129/2c2edc4b550d495f8bb1f20a21d6f17e/c.html.

Index

For EU product safety concerns, contact us at Calle de José Abascal, 56–1°,
28003 Madrid, Spain or eugpsr@cambridge.org.